COMPLEXITY

SOFTWARE DESIGN PHILOSOPHY IN THE SWIFTUI ERA

HUI WANG

First Published: 2025

WRITTEN FOR THE FUTURE YOU

I often wonder: if one day in the future a young developer opens this book, what will they expect to read? Is it a SwiftUI API tutorial? Is it a practical guide to an architectural pattern? Or a checklist of performance optimizations?

No, this book will not provide those. It deals with something deeper than techniques and more enduring than patterns: complexity.

Over the past decade and more, I have continually explored the intersections of technology, business, history, and psychology. I have studied how wars failed because of the complexity of supply lines, how empires declined because of bureaucratic complexity, and how companies collapsed because of organizational complexity. When I returned to the daily work of software development, I suddenly realized: complexity is the central enemy here as well.

Software doesn't die from bugs; it dies from complexity. Bugs can be fixed; complexity accumulates. It is like sand blown by the wind—unseen and intangible, yet over time it can bury everything.

In my years as an iOS developer, I've seen too many teams fall into the same trap:

A feature ships quickly, but becomes everyone's nightmare three months later;

An architecture seems elegant, yet it takes newcomers weeks to understand;

A cross-platform choice saves time in the short term, but creates twice the chaos in the long term.

Airbnb once attempted to unify development with React Native but, eroded by complexity, had to return to native development;

Dropbox, while exploring multi-platform unification, made painful adjustments because of the costs of complexity;

NASA's Apollo moon landing program showed us that complexity must be suppressed to a level manageable by the human mind, or it will become a disaster;

The stories of companies like Netflix, Spotify, Slack, and Uber are all a tug-of-war between complexity and the human mind.

I want to write these down not out of curiosity, but to make more developers realize: complexity is our only true enemy.

So, who is this book written for?

It is written for iOS developers. Especially those who have moved beyond the beginner stage, who are no longer satisfied with "the code runs" and have begun to ask: "Why does our system become so complex? Why does nobody dare maintain this project after a few months?" You might be a solo indie developer, or a senior engineer leading a team of dozens. Regardless of size, complexity will find you.

It is also written for teams. Complexity is not an individual problem; it is always the product of the collective. A team's way of communicating determines the direction of complexity. An organization's boundary design determines the lifespan of its architecture. If you are a team manager, architect, or technical lead, you will find in this book methods to help you "hold the boundaries."

It is written even more for the future you. Because code that feels clear today may become a riddle three months from now.

The essence of complexity is to entangle your future self. The sole criterion of this book is to help your future self understand quickly.

Why am I writing this book?

Because in my decades of exploration I have repeatedly seen the same law: the human mind is limited, while complexity is unlimited. History is like this, war is like this, business is like this, and software development is no different. If On War is the classic study of the complexity of warfare, and Foundation is a parable about the complexity of civilization, then I hope this book can become a coordinate system for SwiftUI-era developers facing complexity.

I don't want to write a manual full of tips — those things will be outdated in two years. I want to write a philosophy, something you can read ten years from now and still find clear and valuable. Just as Nintendo insists on being "player-friendly" and can create timeless classics even with inferior hardware, software architecture must insist on being "human-friendly" and, when faced with complexity, must preserve comprehensibility.

The core idea of this book can be summed up in one sentence:

The ultimate goal of software architecture is not to make machines run faster, but to make it easier for humans to understand.

Machines don't care about your code. They only care about zeros and ones. Those who truly coexist with the code are humans: your future self, newcomers who haven't joined yet, your teammates. If they cannot understand quickly, then that code has failed.

Therefore, this book, starting from complexity, discusses:

- How design principles are reinterpreted in the SwiftUI era;
- How architectural patterns help reduce our cognitive load rather than increase it;

- Why the illusion of cross-platform development ultimately cannot escape the price of complexity;
- Why native development is a friend of time;
- Why testing, performance optimization, and CI/CD are essentially all guardians of comprehensibility;
- Why AI can help us write code but cannot replace us in making design decisions;
- Why team culture and communication styles determine the direction of complexity more than any pattern.

Each chapter will open with a story — Airbnb's cross-platform experiment, Dropbox's trade-offs, NASA's moon-landing program, Netflix's evolution, Spotify's predicament, and Nintendo's philosophy.

These stories are not curiosities; they are parables.

Their details may differ, but the endings are similar: complexity is never absent.

What will this book give you?

Not a new API checklist, but a new way of thinking.

Not an operational manual for a framework, but a mental model for facing complexity.

Not to make you write faster today, but to make today's code readable three years from now.

I hope it will become your companion, helping you see where the oases and the traps lie in the desert of complexity.

It is not a mentor, but a map.

A map will not walk for you, but it will help you take fewer detours.

This is not a cold, technical book, but a book about humans and complexity.

Its goal is not only to teach you how to write code, but how to survive in the winds and sands of complexity.

As an author who has long studied history and technology,

and also an iOS developer who writes SwiftUI every day, I know these two worlds are not really far apart.

The fall of empires and the failure of projects are essentially both cases of complexity overwhelming humans.

Victory in war and success in architecture are both essentially about cognitive load being sensibly distributed.

I hope to use this book to connect the two.

If it can give you an extra measure of clarity when facing complexity, then it will have fulfilled its mission.

Complexity is like a desert.
It is silent and imperceptible, yet it can devour everything.
Architects and developers are like travelers in that desert.
You cannot eliminate the desert, but you can carry a water bag, travel in company, and remember the landmarks.
The true enemy is not the wind and sand, but losing your sense of direction.
This book is a flag planted atop the dune, reminding you:
The direction is always — make code human-friendly.

CONTENTS

PART FIVE
ENGINEERING PRACTICE

PART SIX
AI AND THE FUTURE

PART SEVEN
BATTLEFIELD NOTES ON COMPLEXITY

PART EIGHT
TEAMS AND CULTURE

PART NINE
THE POWER OF KEEPING IT SIMPLE

PART TEN

APPENDIX

PART ONE
THE FATE OF SOFTWARE

CHAPTER 1
WHY ALL APPS DIE OF COMPLEXITY

An empire is not destroyed by its enemies, but by its own weight.
So is software; complexity is its gravity.

Winds rise without form, sand falls without sound. Complexity is not an explosion, not a collapse, but a long-term erosion.

Historians recorded the decline of empires: not the failure of a single battle, but the cracking of roads, the rot of granaries, the imbalance of taxation.

Software is the same. No application dies because it lacks a "feature"; they die of complexity: accumulated logic, haphazardly stacked abstractions, repeatedly compromised decisions.

When Airbnb first rose, it was nothing more than a small apartment in the hands of its three founders. A few air mattresses, a website, the simplest of ideas: let people find a place to stay in a strange city. Like the first brick of an empire, it always appears in a border market, not in the capital's hall.

As Airbnb grew, that idea quickly ballooned into an empire. The app was no longer just a window to list rentals; it had to handle identity verification, payment flows, review systems, customer support, mapping and location, push notifications... The empire's territory expanded with each iteration of requirements.

The empire's expansion brought glory: more users, higher valuation, larger market share.

But beneath the glory, the gravity of complexity began to accumulate.

Each new feature was a stone placed on the empire's tower. The tower grew taller, but also heavier.

Complexity's earliest manifestations are always trivial.

A tiny branch in logic to handle the tax rules of a particular country;

A temporary utility function to ship before Black Friday;

A "temporary" architectural change to be compatible with a newly released API.

These are like the small taxes and levies on an empire's border. Seemingly minor, they accumulate silently.

Airbnb's engineering team at first did not notice. They were in the frenzy of growth; everyone was running, everyone chasing features. The cost of complexity was deferred, like an empire's fiscal deficit, always inherited by the next generation of officials.

The turning point came in the cracks of the user experience.

Airbnb's app was renowned for its refined experience. Whether it was the speed of image loading or the smooth interaction of the maps, users were once amazed. However, when complexity accumulated to a certain critical point, those experiences began to change subtly. The smoothness of map zooming declined, price displays lagged, and error messages in the payment flow increased.

These cracks were not catastrophic. They did not cause users to immediately uninstall the app, nor did they lead investors to pull out at once. They were like fissures in an empire's roads:

caravans could still travel, but more slowly, with increased friction and more complaints.

Such is complexity: it does not destroy a system in the form of a battle, but through everyday inconveniences that gradually erode trust.

Inside Airbnb, the gravity of complexity was even more apparent.

Developers found that it took longer and longer to fix a bug. In the past, they only needed to locate the problem within a single module; now they had to shuttle across three layers of architecture: React Native, iOS, and Android. Each bug was like a maze, with a vague entrance and a distant exit.

Teams also found that iteration speed was slowing. Previously, a two-week sprint could bring two features live; now, an entire sprint might only be enough to fix legacy issues. New feature development was delayed, product managers grew more dissatisfied, and the air in the meeting rooms grew tense.

The weight of complexity was not just a technical weight — it was emotional weight, communication weight, cultural weight.

The empire's weight also showed up in the organization.

Airbnb had to set up more and more cross-team coordination meetings:

- The cross-platform group had to align with the native teams;
- The native teams had to confirm interactions with the design team;
- The QA team had to align test plans with third-party developers.

Meetings, like taxes, began to erode productivity. Every hour of meeting was a gold coin deducted from development time. The empire's finances looked prosperous on the surface, but were actually deeply in deficit.

The gravity of complexity gradually wore down the team's

mental capacity. Young engineers joined the company full of enthusiasm, only to find months later that most of their time was spent understanding legacy code. Senior engineers grew exhausted; in one rescue after another they lost their creativity. This was not the roar of failure, but slow quicksand.

"The decline of an empire always begins with the loss of morale."

Airbnb's engineers were once excited by rapid innovation; they were proud to be changing the world. But as the gravity of complexity pressed down, their language gradually changed.

From "we can do this" to "how long can we keep this up";

From "we are innovating" to "we are maintaining."

Complexity is like that: it does not destroy your code, it destroys your language.

When language changes, the empire has already begun to decline.

At this stage, Airbnb's app was still running, and users were still growing.

The outside world could not see the cracks in the empire.

But those inside already felt it:

Complexity was changing their breathing, quietly suffocating them.

The empire's weight is invisible, yet everywhere.

The burden of the empire is not in its territory, but in its order.

When complexity exceeds what people's capacity can bear, the empire is bound to collapse.

The gravity of complexity is not lessened by external applause.

Airbnb's app continued to expand worldwide, user numbers kept climbing, media coverage was frequent, and investors' funds kept coming.

On the surface, it was a miracle of a digital empire.

Yet behind the miracle, complexity had already, like invisible dust, filled the empire's lungs.

In day-to-day engineering tasks, complexity manifested as "delay."

A simple requirement — for example, adding a new payment method on the checkout page — was estimated at planning to take two weeks, but ultimately took two months.

The reason was not developer laziness, but the length of the path.

Every requirement had to pass through a threefold maze:

The component layer of React Native,

The native modules of iOS,

The implementation details of Android.

Between the three layers were bridges and mismatches.

Every change could produce unexpected side effects in some layer.

So engineers had to spend countless hours cross-checking and retesting.

Time is the currency of an empire.

When time is devoured by complexity, the empire's finances inevitably run a deficit.

Airbnb's developers gradually discovered that they had lost their advantage in iteration speed.

Complexity also manifests as "ambiguity."

Once, the source of a bug was obvious.

In the native era, a crash often pointed to a particular module or API.

But in the React Native era, a crash could be:

- An exception in the JavaScript runtime,
- Delays in the bridge-layer communication,
- Incompatibility in native code,
- Or a chain reaction of all three combined.

Ambiguity is complexity's deadliest weapon.

It makes developers wander in the fog and causes teams to waste effort on guessing.

When ambiguity becomes the norm, morale will wither.

The gravity of complexity also reveals itself through "communication."

Airbnb was once known for efficient collaboration. Small teams were self-driven, iterating quickly, and everyone could see the results of their work in a short time.

But when React Native introduced a three-layer architecture, communication became a new tax.

A requirement had to be confirmed by three parties:

- The cross-platform group,
- The iOS team,
- The Android team.

Every meeting involved lengthy explanations: which layer does a bug actually belong to? Who is responsible for a particular latency?

Meeting notes grew longer, actions grew slower.

Developers got lost in Jira and emails; they spent more time writing explanations than writing features.

Bureaucratization of the empire happened this way.

Not because people grew lazy, but because complexity forced them to create more processes to combat uncertainty.

Yet with every added process, the empire grew that much heavier.

The most insidious force of complexity lies in "cultural erosion."

Airbnb's culture once centered on "move fast, keep it simple."

This is an entrepreneurial spirit: small, rapid steps; iterating to survive; unafraid of failure.

But when complexity accumulated to a certain degree, the language of the culture began to change.

Engineers no longer spoke of "speed," but of "regressions."

They no longer asked "how to innovate," but "how to fix."

Their eyes no longer looked to the future, but were trapped in the mire of legacy problems.

This cultural shift is a sign of an empire's decline.

When soldiers no longer crave victory but only survival, the empire's glory is gone.

The gravity of complexity even shook Airbnb's strategy.

The board once believed that React Native would save the company money and improve efficiency. But the reality of the data gradually confronted them:

- Feature release cycles were twice as long as expected;
- Bug fix rates declined;
- Complaints about user experience increased;
- Engineer turnover rose.

The data were cold and merciless; like stone tablets, they etched the truth of complexity. No argument could hide those numbers.

So management began to split. Some held on to the dream, believing React Native was merely "not yet mature" and would improve in time. They were like the empire's expansionists, convinced that the larger the territory the better.

Others called for contraction, pointing out that complexity had exceeded the team's capacity. They were like the empire's conservatives, advocating a return to the core and the abandonment of illusions.

This split was not just a technical debate but a cultural rift. When leadership fractures, the empire's voice no longer speaks with one accord.

Complexity also changed the identity of engineers.

Under the React Native regime, developers were no longer creators but translators. They spent huge amounts of time switching between JavaScript and Swift, Kotlin—like interpreters of ancient empires. They had to understand three cultures, three toolchains, three debugging approaches.

The result was that engineers' focus was diluted. They could no longer go deep in any one area or exercise true expertise. They became generalists, no longer specialists.

An empire's greatest strength lies in its experts—those who can solve problems at critical moments. When experts are forced to become generalists, the empire loses its true moat.

The gravity of complexity even extended to hiring and retention.

Airbnb once attracted the world's best iOS and Android engineers. These people wanted to dig deep in native domains, pursuing peak performance and experience. But under the React Native regime, they found their expertise undervalued. They were asked to learn JavaScript and forced to deal with tedious cross-platform minutiae.

Some chose to leave, seeking places where they could truly contribute. Others stayed, but with a sense of loss. The loss of talent was not a thunderous collapse, but a quiet one. But once the exodus began, the empire's cornerstone had already been shaken.

The gravity of complexity was further amplified by the "external environment."

Mobile platforms evolve extremely quickly.

Apple releases new APIs, new frameworks, and new design guidelines every year.

Android's ecosystem is also updated frequently, and hardware differences are everywhere.

When Airbnb tried to unify the two major platforms with React Native, they actually took on double the complexity:

they had to keep pace with Apple's cadence, keep pace with Google's cadence, and maintain React Native's own updates.

The convergence of these three tides kept them constantly on the run.

No team can endure that kind of gravity long-term.

"An empire does not die on the battlefield; it dies of debt."

Airbnb's complexity had accumulated into debt.

Every temporary fix, every "we'll do it later" promise was debt.

Debt doesn't disappear; it is merely deferred.

In the end, it will demand repayment with greater interest.

When the debt of complexity reaches its peak, the empire has no room to maneuver.

Against this backdrop, Airbnb's leadership finally realized:

they were not "saving," they were "overdrawing."

They were not "innovating," they were "resisting."

The gravity of complexity had dragged the empire to a turning point.

If they continued, the cracks would only widen and the culture would collapse.

An empire's demise is not because the enemy is strong, but because it can no longer bear itself.

Software does not end for lack of features, but because complexity crushes the human heart.

The gravity of complexity must eventually reach a critical point.

For Airbnb, that point arrived at the height of their glory.

User numbers hit the hundreds of millions, valuation soared, and globalization marched unstoppable.

But behind that splendor, the empire's foundation was already crumbling.

The turning point began with a strategic review.

The glass walls of the conference room were covered with flowcharts, issue lists, and bug statistics.

The cross-platform group, native teams, product managers, designers, and data analysts all gathered together.

The air was heavy, as if the empire's council were taking one last look at the map of its territories.

The data were laid out on the table:

- React Native's bug-fix cycle was more than 30% longer than native;
- The cost of team communication far exceeded expectations;
- Key features—payments, maps, photo uploads—had to be reverted to Native;
- Nearly half of the user-experience complaints were related to React Native.

The numbers were cold, yet more lethal than any rhetoric. No one could deny these facts.

The ledger of complexity was laid bare before their eyes.

What had been thought to be savings was actually an overdraft; what had been thought to be unification was actually division.

However, decisions are never driven solely by numbers; they are a struggle of culture and conviction.

At the meeting, some still clung to the cross-platform dream. They said, "React Native is still evolving, the community is active, it will surely get better." They were like the empire's expansionists, preferring to keep consuming rather than admit retreat.

Others proposed a compromise: "We can keep some React Native modules while gradually migrating back to Native." This was a delaying tactic, like an empire installing puppet regimes on the frontier in exchange for temporary stability.

But most were exhausted. They had endured countless overtime sessions just to fix a single cross-platform bug; they had lost the passion to create, left only with the fatigue of maintenance. The fire was gone from their eyes, replaced by a longing for release.

Then a voice was spoken: "We must return to Native."

The voice was heavy, yet like a sword cutting through the fog. For everyone knew in their hearts that it was the only answer.

In 2018, Airbnb officially announced they would gradually abandon React Native and fully return to Native. It was not only a technical choice, but a cultural one.

In a public blog post they wrote: "We tried React Native; it brought some benefits, but it also brought complexity that could not be ignored. We found that React Native did not reduce our workload; rather, it increased our Cognitive Load. Native is our long-term direction."

These words were like an edict left in the empire's chronicles. Not an admission of failure, but a sober proclamation.

This shift was not completed overnight. The debt of complexity had to be repaid gradually. They began migrating bit by bit, reimplementing key features in Swift and Kotlin. They established clearer boundaries, delineated team responsibilities, and reshaped the architecture.

In the process, the team regained a sense of control. Engineers no longer had to debug across three layers or lose their way in the bridge layer. They confronted the system directly and re-understood every detail.

Complexity still existed, but it was once again contained within controllable boundaries—like water channeled into canals, like wind held back by sand walls.

Rebuilding culture was harder than rebuilding technology.

Airbnb's leadership re-emphasized: "Move fast, keep it simple." The phrase ceased to be a slogan and became a new creed. At every requirements review they asked: "How much Cognitive Load will this feature introduce? Will this architecture make it hard for future us to understand?"

Complexity was placed at the center of meetings, not at the margins. It was no longer an invisible enemy but an opponent to be faced.

This shift restored the team's faith. They knew complexity would not disappear, but it could be tamed. They no longer fantasized about shortcuts; they accepted the reality of long-term coexistence with complexity.

"The greatest empires are not those that never retreat, but those that know how to yield before gravity."

Airbnb's pivot embodied that wisdom. They did not die beneath complexity because they chose to acknowledge its force. They did not cling to illusions but chose to make peace with reality.

This is not just Airbnb's story. It is the fate of all software empires.

Complexity is like gravity; it always exists. You can dance with it, but you cannot ignore it. You can tame it, but you cannot eliminate it.

Every app will ultimately die of complexity. The difference lies in this: some perish because they refuse to admit the illusion of simplicity; others survive because they soberly acknowledge complexity.

Airbnb's experience tells us:

- The gravity of complexity will continually accumulate until it crushes the team's morale;
- The cross-platform dream often ends up costing far more;
- Boundaries and restraint are the only viable moat;
- The goal of architecture is not to pursue uniformity, but to reduce Cognitive Load.

Complexity is the gravity of an empire.
Ignore it, and the empire will perish.
Face it, and the empire can endure.

CHAPTER 2
WRITING CODE ≠ DESIGNING SOFTWARE

Implementation is a temporary encampment;
Design is the city-state that can stand in the wind and sand.
An empire does not collapse because it has too few warriors, but because its roads and codes cannot support the weight of its territory.

The wind whispers in the desert, carrying ancient dust.

Writing code is like drawing lines in the sand: clear in the moment, gone in an instant.

Designing software is like building a levee in the desert: it requires patience, foresight, and leaving a shape for an unseen future.

The story of Dropbox is precisely a testament to this gulf.

When Dropbox appeared on the world stage, it brought an almost magical promise:

Put a file in a folder, and it will appear on all your devices.

At the core of that promise was "sync".

And the word "sync", seemingly simple, hides the most dangerous confrontation between humans and complexity.

In its early years, Dropbox's implementation was stunning.

The combination of Python and C++ let them iterate quickly on the desktop platform.

Their team was small and fast; the founder Drew Houston was even known for "hacker elegance".

Their code was like a sharp sword, striking straight at user needs: file copying, state comparison, conflict merging.

However, a sharp sword cannot build an empire.

A sword can win the present battles, but cannot sustain a long war.

The speed of writing code cannot replace the clarity of software design.

The problem began to appear with the arrival of the mobile era.

After succeeding on the desktop, Dropbox had to enter the world of iOS and Android.

Users were no longer satisfied with syncing between computers; they wanted to access files anytime on their phones.

So the Dropbox team quickly developed mobile apps.

The initial mobile implementation was translational:

The desktop logic was directly ported, with bridging wrappers between Python and native languages.

They thought that as long as the core logic was reused, the mobile side could share the same capabilities.

This is the typical "writing code" approach: taking the shortest path to get the feature done.

Files could be downloaded, uploaded, and displayed, and the team cheered.

But soon they discovered: this was not "designing software".

The gulf revealed itself in the cost of understanding.

Desktop and mobile are not just differences in screen size.

Desktops have stable power and networks; mobile is

constrained everywhere: limited battery, unstable networks, users can switch apps at any time.

Desktops can tolerate tens of seconds of latency; mobile users cannot wait.

Desktops allow multithreading to run continuously; mobile systems may suspend background processes at any time.

These differences turn "sync" into a fundamentally different challenge on mobile.

And Dropbox's initial architecture was not designed for that challenge.

The result was:

Whenever a bug occurred, engineers had to understand three layers of logic at once: the Python core, the iOS bridging layer, and Android's variations.

This was no longer a problem of implementation, but a problem of understanding.

They could fix bugs, but it became increasingly difficult to explain why the bugs occurred.

Inside Dropbox, a story was widely told.

An engineer spent weeks poring over logs and stacks to trace a missing-file issue.

The bug manifested as: files uploaded fine on the desktop, but would occasionally disappear on the phone.

He checked the sync logic and confirmed the Python layer was fine;

He dug into the iOS bridging and found the data transfer was correct;

Only finally, in the Android implementation, did he find a highly obscure thread race condition.

The bug was eventually fixed, but at great cost.

In the postmortem, the team wrote this line:

"We solved the problem, but we do not understand our system."

That line rang like a cold bell.

It exposed the gulf: writing code can make things run; designing software is what makes things understood.

Dropbox's mobile architecture gradually became a maze.

Every requirement added a new passage to the maze.

Every feature added a new fork in the maze.

The maze could keep operating, but no one truly understood its entirety.

This is complexity's favorite trick.

It does not destroy a system outright; instead it makes the cost of understanding the system exceed the cost of implementing it.

When understanding becomes scarce, design is no longer possible.

The team can only keep "fixing" and cannot truly "build".

Dropbox founder Drew Houston once said in an interview:

"We thought we were building a sync system; later we discovered we were building a distributed database."

This sentence is exactly the gulf between understanding and implementation.

Implementation only sees the surface requirements: upload, download, display.

Design must see the hidden essence: distributed consistency, conflict resolution, the switching between offline and online.

Dropbox's early code solved the implementation but did not solve the design.

This made them pay a heavy price in the mobile era.

Engineers' minds are a finite reservoir.

The speed of writing code is like continuously pouring water into the reservoir.

The purpose of designing software is to build a dam so the reservoir will not burst.

Dropbox's story tells us:

When you only keep pouring water and ignore the dam, the reservoir will sooner or later break.

This part of the narrative pauses here for now.

Dropbox's maze continued, and the erosion of complexity had not ended.

The real impact would unfold later.

The power of complexity lies not in destruction, but in attrition.

Not a crushing defeat on the battlefield, but the daily drop-by-drop loss.

What eventually causes an empire to collapse is not the enemy's blade, but the soldiers' unfamiliarity with their domain.

Dropbox's empire entered the mobile era.

Desktop victories brought confidence; a massive user base brought capital and expectations.

And expectations are the most fertile soil for complexity.

At the San Francisco headquarters, during an ordinary product review meeting, the team raised a simple requirement:

Users wanted to quickly preview PDFs, images, and videos on their phones instead of waiting for a full download to complete.

On desktop this was not a hard problem. Desktops have enough memory, broadband, and continuous power.

But on mobile, this requirement meant a completely different battlefield:

- iOS's memory limits are extremely strict; if thresholds are exceeded the app will be killed by the system.
- Android's device diversity means hundreds of resolutions, processors, and OS versions.
- Unstable networks make "partial loading" a gamble.

The team that wrote the code chose the most direct approach:

add a caching layer on top of the existing sync logic, download in chunks and decode.

They did indeed implement the feature, users cheered during the demo, the product manager was satisfied, and the meeting room burst into applause.

However, in the second week after going live, problems came in quick succession.

On some iPhone models, previews caused the app to crash;

On certain Android devices, previews were unbearably janky;

and cross-device file consistency began to produce an increasing number of "ghost bugs" — files showed as complete but were overwritten during background sync.

These issues were not impossible to fix.

Engineers worked around the clock, poring over logs and stacks.

Bugs were pushed back one by one, but new ones kept emerging from the shadows.

Like the empire's frontier, just as one city was repaired, another wall began to collapse.

The real disaster was not the bugs, but the loss of understanding.

Dropbox's mobile architecture consisted of three parts:

The desktop's core logic ported over as the "trusted core";

native bridges for iOS and Android to interface with system capabilities;

And mobile-specific requirements that had to be layered on top of the two, creating new tiers.

Each iteration created new intersection points across these three layers.

Each fix required engineers to shuttle back and forth between them.

Over time, no one could truly understand the entire system anymore.

Young engineers felt frustrated:

"I can implement the feature, but I can't explain why it works this way."

Senior engineers felt exhausted:

"I know where the problem might be, but I don't have the energy to dig through all the layers anymore."

This is the gulf between writing code and designing software.

Writing code only cares whether it runs;

designing software must care whether it can be understood.

When a system can only be run but not understood, it has already begun to decay.

Within Dropbox's team, divisions gradually formed into three camps.

The first camp was the implementation camp.

They believed the most important thing was meeting product requirements.

As long as users could use it, bugs were just a cost of the process.

They were like frontline cavalry—bold and fast, but rarely looking back to see whether the road was collapsing.

The second camp was the design camp.

They saw the growth of complexity and worried about long-term costs.

They proposed refactoring, unified interfaces, and clear boundaries.

But in the fast-paced competitive environment, they were often accused of "slowing down progress".

The third camp was the disillusioned.

They had gone through countless bugs and fixes and gradually lost their faith.

They no longer believed in perfect solutions and simply completed tasks mechanically.

Their eyes were like a well in the desert, already buried by sand.

The empire's crisis was not external competition, but internal fissures.

When the team no longer shared a unified vision, complexity would seize the opportunity.

One winter night, a senior engineer posted a long message on the company Slack:

"We don't need more code; we need more understanding.

Every line of code we write for mobile is a bet against the operating system.

We have forgotten that the purpose of software is not merely to run, but to be understood."

The message was met with a long silence.

Everyone knew in their hearts that it was true.

They did not lack the ability to write code; what they lacked was the courage to design.

The loss of understanding brought a deeper crisis: the collapse of communication.

Product managers could not understand why a seemingly simple feature would take months to ship.

Designers could not understand why moving a button would trigger performance problems.

Management could not understand why, with so many engineers, bugs still could not be cleared.

So blame began to breed:

"Engineers aren't working hard enough."

"The product team doesn't understand technology."

"Management only looks at numbers and not reality."

The deadliest power of complexity is not a technical problem, but that it makes people stop understanding one another.

When a system is incomprehensible, the team becomes incomprehensible.

When the boundaries of the code blur, the boundaries of the team blur as well.

The gulf of writing code becomes an organizational gulf.

By this time, Dropbox already had hundreds of millions of users; great success obscured internal crises.

To the outside, they were still leaders in cloud storage;

inside, they were trapped in an internal war of understanding.

They had to make a choice:

Continue stacking code, trading speed for the illusion of prosperity;

Or stop and redesign the system so the future could be understood.

This was not a technical choice, but a choice of civilization.

The erosion of complexity is like an empire's supply line.

At first, it only slows the speed of transporting grain;

Later, it causes the grain to rot along the way;

ultimately, it starves the frontline troops while the rear still believes the granaries are full.

Dropbox's front line was the mobile client. When the mobile experience collapsed, the desktop glory could not be salvaged. Because users no longer relied only on computers — they lived on their phones. And the complexity inside those phones was silently devouring the empire.

"Our problem is not speed, but understanding. We've written too much code without enough design."

This was a belated awakening. But in the desert of complexity, awakening is always better than sleeping.

Understanding is the only defense against complexity.

A system that cannot be understood can only be sustained by chance;

A team that lacks understanding can only survive on inertia.

And inertia is the most dangerous illusion.

Dropbox's empire had reached a critical turning point. User growth hadn't stopped, investors still watched, and the market still expected. But internally, the fissures of complexity had spread down every corridor.

One night the San Francisco office was brightly lit. In a conference room, a dozen core engineers and technical leaders gathered, and the topic was one: how to save the mobile client.

At the meeting, an engineer took out a sheet of paper and drew three layers: at the bottom, the core sync logic in Python; the middle layer, the iOS and Android bridge code; the top layer, mobile-specific requirements — caching, previews, offline support.

He put the paper on the table and said, "This is not a house, it's a makeshift tent. Every time it rains we tack on another piece of cloth; every time the wind blows we add another pole. The tent still stands now, but no one knows how long it will hold."

The room fell silent. Everyone knew that was true.

The true killer of complexity is not collapse, but unpredictability. On Dropbox's mobile client, every feature launch was a gamble. Even if tests passed, no one could guarantee users wouldn't encounter odd problems. Even if bugs were fixed, no one could guarantee they wouldn't trigger new ones.

This unpredictability gradually eroded the team's confidence. They no longer believed in the code, in the system, or in the future.

At this point, someone proposed the heaviest suggestion: refactoring.

"Refactoring" is a double-edged sword in any team.

It means overturning existing accumulation, entails huge investment, and carries risk.

What management fears most is the word "refactoring."

Because it shows no short-term return yet will consume resources.

But Dropbox had no other choice.

They knew that if they continued as they were, complexity would drag them down completely.

So a plan gradually emerged:

- Return to native and fully embrace Swift and Kotlin;
- Redesign the mobile sync logic instead of simply porting desktop logic;
- Establish clear boundaries so each layer's responsibilities are explicit;
- Most importantly: make the system understandable again.

This was not a technical decision but a rebuilding of civilization.

Dropbox's engineers began a long refactor.

They acted like archaeologists, excavating the ruins of old code and looking for parts that could be preserved.

They acted like architects, designing new boundaries so logic would no longer be entangled but clearly layered.

They acted like translators, converting the ideas in Python into the languages of Swift and Kotlin.

In the process, they gradually recovered what had been lost: understanding.

Understanding is an engineer's most important weapon.

When an engineer can fully explain how the system works, they can control complexity.

When the whole team can align on the same blueprint, they can resist the erosion of complexity.

In the early stages of the refactor, the team's efficiency declined.

Bugs remained, and feature releases were still obstructed.

But the difference was that this time, they no longer felt lost.

They knew the boundaries of problems, the ownership of responsibilities, and the direction of the future.

Complexity still existed, but it had been caged.

The refactor did not happen overnight.

It lasted for years, accompanied by countless arguments and compromises.

But in the end, Dropbox's mobile client stood firm.

The sync logic was redesigned, the UI experience became smoother, and the team regained control of the system.

Most importantly, they rebuilt trust of mind.

Engineers no longer feared bugs because they knew they could understand and fix them.

Product managers no longer feared requirement changes because they knew the system could bear them.

Management no longer doubted the team because they saw continuous improvement.

This is the power of understanding.

Dropbox's story became a parable in the history of software.

It tells us:

Writing code solves today's problems;

Designing software solves tomorrow's problems.

Writing code is translating logic for machines;

Designing software is translating logic for humans.

Machines will never complain about complexity, but humans will. And software, in the end, is written for humans.

Looking back at Dropbox's journey, we can clearly see that gulf:

- They won early by speed, gaining users through execution.
- They sank into the mire in the mobile era because of a lack of design.
- They ultimately refactored, returned to native, rebuilt boundaries, and secured the future with understanding.

This is not an isolated story but a microcosm of software civilization.

"Writing code is erecting tents; designing software is building city-states.

Tents can get you through the night; only city-states can found a nation.

A true architect is not the fastest craftsman but the most patient designer."

Dropbox's case tells us:

- The enemy of software is not missing features but the loss of understanding.
- Writing code ≠ designing software.
- True design is exercising present restraint for future understanding.

And this is exactly what we must remember in the SwiftUI era.

SwiftUI's state-driven model, TCA's single state tree, and protocol-based boundary design — these are not "coding" tricks but the canon of "designing software."

Their purpose is not to make machines smarter but to make humans understand better.

All code will grow old.
Only understanding allows civilization to endure.
Writing code is a fleeting craft; designing software is a millennial philosophy.

CHAPTER 3
COGNITIVE LOAD

An empire's territory is limited, and the mind's territory is even smaller.

The sea of sand is boundless, but there is only one water pouch.

Complexity is not the enemy; it is the mirror of the brain.

The wind does not stop because of an empire's borders, nor does the brain expand because of the size of software.

The human mind is like a small reservoir, limited in capacity, yet required to bear the weight of an entire civilization.

Cognitive load — this is the fate of all developers.

In the 1960s, when the US moon landing program was put on the agenda, engineers faced this fate for the first time.

The Apollo spacecraft had to execute every operation relying on computer instructions hundreds of thousands of kilometers away, in the unforgiving vacuum of space.

Error meant death.

Complexity was not an abstract philosophy, but the lives of dozens of astronauts.

Margaret Hamilton, then a young scientist at MIT, was appointed to be responsible for the Apollo spacecraft's software.

At that time, the term "software engineering" hardly existed.

People had confidence in hardware, in rockets, in fuel, but were filled with doubt about "software."

Even in the eyes of some old-school engineers at NASA, software was merely an "accessory," not worth much attention.

But what Hamilton saw was a different picture.

She understood that the limits of the human brain meant that software had to become a "safety net."

Because astronauts, in moments of crisis, cannot simultaneously process dozens of signals and hundreds of instructions.

Their brains, like today's developers, have only limited working memory.

Experiments in cognitive psychology had long since shown:

Humans can handle no more than seven elements simultaneously in short-term memory.

This is the famous "magical number seven."

When elements exceed this limit, the brain experiences loss, confusion, and misjudgment.

For astronauts, this means:

When ten indicator lights in the cockpit light up at the same time, they cannot accurately judge priority;

When the manual requires entering a dozen or so commands within ten seconds, they may make ordering errors;

When multiple sets of data arrive from the system at the same time, they may not be able to tell which set is critical.

For developers, this means:

When there are ten nested conditions in the code, you cannot track all the branches at once;

When the architecture has ten layers of abstraction, you cannot understand all the calls in one go;

When a project has ten parallel modules, you cannot form a complete dependency map in your head.

The limits of the brain are the boundaries of complexity.

Hamilton's task was to have software shoulder the parts that exceed human cognition.

To that end she devised a principle: software must assume that errors will occur.

Astronauts will press the wrong button, sensors will send false signals, sequences of operations will be disrupted.

If the software cannot cope with those errors, the entire mission is doomed.

Under this principle, she and her team introduced a "priority interrupt system."

When the spacecraft's computer receives many tasks at once, it automatically drops secondary requests and concentrates resources on the most critical instructions.

It's like a calm gatekeeper who, on a chaotic battlefield, preserves only the life-or-death commands.

That design ultimately saved everyone on Apollo 11.

In the final minutes before the lander touched down, the computer repeatedly issued program alarms.

Alarms filled the cockpit and the astronauts were briefly thrown into confusion.

But Hamilton's priority system began to work: it discarded irrelevant radar data and focused resources on landing control.

In the end, the craft touched down smoothly, and humanity set foot on the Moon for the first time.

This is the true footnote of cognitive load.

Without Hamilton's design, the astronauts would have had to process dozens of signals at once, beyond what their brains could bear.

Without the software's filtering, they would have been drowned in a flood of information.

Complexity would have crushed them at the most critical moment.

The fate of developers is no different from that of astronauts.

We are not on the Moon, but we also live in a vacuum of complexity.

Every large application is a spacecraft.

Every release is a launch.

Every bug could be a disaster.

The limits of the brain determine that we cannot expand indefinitely.

We must, like Hamilton, build "priority interrupts."

We must admit: humans cannot understand all the logic at once.

Therefore, we need to design so that complexity is tamed within boundaries.

In the world of SwiftUI, this problem is especially pronounced.

SwiftUI's declarative philosophy brings developers closer to the natural expression of the mind.

However, when state is scattered across multiple places, when view update logic is hidden in the framework's "magic," cognitive load can still exceed the brain's limits.

Developers can get lost in a storm of state just as astronauts get lost in a noise of signals.

Hamilton's story reminds us:

Software is not about showing off; it is about protecting the human brain.

Architecture is not about elegance; it is about enabling future developers to quickly understand.

The struggle against complexity is essentially a struggle against the capacity of the mind.

NASA's moon landing is a miracle in human history.

But behind that miracle lies a sober truth:

Humans succeeded not by infinite wisdom, but by acknowledging their limitations.

Margaret Hamilton said in a speech:

"Errors are inevitable, and we must design protections for them."

This sentence is both a safeguard for astronauts and a reminder to all developers.

The wind is silent in the vacuum of space,

complexity is invisible in the world of software.

It will not crush you all at once; it will eat away at your mind.

If you refuse to acknowledge the brain's limits, it will strike you down at the most critical moment.

Humans can see the stars, yet cannot see the abyss of their own minds.

The vacuum of space will not forgive, nor will the flood of complexity.

The power of complexity lies not in its ferocity, but in its constancy.

It is like the gravity of the universe—unseen, yet never stopping.

Hamilton's deepest realization in the Apollo program was not the thrust of rockets, but the brain's capacity to endure.

After Apollo 11's successful landing, the whole world rejoiced.

Viewers in front of their TVs saw the moment humans first set foot on the Moon, but did not see the tension and chaos inside the cockpit.

In the final minutes before landing, the computer issued 1201 and 1202 program alarms.

If the astronauts had been untrained, or if the software had not been designed clearly enough, that moment would have been enough to turn the entire mission to ashes.

Fortunately, Hamilton's "priority interrupt system" saved the situation.

It automatically discarded unnecessary data and ensured the spacecraft could continue its landing.

This is the truth about cognitive load: astronauts cannot instantly tell which signals are important, so the software must make the trade-offs for them.

But the moon landing was only the beginning.

NASA's subsequent missions—Apollo 12, 13, 14, and later Skylab—faced even more complex challenges.

Spacecraft had to carry out longer missions and confront more uncertainties.

Hamilton and her team had to write software that could handle infinite possibilities within very limited computing resources.

Apollo 13 is the most famous crisis.

It was April 13, 1970, and the spacecraft was about 300,000 kilometers from Earth when an oxygen tank exploded.

The cockpit descended into chaos: lights flickered, alarms sounded continuously, and the air began to thin.

Complexity fully erupted at that moment.

The astronauts had to determine, in extremely short order, which systems were still usable and which were damaged.

They had to decide how to shut down unnecessary modules, how to conserve power, and how to recalculate a return trajectory to Earth.

This was not a drill; it was a real life-or-death decision.

The limits of working memory were fully exposed.

No human could, in a matter of minutes, simultaneously process dozens of indicators, update complex orbital data, and operate exquisitely delicate hardware.

Without software assistance, they would inevitably have descended into chaos.

Hamilton's team at mission control on Earth quickly provided instructions to the astronauts.

They handed the complex calculations to the computer and the simplified steps to the crew.

Software became the bridge, and the human mind was protected within a tolerable range.

In the end, Apollo 13 miraculously returned to Earth.

It was a failed mission, yet a victory in the struggle between human cognition and complexity.

Hamilton wrote in her recollections:

"We must assume that astronauts will make mistakes. We must assume that hardware will fail. We must assume that all complexity will concentrate and erupt at the worst possible moment. If the software cannot cope with all of this, then the mission is doomed."

This is her philosophy:

The essence of software is not functionality, but the management of cognitive load.

Developers face the same situation in their daily work. In an iteration of a large application, dozens of features move forward at once and hundreds of tasks hang on the board. Every meeting is a mini "Apollo 13." You must, within limited attention, distinguish what truly matters. You must decide what can be discarded and what must be protected.

But the human brain often fails at this. We get held back by details, drowned in noise, tempted by short-term gains. So complexity quietly grows until it becomes irreversible.

Hamilton's priority system is the way to fight this. It reminds us: don't try to process all information at once; instead, have a clear "interrupt system" that automatically drops what's unimportant.

SwiftUI's declarative programming is one such attempt. It tells developers: don't worry about how a view is drawn step by step; just care about what the state is. Don't chase every change; only update the UI when necessary.

This is a relief for cognitive load. It lets developers step away from implementation details and focus on the core logic. But the problem is, if state management is unclear and data flow is scattered everywhere, cognitive load can instead multiply.

Like Apollo's astronauts, without a priority system they would be drowned by signals; likewise, SwiftUI developers without a single source of truth will be drowned by state.

Another key principle of Hamilton's was that "errors must be recoverable." She rejected any design that assumed errors would not occur. She required the team to add safeguards at every possible point. Even for seemingly impossible errors, she insisted on having a contingency.

At the time, many criticized this as "overly cautious." Some even mocked her: "You're wasting time." But history proved that this caution saved the mission.

Developers today often repeat the same mistake. They assume users won't press the wrong buttons, that the network will always be stable, that third-party libraries will always be reliable. So, when errors occur, systems crash, users churn, and teams descend into chaos.

A trap of cognitive load is "over-optimism."

The human brain tends to ignore low-probability events.

But in complex systems, low-probability events inevitably occur.

If the software lacks safeguards, the brain will inevitably be overwhelmed.

The success of the Apollo program was not because humans were greater than the universe, but because humans acknowledged their fragility.

Hamilton made software an extension of the mind, a shield against complexity.

Her philosophy can be summed up in one sentence:

"Acknowledge the limited capacity of humans, and let systems bear the overload for us."

What developers need to learn is precisely this attitude.

Don't pretend you can understand ten modules at once; don't pretend you can control every abstraction.

Acknowledge the limits of the mind, and corral complexity into the system.

Let architecture be a filter, let patterns be a safety net.

This is not cowardice, but wisdom.

The return of Apollo 13 is the embodiment of that wisdom.

Complexity was not eradicated, but it was confined within a controllable boundary.

The wind is still silent in space.

Complexity remains invisible in software.

It will not dissipate because of a single success; it will reappear in the next mission.

All humans can do is repeatedly acknowledge it, repeatedly design, repeatedly guard against it.

Errors are inevitable.

Human capacity is limited, while the growth of complexity is boundless.

If civilization is to endure, it must establish institutions that reconcile the finite and the infinite.

The success of Apollo 11 and the dramatic return of Apollo 13 gave the world endless cheers.

Yet in NASA's control center and in MIT's laboratories, Hamilton and her team did not indulge in romantic narratives.

What they saw was a starker picture: complexity had never disappeared, only been temporarily tamed.

The astronauts' courage was recorded in history;

The president's speech was replayed repeatedly;

While Hamilton's notes, flowcharts, and annotations were thickly sealed in the archives.

Those lines of handwritten marks carried a deeper truth:

the human brain cannot bear the full complexity of software systems.

Therefore, software must become an institutional protection, not a spectacle of showmanship.

Hamilton said in an interview:

"We are not writing code; we are writing laws.

Code is law; it defines how a system acts, how it responds to errors, how it protects humans."

This statement laid the true meaning of software engineering.

Software engineering is not a pile of techniques, but the establishment of institutions.

It is like the laws of an empire, like the doctrines of a religion, like the restraints of a constitution.

Its goal is not to make machines smarter, but to make humans safer.

The Apollo experience was summarized by Hamilton into several core principles:

First, errors will inevitably occur.

No system, no human, no task can avoid mistakes.

Assuming errors will not occur is arrogance.

Software must assume errors will happen and be designed with safeguards.

Second, priorities must be clear.

When the system is overloaded, there must be a clear mechanism to know what can be discarded and what must be preserved.

Ambiguity and hesitation only amplify chaos.

Third, boundaries must be clear.

Each module must absorb complexity within its boundaries.

Do not scatter complexity across the whole system and drag everyone in.

Fourth, the institution is above the individual.

Do not rely on a single person's cleverness to save the system.

Processes must ensure that even the most ordinary member can execute the correct steps amid chaos.

These principles later became known as the cornerstones of software engineering.

In Hamilton's context, they carried a deeper meaning:

they are the institutionalized embodiment of cognitive load management.

The Apollo archives record a scene like this.

In a simulation, an astronaut intentionally pressed the wrong button.

As a result, the spacecraft's software did not crash; it calmly reassigned tasks and dropped unrelated requests.

The astronaut laughed: "It's like you anticipated I would make a mistake."

Hamilton replied: "Of course — because you will."

It was a stark yet gentle answer.

It acknowledged human limits, yet left room for humans within the system.

This is precisely the mindset developers need today.

In SwiftUI projects, we are often troubled by state management.

Variables are scattered everywhere, data flows are inconsistent, and view updates are unpredictable.

This chaos is like astronauts surrounded by dozens of signals, at a loss.

If we assume developers will not make mistakes, we will inevitably be overwhelmed by complexity.

If we assume everything will sync perfectly, then the system is destined to fail at a critical moment.

We must, like Hamilton, acknowledge the inevitability of errors.

We must design fault-tolerant boundaries into the architecture.

We must establish clear "priority interrupts" within the team.

This is SwiftUI's "single source of truth" philosophy.

It is not a flashy slogan, but a protection against cognitive load.

It tells us: data can have only one truth; views are merely mappings.

Once the truth is split, the human brain cannot cope.

Hamilton's ideas also have a profound social dimension.

At NASA at the time, many male engineers did not take software seriously.

They believed hardware was the key, the rocket was the core, and software was only an accessory.

Hamilton had to keep fighting to make people admit: software itself is the lifeline of the mission.

That struggle was not merely about gender, but about philosophy.

It required the entire organization to acknowledge: the core of complexity lies not in hardware but in cognition.

If that point is not admitted, no matter how powerful the rocket, it can fail because of cognitive collapse.

The same situation still exists in teams today.

Many managers emphasize the number of features while ignoring cognitive load.

They believe "more is better" and "faster is winning."

But complexity accumulates in the dark and will eventually bring the system down.

Hamilton's victory was not only a victory for women or for software, but a victory for cognition.

She made an empire admit: the human brain is limited and therefore must be protected by institutions.

The NASA story has a clear echo in the context of SwiftUI.

SwiftUI's design philosophy is, in fact, "institutionalized cognitive protection."

It frees developers from imperative chaos and makes state drive everything.

Its essence is not simplifying code, but simplifying the mind.

However, if developers misuse it, if state becomes fragmented, if boundaries are unclear, SwiftUI can become a new complexity trap.

It can, like an unprotected Apollo spacecraft, hurl astronauts into a chaotic storm of signals.

Therefore, SwiftUI's true value lies not in letting you write less, but in letting you have to understand less.

This is the core of cognitive load.

Hamilton's philosophy also influenced the team's culture.

She required the team, in every commit, to assume that future readers know nothing.

She required every document to prepare for the worst-case scenario.

She required every test to simulate the most absurd error conditions.

This exhausted the team, but it made the system strong.

Because complexity never chooses the most reasonable moment to appear; it always appears at the most absurd moment.

Today's teams must do the same.

Code review is not about finding faults, but about reducing future cognitive load.

Testing is not about meeting KPIs, but about protecting the system at its most absurd moments.

Documentation is not for archiving, but for helping future readers understand.

This is Hamilton's legacy:

Elevating the management of cognitive load into culture and institution.

Historians wrote in the annals:

"Civilization endures not because humans are smarter, but because humans are more clear-headed."

The Apollo program's success was not because the astronauts made no mistakes, but because their mistakes were absorbed institutionally.

The value of software engineering is not that developers are more powerful, but that developers acknowledge their own limits.

In the desert of complexity,

We cannot eliminate the sandstorms;

We can only build windbreaks,

Only design reservoirs,

Only prevent finite minds from being swallowed by infinite complexity.

This is Hamilton's revelation.

This is the philosophy of software design.

When you write a state in the world of SwiftUI, when you draw a boundary in your architecture, when you establish a process in your team,

Remember:

You are not writing code; you are writing laws.

You are not designing features; you are protecting minds.

You are not chasing elegance; you are guarding the future.

Errors are inevitable.
Complexity is eternal.
The sole goal of software engineering is to allow humans to survive within their limits.

CHAPTER 4
SOURCES OF COMPLEXITY

The cracks are not in the stones, but in the gaps between them.

Branches are not the problem; it is the combination of branches that brings empires to collapse.

The arrival of complexity never comes with a roar.

It is like nightfall, inch by inch consuming the realm.

In the world of Microsoft Office, such nightfall once quietly descended.

Office is a vast empire.

Word, Excel, PowerPoint — each is a long-established city.

In the desktop world, they each governed themselves, with complex features and a solid foundation.

But on mobile, they had to be unified:

A unified UI specification, unified interaction logic, unified synchronization mechanism.

More importantly, the empire's territory had to span not only iOS and Android, but also Web and desktop.

The empire's ambition was the breeding ground of complexity.

To make these cities run in different territories, the initial choice was natural:

Use branches to cope with differences.

Different platform, write a condition;

Different requirements, add a logic;

Different countries' language habits, add another check.

At first, this was an elegant victory.

Engineers, like gardeners, used a few branches to make a tree of features adapt to different climates.

They even felt proud:

"Look, our code is so flexible, it can handle any situation."

However, the trap of complexity was quietly opened at that moment.

Years later, when an engineer tried to modify a piece of logic, he no longer faced a few clear branches, but a jungle:

- If the platform is iOS, go to path A;
- If it is Android, go to path B;
- If the user is newly registered, go to path C;
- If it is an enterprise account, go to path D;
- If the system version is lower than a certain number, go to path E;
- If an experimental feature is enabled, go to path F.

The explosion of branches is not linear, but exponential.

Each new condition doubles the overall possibilities.

When conditions intertwine, no human brain can mentally simulate all possible outcomes.

Branches themselves are not frightening; what is frightening is their combinations.

When a logic tree has thousands upon thousands of paths, no matter how large the testing team, it cannot cover every possibility.

Developers can only rely on intuition to test selectively, and intuition is the most fragile defense against complexity.

In an internal postmortem, the Microsoft Office team admitted:

The trickiest problem they encountered was not the bugs themselves, but the unpredictability of bugs.

Bugs were no longer "inevitable errors" but "traps of possibility."

A feature works correctly in 99% of scenarios, but utterly collapses under that 1% combination of conditions.

This plunged developers into endless anxiety.

Because they could neither foresee nor reproduce it.

Complexity turned them from "masters of the code" into "prisoners of the code."

Historical records tell us:

An empire's decline is not because its territory is too large, but because its governance remains stuck in an old era.

Office's branching strategy was such governance.

It worked at first, but after the empire expanded it became a shackle.

In the mobile era, Office had to satisfy the needs of different devices, different markets, different languages.

This means the number of branches will not decrease, only continue to increase.

When the logic tree grows so large it cannot be controlled, complexity has already exceeded human cognitive capacity.

The source of complexity is not the number of features, but the combinatorial explosion of branches.

It turns everything that was once clear into the unpredictable.

In a real meeting, an Office engineer said helplessly:

"We are not writing logic, we are building a maze.

Every change is like lighting a torch in the maze — it illuminates what's before you, but deepens the darkness in the distance."

The maze of branches does not collapse in a single day.

It simply keeps adding new forks, so those who enter can no longer find an exit.

This is the first source of complexity.

Not an explosion, not a collapse, but the day-by-day, month-by-month accumulation of branches that turns the system into a jungle.

In this jungle, any step may trigger an unknown trap.

The original purpose of inheritance is to spare successors from rebuilding the city.

However, when citadels are piled layer upon layer, waterways become clogged, and streets maze-like, inheritance becomes a shackle.

Inheritance runs deeper than an ocean trench.

The jungle of complexity did not stop at branches.

When Microsoft's Office empire expanded to mobile and cross-platform, they faced not only an explosion of conditions but also the weight of history.

The history of Office ran too deep.

In the desktop era, Word, Excel, and PowerPoint had already built vast and sophisticated feature systems.

No feature was isolated; each was built on the foundations laid by predecessors.

Decades of accumulation made these apps' features so rich as to be nearly perfect, but they also made their internal structures like ancient palaces: layer upon layer, generation upon generation.

When mobile demands arrived, the team faced not the freedom of starting from scratch, but the difficulty of carving from monoliths.

They had to inherit existing logic, reuse historical modules, and ensure documents opened the same on any platform.

Inheritance became the only path.

At first, inheritance seemed reasonable.

New platform features could be added on top of base classes;

New functionality could be implemented by extending existing structures.

It was like an empire building a new city outside the old city's walls, avoiding duplicated labor.

However, complexity quietly accumulated within that "reasonableness."

Office's editor module was a typical example of the abyss of inheritance.

To keep Word and Excel consistent, the team designed a "base document class."

All document-related logic was placed there.

Word inherited it and added paragraphs, styles, and comments;

Excel inherited it and added cells, formulas, and tables;

PowerPoint also inherited it and added slides, animations, and slide masters.

At first, it was all clear and orderly.

However, as time passed, this "base document class" kept expanding like an avalanche.

It had to handle text, and it had to handle tables;

It had to be compatible with comments, and it had to be compatible with formulas;

It had to understand slide layouts, and it had to support embedded objects.

Ultimately, this class grew so large that no one dared to touch it lightly.

It stood like a temple that everyone worshipped, but no one was willing to enter.

The real trap of complexity lies not in how many features there are, but in the depth of dependencies.

When an inheritance hierarchy becomes deep enough, every modification creates ripples.

A team, trying to fix a paragraph indentation problem in

Word, had to gingerly adjust logic in a parent class; as a result, Excel's cell rendering skewed and PowerPoint's text-box alignment failed.

This is the abyss of inheritance:

it ties all functionality together, making any single change capable of triggering a chain reaction.

In such a system, bugs are no longer isolated errors but tremors through the entire system.

On Office's mobile side, these tremors are especially lethal.

Because the team must both preserve historical compatibility and adapt to mobile platform differences.

They inherited a massive structure from the desktop era, and on mobile were forced to add new layers on top of it.

Parent classes wrapped by subclasses, subclasses wrapped by further subclasses.

Each generation of engineers continued building on the legacy of the previous one.

Years later, these inheritance levels ran so deep that no one could fully understand them.

Fixing a bug often required tracing a dozen or more layers of calls;

adding a new feature often required modifying several levels simultaneously.

When debugging, developers felt as if they were in an underground maze.

Every tunnel led to another tunnel, light refracted within, sound echoed.

They kept descending but could not see the end.

This is not a dilemma unique to Office.

In the history of software civilization, the abyss of inheritance has appeared countless times.

Its temptation is reuse; its cost is coupling.

It brings short-term convenience but, in the long run, produces unbearable complexity.

Microsoft's team recognized this early.

They tried to replace inheritance with composition, to reduce dependencies through modularization.

However, the weight of history prevented them from fully escaping inheritance.

Because countless features had long been deeply embedded in parent classes, extracting them would cost more than maintaining the status quo.

So inheritance continued.

The abyss continued.

A hypothetical but plausible scenario is enough to reveal the full scope of the predicament:

In Mobile Office, there was a requirement to allow Excel tables to be embedded in and edited within Word.

To users, this was a natural request:

Insert an Excel table into a Word document and, when clicked, enter the table editing interface.

However, within the inheritance system, this amounted to disaster.

Word's parent class did not understand table logic; Excel's subclass depended on formula calculations; and the intersection between the two had to be implemented through the parent class.

Engineers were forced to add new logic to the parent class so it could support both text and tables.

That change set off a chain reaction, affecting Word, Excel, and PowerPoint all at once.

In the end, implementing this requirement took months and involved multiple teams.

And the benefit it delivered was merely convenience for users in a few scenarios.

The cost of complexity is strikingly asymmetric.

Short-term requirements are exchanged for long-term burdens.

Local convenience is exchanged for global risk.

Another consequence of the inheritance abyss is the uncontrollable Cognitive Load.

When new engineers join the team, they must spend months just to understand the vast inheritance system.

They need to trace parent-class logic, understand subclass extensions, and untangle their interdependencies.

When debugging, they shuttle constantly between different files and modules, like historians trying to sort through an empire's annals.

This learning cost far exceeds the complexity of the features themselves.

Complexity is amplified not because there are more requirements, but because inheritance entangles all requirements together.

The power of complexity is manifested most vividly in inheritance.

It traps human cognition, makes team communication inefficient, and renders bug fixes unpredictable.

The original vision of reuse ultimately became a maintenance nightmare.

Office's inheritance system is like an island that keeps sinking.

It still stands on the surface, but seawater has already poured into its cracks, and the sand is washing away beneath it.

Any new construction only accelerates the sinking.

This is the truth of the inheritance abyss:

It is not a design mistake, but a burden of history.

It is not a failure of functionality, but a cost of civilization.

The second source of complexity is inheritance.

It is like a poison, slow and lethal.

It gives teams short-term gains but, in the long run, traps them in a quagmire.

In the story of Office, this abyss of inheritance did not immediately destroy the system.

It merely slowed the system's evolution and gradually sapped the team's morale.

Until one day people realized: they were no longer designers, but custodians of history.

Abstraction is humanity's weapon against chaos.

But when there are too many weapons, they conflict with one another and create new chaos.

Magic is not a miracle, but a fog that obscures understanding.

The sources of complexity are not limited to branching and inheritance.

Within Microsoft Office's empire there are two other deep fissures: fragmentation of abstractions and the enchantment of frameworks.

The first comes from human over-design, the second from tools' over-promises.

They tangle with branching and inheritance and push complexity to the limit.

Abstraction, at first, is a gift of civilization.

When a system becomes too large for humans to confront every detail, abstraction becomes a shield.

Like city-states codifying laws to replace customs;

Like empires building roads and using standardized milestones to replace the chaos of dirt tracks.

Office's teams did the same.

They faced a world spanning desktop, web, iOS, and Android.

If each platform implemented the same logic independently, engineering would devolve into chaos.

So they chose abstraction.

They designed a "document interface" to unify the behaviors of Word, Excel, and PowerPoint;

They designed a "storage protocol" to unify local storage and cloud sync;

They designed a "rendering layer" to standardize presentation across devices.

At first, these abstractions brought clarity.

Engineers could program against interfaces without worrying about underlying differences.

Code looked clean, the architecture seemed elegant, and team productivity appeared to improve.

However, the trap of abstraction was quietly unfolding.

Because each new requirement brought new abstractions.

New features did not always fit old interfaces perfectly, so new interfaces were created.

New scenarios did not always conform to existing protocols, so new protocols were introduced.

The number of abstractions kept increasing, like shards of pottery scattered across the ground.

Engineers no longer face a single clear interface, but a dozen or so similar yet slightly different interfaces.

When developing, they must first choose which one to use;

when debugging, they must first trace which one was called.

Abstraction was supposed to reduce complexity, but after accumulating in number it created new complexity.

Inside the Office teams a joke circulated:

"The hardest bugs are not in the code, but between the interfaces."

They found that bugs were often not errors in a particular implementation, but conflicts between different abstraction layers.

One interface assumes a document is linear, while another assumes the document is a tree;

one protocol emphasizes immediacy of synchronization, while another emphasizes tolerance for sync delay.

When these assumptions meet, chaos is born.

This is the truth of fragmented abstractions.

Abstractions are not wrong, but when there are too many, too scattered, and conflicting, they lose their original meaning.

They cease to be a unified code and become fragmented local ordinances.

The third fissure in complexity is the magic of frameworks.

The lure of magic has always been powerful.

When teams are troubled by complexity, someone will always say, "We can solve this with a framework."

Frameworks promise:

If you follow my rules, I will handle the tedious details for you.

If you trust my mechanisms, I will make your development more efficient.

In the Office story, such magic was inevitable.

To adapt quickly on mobile, the team adopted a large number of third-party frameworks:

Cross-platform rendering engines, libraries for network requests, tools for data storage.

These frameworks did bring convenience at first.

They were like magicians performing complex operations inside a black box, allowing developers to call a few methods and get results.

Engineers cheered because complexity seemed to be swallowed by the frameworks.

However, complexity is not swallowed; it is merely transferred.

Over time, the framework's magic began to turn on them.

When a framework is upgraded, API changes stall the whole system;

When a framework's internal implementation conflicts with platform updates, bugs suddenly surface;

When the team tries to debug, they find they cannot penetrate the black box and must rely on scattered documentation and community information.

Complexity now manifests as invisibility.

It is no longer traceable logic, but unknowns buried inside frameworks.

Developers face bugs but cannot determine whether they belong to their own code or to the framework.

They spend countless nights tracing problems, only to find the root cause is a library they cannot control.

Microsoft's teams felt anger as a result.

They thought the magic would save them, but discovered the magic created new dependencies.

These dependencies were both technical and psychological.

The teams gradually lost autonomy and their sense of control over the system.

The most terrifying aspect of complexity is not its quantity but its invisibility.

Branch explosion makes possibilities inexhaustible, the inheritance abyss makes dependencies inseparable, fragmented abstractions make interfaces ununifiable, and framework magic makes problems invisible.

Together they form the four horsemen of complexity, driving teams toward fatigue and loss of control.

Office engineers wrote in an internal document:

"We have the most powerful productivity suite in the world, yet we are gradually losing productivity to the complexity of maintaining it."

The sentence stings, but it is unavoidably true.

After all this, Microsoft had to undertake a large-scale architectural refactor.

They began to break down abstractions and clean up redundant interfaces;

They began to reduce framework dependencies and return to core logic;

They began to try modularization, confining each module's complexity to a limited scope.

It was a painful shift.

There were no shortcuts, no magic, no instant results.

It could only be through long-term governance that complexity would be gradually reduced.

Historians wrote:

"Complexity is never destroyed; it can only be tamed.

When humans chase illusions, it appears in more complicated forms;

When humans confront it, it will slowly withdraw."

The story of Microsoft Office is precisely an illustration of this rule.

They were lost in branch explosions, struggled in the inheritance abyss, and indulged in fragmented abstractions and framework magic.

In the end, they had to admit:

Complexity is not a war that an enemy can be slain in, but a river that must be guided.

At the end of this chapter, we must remember:

- Branch explosion reminds us that the power of composition far exceeds the human mind;
- The inheritance abyss reminds us that the weight of history can crush the future;
- Fragmented abstractions remind us that unity is the true value;
- Framework magic reminds us that invisibility is the greatest risk.

The four horsemen of complexity are not fictional, but the fate every large project must endure.

Their arrival is not due to team incompetence, but the inevitability of civilization.

True wisdom is not to avoid them, but to acknowledge them and to leave breathing room in designs for future readers.

Branches are sand, inheritance is stone, abstractions are pottery shards, frameworks are mist.
Sand will pile up, stone will grow heavy, shards will break, mist will obscure.
But the human mind can still build roads within them, so long as it remembers:
The goal of the road is not to conquer complexity, but to make complexity yield to understanding.

CHAPTER 5
THE ONLY CRITERION OF MEASUREMENT

The greatest metric is not lines of code, nor performance curves, but whether your future self can bear it.

The measure of a city is not how many streets it has, but whether a stranger can find their way within it.

The only criterion of measurement: whether your future self can quickly understand it.

This sentence sounds like a maxim, but it is the most ruthless law of software civilization.

Code is not stone; it changes. Frameworks are not rails; they depreciate.

The only constant is the limits of human understanding.

Today you write logic you believe to be clear; tomorrow you may have forgotten your original intent.

In the vast history of code, countless projects die not from lack of performance but because future readers cannot understand them.

The story of Instagram is the clearest illustration of this law.

At first, it was not called Instagram.

The app Kevin Systrom founded in 2010 was called Burbn.

Burbn was a location-based social app with complex features like check-ins, dating, points / rewards, and photo sharing.

At that time, Foursquare was riding high, innovation in social apps was like a spring tide, and Burbn wanted to fight its way through.

However, the shadow of complexity already loomed at birth.

Burbn had every feature, but no clear main thread.

Users were confused by the interface: is this for check-ins? For dating? For sharing photos?

The team poured in a lot of effort but could never find the core.

Complexity is like that: it doesn't need a large system to appear; it lurks in fuzzy boundaries from the start.

Burbn's code and features piled up together like a city without a map.

The future readers are not the users, but the team itself.

When even the founders cannot quickly explain the product's purpose, complexity has already completed its first erosion.

The turning point of fate came during a conversation between Kevin Systrom and Mike Krieger.

They realized that Burbn's problem was not too few features, but too many.

So they made a ruthless decision: cut everything, keeping only photo sharing and filters.

This decision, seemingly simple, was a great turning point in the history of software.

They did not chase more features; they chose understanding.

When an app does only one thing, future readers (whether users or engineers) can quickly grasp it.

This was the moment Instagram was born.

In October 2010, Instagram officially launched.

Its main interface had only a few buttons: take a photo, add a filter, share.

Just like that, Instagram attracted one million users within a few months.

Simplicity is not sacrifice; it is strength.

Future readers can understand its purpose without being blocked by complexity.

Instagram's early code architecture, like its product philosophy, remained extremely simple.

Kevin and Mike were only two people; they had no time to build large, complex systems.

They implemented requirements in the most direct way and expressed logic in the clearest way.

At that stage, no one cared about "elegant architecture" or "perfect patterns"; they cared about one thing:

When we look back in three months, can we quickly understand what we wrote?

This was Instagram's early "measure."

Not flashy design patterns, not perfect abstractions, but whether the future can understand.

However, complexity never leaves easily.

After Instagram exploded in growth, new demands came like a tide.

Users wanted direct messages, wanted video, wanted a tagging system, wanted an Explore page.

The shadow of Facebook also gradually drew near, and rumors of acquisition filled the air.

The team expanded, features expanded, and complexity expanded with them.

Instagram was no longer the two-person workshop but a collaborative body of dozens, then hundreds.

Every feature required multiple people to collaborate; every line of code had to pass through many hands.

At this stage, complexity appeared in new forms:

- Dependencies between features made changing one piece of code affect the whole body;
- Coupling between modules turned debugging into a maze;
- Lack of documentation left new members bewildered when onboarding.

The future readers were no longer just Kevin and Mike, but the entire team.

The cost of understanding became the team's lifeline.

During an internal retrospective, an engineer wrote:

"We are not racing against competitors; we are wrestling with our own code.

If our future selves cannot quickly understand today's choices, our failure is only a matter of time."

This sentence reads like a commentary on the entire software civilization.

Instagram's success was not just because of filters and sharing, but because at critical moments they chose "comprehensibility."

And during their expansion, they had to reaffirm this principle again and again.

The story of complexity always carries the irony of fate.

Burbn was eliminated for having too many features; Instagram succeeded because it was simple.

But when Instagram itself grew into a behemoth, it too had to face the shadow of complexity.

Simplicity is not a one-time protective charm; it is a philosophy that must be constantly guarded.

Kevin Systrom once said in an interview:

"We kept asking ourselves: if today's design is something we can't even understand three months from now, then it's the wrong design."

This sentence is both product philosophy and software philosophy.

The only criterion of measurement is not whether something is elegant today, but whether it can be understood in the future.

Instagram's early architecture and evolution are an annotation of this law.

It shows us:

- There can be many features, many users, and a large team, but if the future cannot understand, everything will collapse.
- Simplicity is not compromise; it is survival.
- Comprehensibility is not a luxury; it is the only measure.

Complexity does not disappear; it only lies dormant.

A city's original streets are clear; later they become twisted by repairs and detours.

When strangers can no longer walk from one end to the other, the city has lost its soul.

Software is the same: it does not collapse because of too many features, but because future people cannot understand it.

Instagram's dawn belonged to simplicity.

One filter, one button, one share.

It allowed humanity, for the first time, to record everyday life in such a light way, shortening the world's distances through the flow of images.

But when the morning passed and the sun rose, complexity also followed.

User expectations surged like a tide.

When millions of users became tens of millions, and photos were no longer singular but carried travel, advertising, politics, and culture, Instagram could not remain forever with those three buttons.

The Explore page, direct messaging, short-form video, ad systems… each new feature was a territorial expansion of the empire.

And with each expansion, complexity accumulated in the dark.

Kevin Systrom and Mike Krieger faced a familiar dilemma:

how to choose between rapid iteration and future comprehensibility.

This is the choice every software empire must confront.

The first form of complexity appeared in team collaboration.

In the early days, two people could work with tacit understanding; the code was the conversation.

But as the team grew to dozens, conversation became meetings, meetings became documents, and documents became transmission errors.

Instagram's engineers found that:

They were no longer facing users directly, but each other's code.

A change in logic required approval from three people;

Launching a feature required coordination among four teams;

An omission in a document could lead to a week of rework.

Complexity is an amplifier of communication.

It magnifies a simple requirement into dozens of meetings and turns a small adjustment into a weeks-long war.

The story takes place in 2013, the second year after Instagram was acquired by Facebook.

The team expanded rapidly, and calls for new features grew louder.

Especially the Explore page.

Users wanted to discover new accounts and new content there, not be limited to the people they followed.

The logic behind the Explore page was far more complex than it appeared.

It required recommendation algorithms, caching mechanisms, fast rendering, and integration with the ad system.

For Instagram's engineering team, it was not just a feature but an architectural challenge.

The initial version was rushed to launch.

The code was filled with temporary calls and emergency patches, all just to deliver by the deadline.

At launch, users cheered and usage spiked.

- Debugging became extremely difficult; any change could affect the whole system;
- Bugs kept appearing, and the team fell into a continuous repair loop;
- New members could not quickly understand this portion of the logic; onboarding took weeks or even months.

Future readers were utterly lost in front of this code.

They were like people entering a city without a map—streets crisscrossed, signage was missing, and any step could lead into a dead end.

Complexity is not purely a technical problem; it is also a culture.

Under the pressure of rapid iteration, the team gradually formed a consensus:

"Ship first, refactor later."

This is a short-term victory but a long-term poison.

Because the "we'll refactor later" days often never arrive.

Engineers wrote in internal documents:

"Our Explore page is like the shadow of Burbn.

Features are increasing, but our future selves are nearly unable to understand it."

History always likes to joke.

Burbn failed because of complexity, and Instagram succeeded because of simplicity.

But when Instagram itself followed the path of expansion, it inevitably touched the trap of complexity again.

Kevin Systrom once tried to remind the team at an all-hands:

"Don't forget why we succeeded at the beginning.

It wasn't because of more features, but because it was simple and understandable."

However, the empire's pace had already quickened.

The ad system needed integration, video features needed expansion, and cross-team collaboration was unavoidable.

Complexity swept in like a storm; no one could completely stop it.

Another form of complexity appeared in the experience of newcomers.

When a new engineer joined the team, he needed weeks to understand the Explore page's logic.

Onboarding documents were often out of date, and the only option was to read the code.

But the code had already become a maze.

No one could explain all the dependencies in a single day, and even long-time employees often forgot certain details.

Future readers were no longer an abstract concept but these newcomers.

Their confusion was the direct consequence of "being unable to quickly understand."

The team's learning costs rose, morale declined, and complexity quietly devoured efficiency.

The third form of complexity is the suppression of experimentation.

In the early days, Instagram's engineers could quickly try new ideas.

One filter, one interface, a few days was enough.

But as complexity grew, any experiment became expensive.

Adding a new recommendation logic to the Explore page

could take weeks, simply because countless dependencies and compatibilities had to be handled.

As the cost of experiments rose, the pace of innovation slowed.

The team fell into another dilemma:

They were still iterating quickly, but what they iterated on was maintenance, not creation.

They were wrestling with complexity, not racing competitors.

The fourth form of complexity is invisible fear.

When a system becomes sufficiently complex, engineers dare not touch it.

They fear a small change will trigger a chain reaction.

So the code becomes wrapped in layers and grows rigid.

Features keep being added, but flexibility is gone.

This fear is the real killer.

It stops the team from taking risks, from questioning, from refactoring.

The victory of complexity is not that the system collapses, but that the team loses its courage.

An internal Instagram document once recorded this scene:

A new engineer spent a full three weeks just to understand the Explore page's logic.

When he finally could change the code, he found he hardly dared to commit.

He wrote in the document:

"This is not code; this is a trap.

I'm afraid I'll be the one to set it off."

Future readers were utterly desperate here.

Understanding was no longer a threshold but a prison.

Facebook's acquisition gave Instagram enormous resources.

But resources cannot eliminate complexity.

More people, more meetings, more documents sometimes only create more complexity.

The real way out is still to return to that cold law:

The only standard of measurement is whether the future can quickly understand.

Yet, in the tide of expansion, adhering to this law is harder than ever.

Instagram's team is struggling along this path.

In any civilization, the true measure is not its territory, but whether its records can be understood by those who come after.

Cities can collapse, empires can fall, but if the writings and rules remain clear, they continue to endure into the future.

Instagram fell into a quagmire of complexity after expanding its features.

The maze of the Explore page, the coupling with the ad system, the chaos of the direct messaging system—all like a storm on the dunes, pushing the team to the edge of comprehension.

They had to make a choice: keep accelerating until they lost control; or slow down to guard understanding.

The turning point came in 2015.

That year Instagram already had hundreds of millions of users and had become one of the fastest-growing apps in the world.

But internally, the pain caused by complexity had reached a critical point.

New engineers needed months before they could independently own features, bug-fix cycles stretched out, and team communication consumed almost all their energy.

At an all-hands meeting, Kevin Systrom said, "We must stop and ask ourselves one question:

When future people read this code, will they be able to understand it quickly?"

That sentence was not a product slogan but a declaration of software philosophy.

It reawakened the team's memory—Instagram succeeded not because of many features, but because of simplicity and clarity.

If they lost that, complexity would become the real enemy.

So Instagram began a long "comprehensibility reform."

This reform was not a one-time refactor but a series of institutional and cultural measures.

First was the remaking of documentation and knowledge.

They mandated that any new feature must be accompanied by clear documentation, and any architectural decision must leave comments.

Documentation was no longer an optional accessory but the team's contract.

Future readers would no longer be forced to infer from code but would have a clear trail.

Second was the redrawing of boundaries.

Instagram's engineers found that much complexity came from fuzzy boundaries.

Dependencies between modules had no clear contracts, and relationships between features had no defined borders.

So they began promoting the idea of "single-responsibility modules":

Each module must have clear boundaries, and every piece of complexity must have a clear owner.

This was not a pursuit of "elegance," but a pursuit of "future understandability."

Third, the strengthening of testing and verification.

At that time Instagram invested heavily in automated testing and continuous integration.

They understood that what future readers feared most was not the complexity of the code, but the uncertainty of the code.

When a change can be validated automatically, it becomes understandable.

Testing was not about achieving 100% coverage, but about providing future people with a guarantee:

"You can change boldly; this won't break."

In this reform, one case was mentioned repeatedly by the team.

A newly joined engineer was assigned to maintain the ad-serving module.

At first, he was lost in the code, like all newcomers.

But this time he found clear documentation, single-module boundaries, and comprehensive tests.

Weeks later, he could not only maintain the code independently but also confidently propose improvements.

He wrote on the internal forum:

"For the first time I felt my future self was respected.

I don't need to guess the intentions of those before me; I only need to understand the rules they left behind."

This sentence became a symbol of Instagram's internal reform.

Future readers were no longer victims, but people who were treated well.

Complexity did not disappear, but it was tamed.

It still grew, but as it grew, guardrails for understandability were also put in place.

Instagram's team learned a new attitude:

We cannot avoid complexity, but we can make complexity understandable.

This attitude gradually became Instagram's culture.

In code reviews they no longer only asked "Is it usable?" but also "Is it understandable?"

In architecture discussions they no longer only pursued "Is it elegant?" but asked "Can future people understand it?"

In feature planning they no longer only considered "Is it fast?" but asked "Can it still be maintained in the future?"

The single standard of measurement gradually seeped into every corner.

However, this reform was not smooth sailing.

Some still believed that shipping fast was the most important thing.

They worried too many rules would slow them down, and worried that documentation and tests would become a burden.

But history has repeatedly proven: the price of speed will ultimately be paid by the future.

Kevin Systrom wrote in an internal email:

"We save a minute today, and the future will make the team pay an hour.

Our silence today will make the team pay a day in the future.

Our compromise today will make the team pay a week in the future."

This email later came to be called the "Warning of Time."

It reminded everyone: the standard of measurement has never been present speed, but future understandability.

Under Facebook's aegis, Instagram gained unprecedented resources.

But they did not once again chase the illusion of "unification," nor did they stack features again; instead, they cautiously guarded understandability.

Complexity still existed, but it was no longer devouring—it was being tamed.

Instagram's team gradually formed a creed:

"Code is not written for machines, but for future people."

Machines only need results; people need understanding.

If future people cannot understand, then that code is a failure.

At this point, we can see Instagram's three journeys:

Burbn's complexity → Instagram's simplicity → Instagram's expansion and complexity → Instagram's reform and understandability.

These three journeys precisely form a microcosm of software civilization.

Complexity never disappears; it only appears in different forms.

The only victory is not to avoid complexity, but to make it quickly understandable to future people.

The sole standard for judging good code is not whether it looks elegant today, but whether it can be quickly understood in the future.

Instagram's story tells us:

- The more features and the greater the complexity, as long as the future can understand it, the team can survive.
- The fewer the features and the simpler the architecture, if the future cannot understand it, the team will collapse.

This is the law of software civilization, and one of the core philosophies of this book.

The future you is the only reader.

If the future you cannot understand the code you write today, then it is a failure.

If the future you can quickly understand it, then it is a victory.

Great civilizations are not built on stone, but on understanding.
Great software is not built on showmanship, but on whether the future can quickly understand it.

PART TWO
THE PHILOSOPHY AND PRINCIPLES OF DESIGN

CHAPTER 6
A REINTERPRETATION OF SOLID

Laws are not eternal, but a balance of a stage. Design principles are likewise: born in the old world, grown in a new realm, dying in illusion.

Complexity is a persistent force, and design principles are the defenses set up by humans.

In the history of software, SOLID has been hailed as the golden rule; it is like the charter of an empire, guiding countless engineers through long nights.

Single Responsibility, Open/Closed, Liskov Substitution, Interface Segregation, Dependency Inversion — five decrees, like five stone pillars, once supported the hall of object-oriented programming.

However, when SwiftUI appeared, when declarative and functional thinking seeped into the iOS world, these pillars began to look outdated.

They had not collapsed, but the shadows they cast did not always align with the new architectures.

Like an empire's old code being reinterpreted on new territory.

Netflix is such an empire.

Its territory is not land, but screens.

Hundreds of millions of users watch on different devices: iPhone, iPad, Apple TV, and every experience must be consistent and smooth.

The Netflix app must withstand the flood of users online simultaneously around the globe and remain stable under countless edge conditions.

This is not an ordinary city, but a giant metropolis that never sleeps.

In this context, the SOLID principles are both a beacon and a burden.

They once helped Netflix establish a solid order, but in the SwiftUI era they also created new illusions.

In Netflix's early days, the team relied on the classic MVC architecture.

View, Controller, Model — the three were like the empire's three major departments, each fulfilling its duty.

But as features expanded, controllers became behemoths.

They took on too many responsibilities, from network requests to data binding, from driving animations to state management.

A controller was like a prime minister managing military, governance, and finance at once, and would eventually be crushed by the burden.

So the flag of SOLID was raised.

Single Responsibility became the weapon against bloated controllers.

Each piece of logic was split, each module doing only one thing.

Netflix's engineers wrote in internal documentation:

"We must build boundaries of responsibility as if building high walls, so that every brick is clearly visible."

At first, this brought order. Controllers were no longer bloated; logic was distributed across multiple small modules.

Dependency inversion freed higher layers from depending on concrete implementations, and interface segregation meant callers only needed to know the parts they required. The whole architecture seemed elegant, like a finely crafted palace.

But complexity never exits easily. It merely dons a different mask.

When SwiftUI appeared, it brought another philosophy: the UI was no longer a pile of imperative commands, but a declaration of state. The interface was no longer a collection of operations, but a projection of data. "Let the view be a mirror of state." This is SwiftUI's creed.

However, this declarative way of thinking does not always align with some of SOLID's principles.

Single Responsibility demands modules be split more finely; SwiftUI, meanwhile, leans toward composition, allowing a view to naturally embody multiple mappings of state. The Open/Closed Principle requires extension rather than modification; SwiftUI views often achieve clarity by directly changing declarations. Liskov Substitution carries deep meaning in a polymorphic world; in SwiftUI's world, composition often trumps inheritance, and substitution is no longer the central concern.

Netflix's engineers soon discovered: if they rigidly applied the old SOLID canon, they would fall into overengineering. A simple playback interface was dissected into dozens of tiny responsibilities, each with its own protocol and implementation. The result was not clarity but fragmentation. Every requirement change required crossing multiple small modules, like traversing a maze made of countless little doors.

The truth about complexity revealed itself here. SOLID was once a weapon against complexity, but in the world of SwiftUI it can become a new source of complexity. Because the principles themselves can become illusions. When you blindly follow them, you are led into another extreme.

Debate arose within Netflix's team. Some insisted SOLID was an eternal law and any deviation was dangerous. Others argued that SwiftUI had already changed the world and we needed new interpretations. The debate continued for months, like an empire's internal dispute over old codes and new statutes.

Complexity takes no side; it simply watches humans contradict themselves.

At an internal seminar, a senior engineer raised a question: "Where is the limit of Single Responsibility? If we split every detail, what do we end up with? Depth, or fragmentation?"

The question struck the core. The original purpose of Single Responsibility is to make modules easier to understand. But when responsibilities are over-split, the cost of understanding actually rises. Human minds are not good at finding paths through a fragmented maze.

The Netflix app has to serve hundreds of millions of users, not a perfect textbook case. The struggle with complexity is not philosophical purity, but the economics of cognition.

SwiftUI gave Netflix a new opportunity. They began to try using declarative composition, rather than rigid decomposition, to tackle complexity. A playback interface can be composed of many small views, each clearly expressing its own intent. Not by layering isolation through protocols and interfaces, creating superficially elegant deep abstractions.

This shift is not a rejection of SOLID, but a reinterpretation. Principles are not ruins, but cornerstones. Yet on new ground, the cornerstones need new placement.

Complexity still exists; it will not disappear because of SwiftUI's elegance. It simply changes its disguise—from bloated controllers to excessive responsibility splitting. What humans need is not blind obedience, but clear-headed choice.

Netflix's story is only just beginning. They must find balance between the old canon and the new philosophy, and a way out between principles and reality.

The dust of complexity still drifts in the wind. No one can be certain they are on the right path. But at least they are beginning to realize: SOLID is not eternal; it is only a temporary defense.

Once law becomes faith, it transcends its original purpose.

Humans no longer obey reason, but illusion.

Complexity is not a sudden collapse, but a gradual accumulation. Netflix's engineering team first raised the flag of SOLID to resist bloated controllers and the chaotic piling up of logic. At that time, the five principles were like the empire's charter, restoring order to chaos. However, any charter, once absolutized, will lose its original meaning. SOLID is no exception.

Within Netflix, there was a playback team. They were responsible for core features: video playback, quality switching, subtitles, and recommendations. This was one of the earliest groups to embrace SwiftUI and also the most rigorous in applying SOLID. They believed that by strictly enforcing Single Responsibility and Dependency Inversion, they could keep the complex playback interface clear.

The initial results were encouraging. The playback module was split into dozens of small components: a subtitle manager, a network buffering controller, a quality strategy, a UI rendering layer—each part with a clear boundary. Interfaces were segregated, dependencies inverted; each module stood like a sturdy little city. The team took pride in this, as if they were building an impregnable imperial fortress.

But complexity doesn't care about your pride. It quietly breeds in the gaps between these boundaries.

A new requirement arrived: users wanted to be able to switch audio tracks and subtitles instantly during playback. This meant the UI had to respond, the network had to be rescheduled, and the playback engine had to stitch things together seamlessly.

Problems emerged. Although the requirement was logically simple, it involved too many modules. The subtitle module, the audio-track module, the playback engine, the UI rendering layer—each had a clear single responsibility, but each needed to be coordinated. The team found they had to cross a dozen interfaces to complete a simple state change. A single requirement felt like running between city-states of an empire, delivering orders.

Developers said in a meeting, "We thought splitting would reduce complexity, but now we're just wandering in a maze of interfaces."

This situation is even more pronounced in the context of SwiftUI.

SwiftUI's philosophy is composition. A playback interface is not pieced together from countless tiny, responsibility-split modules, but is naturally composed from a few clear states and views. Composition emphasizes bringing things together, not cutting things apart. Yet an extreme interpretation of SOLID demands that every responsibility be split.

As a result, Netflix's playback interface displayed a strange phenomenon: a SwiftUI view that looked simple actually depended on a dozen protocols and objects behind the scenes. Every change required traversing multiple layers of abstraction to find the real logic. This was not depth, but fragmentation.

Complexity changed its face—from bloat to fragmentation. But it still exists, still devouring minds.

Conflicts gradually erupted during the team's internal review.

One camp insisted, "We must be faithful to SOLID. It is the industry's golden law; we cannot betray it lightly." The other camp retorted, "We are not writing academic papers; we are facing real users. SwiftUI's philosophy of composition conflicts with certain SOLID dogmas. We need a new interpretation."

The debate was fierce, like a legal argument within an empire. The old guard believed any problem arose from insufficiently thorough application of the principles; the new guard believed over-application itself was the problem.

Complexity accumulated in that debate. With every delayed requirement, every postponed release, every team argument, complexity silently increased.

Historians would call this "the trap of legalism." When principles are absolutized, they depart from their original intent. Single Responsibility was meant to reduce cognitive load; over-splitting, however, makes the Cognitive Load heavier. Dependency Inversion was meant to reduce coupling; over-abstraction forces every act of understanding to cross multiple layers of interfaces. Liskov Substitution was meant to ensure clarity in polymorphism; in a composition-first SwiftUI world, it instead becomes an unnecessary shackle.

Netflix's team thus fell into an illusion. They thought they were obeying the golden rules; in reality, they were being enslaved by them.

A turning point came in a real incident.

It was a global launch day. Netflix released a new feature: users could preview the next episode during playback and decide whether to skip the intro.

After release, they quickly received a flood of user complaints. On some devices, clicking "Skip Intro" caused playback to freeze. Engineers urgently investigated but found the problem hard to locate.

The cause soon surfaced: the feature's implementation involved the playback engine, UI rendering, network requests, and synchronization of subtitles and audio tracks. Each part had a single responsibility, but they were isolated from one another. To debug, engineers had to cross dozens of interfaces, tracing the transfer of state between modules. It took a full three days before they found the root cause: a piece of state was lost while crossing multiple responsibility boundaries.

"We were not defeated by complexity, but trapped by our own principles." An engineer wrote this in the postmortem.

The incident shook Netflix internally. Management demanded the team reassess their design philosophy. New voices gradually emerged within the team.

These voices emphasized: "Our goal is not to be faithful to principles, but to reduce cognitive load. SOLID once helped us resist complexity, but in the context of SwiftUI we need a new balance."

This was the embryo of "Cognitive Load First." It was not a denial of SOLID, but a reinterpretation. Single Responsibility is not infinite splitting, but keeping modules at a size that humans can understand. Dependency Inversion is not layer upon layer of abstraction, but appropriate isolation so boundaries are clear without being excessive. Interface Segregation is not countless tiny interfaces, but avoiding exposing irrelevant information. Principles are no longer the goal, but the means.

At a workshop, an architect quoted a metaphor: "SOLID is the canon of the old empire, while SwiftUI is the climate of the new land. We need to adapt the canon to the land, not force the land to submit to the canon."

The metaphor dawned on many. They realized they had been trying to govern a new world with old decrees. Complexity was hiding in that mismatch.

However, the shift was not easy. The old guard remained steadfast, believing any deviation was dangerous. The new guard advocated practice; they experimented on a small scale with "composition-first" approaches, trading fewer abstractions for lower cognitive load.

The struggle was like a civil war within an empire. There were no guns, but morale and time were consumed. Complexity remained, still quietly accumulating.

Netflix's team was still wandering this path. They wavered between the old canon and the new philosophy, between principles and reality. Complexity never exited the stage; it simply watched coldly as humans were swayed by illusions.

If the canon is blindly believed, it becomes a shackle;

If the canon is understood, it becomes a weapon.

True wisdom does not lie in obeying rules, but in mastering cognition.

Complexity continued to accumulate in the shadows. Netflix's team had already realized that SOLID could no longer be treated as an absolute decree. But realizing the problem did not mean finding the answer. The empire's canon needed rewriting, yet the new words had not been formed.

At that moment, a new attempt quietly began.

In the mobile client team, there was a senior engineer responsible for the "Resume Playback" feature: when users return to the app, they can continue watching from where they last left off. The feature seemed simple, but it involved three major modules: the playback engine, network synchronization, and UI rendering. In the past, in order to strictly adhere to Single Responsibility, they split the logic into countless small units: a playback state manager, a timestamp synchronizer, a UI update coordinator—each connected via protocols.

However, this time he chose a different approach. He decided to use SwiftUI's composition philosophy: have the "Resume Playback" view bind directly to the playback state, letting the state naturally drive the UI instead of going through layers of abstract interfaces. He only kept the most critical boundary—the isolation between network synchronization and local state.

This meant fewer modules and reduced levels of abstraction. The logic remained clear, but the cognitive cost of reading it dropped significantly. A newly onboarded engineer only needed to understand a few states to grasp how the whole feature worked.

"This is not violating SOLID, but reinterpreting it," he said in the team's presentation. "Single Responsibility is not infinite splitting, but keeping modules at a size that humans can quickly understand."

This attempt triggered a chain reaction.

Other teams began trying similar approaches in their SwiftUI projects. They gradually discovered:

- Sometimes, composing logic directly in the view is clearer than abstracting countless protocols;
- Sometimes, reducing the number of interfaces is more effective than interface segregation;
- Sometimes, dependency inversion doesn't require grand abstractions, only a lightweight boundary.

The SOLID principles were not discarded. They still existed, but their interpretation changed. They shifted from being "sacred laws" to "tools for cognitive optimization."

At an interdepartmental architecture workshop, Netflix's technical lead proposed a new definition:

"We are not discarding SOLID; we are making it serve a higher goal — reducing cognitive load. This means:

Single Responsibility should be measured by the human mind, not by abstraction;

The Open–Closed Principle should be bounded by the cost of understanding, not by the fear of change;

Liskov Substitution should be valued only when true polymorphism is needed, not treated as a formal dogma;

Interface Segregation should avoid exposing irrelevant information, not split everything into countless fine-grained interfaces;

Dependency Inversion should isolate complexity at the boundary, not create layer upon layer of abstraction."

This is not denial, but rewriting. Like a new charter for the empire, it inherits the spirit of the old canon while using new words to suit new lands.

Complexity still exists, but it is being re-governed.

In the new practice, Netflix's SwiftUI interfaces were no longer a fragmented maze, but a deep-yet-simple composition. A playback screen might be driven by only a few key states: playing, paused, buffering, failed. All logic revolves around those states, rather than being scattered across dozens of responsibility units. The path to understanding was shortened, and the cost of comprehension lowered.

Engineers felt relief again. They no longer had to wander a maze of interfaces, nor memorize countless abstract definitions. They regained mastery over the system, instead of being enslaved by it.

The shift did not happen overnight. Some still questioned it, fearing that simplification would lead to long-term chaos. But the facts showed that reduced cognitive load brought faster iteration, fewer bugs, and a more stable user experience.

Data convinced the skeptics. Average bug-fix time dropped, feature iteration cycles shortened, and new hires ramped up faster. Complexity still existed, but it was locked inside deeper modules instead of scattered among innumerable fragments.

"The value of the old canon is not its words, but the spirit it fosters. When the words obstruct the spirit, new words must appear."

Netflix's practice is exactly such a footnote. They did not abandon SOLID; they reinterpreted it. They made SOLID a tool that serves cognitive load, not a decree that stands above humans.

This brings a deeper insight:

The goal of software design has never been "to follow principles," but "to reduce complexity." Principles are tools, not ends. When a tool becomes an end in itself, it turns into an illusion. Illusions create new complexity instead of solving it.

The design philosophy of the SwiftUI era is to expose those illusions. It tells us:

Composition can replace inheritance;

Plainness can beat excessive abstraction;

A single source of truth for state is more reliable than layer upon layer of isolation.

This is not a betrayal of SOLID, but a return to its essence. The essence of SOLID has always been to reduce cognitive load.

Netflix's story ultimately became an industry case study. They candidly wrote on their tech blog: "SOLID still has value in SwiftUI, but we must be wary of its illusions. In the new context, reducing cognitive load is our true goal."

That sentence, like a seal, was stamped on the record of software design civilization. It reminded all who came after: do not blindly worship rules, do not fall into illusions. Complexity will not vanish because of your devotion; it will yield to your clear-headedness.

Here we arrive at the ultimate philosophy:

The sole goal of software design is to reduce complexity. SOLID is a tool, not a decree. The world of SwiftUI needs a new balance: measured by cognitive load, bounded by the human mind.

True architecture is not showy patterns, but comprehensible order.

When humans remember: principles are not faith, but weapons;
When humans understand: complexity cannot be eliminated, only constrained;
When humans acknowledge: boundaries are not walls, but bridges;
then the civilization of software truly begins.

CHAPTER 7
FROM CLEAN CODE TO COGNITIVE LOAD

Excessive order is also chaos.

When statutes outweigh thought, when rules override intuition, an empire falls not to enemies but chokes on itself.

The wind does not stop because the dunes are neatly arranged.

Complexity does not dissipate because of "cleanliness".

Humans crave order, so they write codes, build roads, and compile regulations.

But when the codes become overly complex, the roads overly winding, and the regulations overly fragmented, order reverses into a new chaos.

The "Clean Code" of software engineering is precisely such a code.

It arose from developers' fear of chaos: variables named arbitrarily, bloated functions, heavily coupled modules.

Thus the slogan of "clean code" sounded, spreading through teams like imperial decrees.

Names must be clear, functions must be short, classes must have a single responsibility.

All of this was originally intended to tame complexity.

But complexity never yields.

It only dons a different coat.

Google's Android team was once one of the most devout adherents of Clean Code.

Their apps run on billions of devices worldwide; any single bug could affect tens of millions of users.

Therefore, they pushed Clean Code principles to the extreme:

Any function longer than ten lines must be broken up;

Any possible responsibility should be its own class;

Any module should be isolated by interfaces to guard against future changes.

On the surface, it was an extremely tidy land.

The classes in the codebase stood in neat rows like soldiers, and the functions were short and lean like ranks of an army.

Code review comments were full of "this should be split further" and "this function is too long."

Everything conformed to the laws of Clean Code.

However, complexity did not decrease.

It merely shifted from the implementation layer to the cognitive layer.

When a new engineer joins, they do not face bloated functions but hundreds of fragmented methods.

They must jump between dozens of files to understand the full picture of a single logic.

They must trace back and forth between interfaces and implementations to confirm the true source of a value.

Beneath the tidy surface lies a fractured cognitive experience.

The empire's code did not reduce corruption; it only made corruption more concealed.

The overzealous enforcement of Clean Code did not lower complexity; it merely shifted complexity onto the burden of understanding.

Developers of Swift and SwiftUI often find these stories familiar, because they have experienced a similar illusion. When the Swift language introduced protocols and extensions, many teams excitedly abstracted everything into interfaces. The networking layer was split into dozens of protocols, the service layer wrapped in multiple layers, and ViewModels were cut into countless tiny components. The result: implementations looked "elegant," but reading them was extremely painful.

Complexity did not disappear.

It merely transformed into Cognitive Load — the burden on cognition.

This is the truth we must face:

the goal of software design is not to make code "clean," but to make it understandable by humans.

Clean Code is a means; Cognitive Load is the end.

Google's Android team eventually admitted in an internal review:

their Clean Code culture created huge onboarding costs.

New engineers needed months to become familiar with the system, not because the logic was complex, but because the abstractions were excessive.

Their toolchain showed: lines of code decreased, but the number of files exploded.

Bug-triage times lengthened, development slowed, and team morale fell.

They began to adjust.

They found that the most important thing was not "functions must be short," but "the logic must be clear at a glance."

Not "classes must have a single responsibility," but "modules should be deep and stable."

Not "interfaces should exist everywhere," but "boundaries should be just right."

This is the shift from Clean Code to prioritizing Cognitive Load.

From rule-driven to cognition-driven.

From the statutes of law to the human mind.

In the world of SwiftUI, this shift is especially important.

SwiftUI views are declarative and seem to naturally split into countless small components. If developers blindly chase the Clean Code virtues of smallness and reuse, they will split a simple page into a dozen Views, each showing only a few lines of content. The result is: to understand a single screen, you must jump between dozens of files. This does not reduce complexity; it merely transforms it into another form.

When developers prioritize Cognitive Load, they make different choices: rather than fragmenting logic, they keep a clear structure in a single file. Rather than over-reusing, they tolerate local duplication so the logic remains intact. Rather than pursuing surface elegance, they pursue overall comprehensibility.

This is not an opposition to Clean Code but a transcendence of it. Clean Code is necessary but not sufficient. It must submit to the principle of prioritizing Cognitive Load.

An empire's codes that do not reduce the burden on the people are useless. Coding rules that do not reduce developers' comprehension cost are shackles.

Google's Android team taught us with their experiment: excessive Clean Code creates new chaos. SwiftUI developers must also learn from this: the true goal is not the illusion of neatness but clarity of cognition.

Complexity will not vanish because of rules.

It will only be moved into the human mind.

And the human mind is the scarcest resource.

When the code of laws grows long, memory grows short; when rules proliferate, the mind fragments.

True order is not the accumulation of statutes but the saving of cognition.

The power of complexity has never lain in the code itself but in human understanding. Google's Android team proved this with their own experience.

Under the laws of Clean Code they built a city that looked perfect. Streets were straight, houses orderly, every corner conformed to the rules. But when new residents entered that city, they found themselves lost. Because although the city was tidy, it lacked intuition. The roads were too similar, the houses too repetitive, and the entrances and exits were fragmented by the rules.

This is the real consequence of excessive Clean Code:

Seemingly concise, but actually complex;

Seemingly tidy, but actually chaotic;

Seemingly elegant, but actually exhausting.

At internal retrospectives, Google's engineers repeatedly mentioned one word: onboarding.

When new engineers join the team, they do not face a large, coherent logic, but hundreds or thousands of tiny fragments.

They must build connections between the fragments to understand the whole.

It's like sending a recruit into an empire with a hundred thousand laws without giving them a map.

They must rely on their own memory and experience to find patterns among the statutes.

Such a burden is almost certain to end in failure.

A senior engineer wrote:

"The more we split things, the harder it is for newcomers to understand.

Clean Code was supposed to be a bridge, but it became a maze."

That quote was posted on the internal Wiki's front page as a warning for the whole team.

So the shift began.

They proposed a new principle:

The primary goal of code is not to obey rules, but to reduce the cost of understanding.

This principle was later called Cognitive Load first.

In practice, what does this mean?

First, they began to re-examine function length.

The traditional Clean Code requirement is: functions should be as short as possible, each doing one thing.

However, under the Cognitive Load–first philosophy they discovered:

An overly short function actually increases the cost of context switching,

Because the reader must jump frequently to piece together the logic.

So they stopped splitting blindly.

Instead, they used "Cognitive Load" as the standard:

If a function is longer but its logic is coherent and highly readable, keep it together.

If splitting it would force frequent jumps, keep it intact.

In short: smallness is not the goal; clarity is.

Second, they began to adjust their interpretation of "single responsibility."

The Clean Code slogan is: each class should do only one thing.

So they split classes into extremely small pieces:

One class responsible for one data transformation, one class responsible for one interface call, one class responsible for one small piece of logic.

The result was thousands upon thousands of tiny classes filling the system.

When reading the code, engineers had to shuttle between countless files.

This kind of "single responsibility" actually increased Cognitive Load.

After the shift, they adopted a new criterion:

Responsibility is defined not as the smallest unit of logic, but as the smallest unit of understanding.

If a class carries more logic but is essentially a coherent whole, keep it together.

If splitting it would interrupt comprehension, refuse to split.

This shift applies equally in the world of SwiftUI.

SwiftUI Views are, in essence, declarative functions.

Followers of Clean Code often pull every small component out into its own View, pursuing so-called reuse and neatness.

The result can be a single screen requiring jumps across twenty files.

Developers' Cognitive Load becomes far greater than the burden of a single file.

When Cognitive Load is prioritized, developers find that rather than splitting into twenty files, it's better to keep things in one file and organize them with clear sections.

Rather than chasing extreme reuse, accept local duplication so the logic stays intact.

That is the real optimization: not reducing lines of code, but reducing the burden of understanding.

Google's engineers also redefined "abstraction."

In the Clean Code culture, abstraction was almost a religion.

Any similar logic had to be extracted into a function or class.

Any potential difference had to be isolated behind an interface.

The result was a large number of "extensible" abstractions that were seldom actually extended.

The system appeared elegant on the surface, but maintainers were lost in countless layers of abstraction.

They finally realized:

Abstraction is not the goal; cognitive clarity is.

Rather than creating premature abstractions, accept local duplication.

Rather than designing complex interfaces, express intent directly.

Rather than pursuing hypothetical future possibilities, serve present understanding.

This shift resonates deeply in the iOS world.

Swift's protocols were once seen by developers as a powerful tool for abstraction. Many teams, when designing architectures, abstracted almost all logic into protocols in the name of "flexibility." The result was that they had to jump between a dozen protocols to find a single implementation. That was not flexibility; it was confusion.

The Cognitive Load–first philosophy tells us: protocols should be used for real boundaries, not as an abused wrapper. The definition of a boundary should be judged by "cognitive clarity," not by "theoretical perfection."

Google's team also found in practice that Cognitive Load–first changes team culture.

Under the laws of Clean Code, code review focused on: Are functions too long? Do classes have a single responsibility? Is there duplication? This led the team into a formalistic obsession. They chased rules and neglected the true goal.

After adopting Cognitive Load–first, code review focused on: Can future readers quickly understand this? Is the logic immediately clear? Are modules placed within the correct boundaries?

This shift may seem subtle, but it is profound. It brought software engineering back from "rule worship" to "human-centeredness."

In SwiftUI teams, this cultural shift is equally important.

Code review is no longer about nitpicking "can this be split further," but about discussing "is this clear enough." No longer about pursuing "minimal duplication," but about pursuing "maximum readability." No longer about emphasizing "perfect abstraction," but about emphasizing "clear boundaries."

This is real progress:

From legalism to Cognitive Load–first.

From the appearance of rules to the essence of understanding.

In Google's reflections there is a passage that was widely quoted later:

"Clean Code gave us order, but Cognitive Load–first gave us freedom.

Order is the order of rules; freedom is the freedom of understanding.

We would rather have imperfect code that humans can quickly understand.

Because software is written for humans to read; machines just happen to run it."

That passage is etched like an inscription in the team's memory.

Complexity does not decrease because of rules.

It only shifts between different layers.

Clean Code can reduce implementation chaos, but it may increase cognitive chaos.

Cognitive Load–first is the real antidote.

Rules make people fearful; understanding makes people free.

When complexity becomes a flood of civilization, the only levee is not more statutes, but less Cognitive Load.

Complexity will not disappear.

It only waits, waiting for human minds to grow weary.

After Google's Android team shifted to Cognitive Load–first, they finally understood: the true victory is not making code conform to the canon, but making it easy for future readers to understand.

This shift changed their architecture.

In the past, their system was full of countless tiny classes and functions.

Like a city divided into thousands upon thousands of blocks.

Each block was neat and uniform, yet it made people lose their way.

Under the philosophy of Cognitive Load–first, they began to refactor:

- Merge overly split classes back together so logic remains whole.
- Preserve local duplication and avoid premature abstraction.
- Introduce clear modules at key boundaries, instead of creating interfaces everywhere.

This refactoring was like digging deep wells.

No longer spreading water across countless shallow pits, but concentrating it in a few deep wells.

That way, people fetching water don't have to run around; they can satisfy their needs in one place.

The SwiftUI world is undergoing a similar evolution.

In early SwiftUI projects, many teams were obsessed with "splitting."

They pulled every button, every piece of text, every small component out into its own View.

The result was that a simple interface was split into dozens of files.

When reading, developers had to constantly jump around, and Cognitive Load was mercilessly raised.

Later, they gradually realized:

Rather than pursuing extreme reuse, it's better to maintain a clear structure in a single file.

Rather than abstracting a button into ten files, let it remain in context and coexist with the surrounding logic.

SwiftUI's philosophy is, after all, "state-driven," not "fragment assembly."

This shift is precisely the embodiment of Cognitive Load–first.

Prioritizing Cognitive Load also changed the team's way of communicating.

In the past, under the culture of Clean Code, code review discussions often fell into formalism:

"This function is too long."

"Can an interface be extracted here?"

"Does this logic violate single responsibility?"

These discussions, while outwardly pursuing cleanliness, actually increased friction.

Engineers, caught in endless arguments, lost focus on the real problems.

In a Cognitive Load–first culture, the discussion shifted to a different mode:

"Can future readers quickly understand this?"

"Is this logic clear enough?"

"Are this module's boundaries natural?"

These discussions were no longer judges of rules but guardians of understanding.

They transformed the team from slaves of doctrine into stewards of cognition.

In the iOS world, this cultural shift is especially critical.

The combination of SwiftUI and TCA gave teams a new perspective:

State-driven means logic is not cut into countless tiny functions but concentrated in Reducers.

Reducers are not about obeying rules but about making all changes understandable in one place.

This concentration is precisely the embodiment of Cognitive Load–first.

A complex business scenario that, under Clean Code thinking, might be split into dozens of small methods, under TCA's philosophy is centralized in a Reducer, forming an organic whole.

This lets developers read without jumping between countless files and understand the whole in one place.

In the long run, Cognitive Load–first brings a deeper change: the team's psychological safety.

Under the culture of Clean Code, engineers often feared "violating the rules."

They feared functions being too long, classes bearing too many responsibilities, and being told in review "this could be further abstracted."

This fear led them to continually pursue superficial neatness while neglecting true understanding.

In a Cognitive Load–first culture, engineers no longer fear "breaking the rules." Because the rules themselves are no longer the goal. The sole goal is to reduce cognitive load. As long as the code is clear and the logic understandable, it is reasonable for a function to be a bit long or for a class to take on more responsibilities.

This culture brings a new kind of freedom. Freedom is not arbitrariness, but clarity. Freedom is not chaos, but restraint.

Google's team wrote in a retrospective: "We stepped out of legalism and entered the philosophy of cognition. This made us masters of the system again, not servants of the rules."

There are similar stories in SwiftUI teams.

A small startup, early on following Clean Code's dogma, split all logic into extreme fragments. Their app was only a simple scheduling manager, yet it had hundreds of small View files. Each View file was responsible for displaying just a small piece of text or a button. As a result, newcomers spent weeks before they could understand the rendering logic of a simple page.

Later they shifted to Cognitive Load–first. They merged files, reduced jumping, and accepted local duplication. They found that development speed not only did not decline but actually improved. Because the team's cognitive load decreased, the efficiency of understanding increased.

This is the long-term power of Cognitive Load–first. It not

only changes the shape of code but also the team's culture and mindset.

Complexity does not disappear because of Clean Code; it only changes form. Only when a team makes Cognitive Load its primary goal is complexity truly controlled.

This also reveals a deeper philosophy: software design is not for machines but for humans.

Machines do not care about function length, class responsibilities, or whether something is abstracted. Machines only execute. Humans need to understand. Understanding is the true goal of software design.

Clean Code is a stage in history. It was like an empire's codex, once bringing order and hope. But the end of the codex is not more rules, but less Cognitive Load.

Cognitive Load–first is a new phase. It is like a new order, bringing clarity, bringing freedom, and bringing more lasting vitality.

In the world of SwiftUI, developers will continue to walk this path. They will face new complexities: state bloat, asynchronous traps, and architectural choices. They will continue to choose between Clean Code and Cognitive Load. And the ultimate answer will always point in the same direction: Cognitive Load–first.

The greatest software is not the cleanest, but the most understandable. The most enduring teams are not the most rule-abiding, but the most committed to clarity.

CHAPTER 8
DEEP MODULES AND SHALLOW MODULES

The water of a shallow shoal can be stepped on by anyone, yet it is muddy everywhere.
The water of a deep well has a narrow mouth, yet the sweet spring is reached directly.

The appearance of complexity always tempts us to disperse it.

Every small module, every thin layer, seems clear, but in reality is like a field of gravel in the desert.

Walking through it, steps become cumbersome, attention scatters, and energy is exhausted.

A deep module, however, is like a well: the entrance is small, but it pulls complexity inward and only presents the most necessary results.

In the history of iOS development, this contrast has a typical example:

the evolution of the networking layer.

In the early years of the empire, people used NSURLConnection.

Network requests then were like waystations scattered across the frontier.

Each request required engineers to handle it personally: setting delegates, managing callbacks, handling caching, listening for errors.

These waystations had no unified system, only scattered conventions.

For small-scale applications this seemed acceptable.

Like a village, a few dirt roads were enough to meet travel needs.

However, when an app scaled, when hundreds of network requests intertwined, problems inevitably arose.

Engineers had to repeat similar logic in each module.

Each request had subtle differences, and every error had to be caught separately.

When a bug appeared, you had to go into every "dirt road", check them one by one, and fix them one by one.

These "shallow modules", superficially appearing to have clear divisions of labor, in fact let complexity diffuse throughout the system.

The biggest problem with shallow modules is not the complexity of implementation, but the dispersion of understanding.

When an engineer wants to understand the entire networking layer, they must jump back and forth among countless files to piece together the whole.

Each request is a story, but there is no common language.

Over time, the team lost the "global narrative", leaving only fragmented comments and oral legends.

Complexity grows in this diffusion.

It is not like a centralized monster, but like countless tiny grains of sand that, accumulating over time, form dunes that cannot be crossed.

Apple's engineers also saw this limitation.

They knew that while NSURLConnection worked, its shallow-module design was destined to be unable to support an increasingly complex ecosystem.

So, they began to plan a major shift.

Just as an empire needs to build a central avenue to bring scattered waystations under a unified system, iOS also needed a deep module to concentrate the complexity of network requests and hide it behind a clear boundary.

This deep module is URLSession.

Before URLSession appeared, developers' daily life was a scene of chaos:

- Some wrote their own caching logic, others relied on third-party libraries;
- Some used synchronous calls, others used asynchronous callbacks;
- Error handling had no unified convention, and retry mechanisms were haphazardly stitched together.

The result was: as an app scaled, the networking layer became the most fragile part. A single system upgrade could cause multiple requests to fail simultaneously. A single team member's departure could leave a feature completely unmaintainable.

This is the cost of shallow modules: they make complexity appear dispersed while in fact making it ubiquitous. They make a team seem flexible, while in reality they strip the team of the possibility of centralized governance.

The arrival of URLSession carried a certain institutional temperament. It was like a code of laws issued by the empire, requiring all waystations to follow the same set of rules. It centralized the management of sessions, tasks, caching, and error handling, drawing the logic that had been scattered everywhere into a single boundary.

For developers, this meant the centralization of complexity. They no longer needed to repeat logic in every request, but instead could obtain consistent behavior through a single unified entry point.

But when URLSession first appeared, not everyone welcomed it.

Some developers felt it was too large and had a high learning cost. They longed for the simplicity of NSURLConnection, feeling that "writing a few lines to make a request" was more direct. They couldn't see the ledger of complexity; they only saw immediate convenience.

It was like the frontier villagers complaining when the empire built the avenue: "We only needed a small path; why build such a wide road? The avenue requires taxes, requires regulations; we've lost our freedom."

However, they overlooked a fact: freedom is never free. The freedom of the small path comes at the cost of long-term chaos; the avenue's rules bring sustained order.

The design of URLSession is a paradigm of a deep module: it hides most implementation details and exposes only the necessary interfaces. It concentrates complexity internally, making external usage consistent and clear.

The philosophy of this design is not about making functionality more powerful, but about lightening the Cognitive Load. When developers no longer need to remember countless details or jump between multiple files, they can focus their attention on higher-level logic.

This is the value of deep modules: they do not make complexity disappear, they centralize it. Centralization means governability, predictability, and that the team's cognitive capacity can bear it.

In the records of history, shallow modules are always a brief prosperity; deep modules are the lasting foundation. The shallow flexibility of NSURLConnection let early development expand quickly; but it was the deep centralization of URLSession that allowed the iOS networking layer to mature.

The flood of complexity never disappears. The only way out

is to build deep modules that channel the flood into reservoirs rather than let it spread boundlessly.

Airbnb's cross-platform experiment tells us that the diffusion of complexity brings fragmentation and collapse. In URLSession's design, Apple showed another path: centralizing and hiding complexity can keep an ecosystem stable over the long term.

Depth is not darkness, but shelter.

Hiding complexity in a deep well is what allows the surface to remain clear.

The birth of URLSession was not an accidental technical update, but a civilizational choice. When NSURLConnection's dirt roads could no longer bear the load, when complexity kept breeding at the frontiers, Apple's engineers saw the outline of the flood. They knew that without restraint, future iOS apps would be dragged into the abyss by fragmented logic.

The design of deep modules is not only to meet present needs, but to resist future complexity. The significance of this design is not in current features, but in whether the minds of hundreds of thousands of developers can remain clear over the next decade.

The philosophy of URLSession can be summed up in one sentence: concentrate complexity where the system can bear it, not scattered across the minds of every developer.

Imagine a simple operation: downloading an image.

In the era of NSURLConnection, this meant:

- Create a request object;
- Set a delegate;
- Handle callbacks;
- Check for errors;
- Decide on caching yourself.

Each step was like a dirt road that the developer had to walk personally.

One image demanded such a cost.

When dozens or hundreds of images were requested simultaneously, those dirt roads crossed into a web, and no one could see the whole picture.

After URLSession appeared, developers only needed to express intent:

"I need this image."

The connection details, the caching strategy, and error handling were all taken on by the deep module.

Complexity did not disappear.

It still existed, but was hidden beneath the well.

Developers only needed to draw water from the well's mouth without having to understand the construction of the well walls or the course of the water.

This is the power of information hiding.

Many people misunderstand information hiding, thinking it is a form of "defensive encapsulation."

In fact, its true purpose is to reduce cognitive load.

When outsiders do not need to understand every detail, they can use limited mental resources to handle higher-level problems.

A real example appeared in 2015.

When iOS 9 introduced App Transport Security (ATS), requiring all network requests to use HTTPS, for projects still relying on NSURLConnection this meant countless changes and tests.

Developers had to inspect requests one by one to confirm they met the new standard.

For projects based on URLSession, this was almost no problem.

Because URLSession centralized the management of security policies, developers didn't need to configure each request individually.

When the system upgraded, complexity was concentrated in the deep module and the outside simply enjoyed the new order.

This is the advantage of deep modules:

When the external environment changes, they can absorb the impact and keep complexity behind the scenes.

Developers' world thus remains stable.

A deep module is like the empire's capital.

It is the concentration of complexity and the source of order.

The capital's institutions can constrain the chaos at the frontiers;

The design of a deep module can constrain the system's fragmentation.

URLSession is more than an API; it changed the way developers work.

In the era of NSURLConnection, teams often got into disputes because of the networking layer:

- How should caching be implemented?
- Should error handling be unified?
- Who decides the timeout strategy?

These disputes consumed countless attention yet produced no stable order.

After URLSession appeared, these issues were institutionalized. Caching, errors, and timeouts all had unified answers. Teams no longer needed to debate repeatedly, and instead turned their attention to more valuable problems: how to design better user experiences, how to optimize business logic.

Complexity was not eliminated, but it was moved to the most appropriate place. This transfer is at the core of software design.

In the world of SwiftUI, this philosophy is continued.

SwiftUI's core idea is state-driven. It asks developers to only describe "the state I need," rather than manually manage "every step of the UI's changes." The UI update logic is hidden inside the framework's deep module. Developers no longer need to maintain "when to call refresh," nor track countless observers; they only need to declare "the state changed."

This mirrors URLSession's design. URLSession says: you just express "I want data," and leave the rest to me. SwiftUI says: you just express "I want UI state," and leave the rest to me.

This is the philosophy of deep modules: concentrate complexity, hide details, and let developers focus on higher-level expression.

The value of information hiding lies in concentrating Cognitive Load.

Shallow modules make everyone carry a bit of complexity—seemingly fair, but actually cruel. Deep modules make the system carry the complexity, thereby liberating developers.

A concrete analogy: the world of shallow modules is like farmland without irrigation channels—each farmer must dig a well and carry water. The world of deep modules is like fields covered by an irrigation system—farmers only need to focus on planting; the water will come naturally.

The former consumes the energy of countless farmers; the latter consumes centralized system design. This is the difference of civilization.

However, deep modules are not without cost.

When Apple designed URLSession, they had to handle enormous complexity. How should caches interact with disk? How to ensure thread safety? How to maintain performance across millions of requests?

These complexities did not disappear; they were concentrated within Apple's engineering teams. They bore that weight so developers around the world could travel light.

This is the division of labor of civilization. Just as an empire's capital must sustain a bureaucracy to keep institutions running, deep modules must shoulder the burden of implementation to preserve clarity on the outside.

Historians say that the greatness of an institution lies not in whom it benefits, but in how it spares countless people from chaos. URLSession's greatness lies in this as well.

It did not make network requests simpler; it made them more uniform. It did not make errors vanish; it made errors more predictable. It did not make complexity disappear; it made complexity more manageable.

At a developer conference, an Apple engineer once said, "We want developers to put more attention on the app experience, not the infrastructure." Behind that sentence is precisely the design philosophy of deep modules.

The complexity of infrastructure should be managed centrally. The creativity of experience should be unleashed. This is the direction in which civilization advances.

The emergence of URLSession made countless teams rethink: should our own systems also build such deep modules? Should we concentrate complexity at a single boundary instead of scattering it everywhere?

So new practices gradually emerged. Some teams began building "network-layer frameworks" for their businesses, centralizing logging, caching, retries, and encryption. Other teams began establishing a "single source of truth" for state management so UIs would no longer be driven by dispersed events.

This idea gradually took root in the iOS community. It changed not only code but culture.

Deep modules are a milestone of civilization. They turn chaotic dirt roads into avenues, fragmented logic into institutions, and dispersed complexity into a centralized burden.

Without URLSession, the iOS networking layer might still be trapped in an era of chaos; with URLSession, the whole ecosystem can move forward under a unified order.

Shallow freedom is a waste of mental capacity;
Deep institutions are the gift of civilization.

The emergence of URLSession was a watershed moment in iOS history. It not only changed the way developers interact with the system, but also transformed the culture of the entire ecosystem. But its true significance is not limited to the "network layer."

It revealed a larger truth: deep modules are not merely a technical choice, but a cognitive strategy.

In the world of software, humanity's greatest enemy has never been bugs, but understanding. Bugs can be fixed, performance can be optimized, but the cost of understanding grows without bound over time. When a system's complexity is dispersed everywhere and no one can explain the whole picture, that system is doomed to decline.

The value of deep modules lies in making understanding possible. They gather complexity into a narrow entrance; the outside only needs to remember a "door." Behind that door may be a massive mechanism, but that weight is borne by the system, not by the human mind.

Imagine an ancient city. If every citizen had to handle water supply, sewage, and road construction themselves, the city would soon fall into chaos. A system of shallow modules is such a city. Everyone needs to know too many details, and anything can go wrong.

Deep modules, on the other hand, are like a centralized municipal system. Water supply, sewage, and roads are all handled by institutions. Citizens do not need to understand the pipe network behind them; they only need to turn on the tap. This centralization allows the city to expand and civilization to continue.

URLSession's relation to iOS is like a water supply system's relation to a city. It frees countless developers from being distracted by details so they can continue building on a stable system.

In the world of SwiftUI, this idea is once again validated.

The design of SwiftUI is not merely a "UI framework innovation" but a liberation of cognition. The traditional UIKit world is like the chaos of shallow modules:

- Every button needs to be bound manually;
- Every state update needs to be tracked;
- Every change can be missed, leading to bugs.

This shallow control appears flexible, but in reality disperses complexity throughout the code.

SwiftUI's philosophy is that state is the single source of truth. It asks you to concentrate complexity: all UI changes originate from state, and all core logic is centralized in a single source.

This is the power of deep modules. They hide the details of UI updates and concentrate complexity in state management. Developers are thus liberated, no longer lost among countless callbacks and notifications.

TCA (The Composable Architecture) pushes this idea to the extreme.

At TCA's core is the Reducer. It requires you to concentrate all state changes into a single function. This seems strict, even constraining to beginners. But it is precisely this centralization that ensures complexity does not diffuse.

When a bug occurs, you don't need to search through countless files. You only need to look at the Reducer and understand the flow of state. Complexity is locked in a cage, not scattered across the wilderness.

TCA's philosophy is of the same lineage as URLSession: both are about centralization and hiding. The former centralizes state changes; the latter centralizes network requests. Different domains, the same wisdom.

Deep modules are not only a technical choice but also a team choice.

In a small team, the flexibility of shallow modules can barely be sustained. With a few people sitting together and communicating, the diffusion of complexity is still tolerable. But in a large team, shallow modules are a disaster.

When a feature needs to span multiple small modules, when a bug must be passed between different teams, the cost of complexity is no longer just a technical burden but a communication nightmare.

Deep modules can reduce this nightmare to a minimum. When a module with a clear boundary exists, communication between teams can focus on the interface rather than the details. This is the truth of "one module = the cognitive boundary of one team."

Imagine a hypothetical team case: a large e-commerce company with hundreds of iOS engineers. Their app contains countless features such as shopping, payments, logistics, and customer service. In the early days, they chose "shallow modularization": each team developed its own features and called each other freely.

At first, this seemed very efficient. Teams could act independently and quickly roll out features. But years later, they found that the app could no longer be understood by any single person. The root cause of a bug could span three teams, and fixes could take weeks. Complexity, like a sandstorm, buried everyone.

In the end, they had to refactor: they established "deep modules." Payments became a module, shopping became a module, customer service became a module. Each module hid complexity internally and only exposed clear interfaces.

From then on, bugs no longer needed to cross the entire empire; they could be resolved within a single module. Communication costs fell and the boundaries of understanding became clear. Deep modules saved the team.

The cost of deep modules lies in centralization. Centralization means power, and it also means responsibility. URLSession centralized the responsibility for bearing network complexity; SwiftUI centralized the responsibility for bearing UI update complexity; TCA centralized the responsibility for bearing the complexity of state changes.

This centralization liberates developers, but it also places a heavy burden on designers. Apple's engineers must design modules deep enough to ensure that complexity does not turn back on them. TCA's designers must endure criticism and explain why a centralized Reducer is necessary.

This is the price of civilization. Institutions are not free, and deep modules are not free. Their cost is the effort behind centralization.

But as history has shown: costly institutions are often more worthwhile than cheap freedom. Short-term flexibility brings long-term chaos; short-term centralization brings long-term stability.

The success of URLSession, the rise of SwiftUI, and the philosophy of TCA all attest to the same fact: deep modules are the only future of software civilization.

Complexity will not disappear; it is everywhere like windblown sand. The only thing to do is build deep modules—keep the sand inside the walls and keep clarity outside.

Apple used URLSession to build such a wall, protecting the minds of countless developers. SwiftUI used state-driven design to build such a wall, protecting the clarity of countless UI logics. TCA used the Reducer to build such a wall, protecting the stability of team collaboration.

Each deep module is an embankment of civilization.

- Shallow modules are the diffusion of complexity. They make everyone carry the weight of fragments, ultimately dragging the team down.
- Deep modules are the concentration of complexity. They let the system bear the weight and free the human mind.
- Deep modules are not showmanship, but mercy; not a luxury, but survival.

Great design is not about creating infinite possibilities, but about protecting finite minds.
Deep modules are the walls humans build in the face of complexity.
Walls cannot stop the windblown sand, but they allow civilization to breathe.

CHAPTER 9
SINGLE SOURCE OF TRUTH

When truth is scattered across multiple documents, an empire falls into internal conflict.

When state is scattered across multiple corners, software falls into chaos.

There is only one truth; facts can exist in only one place.

One of complexity's most effective weapons is the fragmentation of state.

In the history of software, almost no empire has fallen for lack of logic.

They fell because that logic was scattered across different documents, contradicting and pulling against one another.

Spotify's mobile app is a typical battlefield.

Its territory is vast, its features numerous: playback control, playlist management, recommendation systems, download caching, social interaction, device switching...

Every functional pathway is tightly related to state.

When these states cannot be managed uniformly, complexity, like silent dust, gradually covers the entire empire.

At first, Spotify's mobile team adopted the most straightforward approach:

Different modules each managed their own state.

The player module managed the current song, progress bar, and play queue;

the playlist module managed favorites, track order, and sync progress;

the recommendation module managed candidate tracks, cache flags, and user preferences.

On the surface, this seemed reasonable.

Each module was independent, did not interfere with the others, and had its own control.

However, complexity often lurks in the places that seem most reasonable.

Imagine this scenario:

A user taps play in the playlist view; the player module receives the command and its state updates to "playing."

Meanwhile, the recommendation module is also listening to state and adjusts recommended tracks based on user behavior.

But because the two modules each maintain their own state, the recommendation module receives a "paused" state at that moment—because its cache hasn't had time to refresh.

The result is:

The player is playing, but the recommendation module thinks the user is paused.

The recommendation list is wrong, and the calculation for the next song fails.

What the user sees on the interface is not the "smart recommendations" they imagined, but chaotic logic.

This misaligned experience is like an empire issuing two conflicting edicts.

One official says "march," another says "rest," and the army is left unsure what to do.

The chaos in software grows precisely out of such "multiple facts."

Complexity does not explode immediately.

It chooses to lie dormant, waiting for boundaries to become increasingly blurred.

Spotify's app needs to support multi-device switching: users can switch from phone to computer, from computer to a smart speaker.

This means state must be synchronized across devices.

But at the time, each module still managed its own state.

The player module updated the state, but the playlist module was still waiting for sync; the recommendation module received the signal late; the cache module had no idea the switch had happened.

The result was:

A user paused music on their phone while the speaker kept playing;

A user added a song on their computer while the phone's playlist lagged behind and didn't update;

the recommendation system suggested songs that had nothing to do with what was actually playing.

To users, these problems looked like "the app has a bug";

to developers, they were "state fragmentation."

The terrifying thing about state fragmentation is not a single bug, but its unpredictability.

Fix A today and it will reappear in scenario B tomorrow.

Every developer knows where the problem manifests, yet no one can guarantee it won't happen again.

The empire's roads remain, but the caravans are lost.

The software's features remain, but the logic is wavering.

Spotify's engineers began to feel exhausted.

They found that every new feature could trigger old bugs.

They found that every fix could create new contradictions.

They found their work was not construction but firefighting.

In an internal meeting someone said:

"We don't have a single truth.

The playback module has its truth, the playlist module has its truth, the recommendation module has its truth.

But truth shouldn't be threefold; it can only be one."

That sentence echoed like a bell in the team's minds.

The shadow of complexity had already suffocated them; the only cure was a single source of truth.

A single source of truth is not a novel idea.

In psychology it corresponds to "cognitive consistency";

In management it corresponds to "a single authority";

In software it corresponds to "a unified state tree."

But there is a gulf between idea and practice.

How do you unify the states scattered across countless modules into one place?

How do you ensure all modules depend on the same fact?

How do you make the flow of state traceable amid complex interactions?

Spotify's team had to find the answer.

Otherwise, their app would sink into an endless quagmire of complexity.

The terrifying thing about complexity is its "hidden" nature.

When a bug erupts, it is obvious;

When state becomes chaotic, it is shocking;

But in daily life, it merely lurks at the boundaries, waiting for an opportunity.

Spotify's developers realized they needed not just bug fixes, but a change in philosophy.

They were no longer satisfied with "module self-consistency"; they needed "global consistency."

They were no longer satisfied with "rapid iteration"; they needed "long-term understandability."

They were no longer satisfied with "local facts"; they needed a "single truth."

So a new philosophy began to take root within the team.

Its core was:

State is not a collection of scattered variables, but a unified tree.

All features must read from and update this tree.

All changes must be propagated through clear paths.

This was not a choice of tools, but a turn in civilization.

From "local autonomy" to "global consistency,"

From "individual understanding" to "team consensus,"

From "multiple facts" to "a single fact."

Spotify's story reached a turning point here.

The shadow of complexity remained, but they finally saw the direction of the light.

Chaos is not the work of a single day, nor is unification the work of a single day.

An empire's code of law needs years to be carved; the truth of software needs institutions to sustain it.

In Spotify's archives, 2016 to 2018 are called "the years of fragmentation."

During that period, their mobile app resembled a grand but precarious empire: vast territories, a thriving population, but crumbling roads, split commands, and low morale.

Developers repeated the same complaints in meeting after meeting:

"The playback module thinks the music is playing, while the recommendation module thinks it's paused."

"The playlist updated, but the cache still shows the old order."

"A user added a favorite on desktop, but the phone takes minutes to show it."

This was not a bug; it was a fracture of civilization.

At one cross-department meeting, a senior engineer wrote

five words on the whiteboard:

Single Source of Truth.

He said nothing more.

Those present were silent for a few seconds.

The words, like the inscription of an ancient empire, suddenly reminded people that order had once existed.

He continued and wrote the second line:

"There can only be one truth."

Ideas are always simpler than practice.

When Spotify decided to push for a single source of truth, they faced not only technical problems but organizational and cultural resistance.

The playback team said:

"We maintain our own state for efficiency. Putting all state in one place—won't that hurt performance?"

The recommendation team said:

"Our algorithms rely heavily on caches; if we have to wait for global state updates, the real-time nature of recommendations will suffer."

The cache team said:

"Network latency is unavoidable; a single source of truth will force us to depend on remote services frequently, and that's uncontrollable."

Every objection was reasonable.

The terrifying thing about complexity is that it always disguises itself as reasonableness.

When an empire tries to legislate, it will encounter resistance from local powers.

Spotify's team had to find a way to build a new balance between unification and autonomy.

They decided to run an experiment:

choose one feature to pilot the single source of truth.

The feature was neither the most complex nor the simplest, but "cross-device playback state."

Cross-device playback state is one of Spotify's souls.

It allows a user to pause music on their phone and continue playback on a speaker;

It allows a user to switch tracks on a computer and hear the change immediately in their headphones.

In the past, this feature was maintained by multiple modules:

The player had a state, device management had a state, the recommendation module also had a state.

This led to frequent sync delays and repeated poor user experiences.

The engineers decided to make this feature the pilot:

The playback state for all devices would be managed only by a single global state tree.

Any module that wanted to read had to get it from that state tree;

Any module that wanted to update had to go through a strict Reducer flow.

The first attempt was not smooth.

They found that the logic originally scattered around had to be migrated into the new state management system.

That meant a large amount of refactoring.

And refactoring means risk.

The playback engineers worried:

"If we hand over the state, many of our performance optimizations will no longer be directly controllable."

The recommendation engineers questioned:

"Our experiments require rapid iteration; if every change must touch global state, won't that be too slow?"

The cache engineers warned:

"Network latency and local caching are inherently in conflict; a single source of truth cannot resolve these contradictions."

The meeting was tense, as if the empire's vassals were protesting the new code.

But the shadow of complexity had already closed in; no one could deny the collapse of the status quo. The pilot project began.

In the first week, they migrated the playback state into the global state tree. All modules had to obtain playback information from the same place. Bugs appeared immediately: the recommendation module crashed, the cache module threw errors, the player stuttered.

In the second week, the team began to fix things. They added logging to record every state change. They built debugging tools that could show the flow of the state tree on a single diagram. Gradually, the problems were unraveled.

In the third week, the first user test took place. The results were astonishing: cross-device playback state was finally consistent. When users paused on their phones, the speaker responded instantly; when users skipped tracks on their computers, the headphones synchronized immediately.

For the first time someone on the team smiled. Someone said, "We've finally found the truth."

Complexity wasn't eliminated, but it was concentrated. When all state lived in one tree, bugs didn't disappear, but they became traceable. For the first time engineers had confidence: they could explain the problem instead of being explained by it.

However, this was only a pilot. The real challenge was rolling it out.

After the pilot succeeded, management required that other modules be gradually migrated into the single state tree. The playlist team objected first. They said, "Our logic is highly complex and the state is large. The cost of migration will be very high."

The recommendation team worried again. They said, "Our experiments need rapid iteration; the single state tree will slow us down."

The cache team remained skeptical. They said, "Network uncertainty cannot be solved by a single state tree."

The team became mired in a tug of war. Every architectural evolution was a political struggle. Spotify's developers had to find a balance between technology and organization.

They decided on a progressive migration. Each iteration would migrate only one module. Each migration had to include strict monitoring and logging. Every failure had to be analyzed for lessons, not blamed on individuals.

This incremental strategy gradually accustomed the team to the new philosophy. Bugs still existed, but they became visible. Complexity remained vast, but it was managed in a concentrated way. The Cognitive Load remained heavy, but it was distributed fairly.

During the migration, Spotify's team gradually developed a new language. They began using "Reducer" to describe state changes; they began using "single state tree" to describe the global truth; they began using "traceable" to describe the value of a bug.

This language did not appear out of thin air, but was the accumulation of experience. It gave the team a common syntax and a new order. This was the nascent form of the TCA philosophy: state must be unified, changes must be controllable, truth must be singular.

Complexity still lurked in the dark, but Spotify's team already saw the direction. They knew the road ahead remained long, migration would be difficult, and resistance would persist. But they also knew the era of chaos was over and the flame of order had been lit.

When truth is singular, chaos has nowhere to hide.

When state is unified, complexity can be contained.

The foundation of civilization is not speed, but order.

Spotify's migration was not a lightning campaign but a

sustained campaign. It lasted three years, spanned multiple teams, and involved over a million lines of code. Complexity was not an enemy; it was a sandstorm. Sandstorms cannot be eliminated; they can only be corralled. Spotify's team learned to build walls, to dig wells, to tame the sandstorm into institutions.

After the cross-device playback pilot succeeded, the team's confidence rose. But this was only a victory on the empire's frontier. To truly restore order they had to push into tougher modules: playlists and recommendations.

The playlist module is Spotify's emblem. Users' favorites, ordering, syncing, and sharing almost all depend on playlists. This part of the logic is like an ancient and vast palace—countless rooms and interwoven secret passages. Every change could trigger unknown traps.

In the past, playlist state was scattered across different places: a copy in local cache, one on the server, one in the UI module. They passed information via callbacks, notifications, and refresh mechanisms. Such mechanisms could be sustained at small scale, but under tens of millions of users, problems became frequent.

A user deletes a song on their phone, and the computer still shows it; a user edits a playlist offline and finds conflicts with the server when going online; the sharing feature works on one client but fails on another.

These contradictions were not bugs, but the inevitable result of multiple sources of truth.

Migrating the playlist module meant enormous risk. Any synchronization failure could trigger large-scale user complaints. Therefore, Spotify adopted a progressive strategy: they did not immediately decommission the old system, but ran two mechanisms in parallel. The new system centered on a single state tree, while the old system continued to provide functionality. Once the new system was validated, it would gradually replace the old logic.

This process was like an empire enacting a new code. The old laws still existed but were gradually superseded by the new articles. During the transition, chaos was unavoidable. But each replacement brought the team closer to order.

The migration of the recommendation module was even more difficult.

Recommendation algorithms depend on real-time performance; latency must be controlled at the millisecond level. That meant any additional state synchronization could impact the experience. The team split internally: some insisted that the recommendation system should remain independent and not depend on global state; others insisted that all modules must submit to a unified system, otherwise order would collapse again.

The debate lasted for months. It was not just a technical dispute but a philosophical one.

In the end, management decided: the recommendation module must migrate. Because if truth can be two, then tomorrow there could be three or four. Order must be total; it cannot be abandoned halfway.

Once migration began, the recommendation engineers suffered. They had to integrate the algorithms with the state tree and fold the previously loose logic into a strict Reducer flow. But months later they discovered a surprising fact: recommendation quality did not decline; it became more stable. Because state no longer relied on cache-based guesses but fetched facts directly from the global tree. The algorithms no longer got lost in latency and contradictions; they ran atop a consistent truth.

This was a victory of philosophy. Unification did not bring the expected slowdown; instead, it provided a stable foundation. Once complexity was centralized, it became not a drag but a source of strength.

The year the migration completed, Spotify's internal toolbar gained a new feature: time-travel debugging.

Engineers could replay every state change like historians leafing through the empire's archives. They could see how the state tree updated when a user hit play; they could see how the recommendation module adjusted based on state; they could see how playlists remained consistent within the global truth.

Bugs were no longer ghosts. They had origins, trajectories, and causality. Complexity still existed, but it had been written into the system.

It was then that Spotify's team truly understood the philosophy of a single source of truth. It was not a technique, but an order. It did not make code elegant; it made the future comprehensible. It was not about showing off, but about compassion.

This philosophy aligned with the principles of TCA. TCA emphasizes:

- State must be centralized;
- Changes must go through Reducers;
- Side effects must be handled explicitly;
- Logic must be traceable.

Although Spotify's team did not adopt TCA completely, the path they took was remarkably consistent with TCA's ideas. This was a resonance of civilization: different empires ultimately discover the same laws.

After the migration, Spotify's team regained confidence. They no longer feared feature expansion because state had a single root. They no longer dreaded bugs because they could be traced. They no longer blamed one another because there was only one truth.

This confidence is the foundation of software civilization.

The philosophy of complexity completed a cycle here: it began in chaos, it was awakened through pain, it was tamed through migration, and it was sublimated through unification.

Spotify's story tells us: complexity will not disappear; it can only be concentrated; state will not be reduced; it can only be unified; truth cannot be multiple; it can only be one.

When we look back on this history, we find it belongs not only to Spotify but to all software teams. Whether small apps or large platforms, the shadow of fragmented state is everywhere. The only antidote is a single source of truth.

It reduces cognitive load, it lowers communication costs, it protects the readers of the future.

This is one of the greatest codes of software civilization.

Making state singular is making truth singular.
Making truth singular is making the future clear.
The ultimate compassion of software is not the abundance of features, but the restraint of complexity.

CHAPTER 10
THE TRUE MEANING OF DEPENDENCY INVERSION

The strength of a city does not lie in the height of its walls, but in the clarity of its entrances and exits.

The design of boundaries is not about blocking, but about order.

The favored soil of complexity is chaotic dependencies.

When, in a system, every module reaches outward directly to take, its shape resembles an unplanned marketplace.

Vendors erect stalls randomly in the streets, overlapping each other; communication relies on shouting, rules rely on tacit understanding.

At first, such a market is bustling, flexible and free.

However, as the crowds grow, conflicts inevitably accumulate: the flow of goods is obstructed, disputes are hard to resolve, information transfer becomes muddled.

Without clear boundaries, everyone is swallowed by noise.

Software is no different.

In iOS development, dependencies are invisible roads.

They connect modules, pass data, and make features possible.

But when dependencies spread disorderly, complexity begins to erode.

This is why "dependency inversion" is not just a principle, but a philosophy.

The client team at Spotify once experienced such a moment.

As one of the world's largest music streaming platforms, Spotify's iOS app had to handle more than just "playing a song".

It needed to display huge playlists, real-time updated recommendations, synchronization with the backend, offline caching, search, and social sharing.

Behind every feature lies complex dependencies.

Initially, Spotify's iOS client, like many startups, iterated quickly, called backend interfaces directly, and wrote logic in controllers.

Requirements drove speed, and speed concealed complexity.

But as scale grew, problems gradually emerged:

A playlist page might directly depend on the network layer, directly call caching logic, and also be directly responsible for data parsing.

Any change to an API could trigger a chain reaction in a dozen places.

Complexity does not show itself openly; it simply makes the cost of every change gradually rise.

What used to be a small feature tweak now required crossing multiple modules, notifying multiple teams, and modifying multiple files.

No one could complete a task independently; everyone was trapped by an invisible web of dependencies.

So Spotify's engineers began to reflect:

If dependencies are the breeding ground of complexity, then boundaries are the remedy.

But boundaries are not walls, boundaries are a contract.

They decided to refactor core modules and establish a protocol-based Service layer.

This meant the playback module no longer depended directly on network requests, but on an abstract "music source";

The download module no longer cared where data came from, but depended on an abstract "resource provider."

This design made the upper layers only know the protocols, not the concrete implementations.

Implementation details were hidden deep inside, and changes were isolated within the boundaries.

Like an empire's capital that does not have to manage every village directly, but uses provincial governors so affairs are handled within their borders.

But establishing boundaries is not accomplished in a single stroke.

Spotify's team found they had to confront two challenges.

First, how to delineate boundaries.

The number of protocols is not "the more the better."

Over-abstraction can create nominal boundaries while increasing cognitive load.

They had to judge which complexities were worth isolating and which could be exposed directly.

This is a philosophical trade-off, not just an engineering calculation.

Second, how to make the team respect the boundaries.

In a fast-iterating environment, engineers often tend to "take shortcuts."

Directly calling an internal method seems faster; bypassing the protocol seems to save time.

But this convenience is precisely the crack complexity loves.

They had to establish processes so that boundaries become a contract of trust, not an optional convention.

The true meaning of dependency inversion is not the mechanical phrase "invert dependencies."

Its true meaning is to extract the system's fragile parts from the high level and concentrate changes so they are isolated at the low level.

This is not only architectural wisdom, but also cognitive mercy.

In Spotify's practice, these boundaries greatly reduced developers' cognitive load.

They no longer needed to understand the entire system's details, only the contract of the protocols.

When backend APIs changed, only the implementation layer needed adjustment; upper modules could remain unaffected.

Complexity was corralled rather than allowed to run rampant.

However, none of this came without cost.

Designing protocols requires foresight, patience, and anticipation of future changes.

Maintaining boundaries requires discipline, tools, and continuous cultural work.

Complexity was not eliminated; it was merely tamed.

And any taming comes at a cost.

Spotify's team embarked on a long road.

They knew this was not a battle to be won quickly, but a long-term governance.

Dependency inversion was their wall against complexity;

Protocols were the rules they established;

And rules only truly take effect through persistent day-by-day adherence.

Complexity still lurks in the shadows.

It does not disappear; it only waits for a new opportunity.

But Spotify's story tells us:

When you design boundaries with protocols, you at least leave a lamp for future readers.

The power of rules is not to eradicate chaos, but

to delay its erosion.

Boundaries cannot make complexity vanish; they can only confine it to a controllable scope.

And once discipline slackens, complexity will come rolling back.

Complexity is most like the wind.

It does not need to destroy; merely by blowing it lets grains of sand seep into the cracks.

Spotify took the first step on the road to protocol-ization, replacing concrete dependencies with abstract contracts.

These boundaries brought a brief period of stability.

Developers found that they no longer had to chase every change in the underlying layers.

The playback module depended on a "music source protocol," not on specific HTTP requests.

Offline downloads depended on a "resource provider protocol," not on direct access to cache files.

In their daily development, they could finally focus on business logic instead of struggling in the quagmire of complexity.

But complexity would not be defeated.

It merely stepped back, waiting for a new moment.

That new moment arrived soon.

Spotify's recommendation system kept evolving.

In the early days it was just a static playlist manually curated by an editorial team.

Later, with the development of machine learning, they introduced personalized recommendations.

Each user's play history, skip behavior, and favoriting habits were fed into the algorithms.

Recommendation results changed daily; every refresh was a unique experience.

For users, this was delightful.

But for the client team, it was a storm of complexity.

The recommendation result interface was no longer stable.

Different experimental versions might require different fields;

Different algorithmic models might return different data structures.

The client must still ensure a stable presentation in an uncertain environment.

The protocolized boundary was challenged here.

If a protocol is designed too rigidly, it will need constant changes as fields change frequently.

If it is designed too broadly, it will lose its constraints and become a "universal pocket" where any data can be stuffed.

Once a boundary fails, complexity will overflow again.

Spotify's engineers had to make hard trade-offs.

They further split the protocols, abstracting recommendation results into "content units," not exposing fields directly but providing a unified access interface.

This abstraction let the upper layers avoid worrying about the details of the data structure, only needing to know it can provide a "title," a "cover," and a "navigation target."

Changes to these fields were isolated within the boundary and adapted by the lower layer.

This was a new victory.

But the price of victory was the rising complexity of the protocol layer.

The team that maintained the protocols had to constantly follow backend experiments and frequently modify adapters.

They became the new gatekeepers.

Complexity had not disappeared; it was concentrated in the hands of a few.

The second direction of complexity's attack was offline caching.

Spotify's users are spread across the globe; some live in regions with unstable networks.

Offline caching became their lifeline.

Users wanted to listen during flights and have playlists play in the mountains.

This meant the client had to maintain a complex local caching system.

Cache logic was far more than "saving files":

- It needed to manage a download queue and ensure reasonable allocation within limited space;
- It needed to handle copyright/licensing changes and ensure expired songs are automatically removed;
- It needed to handle network interruptions and ensure downloads can resume from breakpoints;
- It needed to handle multi-device synchronization to avoid inconsistencies across devices.

These responsibilities made the cache system itself into a vast empire.

Spotify tried to use protocols to isolate caching from business logic.

The playback module only needed to depend on a "resource provider protocol," not care whether resources came from the network or locally.

The download module only needed to depend on a "storage service protocol," not care whether storage was on disk or in a database.

This kind of abstraction was effective at first. But as caching logic grew more complex, the protocol layer began to bloat. A simple "resource provider" now had to support many states: online, offline, partially available, expired. With each new requirement, the protocol gained another method. The protocol had turned from a "gatekeeper" into a "beast"—instead of isolating complexity, it had itself become bloated.

Engineers began to feel uneasy. In meetings they argued: "Have we gone too far? Protocols were meant to simplify, yet we've created new complexity."

This argument was not only technical. It was philosophical:

how deep should a boundary be? If too shallow, complexity leaks out; if too deep, the boundary itself becomes complexity.

Spotify's team had no standard answer. They could only iterate, adjust, and seek balance again and again.

The third direction of complexity was team collaboration.

As Spotify scaled, the client team was split into multiple squads: playback, recommendations, downloads, search. Each squad owned a module, but all modules ultimately had to converge in the same app.

Protocols were supposed to be their contract. The reality, however, was that each squad had its own interpretation. The playback squad wanted simpler protocols for faster implementation; the recommendations squad wanted more flexible protocols to accommodate experiments; the downloads squad wanted stricter protocols to avoid data inconsistency.

Conflicting needs turned protocols into a battlefield. Adjusting a boundary could require weeks of cross-team coordination. In meetings, engineers argued incessantly, each standing their ground, yet finding it hard to reach consensus.

Here complexity revealed a new form: communication complexity. Code complexity can be isolated by protocols, but the complexity between teams must be constrained by process.

Spotify eventually introduced a "protocol committee" composed of representatives from each squad to unify boundary definitions. This made protocols no longer a tool of a single squad but a contract for the whole team. However, the cost of this process was slower decision-making. A new requirement's rollout had to go through discussion, voting, and validation. Speed was sacrificed in exchange for order.

Complexity is cunning.

It will not be satisfied with a single form; it keeps changing.

In Spotify’s story, it first lurked in the chaos of dependencies, then hid in the bloat of protocols, and later transformed into conflicts in team collaboration.

Engineers gradually realized:

dependency inversion is not a one-time solution but a long-term struggle.

Protocols are not a silver bullet; they themselves can become containers of complexity.

All they can do is continuously adjust, continuously govern, and repeatedly seek balance between chaos and order.

Spotify's client team kept moving forward.

Their app remained the window for hundreds of millions of users worldwide.

Complexity still eroded them, but they learned how to delay it, how to resist it, and how to maintain order amid storms.

Boundaries are not walls but channels.

They are not about blocking, but guiding.

Build walls too high and the water chokes; leave things unbounded and floods ensue.

The way of dependency inversion is a way of managing water.

The storm of complexity never ceased.

Spotify's client team had learned to pitch tents in the wind and use protocols to hold order.

However, they also saw a new truth: protocols are not the answer themselves; they are only a means.

Excessive protocols become redundant rituals.

A lack of protocols plunges you into disorderly dependencies.

True wisdom is not about "whether to protocolize," but about "when to protocolize."

In one iteration, the product team proposed adding a "lyrics sync" feature to the player UI.

It was a feature strongly requested by users.

The problem was: the source of lyric data was unstable.

In some markets, Spotify cooperated with third-party rights holders and needed to fetch lyrics remotely;

In others, lyrics needed to be cached locally to ensure availability when networks were poor.

More complicated still, some songs had no lyrics and needed to degrade gracefully.

The engineers' initial reaction was to design a "lyrics service protocol."

That way, the player would depend on an abstraction rather than on specifics.

Lyrics could come from remote sources, from local sources, or even be empty.

But during the design process, arguments arose.

Some argued: we don't need to create an entirely new protocol for a single feature; that would increase layers of abstraction.

The lyrics logic could be accessed directly by the player through the "resource provider protocol"—after all, lyrics are a kind of resource.

Others insisted: lyrics have unique characteristics, and mixing them with other resources would blur the boundary.

The debate lasted several days.

The whiteboard in the meeting room was covered with arrows and boxes.

Each arrow represented a possible dependency.

Each box was a candidate abstraction.

In the end, the team reached a consensus:

They would not create a separate protocol for lyrics, but would extend the existing "resource provider."

This way, the boundary remained clear and abstraction levels would not bloat.

This was an important turning point.

It marked the team's realization that the true meaning of dependency inversion is not "the more protocols the better," but "the right number of protocols."

Selective abstraction is the long-term way to survive.

This selectivity is not an innate gift, but a culture.

Spotify gradually formed a set of cultural guidelines internally:

- If something changes frequently, it must be isolated by a protocol.
- If a dependency is stable, there is no need to force an abstraction.
- If a feature spans multiple teams, a protocol is the contract for collaboration.
- If logic is used in only one place, abstraction only adds cognitive load.

These guidelines, like invisible laws, were etched into engineers' daily thinking.

When designing, they no longer abstracted blindly, but first asked:

"Is this complexity worth isolating?"

Building this culture was not done in a day.

It came from countless debates, failures, and retrospectives.

It came from the pain of complexity and the clarity brought by protocolization.

Eventually it became a consensus, like an imperial code, maintaining order.

Culture needs tools to guard it.

Spotify's team knew human memory is limited.

Relying on verbal agreements will be forgotten; relying on cultural transmission will be diluted.

So they built tools and institutions to protect boundaries.

They introduced static analysis tools into the continuous integration pipeline.

Any code that directly called lower-level dependencies would trigger warnings.

Any implementation that bypassed protocols would be rejected from merging.

These tools, like guards at the city gates, patrol automatically and tirelessly.

They established new standards in code review. The goal of a review was no longer to point out mistakes but to confirm whether boundaries were being upheld. Each review was a judgment of the boundary. Any attempt to cross a boundary had to have a sufficient justification, otherwise it was immediately rejected.

They recorded the intent and boundaries of every protocol in documentation. These documents were not just manuals but constitutions. When the team expanded and newcomers joined, the documentation was their first threshold for understanding the system.

Tools, processes, and culture—combined, they became the moat protecting the boundaries. Complexity still existed, but it was constrained outside the moat.

However, complexity never fully retreats. It waits for new opportunities.

When Spotify began expanding into podcasts, new complexity struck again. Podcasts are different from music: their files are longer, update frequency is higher, ad insertion is more complex, and playback behavior is less predictable.

The protocols originally designed for music suddenly faced new challenges. The "resource provider protocol" had to support segmented loading of long-form audio; the "playback control protocol" had to support dynamic ad insertion; the "recommendation protocol" had to support mixed ordering, presenting music and podcasts together.

The boundaries of the protocols were once again torn. The team had to rethink: continue extending existing protocols, or establish separate boundaries for podcasts?

This time they chose a compromise. They created an "audio resource protocol" that could encompass both music and podcasts. Under that protocol, they then separated the specific logic for each.

This design kept the system consistent while allowing flexible extension. Complexity was tamed again rather than allowed to run rampant.

Spotify's story tells us: dependency inversion is not a static answer but a form of dynamic governance. Boundaries are not once-and-for-all; they continuously evolve. Protocols are not omnipotent and must be used selectively.

Such governance requires courage and humility. Courage is not compromising in the face of complexity; humility is admitting that protocols themselves can introduce complexity.

In the world of SwiftUI, this philosophy is even more important.

SwiftUI itself is a philosophy of boundaries.

It makes the UI depend on state, rather than the state depend on the UI.

This is a natural form of dependency inversion.

The UI no longer directly calls data, but receives input through state in a protocol-driven way.

Complexity is compressed inside Reducers and State, rather than scattered across Views.

If these boundaries are not upheld in SwiftUI, complexity will immediately strike back.

When a View also bears business logic, when state is dispersed in many places, when dependencies are chaotic and unordered, SwiftUI's clarity vanishes at once and becomes a new quagmire.

Therefore, in the world of SwiftUI, the true meaning of dependency inversion is even clearer:

use protocols to guard boundaries, keep Views innocent, and hide logic deep within.

"The greatness of an empire lies not in the size of its territory, but in the clarity of its institutions.

The longevity of software does not lie in the abundance of features, but in the simplicity of its boundaries."

Dependency inversion is not a technical detail but an institution.

Protocols are not syntax, but contracts.

Boundaries are not constraints, but acts of kindness.

Spotify's client team keeps moving forward.

Their protocols continue to evolve, their boundaries continue to be adjusted.

Complexity still exists, but they have learned to coexist with it.

They know that dependency inversion is not a final victory, but a way to survive.

And for every iOS developer, the road is likewise long.

SwiftUI has given us new weapons, but complexity will not retreat for that reason.

True victory comes from whether we learn to design boundaries with protocols, and whether we learn to remain clear-headed in the face of complexity.

Boundaries are civilization.
Protocols are not tricks, but symbols of order.
The true meaning of dependency inversion is not reversal, but humility:
we acknowledge the limits of our own minds,
and therefore let boundaries guard our future.

PART THREE
FROM PATTERN TO PRACTICE

CHAPTER 11
THE EVOLUTION OF MVVM

Patterns are not salvation, but habits.
If habits are not restrained, they will eventually become new shackles.

An oasis in the sand always attracts travelers with its clear water.

The birth of MVVM was like such an oasis.

It promised clear boundaries: the Model manages data, the View presents the interface, and the ViewModel acts as a bridge, isolating the two from chaos.

From its naming, the pattern was a parable telling people: division of labor and boundaries are the only way to govern complexity.

The arrival of SwiftUI made MVVM seem to return to its homeland.

Declarative syntax and state-driven updates naturally fit the role of the ViewModel.

The View no longer needs to manage its own lifecycle, but is driven by state;

the ViewModel no longer needs to notify explicitly, but propagates changes naturally through bindings.

Many marveled: SwiftUI has brought MVVM back to its golden age.

But gold is always accompanied by greed.

When a pattern turns from a solution into a habit, it begins to create complexity in return.

Massive ViewModel is precisely a product of that greed.

Netflix's story can serve as the clearest illustration.

This streaming empire controls the distribution of countless pieces of content.

Their app is not just a player, but a gateway to a world:

personalized recommendations, category browsing, search, trailers, playback, downloads, offline, parental controls...

Each feature is a source of complexity.

In the early days, Netflix's mobile team adopted MVVM.

At that time, their goal was to let different platform teams — iOS, Android, TV — use similar architectural thinking to reduce communication friction.

MVVM offered a simple promise: put all business logic into the ViewModel, and let the View only handle presentation.

In the first few years, this brought significant efficiency gains.

Teams could quickly build new features, ensure consistent patterns, and facilitate testing.

But the shadow of complexity always quietly appears in times of prosperity.

The recommendation page is at the heart of Netflix.

It needs to dynamically generate content based on the user's historical behavior, regional licensing, and device type.

When a user opens the app's home screen, thousands of data requests and logical decisions are carried out in the background, then stitched together into one recommendation card after another.

These cards appear simple, but behind them lie countless strategies:

- Which titles need to be promoted first;
- Which categories are suitable to appear during the user's time slot;
- Which experimental groups are running.

In the MVVM context, all of this logic is concentrated in the ViewModel.

Thus, the ViewModel for a recommendation page gradually becomes a monster.

It is no longer just a simple bridge, but a microcosm of an empire:

It must handle network requests, manage data caching, control UI state, and even participate in experiment traffic-splitting.

Developers call it the "God ViewModel."

In an internal talk, someone joked:

"If this ViewModel crashes, it's like cutting off the capital's food supply."

This is not an exaggeration.

A single file with thousands of lines, dozens of properties, hundreds of methods.

Every new requirement can only be stacked onto this behemoth.

No one dares to change it lightly, because any modification may trigger a chain reaction.

Massive ViewModel is not a problem unique to Netflix.

It is a kind of fate.

When a pattern brings initial convenience, people habitually put everything into that "middle layer."

Views become too thin, Models too distant, logic has nowhere to live, so everything flows into the ViewModel.

At first, it is a shortcut; later, it becomes a trap.

The erosion of complexity is never sudden.

It shows up as a kind of fatigue.

Engineers find that every new feature requires first reading thousands of lines of legacy code and understanding countless contexts.

They find that bug localization is no longer "find the error" but "search for the exit in a maze."

They find that tests may exist, but coverage is essentially meaningless, because the logic has become deeply entangled.

The most dangerous thing is not the length of the code, but the Cognitive Load.

When any person needs to spend weeks to understand a module, that module has already lost its reason to exist.

Of course, Netflix's team had noticed. They began trying various measures: modularization, layering, and service-orientation. They introduced new boundaries, extracting some logic into independent managers. They hoped that by "abstracting one more time" they could reduce the ViewModel's burden.

But abstraction itself is also a form of complexity. When abstraction is excessive, new fragments appear. Logic gets scattered across multiple places, and the cognitive cost doesn't decrease—it increases. Developers joked: "We used to have one hard-to-understand file; now we have ten hard-to-understand files."

This irony is almost a constant in the history of software. When people try to solve problems with patterns, the pattern itself often becomes part of the problem.

The arrival of SwiftUI gave them new hope. The declarative approach binds UI logic to state, reducing a large amount of repetitive boilerplate. In SwiftUI, the state-driven update mechanism made many complex ViewModel methods unnecessary. Netflix's iOS team began experimenting: if they migrated parts of the recommendation page logic to SwiftUI, would that lighten the ViewModel?

The initial results were encouraging. Some small pages, after being rewritten in SwiftUI, saw a noticeable reduction in ViewModel code and more straightforward logic. Developers exclaimed: "This is what MVVM should look like."

But complexity doesn't disappear because of a new tool. It only puts on a new outfit, waiting for a new opportunity.

In Netflix's experiments, a new contradiction emerged. SwiftUI's declarative updates are certainly concise, but when the state itself becomes large, managing it remains a burden. The recommendation page's state still contains countless pieces of logic: user cohorts, experiment toggles, network state, caching policies. If all the state is put into the ViewModel, then that ViewModel will still bloat. It may no longer be a "God ViewModel", but it's still an "Empire ViewModel".

This is SwiftUI's paradox.

It makes MVVM look more elegant, but without restraint it can still slide into the same trap.

A pattern is never the destination; boundaries are.

Netflix's story so far is only the beginning.

They have awakened from the fatigue of the Massive ViewModel and begun to explore new boundaries.

But the sands of complexity continue to accumulate.

The real choice is still ahead.

The desert doesn't shrink because of a new well; it only gathers sand in a different place.

A pattern doesn't become clear because of a new syntax; it merely appears in a new form.

In Netflix's experiments, SwiftUI once brought hope like the dawn.

The declarative syntax simplified the relationship between UI and state to something almost poetic.

For the first time, engineers felt they could spend more energy on user experience instead of struggling with notifications and callbacks.

But complexity has never been determined by syntax.

It is like a shadow that stretches at your feet no matter how bright the sun.

The recommendation-page experiment was the start of the second wave.

Netflix's iOS team decided to refactor parts of the recommendation logic with SwiftUI.

They wanted to verify whether, under the declarative paradigm, the ViewModel could return to being lightweight.

At first, they centralized the recommendation-page state in a single ViewModel:

It held the user's login info, region info, experiment cohorts, the status of network requests, and various UI flags.

Under SwiftUI's binding mechanism, changes to these states would automatically drive page updates.

Developers marveled: "We no longer need to call updates manually, nor worry about missing things in callbacks."

Everything seemed to be going smoothly.

But as features were added, the shadow reappeared.

The logic of the recommendation page is far more complex than a static list.

When the user scrolls, cards need to load dynamically;

When network conditions change, prompts must appear promptly;

When experiment toggles flip, recommendation ordering must adjust;

When a user taps "Watch Later," the button state must be synchronized to the backend immediately.

All of this logic depends on state.

And all of the state is still concentrated in a single ViewModel.

This ViewModel is like a warehouse that things are stuffed into.

Soon, it swelled again. Properties multiplied, methods became messier, and dependencies grew more complex. SwiftUI's concise syntax did not stop this trend. The ViewModel was still the capital of the empire—every road had to go through it.

Engineers began to complain: "We no longer manually update the UI, but we have to understand the relationships among hundreds or thousands of states."

Complexity had taken on a new face, but it was still devouring their minds.

In an internal tech talk, an engineer displayed the state graph of the recommendation-page ViewModel. The screen filled with dense nodes and arrows. User info pointed to the recommendation algorithm, the recommendation algorithm pointed to experiment toggles, experiment toggles pointed to presentation logic, and presentation logic pointed to caching strategies. Each node connected in multiple directions, forming a massive network.

Someone looked at the diagram and whispered, "This is no longer a ViewModel; it's a maze."

The terrifying thing about a maze is not its walls but its scale. When there are enough paths, any direction can lead you to a dead end. Engineers fell into that sense of dead ends. They found that debugging a bug required crossing multiple state nodes; adding a new feature required carefully adjusting existing relationships; any modification could bring unpredictable cascading effects.

This was the second coming of the Massive ViewModel. It was no longer merely file length but the complex coupling between states.

Netflix's team did not give up. They began trying new boundary definitions.

One group of engineers proposed splitting the state into multiple smaller ViewModels. The recommendation page would no longer have a single ViewModel but would be composed of multiple child ViewModels: one for user info, one for experiment toggles, one for network requests, one for UI state. These child ViewModels each managed part of the logic and were coordinated and composed by a parent.

The approach brought some relief. Files were no longer enormous, and responsibilities were easier to divide. Developers felt that at least they no longer had to confront a "God ViewModel."

But new problems soon followed.

When the state was split, new boundaries appeared.

These child ViewModels still needed to communicate with each other.

For example: whether a network request succeeded needed to affect UI state;

Changes to experiment toggles needed to adjust recommendation logic;

updates to user information needed to be synchronized to caching strategies.

Thus, a new maze emerged.

If the previous maze was one huge center, the new maze was a network of many small nodes.

Engineers had to understand the relationships between these nodes in order to ensure the logic was correct.

One developer wrote in a note: "Our previous pain was a single giant beast; now our pain is a multitude of little beasts."

This shift was not unique to Netflix.

Almost every team that tried MVVM went through similar stages.

From Massive ViewModel, to splitting ViewModels, and then to networked dependencies.

Each step was a negotiation with complexity.

At every negotiation, complexity was waiting for a new opportunity.

In Netflix's meeting room, debates about state management grew heated.

Some insisted on continuing to split, believing finer granularity would reduce cognitive load;

Some proposed introducing the idea of state machines to make state transitions clearer;

Others advocated adopting patterns like Redux or TCA to centralize state management.

These voices were like different factions of an imperial council, each with its own logic.

They were all trying to answer the same question:

How to make MVVM truly effective in the soil of SwiftUI, rather than fall into the Massive ViewModel trap again?

In the process, the issue of cognitive load gradually surfaced.

Netflix's team realized the core problem was not file size, nor the name of the pattern.

The core problem was the limits of the human mind.

When a single engineer must understand more than seven contexts, they become confused;

When a team must coordinate more than ten modules, they become exhausted.

Complexity is not the length of code, but the cognitive weight.

An architect wrote in an internal document: "What we pursue is not the purity of a pattern, but the saving of cognition. The pattern itself is not important; what matters is whether it lets future engineers understand quickly."

That sentence felt like a revelation. It made people begin to reexamine MVVM. MVVM has never been scripture; it is just a tool. The value of a tool lies not in its name but in whether it reduces the cost of understanding.

However, the cost of understanding does not automatically decrease. Netflix's team still had to face countless trade-offs.

In the recommendation-page experiment, they once introduced Redux ideas, concentrating all state into a single Store. The advantage was that the origin of state became clearer and all changes could be tracked. The downside was more boilerplate code and longer logic. Some engineers complained: "We traded development efficiency for tracking clarity."

Other teams tried TCA's reducer approach, distributing logic across different reducers and then composing them together.

This made the state evolution path more predictable, but it also brought more learning overhead. Newcomers joining the team needed weeks to understand how reducers were organized.

The dust of complexity rose again. No matter which approach was chosen, it could not be completely eliminated. It only moved from one corner to another.

Netflix's experiments continued. The introduction of SwiftUI showed them new possibilities; the evolution of MVVM revealed new traps. In this struggle with complexity, they gradually realized: the real goal is not to find a perfect pattern, but to find a pattern that humans can understand.

Complexity does not disappear because the language changes,

Does not dissipate because the framework is updated,

Does not retreat because a pattern becomes popular.

It will only take another form, and in the new soil, wait for a new opportunity.

Netflix's team is still exploring; they have already touched the edge of the truth: patterns are not the answer, cognition is. But they have not yet fully found their way out of the maze. The shadow of complexity still lingers behind them.

The value of an institution lies not in whether it can operate perfectly, but in whether it can sustain human minds over the long term.

The value of a pattern lies not in whether it can solve every problem, but in whether it can resist the erosion of complexity.

Netflix's mobile team, after a long tug-of-war with the Massive ViewModel, gradually arrived at a sober conclusion: they could no longer concentrate all logic in a single ViewModel. Such concentration is like an empire storing all its grain in the capital's granary: once transport is disrupted, the whole empire falls into famine.

They began to look for new paths.

The first attempt was to adopt state machines.

The recommendation page's logic had previously been written as a chain of conditional checks: if the user is logged in, show recommendations; if not logged in, show a prompt; if the experiment toggle is on, use the new sorting; if the network fails, display an error view.

These conditions seemed reasonable on their own, but combined they were a disaster. Countless if-elses intertwined to form an invisible web. When a bug appeared, engineers had to grope through that web bit by bit until they found the break.

So someone proposed, "We should treat the recommendation page as a state machine, not a pile of conditions."

The idea wasn't new, but in the soil of SwiftUI it felt especially natural. Declarative UI is essentially a mapping from state. If you can enumerate all the recommendation page's states and then define clear transition paths, complexity can be constrained.

The team began experimenting: they defined several key states—loading, success, failure, empty data, experiment mode. Each state corresponded to a definite UI, and transitions between states were controlled by a Reducer. In this way, the recommendation page's logic changed from "infinite possibilities" to a "finite set."

For the first time, developers felt the maze was no longer boundless. They had a map.

The second attempt was to design boundaries.

Netflix's team discovered that another root cause of the Massive ViewModel was the lack of boundaries. Putting all logic in one file meant there was no isolation. Any change could have global impact.

So they began to consider:

which logic should belong to the recommendation module,

which to the experiments module, and which to the user module?

Which states must live in the recommendation page, and which can be managed by an upper layer?

This boundary partitioning was not easy.

Because in real-world business, modules always overlap.

For example: recommendation logic needs an experiment toggle, and the experiment toggle depends on user information.

If partitioned improperly, it will create new fractures.

After many discussions, they established a principle:

State should be kept only in the place closest to it.

Recommendation state stays in the recommendation module;

User state stays in the user module;

Experiment state is managed by the experiments module.

Modules communicate through explicit interfaces, not shared global variables.

This approach made ViewModels no longer the empire's capital but autonomous city-states.

Each city-state has its own borders, its own guards, its own order.

Complexity is localized rather than centralized.

The third attempt was measuring cognitive load.

Netflix's architects realized the true enemy of complexity was not code, but cognition.

They began to measure the system in new ways:

- How many days does a newcomer need to understand the recommendation module?
- How many files must be crossed to fix a bug?
- How many states must be prepared to test a feature?

These metrics revealed more truth than code coverage or performance numbers,

Because they directly correspond to human mental burden.

They even put a slogan in internal documents:

"The only standard for judging code is whether future you can quickly understand it."

The phrase, like an oath, gradually spread through the team.

It became the core of code reviews:

not to argue style, not to debate names, but to ask:

"Can future us understand this logic in five minutes?"

As this culture gradually took root, complexity was truly contained.

Of course, complexity never truly disappears.

Even state machines, reducers, and boundary design can only reduce its impact, not eradicate it.

Netflix's team still has to face ever-expanding requirements, still has to deal with cross-platform differences, still has to bear the pressure brought by user scale.

But they had already found an approach. An approach is not a pattern, nor a framework, but an attitude: respect complexity, restrain complexity, and make the burden on human cognition the top priority.

This is the true significance of SwiftUI. It is not only a simplification of syntax, not only the convenience of declarative style; it is also a reminder: UI is merely a mapping of state, and logic is merely a projection of cognition. If state is clear, logic will naturally be concise; if state is messy, logic will inevitably spiral out of control.

Looking back at Netflix's course, we see a clear curve:

At first, they used MVVM to resolve the chaos between View and Model; later, they fell into the trap of Massive ViewModel; in the context of SwiftUI they saw hope again; complexity returned and plunged them into new troubles; finally, through state-machining, boundary design, and measures of cognition, they found a new balance.

This curve is exactly the civilizational curve every team goes through. It tells us: patterns are not the destination, patterns are merely ferries. The significance of the ferry is not in itself, but in whether it can carry us across the river of complexity.

The trap of Massive ViewModel is not unique to Netflix but the fate of all teams. The soil of SwiftUI does make MVVM more natural, but if we forget boundaries and cognition, we will repeat the same mistakes. Complexity always exists; it will not disappear, it will only take another form.

The only weapon is clear-headedness. Be clear-headed in recognizing that patterns are only tools; be clear-headed in accepting that human cognition is limited; be clear-headed in guarding boundaries, keeping complexity within controllable limits.

The power of civilization does not lie in its ability to conquer chaos, but in its ability to make chaos understandable.
The power of software does not lie in its ability to create miracles, but in its ability to be understood by the future.

CHAPTER 12
TRADE-OFFS OF TCA, REDUX, MOBIUS

The unification of power does not always bring order.

Too many voices lead to chaos;

too few voices lead to suffocation.

True wisdom lies in finding a frequency that can carry the human heart.

Wind blows across the plain of data, and servers stand like countless lighthouses.

Spotify, a kingdom whose imperial domain is sound, did not realize the weight of complexity as it expanded.

The distribution of music is light, but the systems behind music are heavy.

Behind every play button, there are state transitions: playing, paused, buffering, disconnected, reconnecting;

behind every recommendation algorithm, there is a downpour of data: user profiles, regional licensing, play order, experiment cohorts.

These states and these data weave into an invisible network.

The network is never silent; it grows every day, like a dense forest.

Complexity whispers in the forest.

It asks Spotify's engineers:

“How do you ensure a song keeps the same rhythm among millions of hands?”

“How do you ensure consistency of state, not torn apart by latency and disconnections?”

“How do you ensure your future self can understand the maze your present self has written?”

Spotify's mobile client is the empire's frontline.

It must carry the usage habits of hundreds of millions of users and handle calls to tens of thousands of songs.

However, as the business grows, the client's complexity rapidly balloons.

At first, Spotify used traditional MVC and MVVM to organize logic.

They once met the needs, until state began to overflow like a flood.

Playback state, cache state, user login state, recommendation experiment state……

Each layer of logic stacked into the ViewModel, becoming increasingly bloated.

A small play button could involve dozens of conditional checks.

And adding a new feature often means adding another layer to the existing logic.

Engineers called it the "beast".

They said:

“Every change is like driving a new nail into the beast's shoulder.

It can still move, but everyone knows that one day it will fall.”

The essence of complexity is the uncertainty of state.

State is like sand, hard to hold between your fingers;

State is like water, constantly flowing;

State is like a shadow, always longer than you expect.

Spotify began to search for new answers.

They turned their eyes to the world of the "single state tree."

In that world, all state is centralized, tracked, and replayable.

This is Redux's promise, and also the inspiration behind TCA.

The single state tree is like the empire's archives.

All laws, documents, and orders are gathered in one place.

Anyone can consult them, anyone can trace them back.

There is nowhere to hide mistakes, nowhere to escape audit.

In this archive, complexity is no longer a hidden wind but a clear dossier.

Redux was born in the world of JavaScript, yet it spread quickly.

Its philosophy is simple: there is only one state, changes happen through Reducers, and all changes are predictable.

This allowed countless teams to feel for the first time that complexity could be tamed.

Spotify saw this possibility too.

They tried to introduce Redux's ideas into the client, hoping to manage playback and recommendations with a unified state flow.

However, the empire's archives also have weight.

Concentrating state in one place does reduce distributed chaos;

but as state keeps growing, the archive becomes a burden.

Engineers began to find that the cost of maintaining a single state tree was also high.

A small interaction might require modifying multiple Reducers;

An expansion of state might necessitate chain adjustments across the entire data flow.

They realized Redux's strength lay in consistency;

But Redux's cost also lay in consistency.

Complexity had not disappeared — it had merely been redistributed.

At the Nordic headquarters, Spotify's architecture committee engaged in months of discussion.

They debated not only technology but philosophy:

How much unity do we need, and how much decentralization?

Do we pursue complete consistency, or allow local autonomy?

Do we force everyone to use the same pattern, or let different features choose freely?

The meetings were like a parliament.

Some were advocates of centralization, arguing for a single state tree;

Some supported local autonomy, arguing for per-feature choice;

Others proposed a third way: Mobius.

Mobius was born inside Spotify as an experiment in architecture. It absorbed Redux's advantages but tried to find a balance between complexity and freedom. Its core is a loop: state and events circulate within the loop instead of piling up in a single tree. It emphasizes testability and well-defined boundaries, but does not enforce centralization.

People at Spotify said, "Redux is a straight road that all cars must pass through; Mobius is a circular track where each feature can run on its own rail."

The problem of complexity is not whether there is a framework, but how the framework aligns with the human mind. Redux is too heavy and can suffocate; MVVM is too loose and can make people lose their way; Mobius sits between the two, like a compromise.

Spotify's choice was not a wholesale overhaul but a gradual experiment. They began using Mobius in some features to observe how it performed. The playback queue, offline caching, and recommendation experiments became the testbed. They hoped that by doing so they could find a balance that both reduced cognitive load and preserved flexibility.

"Every empire must find a balance between center and periphery. Excessive centralization breeds bureaucracy; excessive local autonomy breeds fragmentation. A wise ruler knows how to swing between the two."

Spotify's architectural history is the same. They sought Mobius's circular path between Redux's centralization and MVVM's local autonomy.

All systems have weight.
When a system is too rigid, people are suffocated;
When a system is too loose, order collapses.
Architecture is both law and culture.

Wind passes through the metal racks of server rooms like the pipes of an ancient empire. Spotify's client teams, at the Nordic headquarters, in U.S. offices, and in Asian branches, are scattered like stars, yet together they guard that empire of sound. Their enemy is not the music itself, but the complexity behind the music: the endless branches of users' playlists, the fragmented combinations of recommendation experiments, the tug-of-war between cache and network.

In Redux's centralization, they experienced the clarity of order, yet were also suffocated by its weight.

In MVVM's freedom, they tasted the lightness of getting started, yet were dragged into the mire by uncontrolled branching.

Mobius became their new hope.

Mobius's philosophy is simple and profound:

State is not a single tree, but a river that loops.

Events enter the river, state updates, and new events flow back.

Each feature is like a bend in the river, forming its own loop.

Engineers drew arcs on whiteboards, annotating the flow of events and state.

They said, "In Redux, we are archivists who must centralize every file;

In Mobius, we are sailors, each guarding our own stretch of river."

The first testbed was the playback queue.

The playback queue is one of Spotify's core experiences.

It seems simple: one song plays after another.

But within complex business logic it has long become a maze.

Users can insert songs, reorder, sync across devices, and continue playback when the network is disconnected.

And all these actions must remain consistent on iOS and Android, while coordinating with backend recommendation algorithms.

Under the Redux model, all these states are concentrated in a huge state tree.

Each operation requires updating multiple branches of the state tree.

As a result, the queue logic became hard to maintain, and bugs proliferated.

The arrival of Mobius gave engineers hope.

They isolated the playback queue logic into a loop:

Events enter, state updates, and new events are produced.

Play, pause, insert, delete, sync — all are managed within that loop.

Testing became easier, and the logic became clearer.

For the first time, engineers felt relief.

They said, "We can finally lock complexity in a box, rather than let it wander throughout the whole app."

The second testbed was offline caching.

Spotify's offline feature is one of the most relied-upon experiences for users.

However, it is also a breeding ground for complexity.

When a user downloads a song, it must validate with the licensing system, coordinate with local storage, and interact with the playback queue. When a user operates while offline, it must synchronize changes when the network is restored. This involves countless edge cases: insufficient disk space, expired licenses, intermittent networks, and cross-device conflicts.

Under the Redux model, these logics are stuffed into the global state tree, and any single change can ripple through the whole system. Under the Mobius model, caching becomes an independent loop. It only cares about its own state and does not interfere with the global state. When caching succeeds, it emits an event; when caching fails, it also emits an event. Other modules only need to respond to events without diving into the complexity of the cache.

Engineers said, "It's like moving a noisy market outside the city gates. It's still noisy, but at least it won't disturb the city's order."

However, complexity never leaves easily. It merely takes on a different face and keeps waiting.

Mobius's looping philosophy, while easing the problem of state centralization, brought new challenges. When every feature becomes an independent loop, coordinating among them becomes a new source of complexity.

A single event may propagate through multiple loops. An "insert" event emitted by the playback queue needs to be understood by the caching loop; a "download failed" emitted by the caching loop needs to be understood by the playback loop. Communication between these loops became a new maze.

Someone suggested in a meeting, "We solved local complexity but created global complexity."

The remark dropped into the meeting room like a stone, sending out ripples. The engineers were silent. They knew this is the nature of complexity. You think it's gone; it has merely shifted.

The team's divisions gradually became apparent.

Some believed Mobius was the right path. It made local concerns clearer, made testing easier, and reduced developers' cognitive load. They were willing to accept the complexity of global coordination because it was controllable.

Others worried: as features proliferate and loops multiply, would coordination costs spiral out of control? They missed Redux's centralization—at least everything was on one tree and could be traced.

The disagreement was not only technical; it was cultural. Some are accustomed to central commands, others favor local autonomy. Some believe in uniformity, others pursue flexibility.

Spotify's architecture committee was once again embroiled in debate.

Complexity watched quietly from the sidelines; it knows human nature. People always seek simple answers, yet are repeatedly led by complexity into new predicaments. They chose Redux, thinking centralization would bring clarity, but ended up burdened by an archive. They chose Mobius, thinking loops would bring freedom, but found themselves mired in the mire of coordination. Complexity had only changed its name; it still ruled the scene.

At that moment, the arrival of SwiftUI brought new thinking to some engineers. SwiftUI's state-driven approach, together with TCA's single-state-tree philosophy, offered another option. Some began to imagine: if we could combine the strengths of SwiftUI and TCA, could we find a new balance?

TCA's reducer way of thinking makes state changes clear and traceable; SwiftUI's declarative UI makes the mapping between state and interface natural and smooth. In such a combination, complexity seemed possibly tamed again.

Spotify's iOS team quietly launched a small-scale experiment:

they tried refactoring certain new features using TCA to observe how it differed from Mobius.

This was an imperial frontier probe. Not yet mainstream, it already hinted at the direction of the future.

"Every architectural choice is like institutional reform in an empire. Some support centralization, some support local autonomy, some support compromise. There is no perfect answer, only different burdens."

Spotify's story was reaching this crossroads. They had already witnessed the weight of Redux and experienced Mobius's loop; now they were beginning to glimpse TCA's possibilities.

Systems do not eliminate complexity; they only redistribute it.

Choosing an architecture is like choosing a tax system: some bear lighter burdens, others heavier ones.

True wisdom does not lie in finding the optimal, but in finding a balance that can be sustained over time.

Wind blew through the streets of Stockholm, cold air passing through the glass facade of Spotify's headquarters. The meeting rooms here have long been the battleground for institutional debates. Redux, Mobius, TCA — three philosophies, like three forces, competed here.

Advocates of Redux hoist the banner of the "central archive." They believe only a single state tree can keep a large system predictable. They say, "What we need is global consistency, even if it is heavy."

Supporters of Mobius emphasize the freedom of loops. They argue that decentralized, feature-level autonomy is the salvation in practice. They say, "What we need is flexibility, even if it requires extra coordination."

And the experimenters of TCA are like an emerging school. They don't proclaim loudly, but they show results on a small scale. They say, "We don't need extremes; we need deep modularity."

The first point of conflict is testability.

Spotify's recommendation system is one of their most strategically important features. It makes billions of playback decisions every day and drives user retention. The recommendation logic is extremely complex: it includes experimental groups, real-time data, user profiles, and regional restrictions.

In the Redux model, all this logic is concentrated in the global state tree. Testing one part of the functionality means mocking the entire state tree. This makes testing prohibitively costly.

In the Mobius model, each recommendation experiment is a loop, and testing becomes easier. You only need to simulate that loop's inputs and outputs without loading the global state. This brings great convenience.

However, as the number of experiments increases, coordination between loops begins to run out of control. Some experiments affect recommendation ordering; others affect playback duration. These experiments must communicate with each other. Testing a single loop is simple, but testing the overall effect is extremely difficult.

TCA experimenters found a breakthrough here. They split the recommendation logic into multiple Reducers, each independently testable but composable into larger Reducers. This "depth of composition" creates a new balance: it offers Mobius-like local testability while retaining Redux-like global predictability.

The second point of conflict is cognitive load.

Redux's weight comes from its requirement that all state flows through the same pipeline. This intimidates newcomers. Engineers say, "When I face that massive state tree, it's like looking at an unfamiliar map of an empire. I know it's complete, but I don't know how to read it."

The lightness of Mobius makes it easy to pick up. You only need to understand a single loop to get the job done. However, as the system grows, you have to understand multiple loops at once; the messages between them feel like endless secret missives. Engineers say, "I'm no longer afraid of the map — I'm afraid of the messengers."

TCA's philosophy lies in how it reduces cognitive load. It localizes state yet creates layers through composition of Reducers. Engineers can understand only the Reducer they own, without having to grasp the whole system at once. When a global view is needed, they can expand layer by layer, like reading a volume of history.

This makes engineers feel they have regained power. They are no longer porters in an archive, nor slaves to a network of messengers. They are compilers of history, knowing how to switch between the local and the global.

The third point of conflict is team boundaries.

Spotify is a huge organization with hundreds of teams, each responsible for different features: the playback queue, social sharing, podcasts, recommendations, payments, advertising.

If all teams depend on Redux's global state tree, they must constantly coordinate. It is like every province of an empire relying on the center: any road repair requires approval from the capital. That level of efficiency can hold for small teams but is doomed to collapse at scale.

If all teams rely on Mobius's loops, they can be autonomous. Each team only needs to maintain its own loop and communicate with others via events. This energizes the local level but sacrifices global consistency. Some teams update quickly, others slowly, and the user experience begins to fragment.

TCA offers an organizational answer. It allows teams to maintain their own Reducers as "deep modules." Teams are guardians of modules; modules define a team's cognitive boundary. These

Reducers can be composed at higher levels to form a global whole. This means teams can be autonomous yet be integrated into the larger system when needed.

Spotify's management found this pattern highly compatible with their organizational culture. They have long advocated "small-team autonomy, large-team alignment." TCA's philosophy happens to be an engineered expression of that culture.

Complexity was never eliminated, but it was reshaped.

Redux concentrates complexity, at the cost of weight; Mobius disperses complexity, at the cost of coordination; TCA layers complexity, at the cost of modular discipline.

Spotify's final choice was not to completely abandon any one side, but to mix and make trade-offs. In scenarios that require strong consistency, they still use Redux's ideas; for features that require rapid iteration, they retain Mobius's loops; in experiments with new features and SwiftUI, they adopt TCA at scale.

This is not victory, but maturity. They admit that no one pattern can completely defeat complexity. All you can do is find the most suitable balance for the moment.

At an all-hands sharing session, a senior architect said, "We once thought architecture was about finding the single truth. But now we know architecture is just a way of allocating complexity. You cannot erase complexity; you can only decide where it falls: in the archive, on the messenger network, or in the deep wells of modules."

The room fell silent. Everyone understood that this was not only Spotify's choice, but the fate of all software teams.

"Complexity is like an empire's taxation. You cannot refuse to pay; you can only decide at which level it is collected and who bears it. The worst system is one that leaves everyone trapped under the tax burden; the wisest system makes the burden understandable."

Spotify's story draws to a close here. They did not find a perfect answer, but they found an answer for survival. Redux, Mobius, TCA — they are not opposing banners, but tools in a toolbox. The wisdom of architecture lies not in choosing the one, but in understanding trade-offs.

Complexity does not disappear; it only moves. Redux concentrates it, Mobius disperses it, TCA layers it. The differences among the three are not about technical merits, but philosophical differences about how humans manage cognitive load.

For iOS developers, the combination of TCA and SwiftUI offers us new possibilities: making state clear, making boundaries explicit, and allowing teams and modules to form contracts. This is not the end, but the beginning of a long evolution.

An empire will not endure forever because of a single institutional reform, and software will not enjoy long-term stability because of one architectural choice. Only constant clear-headedness can keep the flame of order alive in the shadow of complexity.

The ultimate truth about complexity is: there is no victory, only balance.
The ultimate goal of architecture is to ensure that people in the future can still understand the choices made today.

CHAPTER 13
REDUCER MINDSET

History is not driven by events, but by state transitions.

The rise and fall of empires, the replacement of institutions, the shocks of culture are nothing more than countless state changes.

The wind rises from the soft click of a keyboard and falls on the user's fingertips. Messages blink, channels switch, notifications appear.

Slack's world is a city-state that never sleeps: its streets are channels, its marketplaces are messages, its squares are groups.

Millions gather here to meet, communicate, and collaborate.

And behind this city hides a vast and dangerous complexity: state.

State is the soul of software, but also its poison.

Is a message read? Is the user online? Is the network connected? Is the file uploaded? Are permissions allowed?

These questions seem simple individually, but when they

intertwine, they form an invisible web that traps the minds of developers.

Slack's early team, like many startups, chose speed.

Their mission was to capture the market as quickly as possible and to get the product onto as many platforms as possible.

Mac, Windows, iOS, Android, Web — all platforms had to be advanced simultaneously.

This was the expansion phase of the empire; everything had to be fast.

However, complexity never compromises for speed.

In Slack's system, states accumulate like grains of sand.

A message marked read on the desktop needs to be synchronized to the mobile;

A push received while a user is offline must be reconciled when they come online;

A failed file upload needs to be retried when the connection is restored;

A channel permission change needs to take effect on all devices immediately.

Every requirement is a new state transition path.

Every fix is a new patch.

The team initially thought they were accelerating forward; in reality, they were building an increasingly complex maze.

The weight of complexity soon became evident.

Slack's engineers found that they could not clearly answer a simple question:

"At this moment, what exactly is a user's message state?"

In different places, they got different answers:

The client shows unread, the server thinks it's read;

The push system shows undelivered, but the database has it recorded;

The Android device thinks it's online, while the iOS device is trying to reconnect.

Like the empire's records diverging across the land:

The capital reports a bountiful harvest while the frontier is starving;

The army sends back tales of victory while the people are wailing.

When the truth cannot be unified, the system collapses.

For Slack, such divergence meant bugs.

The state a user saw on one end was completely different from the state on the other.

Pushes were lost, messages duplicated, unread counts scrambled — the user experience was severely affected.

Complexity began to seep into what users perceived.

Slack's team tried to fix these problems.

They added more flags, more caches, more "temporary fixes."

But each fix was like plastering a new patch over a crack.

The cracks did not disappear; they only extended to new places.

This is the terrifying thing about complexity:

The more you cover it with temporary patches, the more it strikes back in more complicated ways.

In the end, the team found themselves trapped in a paradox:

the more they fixed, the harder the system became to understand.

The more they explained, the heavier the Cognitive Load.

At a critical engineering meeting, Slack's core engineers asked a question:

"Why can we never truly fix these state bugs?"

Some fell silent, some sighed.

Finally, one sentence pierced the fog:

"Because we never actually defined state.

We were just chasing symptoms and never looked at the essence."

That sentence became a turning point in Slack's engineering history.

Complexity, at its core, is not the accumulation of features but the chaos of state.

Without a clear state model, every feature becomes a new branch until the whole tree can no longer be supported.

And the reducer mindset was rediscovered against this backdrop.

The reducer is not a new idea.

In the world of functional programming it has long existed;

In the contexts of Redux, Elm, and TCA it has been proven effective.

Its core is extremely simple:

Treat the system as a state machine: each input transforms the old state into a new state.

It sounds simple, but in a system as large as Slack, it was a revolutionary shift.

Imagine the empire's institutions.

Without a clear code of laws, local officials act independently and the empire would quickly descend into chaos.

The Reducer, however, is like a code of laws:

It defines all the legitimate paths from an old state to a new state.

Every change must be judged by the code;

Every input must yield a consistent result.

Slack's engineers realized that if they could model the messaging system, the push system, and the connectivity system as state machines, then complexity could be constrained.

Not by fighting with patches, but by constraining behavior with rules.

Not by smearing mud over cracks, but by re-piling the foundation.

Yet change never comes easily.

The team was full of debates.

Some argued this would make the system too rigid and slow down development;

Some worried about the cost of refactoring and thought it was an impossible task;

Others questioned, "State machines? Aren't those toys from university lectures? We're dealing with real users."

But complexity gave them no more choices.

Bugs kept increasing and user complaints grew louder.

Slack's reputation was under threat and investor pressure began to mount.

Against this backdrop, the team finally made a decision:

refactor the core systems, adopt the reducer mindset, and treat the software as a state machine.

This shift was like an empire moving from lawless tribes into an era of codified governance.

It would not immediately bring prosperity, but it could prevent collapse.

Slack's engineers began to draw vast state diagrams and exhaustively enumerate every possibility.

Messages transitioning from "unread" to "read," from "sending" to "failed," from "failed" to "retry"—every step had to be specified.

They created reducers that funneled every input into a pure function.

This work was tedious and painful.

Because it forced the team to confront the full extent of the complexity.

Where they had once made local repairs, they now had to lay the entire maze out in the open.

That was terrifying, because the maze was far larger than anyone had imagined.

But after fear came clarity.

When states were explicitly modeled, the sources of bugs began to shrink.

Previously fuzzy boundaries were codified into strict transitions.

Developers no longer needed to hop around three layers of systems; they only had to follow the chain of state transitions.

Complexity remained, but it was contained, constrained, and understood.

Slack's city-state began to restore order.

Channel unread counts became reliable, push deliveries more stable, and message synchronization less error-prone.

Users might not know what was happening behind the scenes, but they felt an improvement in the experience.

That is the power of state machines: they don't make complexity disappear, they make complexity governed by rules.

However, this was only the beginning.

The reducer mindset not only changed the code, it changed the team's culture.

They began to discuss problems in the language of state machines:

"At this moment, which state is our system in?"

"What transition will this input cause?"

They no longer argued about features, but discussed the code.

This lowered the team's communication costs and reduced cognitive load.

But the road remained hard.

Exhaustively enumerating states was far more complex than they had imagined, and cross-platform consistency issues continued to plague them.

Reducer thinking brought order, but order also brought new challenges.

The war against complexity was far from over.

Slack had only taken the first step:

From chaotic patches to orderly state machines.

But greater torrents still awaited them.

The establishment of order was not the end of chaos, but a new form of complexity.

When an empire prides itself on its code, the

generals on the frontier still struggle under the new constraints.

Slack's transformation brought a temporary calm.

When the reducer mindset was introduced, the state-machine code brought engineers a long-awaited clarity.

Bug counts declined, unread counts became steadier, and message synchronization errors dropped significantly.

Team meetings were no longer filled with vague debates, but acquired a new language:

"Is this state covered by the code?"

"Is this input valid?"

Everything seemed to be moving toward order.

However, complexity was never eliminated.

It merely returned in another form.

In Slack's world, the greatest enemy was not the number of features but the infinity of concurrency.

A user posting a message in a channel is just a single input;

but when millions of users communicate across tens of thousands of channels simultaneously, the flood of inputs becomes a roaring ocean.

The advantage of state machines is clarity, but clarity requires exhaustive enumeration.

When Slack's engineers tried to enumerate all possible state transitions, they found themselves facing a map that expanded without limit.

Take the example of "message read."

In a single-user single-device scenario it's just two states: unread → read.

But in Slack's reality, that state chain expands to an unimaginable degree:

- Single user, multiple devices: iOS shows read, Android shows unread, the web browser tab hasn't refreshed.

- Multiple users sharing a channel: one person has read it, another still hasn't; the unread count must reflect the union of the group's state.
- Network conditions: marked read while offline, needing synchronization on reconnect;
- Push mechanisms: push notifications still arrive after a message is read and must be revoked.

Each condition is a dimension;

Each dimension makes the state machine's size explode exponentially.

The state diagrams the engineers drew on the whiteboard grew from one wall to the entire conference room.

They used different colored arrows for different inputs and different-shaped nodes for different states.

The whiteboards filled quickly; they had to bring in more boards and plaster sticky notes everywhere.

This is not an exaggeration; this is reality.

The clarity brought by the state machine let them, for the first time, see the full scope of the complexity, and the sheer scale of that scope was itself a shock.

That shock did not bring collapse, but fear.

The fear was: if we must enumerate everything, can we ever finish?

The fear was: if every input must be strictly adjudicated, will the system become sluggish?

The fear was: if we truly see the complexity, can we bear it?

This fear spread like a shadow through the team.

Some engineers began to doubt the feasibility of the reducer mindset:

"It makes us clearer, but it also makes us slower."

Others insisted: "Only by facing the fear can we truly master complexity."

This debate is not unique to Slack.

In any empire that introduces strict institutions, there will always be this tug-of-war:

Order implies constraints, and constraints imply a loss of speed.

In times of expansion, speed is life; in times of governance, order is survival.

Slack's team was at this turning point.

Another expression of complexity is platform diversity.

Slack's ambition from the start was not limited to a single platform.

They had to maintain Web, Mac, Windows, iOS, Android, and even Linux at the same time.

The state machine's code had to span these platforms and remain consistent.

However, each platform has its own habits and constraints.

On iOS, an app can be suspended by the system and background state requires special handling;

On Android, the notification mechanisms are more open but also messier;

On the Web, tabs can be paused by the browser and socket connections can be interrupted;

On the desktop, a user might have multiple windows open at once, causing state divergence.

The clarity that Reducer thinking brought on a single platform was amplified into new challenges in the cross-platform reality.

The team had to face a question:

Do we pursue global consistency, or local sensibility?

If they pursue global consistency, the state machine's size will balloon without limit;

if they choose local sensibility, user experiences may differ across platforms.

It's like an empire's code: if you demand uniformity across the whole nation, the frontiers may struggle to comply;

If you allow local variations, the unity of the empire will be weakened.

Slack's leadership had to choose between consistency and practicality.

The choice introduced new tensions.

They decided to keep global consistency on core states while allowing differences on non-core states.

For example: a message's read status must be strictly consistent across all platforms;

But the presentation form of notifications can vary by platform.

This was a compromise and a piece of practical wisdom. However, compromise did not mean reduced complexity.

On the contrary, it introduced new boundaries: which states are core, and which are non-core?

That classification itself became a new Cognitive Load.

The team began writing documentation to define core vs. non-core boundaries.

But the documentation quickly became outdated and was repeatedly revised as requirements changed.

In their daily work, developers had to constantly confirm:

"Is this state core or non-core?"

Each confirmation consumed attention and mental capacity.

Reducer thinking gave them clarity, but the price of clarity was new divisions of responsibility and new complexity.

The third source of complexity is time.

In a collaboration tool like Slack, time is not a single linear flow.

Messages can be delayed, backfilled after being offline, edited, or retracted.

Time is not one-way; it can be "rewound" by user actions.

This is an extreme challenge for state machines.

In traditional state machines, inputs are linear and state transitions are irreversible.

But in Slack's reality, states must support rewinding and branching.

After a message is sent, a user may immediately retract it.

Another message may be edited hours later.

These operations change past states, thereby affecting the present and the future.

It's like an empire's history being tampered with:

If the outcome of a battle is rewritten, the entire dynasty's records must be corrected.

Slack's engineers must build a "rewindable" state machine so the system can correctly handle these temporal branches.

This is a wholly new way of thinking.

Reducer thinking is no longer a single straight line but a graph that can roll back and fork.

Engineers must retain clarity within this complex map.

For them, this is an unprecedented test.

The final dimension of complexity is people.

Slack's users are not isolated individuals but teams.

Each person on a team continuously interacts with the system.

Their actions affect one another, forming a collective state.

When a team has hundreds of people online at the same time, the system must handle hundreds of state transitions simultaneously and remain consistent.

This is not merely a technical problem but a philosophical one:

In a multi-user environment, what is the "real state"?

Is it the local truth each person sees, or the global truth maintained on the server?

If the two conflict, who is authoritative?

Slack's engineers had to find an answer between technology and philosophy.

They ultimately chose: the server is the truth, the clients are mirrors.

This is the idea of a single source of truth.

However, this choice also means clients must continuously synchronize with the server, causing latency and performance pressure.

Complexity again transformed into a new form, lurking in the corners of network and performance.

Reducer thinking gave Slack a framework that allowed them to confront complexity. But after confronting it, they truly understood that the scale of the complexity far exceeded imagination. A state machine is not a universal key; it is merely a new code. And the code cannot solve all problems; it can only make problems traceable.

In an internal document, Slack's engineers wrote: "We are no longer blind, but we are no longer naive. The state machine let us see the complexity, but the complexity did not disappear. It merely changed its face and continues to test us."

An empire's code cannot make everyone happy, but it can prevent the empire from collapsing immediately. Reducer thinking, in Slack's practice, was the same. It brought order and also brought new dilemmas. The team stood at a new crossroads: they had to decide how to find a balance between order and flexibility.

Slack's Reducer transformation had only just entered deep water. The real challenges were still ahead.

When an empire learns to admit its own limitations, it truly reaches maturity.

When a team learns to settle within complexity, it truly begins to be civilized.

Order is not the endpoint of chaos, but a new form of complexity. When Slack regained clarity under Reducer thinking, they faced another challenge: how to find a balance between "strict order" and "flexible evolution."

Because software is not a monument but quicksand. It

constantly changes, constantly grows, constantly devours old boundaries. If the code is too strict, the team will suffocate in execution; if the code is too loose, complexity will flood again. Slack's Reducer transformation is searching for a narrow path between these extremes.

The turning point came in a concrete event.

Slack planned to launch a brand-new feature: threaded messages. Users could start a discussion on a particular message within a channel without disrupting the main conversation thread. This seemed like merely a UI-level enhancement, but for the state system it was an earthquake.

A thread means a message no longer has a single context, but can spawn countless sub-contexts.

- The state of a message in the main channel;
- The state of a message within a particular thread;
- Whether a user has read a thread;
- Whether thread messages should trigger notifications;
- Cross-device thread synchronization.

Reducer thinking requires enumerating all possible state transitions.

When engineers drew state diagrams on the whiteboard, they found it looked like a tree growing out of control.

Each parent message could spawn dozens of threads, and each thread had its own read, unread, notification, muted/ignored states.

The number of states grew exponentially.

An engineer stood silently before the whiteboard for a long time and then said, "This is not a state machine, this is a state forest."

The laughter was brief, but no one really felt relieved.

They realized that the order brought by Reducer thinking could also fall into trouble at this scale.

The team fell into debate.

Some argued that they should continue to insist on strict Reducer modeling, even if the cost was a slowdown;

Others countered that the threading feature was critical for market competition, and waiting for complete modeling might mean missing the opportunity.

The debate lasted several days, and finally Slack's leadership decided:

We must find a way of "incremental modeling."

Incremental modeling means not exhaustively enumerating all states at once, but first covering the core paths and then gradually expanding.

It was a compromise and also a kind of wisdom:

Not a denial of the state machine, but an admission that humans cannot see the whole picture at once.

The complexity is too great; it must be digested in batches over time.

Just as an empire cannot establish a complete code all at once during expansion,

It must allow temporary ambiguity at the frontier, letting institutions be refined through practice.

The rollout of the threading feature was the true test of Slack's Reducer transformation.

At first, they only modeled the most core state:

Whether a message was read in the main channel and in threads.

Other states, such as alerts, notifications, and cross-device synchronization, were temporarily marked "to be expanded."

Bugs still existed in the early rollout.

Users complained about inconsistent notifications and incorrect unread counts on some devices.

The team did not deny this, but transparently recorded the issues and gradually expanded new branches in the state machine.

This approach was fundamentally different from the old "patch-style fixes."

Patches are temporary and do not enter the code; incremental modeling is systematic, and all fixes will eventually be incorporated into the state machine.

Gradually, the system moved toward clarity.

Every newly added state fell under the constraints of the Reducer;

Every fix became part of the state machine.

Complexity still grew, but it now had a place in the codebase instead of drifting at the margins.

This approach changed the team's culture.

In the past, engineers were used to applying patches under emergency conditions.

Now they learned to describe problems in the language of "state":

"This is an unmodeled state; we need to extend the Reducer."

Patches were treated as debt, while state extensions were treated as investments.

This cultural shift was more important than the technology itself.

Because it redirected the team's mindset from "putting out fires" to "building institutions."

Complexity was no longer a ghost to be constantly avoided but a guest invited to the table.

People no longer feared it; they discussed how to live with it.

However, the power of Reducer thinking was not limited to technology and culture.

Its deeper impact was the unification of the team's collaborative language.

Slack's developers, designers, and product managers began to use the same concept when discussing features: state.

When designers described user experience, they no longer just said "what happens when you click here," but "this causes the user to enter a particular state."

When product managers planned requirements, they no

longer merely listed features but defined the possible state transitions a user might experience.

When developers implemented features, they no longer just wrote logic but implemented state transitions.

This common language reduced cross-functional communication costs.

Complexity did not disappear, but it was shared and understood at the language level.

That is the real value of Reducer thinking:

It is not only a programming method but a cognitive framework.

Of course, complexity still lurks in the shadows.

Slack's scale kept growing, the user base kept expanding, and requirements became increasingly complex.

The map of the state machine remained dauntingly large.

But unlike before, the team no longer panicked.

They understood that complexity would not go away.

They also knew that Reducer thinking could not make everything simple.

But they believed that as long as states were clearly modeled, complexity would no longer be a black box.

And the black box is the most frightening enemy.

Years later, Slack's engineering wrote in the internal archives: "Reducer thinking made us realize that software is not driven by features, but by state. Features are the surface; state is the essence. When we treat software as a state machine, we are not eliminating complexity, we are making it transparent."

At a philosophical level, this shift has profound implications.

We often regard software as a tool and assume its core is "what it can do." But Reducer thinking reminds us that the true core of software is "what it is at this moment." All features are merely state transitions; all problems are merely state disorders.

When you look at software through the lens of features, you see fragments; when you look at it through the lens of state, you see the whole. This is a revolution in thinking.

Reducer thinking has another value: it forces the team to face human limitations.

Human working memory is limited and cannot grasp too many branches at once. Modeling a state machine breaks complexity into a finite set of states so humans can understand them one by one. It does not make the system simple, but it makes the system comprehensible. Comprehensibility is the only way for people to coexist with complexity.

This aligns closely with the philosophical goal of software: software design is not about pursuing perfect patterns, but about reducing the cost of understanding. Reducer thinking is the engineering embodiment of that philosophy.

Slack's story is not the victory of Reducer thinking, but the truth of complexity. Complexity remains; state machines have not made it disappear. But Reducer thinking gave humans a voice in the face of complexity, institutions, and a language.

In the end, the Slack team learned a phrase: "Complexity cannot be defeated, but it can be modeled."

The most powerful weapon is not to eliminate complexity, but to make it transparent.
The wisest architecture is not the fantasy of being bug-free, but the reality with boundaries.
Reducer thinking is not magic, but a code.
Its value is not in simplification, but in enabling human understanding.

CHAPTER 14
STRATEGY, DECORATOR, ADAPTER, OBSERVER IN THE SWIFT WORLD

Weapons do not destroy enemies, but they can change the order of the battlefield.

Design patterns are not a certificate of victory, but symbols of humanity's dialogue with complexity.

The wind is invisible, yet it can change the shape of the dunes.

Complexity is also invisible, yet it can change the direction of software.

In the archives of the mobile empire, one name expanded like a storm: Uber.

Its territory was not a map, but countless points on screens, from a corner in San Francisco to a district in Mumbai, from a night in Paris to rush hour in Beijing.

Uber's app was originally just a simple ride-hailing tool.

A user entered a location, a driver accepted the request, and a trip was completed.

Simple as a stone dropped into a lake.

However, as it expanded globally, the stone was no longer just a stone, but a vortex that set off countless waves.

Because every city has different rules.

New York taxis have fixed fares; London drivers must comply with black cab regulations; India's payment systems require integration with local wallets; China's map APIs are completely different from other regions.

Uber's engineering team found that their app was no longer a "unified product," but a collection of empires.

Complexity revealed its truest face here:

It was not an increase of features, but an accumulation of differences.

In the early days, Uber's team dealt with differences in the most direct way: conditional statements.

If it's a certain country, follow this logic; if it's another region, follow another logic.

This approach worked at first, like setting up outposts on the frontier.

But as the outposts multiplied, the road was no longer straight, but full of forks and checkpoints.

A payment flow might branch into a dozen paths because cities differ;

A map component might be filled with compatibility logic because of API differences.

Developers were exhausted, and every requirement felt like navigating a maze.

The shadow of complexity fell again.

Uber's engineers had to face a fact: their app could no longer be sustained by simple conditional branches.

They needed new weapons.

At this time, design patterns returned to the stage.

They were not new inventions, but the rebirth of old weapons.

But in Uber's context, they gained new meaning.

Strategy was no longer just the algorithm substitution from textbooks; it became a tool for governing global differences.

Decorator was no longer merely a technique for adding functionality; it became a way to attach different cities' rules onto the core flow.

Adapter was no longer just a bridge between old and new interfaces; it became the key to unifying various countries' payment systems within the Uber ecosystem.

Observer was no longer merely the syntax of notifications; it became the foundation for real-time interactions between passengers and drivers.

In the desert of complexity, these patterns became like water, a resource that sustained the empire's operation.

The true story begins with payments.

Payments were originally Uber's simplest process: a passenger completed a trip, the system calculated the fare, and the credit card was charged.

But when the business expanded to different countries, this process quickly became complicated:

- In India, users tended to prefer paying cash;
- In China, support for Alipay and WeChat Pay was required;
- In Latin America, some regions relied on local bank transfers;
- In Africa, mobile wallets were the primary method.

Each payment method introduced a new difference.

If conditional branches were used, the system would sink into an unmaintainable quagmire.

So Uber chose Strategy.

The core payment logic remained unchanged: calculate the fare, trigger the payment, confirm the result.

Differences were isolated into different strategies: credit card strategy, cash strategy, wallet strategy.

When a user selected a different payment method, the system only needed to swap the strategy instead of rewriting the flow.

This is the power of Strategy:

It tames differences rather than indulging them.

It focuses engineers' cognitive load on "which strategy to choose" instead of getting lost in sprawling conditional logic.

The story of Decorator, meanwhile, happens in pricing rules.

Uber's pricing was never singular.

In New York, surge-hour surcharges might be added;

In London, additional rules related to black cab licensing had to be considered;

In Paris, holidays could trigger extra charges;

In some emerging markets, fuel subsidies or government taxes had to be added.

If all these rules were written into the core logic, the system would become an unreadable monolith.

So the engineers chose Decorator.

The core pricing logic remains simple: base fare + distance * unit price.

Additional rules are layered as decorators: surge surcharge, holiday surcharge, fuel subsidy, tax surcharge.

Each rule can exist independently or be combined with others.

When a new market appears, you only need to add a new "decoration" without modifying the core logic.

The meaning of Decorator here goes beyond the pattern itself.

It becomes a philosophy for governing complexity:

Keep the core pure, and let changes be absorbed at the edges.

The power of Adapter is reflected in system integrations.

Uber's app must integrate with different countries' map services.

In the United States, it can use Google Maps;

In China, it must use Amap (Gaode);

In Russia, it may need to integrate Yandex;

In other regions, there are countless smaller providers.

These map services each have different interfaces and different data structures.

If compatibility logic were written directly into the system, the app would be dragged down by heterogeneous interfaces.

So the engineers used Adapter.

Adapter "translates" external map services into Uber's internal unified interface.

Whether the backend is Google, Baidu, or Amap, Uber's app always sees the same map interface.

This allows the team to focus on business logic rather than be overwhelmed by external differences.

Adapter here is not simple "interface matching," but "protection against cognitive load."

It isolates external complexity behind a wall so internal developers can remain clear-headed.

Finally, Observer.

One of Uber's core experiences is real-time interaction between passengers and drivers.

When a passenger places an order, drivers need to receive a notification instantly;

When a driver accepts an order, the passenger's status needs to update immediately;

While a trip is in progress, the map needs to refresh in real time;

When payment is completed, both parties must be informed.

These real-time interactions are precisely the domain of Observer.

In Uber's systems, event-driven becomes the norm.

Every change is broadcast out, and relevant components subscribe and respond.

This pattern means complex interactions no longer rely on centralized polling, but occur naturally through "observation".

The meaning of Observer here is not "callbacks" but "order."

It makes the empire's communications efficient and orderly, keeping complex interactions within an understandable scope.

Uber's story shows the rebirth of patterns.

Strategy, Decorator, Adapter, Observer — these seemingly stale concepts gain new life in a new context.

They are no longer merely textbook paradigms but weapons for governing complexity.

However, weapons alone do not bring victory.

The key is how, at the right time, in the right way, to use the right weapon.

Uber's empire continues to expand.

Complexity does not stop; it is only temporarily tamed.

New challenges will appear, and new differences will arise.

But at least for now, Uber found a way to prevent the flood of complexity from immediately breaching the levees.

All institutions will eventually bend under their own weight.

All patterns will eventually turn on themselves when overextended.

When complexity learns to disguise itself, it puts on the garb of patterns.

The wind is changing.

As Uber's territory expanded from a single city to hundreds of cities, and from millions of users to hundreds of millions, the dust storms of complexity swept through again.

The once-effective pattern-weapons brought clarity and order.

But weapons are never without cost.

When they are extended without limit, when they are overused, they become new embodiments of complexity.

The cracks in Strategy appeared first.

The diversity of payment logic was tamed by Strategy in the early years.

Credit card strategies, cash strategies, wallet strategies — each independent, each swappable.

This was clear order.

However, as Uber entered more markets, the number of payment methods began to grow exponentially.

A country's credit card payments might have different bank requirements;

A region's wallet payments might be tied to a specific telecom operator;

some places' cash payments might involve government subsidies or coupon deductions.

So Strategy became not a dozen but hundreds.

The payments module turned into a vast forest, each tree a strategy.

When fixing bugs, engineers must first find the correct strategy, then confirm whether it overlaps with other strategies, and then modify it with extreme care.

Strategy was originally a "clear choice," but here it became a "maze of difficult choices."

Human cognitive limits were exposed once again.

When faced with dozens or hundreds of strategies, developers' minds could no longer maintain "quick understanding."

They joked in meeting rooms: "We need a Strategy for Strategy."

Behind the laughter was the relentlessness of Cognitive Load.

The problem with Decorator, meanwhile, spread like vines.

The differences in pricing rules were initially expressed by Decorator elegantly and succinctly.

Base fare, distance fee, holiday surcharges, fuel subsidies... each rule was a leaf attached to the core branch.

However, as markets expanded, those decorations multiplied.

One city required extra charges for nighttime driving; one country required discounts for eco-friendly vehicles; some markets layered two different surcharges on holidays.

The result was that the chain of Decorators grew ever longer.

A pricing request might need to pass through a dozen or more layers of Decorators.

When debugging, engineers had to trace the execution of each Decorator to understand how the final price was derived.

When the chain became too long, Decorator was no longer decoration but a maze.

Every node could hide a bug; every change could trigger a chain reaction.

Engineers described the experience: "like reading a story with no end."

They no longer knew where the boundaries of decorations lay, nor which rule was truly central.

The philosophy of Decorator is "keep the core pure, let changes be at the edges." But when edge changes drown out the core, the core loses its meaning.

The predicament of Adapter, however, came from the diversity of the ecosystem.

Uber's map services initially only needed to adapt to a few major providers.

Google, Baidu, Amap (Gaode), Yandex — each had its Adapter, keeping differences outside the wall.

This was Adapter's most perfect scenario.

However, as Uber partnered with more third parties, the number of Adapters increased sharply.

Payments, push notifications, identity authentication, risk-control systems, customer service systems…

Every external service required an Adapter.

As a result, Adapter itself became a new empire.

Adapters were everywhere in the code.

Engineers had to constantly learn new interface specifications and continually maintain old bridging logic.

Adapter was originally "simplification," but when their number ballooned, they became a new source of complexity.

Worse, when an external service updated, the Adapter needed to be updated in sync.

If an external vendor changed its interface, the whole system could be brought down.

Adapters were no longer protection but shackles.

They made the system overly dependent on external changes and put the team on the defensive.

The chaos of Observer was the most conspicuous.

Uber's real-time interactions relied on Observer's event mechanism.

This made communication between passengers and drivers instant and flexible.

However, as features increased, the number of events also swelled.

Order created, order canceled, payment completed, driver arrived, driver left, location updates, anomaly reports...

Each event had multiple subscribers, and each subscriber could trigger new events.

As the system scaled, this event-driven approach became a storm.

One event could spawn a dozen follow-up events, and engineers found it hard to predict the chain's direction.

Debugging became a game of chasing storms.

"We're like meteorologists," one engineer said, "but the problem is our storms are not natural; they are man-made."

The power of Observer lies in "decentralization."

But when decentralization is excessive, the system loses predictability.

Every module can emit events, every module can subscribe to events, and in the end no one knows where the system's real boundaries are.

Overuse of patterns dragged Uber back into the abyss of complexity.

The maze of Strategy, the vines of Decorator, the empire of Adapter, the storm of Observer.

They were once symbols of order; now they have become symbols of chaos.

Complexity laughs, because it knows: humans think they have tamed it, but in reality they have only changed its form.

This complexity is not only technical but also cultural.

Within Uber's teams, the pride that once existed began to waver.

Patterns were meant to be elegant solutions, but when they are abused, elegance becomes a burden.

Engineers argued in meetings:

"We need a new pattern to manage the existing patterns?"

That debate itself is an embodiment of complexity.

Cognitive load is no longer just a code problem but a team problem.

When newcomers join, they face hundreds or thousands of strategies, countless layers of Decorators, countless Adapters, countless events.

They need months to adapt to the system, yet still cannot fully understand it.

The team's boundaries are torn apart by patterns.

"Patterns are the language by which humans negotiate with complexity.

When language is excessive, the negotiation loses its meaning."

Uber's story is precisely that footnote.

They used patterns to govern complexity, but complexity also used patterns to turn against them.

This is the inevitability of civilization: any system, when stretched to its limits, will expose new cracks.

However, cracks do not mean destruction.

Cracks mean a new evolution is about to occur.

Uber's teams began to realize they must rethink how they use patterns.

They need deeper boundary design and a new philosophy.

The wind is gathering.

A new turning point is about to come.

When institutions ossify, humans must reshape them.

When patterns turn to bite back, humans must reshape the patterns.

Complexity cannot be eliminated, but it can be revered. Reverence is the new order.

After the storm there is always silence.

When Uber's systems were bitten back by patterns, the team stood on the ruins of chaos and, for the first time, clearly saw:

They were not lacking patterns, but lacking boundaries.

The starting point of the refactor was a failed launch.

It was a special requirement from a Southeast Asian market: the government required that order receipts separately list an environmental surcharge and local taxes.

A seemingly simple requirement, yet it brought the entire system to a halt.

The payments module already had hundreds of strategies.

The Decorator chain was as long as twenty layers, each layer potentially affecting the final price.

The number of Adapters was incalculable, with external systems' updates frequently triggering crashes.

Observer's event storm made the logs like battlefield dust, billowing in.

On the night of the launch, the team worked continuously for thirty-six hours.

Bugs were fixed, and new bugs emerged;

Strategies were modified, and other strategies were affected;

Decorators were added, and they overrode other decorators.

By dawn they finally went live, but the system's stability remained fragile.

At that moment, management realized:

Their problem was not functional complexity, but cognitive complexity.

Patterns had lost their meaning as "simplification tools" and had instead become containers of complexity.

Thus, a refactor began.

It was not about overthrowing, but about reshaping.

The team needed to establish a new order out of the chaos.

The first step was to redraw the boundaries.

Payment strategies were no longer allowed to expand indefinitely.

The team divided strategies into tiers: core tier, regional tier, and exception tier.

The core tier contained only the most basic logic;

The regional tier defined regional differences;

The exception tier carried short-term government or market requirements.

This layering meant engineers no longer had to confront hundreds of strategies.

They only needed to look in the correct tier.

Cognitive Load transformed from a maze into a partitioned map.

The chain of Decorators was also truncated.

The team mandated that no pricing logic could have more than three layers of decoration.

Complex rules exceeding three layers had to be split into independent modules and encapsulated as "deep modules."

The core returned to purity, and edge changes were confined to a controllable scope.

The empire of Adapters was pared back.

Adapters were no longer written individually for every external service.

The team established a unified "external services layer," and all Adapters had to connect through it.

It was like setting up customs at the empire's border: external chaos was kept outside the gate, and the interior remained unified.

The storm of Observer events was also contained.

The team imposed an "event bus" constraint:

Not every module could trigger events at will; they had to go through explicit channels;

Events had to have lifecycle management and could not spread indefinitely.

The storm was brought within boundaries; forecasting became prediction again, not chaos.

The second step of the refactor was to establish a "Cognitive Load guardrail."

This was a system of rules, not a technology.

The team agreed: if any module's complexity exceeded what a newcomer could understand within two weeks, it had to be refactored.

They set metrics: limits on the number of strategies, Decorator chain depth, Adapter integration rules, and the number of Observer events.

These metrics were not meant to stifle innovation, but to protect future comprehensibility.

Cognitive load was, for the first time, treated as a resource to be managed.

It was no longer invisible debt but an explicit budget.

Every team had a cognitive budget; if they exceeded it, they had to repay it.

This institutional reform changed the culture.

Developers no longer measured success solely by "feature completion," but by "whether it can be understood in the future."

Their code reviews were no longer just about finding mistakes, but about measuring cognitive load.

Their meetings were no longer just about implementation, but about boundaries.

The third step of the refactor was to acknowledge the role of AI.

In Uber's engineering, AI tools gradually entered the teams: automatically generating tests, automatically detecting diffs, automatically fixing some Adapters.

This brought new power to the teams, but they treated it cautiously.

AI was used to reduce repetitive work, not to hide complexity.

It could generate boilerplate, but it could not design boundaries.

It could assist debugging, but it could not decide patterns.

Engineers recognized:

AI is an assistant, but design still belongs to humans.

Governing complexity requires judgment, trade-offs, and philosophy, not automation.

The final step of the refactor was a cultural shift.

Uber's team adopted a new metaphor:

"We are not builders, but city planners."

Builders care about construction speed; city planners care about whether the city is sustainable.

They realized that software is not a house, but a city.

Patterns are not hammers in a toolbox, but institutions in a city.

Institutions can constrain people, but more importantly, they protect people.

When this culture took root in the team, complexity ceased to be an enemy and became a natural force.

Like wind and sand, it cannot be eliminated, but it can be harnessed.

They no longer sought to eradicate complexity, but to find balance with it.

Years later, Uber's system was still massive, still complex.

But the team had learned a new attitude.

They no longer stacked pattern on pattern, but used boundaries to protect the mind.

They no longer pursued perfect uniformity, but accepted necessary diversity.

They no longer fled from complexity, but acknowledged its existence and coexisted with it within boundaries.

This was the rebirth of patterns.

Strategy was no longer countless branches, but a layered order.

Decorator was no longer an endless chain, but a finite composition.

Adapter was no longer fragments of an empire, but a unified border.

Observer was no longer a storm, but a controlled climate.

They transformed from weapons into institutions; from techniques into philosophy.

"At first, patterns were humanity's resistance to complexity;

Then patterns became an illusion of complexity;

Ultimately, patterns became allies of complexity.

Humans must remember:

The meaning of a pattern lies not in its name but in its ability to reduce Cognitive Load.

Any pattern that increases Cognitive Load has already betrayed its original purpose."

In Uber's archives, that refactor was recorded as a civilizational turn.

It was not a total victory, but it made the team realize:

The true goal of software design is not to write more code, but to enable your future self to understand it.

Complexity remained, the wind and sand still rose, but people had learned to walk among them.

Strategy, Decorator, Adapter, Observer.

They were not dogma, not slogans, not fireworks of showmanship.

They were four keys.
They could open the door to complexity, and they could also trap people in a maze.
The difference was not in the patterns, but in the philosophy.
The rebirth of design patterns is to make them serve people again, not serve complexity.

CHAPTER 15
MISUSED PATTERNS

Patterns are not laws, but shadows.

Shadows change with the light; if you become obsessed with the shadow, you will lose yourself in darkness.

In the depths of the sand sea, people often build phantom cities.

They think the stones are solid, they think the craftsman's skill can resist the wind and sand.

But when the wind changes direction, the stones crack, the phantom city collapses, leaving only an illusion.

In the history of software civilization, design patterns were also treated as stones.

People thought they were universal tools, eternal talismans.

But patterns are essentially shadows of experience.

If you take the shadow as truth, you will be devoured by its illusion.

Client development for large e-commerce platforms is one of the most complex frontlines of the software empire.

Every day millions of users flood in simultaneously; their

actions vary widely, devices differ, and network conditions are unpredictable.

In such an environment, teams always try to find a "stable order", a pattern that can resist chaos.

In Alibaba's client team, design patterns were once regarded as canonical.

Whether new engineers or senior core members, they were taught to be familiar with the classic "twenty-three patterns".

They regarded patterns as lifesaving weapons, believing that as long as they were applied properly, complexity could be tamed.

Thus, in the early stages of projects, the factory pattern and the singleton pattern were almost everywhere.

They were like flags planted on the high ground of each module.

Factories were responsible for producing objects, singletons were responsible for a single point of entry.

It looked orderly, but in reality it planted cracks.

The factory pattern was originally meant to decouple the creation process from the usage process.

In large-scale server-side systems, it can shield complex initialization logic, allowing callers not to worry about details.

However, when this pattern is mechanically transplanted to client development, especially mobile e-commerce applications, problems quietly emerge.

In the order module of the Taobao client, the factory pattern was used to create various service objects: payment, logistics, recommendations, discounts.

Each service object had a corresponding factory.

These factories were further combined into "super factories" managing dozens of sub-factories.

At first, this seemed elegant.

Developers felt they had built a city of order.

By simply calling the factory, they could easily obtain the needed objects.

On the surface, the code looked like a neatly paved plaza.

However, as the business expanded, cracks appeared. Every new requirement introduced new objects. Each new object demanded extensions to the factories. The "super factory" code grew ever larger and increasingly difficult to understand.

The factory's original intent was to hide complexity. But here, it became a collector of complexity. Developers no longer faced a simple interface but a maze. They had to find the right path through the factory jungle, understand layers of dependencies before they could find the entry.

The singleton pattern was an even greater phantom.

In the Taobao client's user session management, the singleton pattern was used extensively. It provided a global entry point that allowed all modules to access user information. Early in the project, this was undoubtedly efficient. Everyone could quickly obtain what they needed without worrying about repeated initialization.

But the price of complexity always arrives later. As the team grew and modules multiplied, the singleton gradually became an invisible shackle. It was like an unseen river that connected all the modules. Any change in one place would affect the entire system.

Once, an error occurred in a session refresh logic inside a singleton. The result was that the entire client experienced login state chaos during a major promotion. Users who had clearly paid were prompted on the order page to "please log in again." The customer service center was instantly overwhelmed, and the team was forced into an emergency fix.

This was not a simple bug. It exposed the fundamental problem of singletons: global sharing means global risk. The complexity here was not the explicit amount of code but the implicit coupling. Developers thought they were saving cognitive load; in reality, they were concentrating risk in an unseen corner.

That night the team's meeting room stayed lit. Engineers

continuously traced logs, repeatedly restarted devices, and tried to reproduce the issue. They found the error was not in the business logic but in the singleton's state synchronization. When multiple threads modified the state simultaneously, the singleton could not guarantee consistency.

This is the power of the phantom. The singleton appeared to provide a unified order, but in fact it produced uncontrollable chaos. It led developers to mistakenly believe they were in control of the system, when in reality they were relying on a rope that could snap at any moment.

Factories and singletons are, at heart, shadows of patterns. In the right contexts they can be hugely effective. But when misused they become obsessions and phantoms.

Alibaba's team was not ignorant. Their engineers were exceptionally smart and experienced. But precisely because of that, they were more easily seduced by the illusion of patterns. They believed patterns were a cure for complexity. Little did they know, patterns are merely another form of complexity.

Complexity does not vanish because you apply a pattern. It only shifts, waiting for you in another form.

In the empire of the sand sea, people once built towering stone spires. They believed that the taller the tower, the more stable the empire. But when the wind and sand came, the tower was the first to fall.

The factory's obsession and the singleton's phantom were that tower. They gave a sense of security in the short term but became amplifiers of complexity over the long run.

During that period, Alibaba's client team was engulfed in fog. They could neither completely abandon those patterns nor avoid paying their price. They marched like a troop across the sand sea, the road ahead unclear and no retreat behind them.

The power of complexity never comes from the enemy, but from internal obsession. When factories are abused and singletons relied upon, complexity has already lain hidden in the system. It does not explode immediately, but one day it will reveal itself in the cruellest way.

The collapse of an empire does not come from invading armies, but from institutions binding themselves.

Once power and tools are misused, they are no longer protection but chains.

The desert wind does not bury a city overnight. Each day it carries off a bit of lime, some bricks, a layer of wall dust. By the time people notice, the whole city has long since tilted.

In the Taobao client empire, factories and singletons are such wind and sand. They were originally bricks that protected order, but through years of accumulated obsession, they turned into chains that trapped the empire.

The expansion of business is like a river breaching its banks. In a large e-commerce platform, the client is not simply a shopping entry. It is a multidimensional universe:

The home page's recommendation feed is an information-flow platform;

The shopping cart's calculations are a financial system;

Order tracking is a logistics network;

Search optimization is an advertising engine;

Live streaming and short videos are part of the entertainment industry.

Every business line is charging forward; every product manager is demanding "faster iteration"; every holiday promotion is pushing the limits.

Within the client, these businesses ultimately converged on the same artery—the App itself. Factories and singletons were treated as valves in the blood vessels, connecting countless modules. However, the more vessels there are, the more valves, and the greater the risk of blockage and rupture.

The cracks first appeared in the home-page recommendations.

Recommendation algorithms were constantly updated, requiring the client to quickly respond to new interfaces. Product managers wanted to display different types of cards in the same recommendation slot: products, videos, ads, coupons. To meet this demand, the team decided to use the factory pattern to generate card objects.

At first the factory was small, responsible for only three types of cards. But as time passed, it rapidly ballooned: new businesses kept joining, and new cards sprang up endlessly. The card factory expanded from three types to ten, then to thirty.

In the end, the factory became a huge list. Every new requirement required adding a new branch to that list. Every developer had to search that list for the correct entry.

On the surface, the factory unified creation logic; in reality, it concentrated all the complexity in one place, forming a new swamp.

Some engineers joked internally: "We're not writing a factory, we're writing the Classic of Mountains and Seas." Each branch in the factory was like a mythical beast from that book—numerous, oddly named, and hard to tell apart.

The singleton's phantom, meanwhile, extended beyond session management into other domains.

For example, the coupon distribution system. To ensure global consistency, the team decided to use a singleton to manage the cache of all coupons. That way, no matter which page a user claimed a coupon on, it would immediately show in the shopping cart and checkout pages.

However, this "global consistency" soon became a global disaster. During a promotion, the singleton's cache logic deadlocked. The result was that the number of coupons users saw in the shopping cart did not match the checkout page. Some users thought they'd received a coupon, only to find it gone at checkout.

In the e-commerce empire, nothing is more sensitive than money. This incident nearly paralyzed the customer service center. Countless users angrily complained, demanding compensation. The development team had to fix it overnight and reissue coupons to affected users.

The singleton's phantom was fully exposed at that moment: it promised simplicity but produced chaos; it promised consistency but brought fragmentation.

As problems began to occur frequently, the team started to fall into a strange cycle.

Whenever a bug appeared, the developers' first reaction was: "Add another layer of logic in the factory." "Add a flag in the singleton."

It was like the empire's guards constantly adding bricks at cracks in the city wall. On the surface, the cracks were patched; in reality, the wall grew heavier and the cracks multiplied.

Years later, when new engineers joined the team, they faced not a clear architecture but a maze. They needed weeks to understand the nested layers in the factory; they needed repeated experiments to figure out the singleton's state flow.

Factories and singletons were supposed to reduce cognitive load; but here they became the main source of Cognitive Load.

The power of complexity exists not only in code but in the organization.

When factories and singletons became the core of the system, team divisions changed accordingly. "Factory teams" and "singleton teams" gradually appeared; they were responsible for maintaining these critical modules. That meant any business team wanting to add a new feature had to get their approval.

At first, this centralization brought order. But soon it turned into power. The factory team controlled the entry point for homepage recommendations; the singleton team controlled the entry points for sessions and coupons. Their decisions affected the operation of the entire empire.

So internal conflicts began to erupt. Business teams complained: "We just want to add a simple feature—why do we have to queue for the factory team's resources?" The factory team retorted: "Without a unified entry, the system will be even more chaotic." The singleton team insisted: "If we don't manage state centrally, the global state will get out of control."

The empire's cracks were not external but internal. When institutions become shackles and patterns become power, complexity has already evolved into cultural conflict.

The rhythm of an e-commerce platform waits for no one. Double Eleven, 618, the New Year goods festival—each holiday is a major battle. When the system's burden is already heavy but the business still demands acceleration, the team's pain reaches the limit.

During preparations for Double Eleven, the team needed to temporarily roll out a new recommendation strategy. This strategy required the homepage to display, in real time, combination bundles the user might like: for example "phone + earphones", "clothes + shoes".

Implementing this feature should have been the work of the algorithm. But on the client side, the card factory was forced to be modified. Because the factory was the only entry point, any new type had to go through it. As a result, during the tense preparation period, the factory's code was massively changed.

On launch day, problems erupted. Some users' homepages failed to load and the app crash rate spiked. The cause was an overlooked branch in the factory that led to card parsing failure.

The incident completely broke the team. They realized: the factory's obsession was no longer a help but a shackle. The singleton's phantom was no longer a convenience but a risk.

Complexity was laughing. It never strikes directly; it patiently waits for humans to bind themselves. When people treat patterns as truth, when people use patterns instead of thinking, complexity has won.

In the desert empire, people often obsessed over building tall towers. They thought the towers could resist wind and sand, but the sand hollowed out the foundations and the towers fell faster.

In the software empire, factories and singletons are that tower. They give a sense of security but steal away flexibility. They bring short-term convenience but create long-term disaster.

Alibaba's client team, in those years, gradually fell into this predicament. They could not completely abandon factories and singletons because they had already penetrated the system's lifeblood. Yet they could not fully rely on them because they had become the main source of complexity.

This was the empire's most dangerous moment. Not an enemy attack, but institutions binding themselves. Not a lack of technology, but obsession taken too far.

If tools are worshipped as gods, they become shackles.

If patterns are treated as laws, they become phantoms.

Only by staying clear-headed can one walk through the sea of sand.

The wind in the sand sea grew stronger. The towers still stood, but their foundations had long since loosened. Alibaba's client empire stood on the brink of a turning point.

An emergency all-platform meeting became the starting point for change. It was a morning just after a large promotion had ended; the meeting room still hung heavy with anxiety and fatigue. The high concurrency of Double Eleven exposed the fragility of factories and singletons: the recommendation factory's extension error caused homepage crashes; lock contention in the coupon singleton triggered checkout chaos; caching defects in the user-session singleton caused some users to be repeatedly logged out.

This was not a single bug, but the result of an accumulated obsession with patterns. At that meeting, the team had to face reality: factories and singletons were no longer means to solve problems, but problems themselves.

The meeting was divided into two parts. The first half was a post-mortem. Engineers presented logs, charts, and analyses. They used data to show that over the past three years, the amount of factory-class code had tripled and the number of singleton objects had doubled. These designs that appeared to be "unified entry points" were, in fact, making the system harder and harder to understand and to test.

Someone displayed a dependency graph. On the projection screen, hundreds of lines intertwined into a tangle. Each line represented a module's dependency on a factory or singleton. The image looked like a spiderweb, trapping the entire system. Everyone fell silent. For the first time, they saw the true face of complexity visually.

The second half was argument. Some people insisted on conservatism: "Factories and singletons have issues, but at least they maintain order. If we abandon them, we might fall into even greater chaos." Others advocated reform: "Continuing to rely on them means every iteration will be slower. The interest on complexity has already crushed us."

The argument lasted late into the night. There was no clear conclusion, but one thing was confirmed: if they continued down this path, it would mean ruin.

So a pilot project was launched. They chose to start with a relatively independent module: the "You Might Like" recommendation feed.

This module had been a heavy casualty of factory-pattern abuse. Dozens of card objects all depended on the massive factory. Any new recommendation type required modifying the factory. The root of bugs was often hidden in one of the factory's bloated branches.

The team decided to refactor. They dismantled the factory and moved object-creation logic back into the modules themselves. They replaced the unified entry with clearer boundaries, allowing each card to be created and managed within its own domain. On the surface, this broke "unification," but in reality it reduced cognitive cost.

Refactoring was not easy. Every change could trigger chain reactions. Old dependencies clung like vines, tightly wrapping the roots of the code. Engineers, like gardeners, had to patiently cut away the vines without damaging the roots.

Once, a refactor caused the recommendation feed to completely crash during a gray-release test. Because the new boundary design did not accommodate the old caching logic, data could not be passed correctly. The team worked overtime for three days to fix it.

Some questioned: "Is this worth it? Are we tearing apart things that still work?" But more people insisted: "Working doesn't equal sustainable. We must endure short-term pain to gain long-term clarity."

Meanwhile, reforms of singletons were also underway. The team split the user-session singleton into smaller state modules. Different modules managed different states: login, payments, coupons, shopping cart. These modules no longer shared state via a global singleton, but communicated through explicit interfaces.

At first, this felt uncomfortable, because the previously readily available global state now had to be passed explicitly. Some complained: "Before it took one call; now we have to write several layers of passing."

But over time, the benefits became apparent. Bug localization became easier because the sources of state were clear. Test coverage improved because modules could be verified independently. Newly onboarded engineers could also understand the system more quickly.

Reforming the empire was never instantaneous. It required institutional adjustments and cultural renewal.

During that period, Alibaba's client team's internal culture shifted. Previously they revered the names of patterns: "Use a factory here," "Use a singleton there." Now they focused more on Cognitive Load: "Will the logic here be understandable to future people?" "Will these interfaces make testing easier?"

The names of patterns gradually receded into the background. Clarity of cognition became the new standard.

Years later, a new order gradually took shape.

The factory for the recommendation feed was completely dismantled and replaced by clearly layered modules. Each card type had its own creation logic. They seemed dispersed but were actually easier to compose. Developers no longer needed to comb through a massive factory; they only needed to understand the module they were in.

The phantom of the singleton gradually faded. User sessions were split and state boundaries became clearer. The team no longer worried about global collapse but could localize issues. Complexity still existed, but it was confined to smaller scopes.

In retrospection, the team wrote the following summary: "Factories and singletons are not evil in themselves. The real evil is treating them as truth rather than tools. Patterns cannot replace thinking. Reducing Cognitive Load is the only measure."

These words, like an inscription, were carved into the team's history.

"The rise and fall of patterns is a parable of software civilization.

When people worship patterns as gods, they become phantoms.

When people treat patterns as shadows, they return to their essence.

True wisdom does not lie in which pattern you use,

but in whether you respect human cognitive boundaries."

At the edge of the desert, people once built countless towers.

Some towers collapsed because of wind and sand, some toppled because of obsession.

Only a few towers stood because their foundations were solid.

Those foundations were not factories, not singletons, but clear boundaries.

This is the lesson left to us by the factory's obsession and the singleton's phantom.
They are not enemies, but they can become traps.
They are not answers, but they can become obstacles.
Patterns are shadows; shadows change with the light.
Complexity will not disappear because the shadow is gone; it will only be tamed by clear-headedness.

CHAPTER 16
ONE MODULE = A TEAM'S COGNITIVE TERRITORY

The boundaries of a territory determine how far an empire can go.

The boundaries of a module determine how long a team can survive.

Complexity is like sand, the monolith like a vessel.

When sand keeps piling up, the vessel will crack.

No empire can expand indefinitely without borders, and no codebase can grow indefinitely without modules.

The story of Facebook Messenger is ironclad proof of this principle.

Initially, it was part of Facebook's main app.

All features—messages, friends, feed, notifications—were inside the same large monolith.

Like an empire without a feudal system, every road led to the same capital.

At first, such a monolithic architecture was not a flaw.

Small teams could collaborate quickly, and any change could be shipped directly.

A single logic change would immediately take effect across the system.

The efficiency was intoxicating.

However, an empire's expansion is never measured by speed alone.

The larger the territory, the heavier the weight of complexity.

Messenger's user growth surged like a flood, and the messaging system became Facebook's lifeline.

With hundreds of millions of users online simultaneously, message delivery latency was magnified to strategic importance.

At that point, the cracks in the monolith had already appeared.

The first cracks appeared in development efficiency.

A tiny change had to navigate through millions of lines of code.

Engineers had to spend days to ensure they didn't break other features.

Even then, regression tests would still reveal unexpected bugs.

The cycle from proposing a feature request to launching it lengthened.

Tasks that once took days now required weeks.

The rhythm of agility was gradually swallowed by complexity.

The empire's capital became the sole bottleneck.

All decisions had to pass through it, all matters converged there.

No matter how wide the roads, they would eventually become clogged.

Cracks also appeared at team boundaries.

As users surged, Facebook had to expand the Messenger development team.

From dozens, to hundreds, to thousands.

However, under the monolithic architecture, everyone collaborated in the same codebase.

- Any change can affect others;
- Merge conflicts erupt frequently;
- Code Reviews become long battles;
- The concentration of knowledge makes it hard for new members to integrate.

An engineer once recalled internally:

"In a monolithic architecture, we worked as if in the same huge warehouse.

Whenever someone put down an item, it would block someone else's way."

A monolith is not evil, but under a massive team it amplifies all friction.

Every collaboration increases the Cognitive Load.

Every new member amplifies the complexity.

The cracks are even deeper in user experience.

Messenger was originally a messaging tool, but it was embedded inside Facebook's main app.

This caused it to have to load all of Facebook's logic at startup.

The app's cold-start time grew longer and users' patience was gradually consumed.

To let Messenger run independently, Facebook decided to split it out into a standalone app.

This step was like an empire creating a new province and devolving some power.

However, this step also revealed the truth about the complexity.

When Messenger was peeled out of the monolith, the team discovered:

logic was intertwined, modules were coupled, and there were almost no clear boundaries.

The messaging system depended on the friends system, the friends system depended on the notifications system, and the notifications system in turn depended on the messaging system.

It was a complex web with neither entrance nor exit.

The separation process was like dividing streets in an ancient city.

Every road crossed, every building connected.

Splitting was not a simple physical act, but a cognitive purgatory.

The essence of complexity lies not in the number of features, but in the blurriness of boundaries.

In the world of monoliths, there are no module territories.

Every team must understand the entire system in order to make the smallest change.

This arrangement can barely hold at small scale;

Once scale increases, it becomes a disaster.

A team's cognitive boundary must align with a module's boundary.

If a module has no clear boundaries, the team's cognition will inevitably overflow, ultimately leading to collapse.

Facebook came to deeply understand this during the process of splitting out Messenger.

They began to push modularization, breaking features into relatively independent units: messaging, friends, notifications, search, payments.

Each module was assigned to an independent team.

A team no longer needed to understand the whole system, but only to guard its own territory.

This step was a philosophical turning point.

A module was no longer just a technical unit, but a cognitive unit.

A module's boundary is the team's boundary.

Complexity was redistributed—not consumed evenly, but concentrated and digested.

However, modularization is not magic.

It is not completed overnight.

Like the institutional evolution of an empire, it requires time, compromise, and sacrifice.

During Messenger's transformation, engineers had to face countless hard problems:

- Which logic should be delegated to modules?
- Which features must remain shared?
- How to avoid duplicated work between modules?
- How to establish clear protocols between modules?

Each of these questions consumed enormous energy.

Because complexity does not disappear with modularization; it only changes form.

From a centralized monolith to distributed modules.

From congestion at the capital to friction at the borders.

Historians say that the feudal division of an empire is a way to govern complexity.

When a territory grows too large for a single capital to sustain, the feudal system becomes inevitable.

But the price of feudalism is new contradictions: border fragmentation and local tendencies toward independence.

Software modularization is no different.

After modularization, Messenger's teams did improve development efficiency.

But they also had to pay new costs:

communication costs between modules increased, and interface design became a new battleground.

If interfaces are not clear, modularization will degenerate into a new chaos.

Modularization is not the end of complexity, but a new form of it.

Its success depends not on technology, but on institutions.

The clarity of boundaries is the core of modularization.

Facebook Messenger's transformation is far from over.

The flood of complexity still lies ahead.

Whether the order brought by modularization can be sustained in the long term depends on how they define boundaries, govern interfaces, and maintain cognitive alignment at the organizational level.

The wind still blows, the sand still falls.

The shadow of complexity has not disappeared; it has only shifted position.

Boundaries do not only bring order; they also bring friction.

Every boundary is protection, and also a potential crack.

Modularization is both a liberation and a predicament.

When Facebook Messenger was peeled out of the monolith, a new order seemed to appear.

Features were broken into modules, and teams were mapped one-to-one to modules.

On the map, these were clear borders; institutionally, this was a reasonable feudal division.

However, imperial historians tell us:

When a territory is partitioned, contradictions do not vanish.

Congestion at the capital lessens, but friction between localities increases.

Complexity has not died; it has merely changed form.

Messenger's modular reform is a portrait of this transformation.

At first, modularization brought obvious benefits.

A team responsible for the messaging module could focus on messaging itself.

They did not need to understand the details of the friends system, nor concern themselves with the evolution of the notifications module.

Their cognitive territory shrank, and complexity was alleviated locally.

But new problems followed:

Interfaces between modules became the new battleground.

Like a country's passes, they are both defense and trade routes.

If a pass becomes clogged, the whole empire's operation can grind to a halt.

The problem of interfaces appears first at design time.

The messaging module needs to know friends' status: whether they are online, whether they are active.

The friends module insists these statuses are private implementation details and should not expose too much.

The two teams argued this repeatedly in meeting rooms:

- The messaging team wants more data to improve features;
- The friends team wants to keep boundaries clear to avoid leaking internal complexity.

This argument is not a technical problem, but a cognitive one.

Every module wants to present a simple face to the outside while keeping freedom inside.

Yet feature demands continually require crossing boundaries to obtain more information.

It is like two neighboring provinces:

One wants to build wider roads to facilitate trade;

the other fears wider roads will let armies pass through easily.

In this contradiction, interfaces become political compromises.

There was a typical conflict in Messenger's history.

When mobile payments were introduced, the payments module had to collaborate with the messaging module.

A user could tap a button in a conversation and transfer money directly.

A seemingly simple interaction hid complex interfaces.

The payments team required the messaging module to

support encrypted transmission and to embed payment information in the protocol.

The messaging team worried this would break existing optimizations and increase transmission latency.

The argument lasted for weeks and ultimately required management to intervene and force a decision.

The result was:

- The messaging module conceded to the payments feature and added new protocol fields;
- Performance was indeed affected, and users experienced latency in some scenarios;
- Bugs followed, and fixing them required cross-team collaboration.

The cost of complexity was clearly visible here.

Modularization had not eliminated complexity; it had only concentrated its explosion at the interfaces.

Beyond interfaces, testing also became a new challenge.

Under a monolithic architecture, tests could cover the entire system in one go.

Although inefficient, at least the scope was clear.

In a modular architecture, each module has its own test suite.

However, interactions between modules are often not fully represented in isolated tests.

Thus, integration testing became extraordinarily complex.

A small change could render several modules' interfaces incompatible.

The testing team had to design large-scale integration scenarios to simulate real user behavior.

This multiplied testing cycles.

Modularization brought improvements in development efficiency, but it moved complexity into the testing phase.

The empire's roads were made smoother, but inspections at the passes became increasingly tedious.

Organizational splits also gradually emerged.

In a modular world, every team has clear boundaries.

This should be good: clear responsibilities, manageable cognition.

However, when team sizes reached into the thousands, new problems arose.

Each team began to develop its own distinct culture, standards, and tools within its module.

- Some teams favored rapid iteration and were willing to take on technical debt;
- Some teams emphasized rigor and strictly followed standards;
- Some teams introduced new toolchains in pursuit of automation;
- Some teams continued to rely on traditional approaches.

The result was a splintered organization.

Collaboration between different teams became difficult; beyond interfaces there were cultural gulfs.

Like provincial states of an empire developing independently, they ultimately weakened the central will.

Complexity also manifests in the transfer of knowledge.

Under a monolithic architecture, although complex, knowledge was at least centralized.

An engineer could understand the system from a global perspective.

In a modular architecture, knowledge is sliced up.

When newcomers join, they can only understand their own module.

The full picture of the system becomes blurred.

Over time, the "overall understanders" of the system gradually disappear.

Like the imperial chroniclers lost, later generations can only see fragmented records.

No one can clearly say anymore what the entire Messenger architecture actually looks like.

This situation creates new risks.

When a module's team is lost, the knowledge goes with them.

A new team that takes over finds insufficient documentation, complex interfaces, and heavy historical baggage.

They are like rulers taking over an abandoned province, having to rebuild order atop ruins.

This is not accidental, but inevitable.

The independence that modularization brings also brings isolation.

Complexity is isolated, but also hardened.

Against this backdrop, management had to introduce a new policy: "module is team, team is responsibility."

This means:

- Each module is fully owned by a single team;
- A module's health is a metric for evaluating the team;
- The clarity of boundaries directly affects the team's assessment.

This was an attempt at governance, binding complexity to organizational responsibility.

It did bring short-term improvements, forcing teams to pay more attention to interfaces and documentation.

However, complexity will not easily yield.

It continues to grow in the gaps of the system.

The Messenger case reveals a profound fact:

Modularization is not the end of complexity, but a new form of it.

In the monolithic world, complexity was concentrated in the capital;

In the modular world, complexity is distributed at the borders.

It is no longer a single weight, but dispersed friction.

Teams must constantly negotiate, coordinate, and compromise.

Every interface is a diplomacy.

Every collaboration is a treaty.

The war of complexity has not ended because of modularization.

It has merely changed its battlefield, moving from the depths of code to the boundaries of the organization.

The wind keeps blowing, the sand keeps falling.

Messenger's modular reform freed teams from the congestion of the monolith, but brought them into a new predicament.

Complexity still exists, only wearing a new coat.

"The evolution of institutions is always a race to catch up with complexity.

When complexity takes on new forms, institutions must adjust accordingly.

Otherwise, the empire is bound to collapse."

The breadth of a realm is not measured by land but by the boundaries people can hold in their hearts.

The depth of a module is not in code but in the scope a team can comprehend.

Complexity is an invisible storm.

It does not tear everything apart overnight; rather, it sneaks along the folds of time.

Facebook Messenger's modular reform brought order, but it also introduced new cracks.

Yet the empire will not halt because of cracks; it must press onward.

After Messenger's teams endured the first wave of modularization, they gradually realized a fact:

modules themselves are not the answer; governance is.

Their architecture had already split into dozens of modules: messaging, friends, groups, payments, stickers, voice, video, notifications, search.

Each module had its own team guarding it.

However, interface friction, fragmented knowledge, and cultural splits continued to drain the organization's energy.

So new policies were established.

The first policy was the module-guardian team.

Every module must have a dedicated team fully responsible for its health.

This means:

- Bugs are no longer shirked; responsibility is clear;
- Interfaces must be documented, and updates must be announced;
- A module's long-term evolution is planned, not just patched ad hoc.

This system was like the provincial governors of an empire.

Each governor must guard their domain and ensure order.

The center no longer intervenes directly but sets boundaries through policy.

This guardianship did relieve some problems.

At least bugs no longer wandered everywhere, and knowledge was not entirely lost.

Modules became true "units of cognition," and teams became true "boundary guardians."

The second policy was cross-team agreements.

Modules must communicate through explicit agreements.

These agreements are not temporary emails or verbal promises, but contracts written into policy.

Like imperial treaties, they define border trade, taxes, and passage.

The presence of agreements made interfaces transparent.

A module cannot arbitrarily change an interface, otherwise it is a breach of contract.

Another module cannot arbitrarily cross boundaries to access it, otherwise it is infringement.

These contractualized boundaries reduced chaos but also increased costs.

Teams must consider the constraints of the contracts with every evolution.

Compromise and negotiation became routine.

The third policy is the balance between knowledge isolation and sharing.

In the monolithic era, knowledge was concentrated but complex;

In the modular era, knowledge is isolated but fragmented.

Messenger's teams realized they had to find a middle ground.

They built a knowledge repository to record each module's architecture, interfaces, and evolution history.

They implemented internal rotations so engineers could work across different modules for short periods and maintain a sense of the whole.

They established an architecture review committee to ensure that different modules' evolution would not become disconnected.

This balance is like the empire's chroniclers and scholars.

Their work is not direct governance but recording, inspecting, and passing things on.

Without historiography, an empire forgets; without the transmission of architecture, software forgets too.

These policies brought new order and a new philosophy.

Facebook Messenger's experience tells us:

A module is not a folder; a module is a boundary of cognition.

The size of a module depends on the scope a team can understand.

If a module is too large, the team's cognition will overflow and complexity will explode internally;

If a module is too small, the team's cognition will scatter and complexity will breed at the interfaces.

The real art is finding the right scale:

Small enough for a team to understand;

Large enough to prevent excessive boundary proliferation.

This is a technical choice and an organizational choice.

Messenger's story also reveals another truth:

Architecture is organization, and organization is architecture.

Conway's Law long ago pointed out that system design will mirror an organization's communication structure.

Messenger's modularization is a vivid embodiment of this principle.

When team sizes expanded into the thousands, the monolith could no longer be maintained.

The rise of modularization was not only technical inevitability but organizational inevitability.

Each module boundary is the reflection of an organizational boundary.

Every argument over an interface is a projection of team culture.

The governance of complexity lies not in code, but in the organization.

However, institutions cannot completely eliminate complexity.

They can only delay it, shift it, or manage it.

Complexity is like a river, always seeking new outlets.

Even with module guardians, agreements, and contracts, it still surges in the dark.

In Messenger's history, the shadow of complexity still remains:

- In the integration of the voice and video modules, performance bottlenecks kept emerging;
- In the security upgrades of the payments module, contractual constraints introduced delays;
- In experiments with new features, cross-team coordination still consumed enormous effort.

Complexity never exits the stage.

It only changes masks and continues to test human intellect.

But this history leaves us a clear philosophy:

Modularization is not a cure, but an order.

It cannot eliminate complexity, but it can make complexity distributed in an orderly way.

It cannot make teams relaxed, but it can make teams bearable.

A module is a team's cognitive territory.

If boundaries are clear, teams can guard their territory and complexity will not spill over.

If boundaries are blurred, complexity will seep in and ultimately consume everyone.

"Facebook Messenger's modular reform was neither a victory nor a defeat.

It was a fate: when systems and organizations reach a certain scale, modularization will occur.

It is not a choice, but an inevitability."

The moral of this history goes far beyond Messenger itself.

In the world of SwiftUI, we still face the same problems.

We build Feature Modules; we establish boundaries in the Swift Package Manager.

These choices are not merely technical conveniences, but a matter of cognitive discipline.

A module is a team's territory.

A team's cognition is the module's boundary.

When we delineate modules, we are also delineating the boundaries of the human mind.

The wind still blows, the sand still falls.

Complexity will not leave the stage; it will only take another form.

And modularization is the fence humans set for themselves.

It is not an eternal bulwark, but it is a shelter for the present.

The clearest boundaries are kindness toward complexity.
The most appropriate modules are a safeguard for teams.
In the empire of software, boundaries are civilization.

PART FOUR
NATIVE AND CROSS-PLATFORM

CHAPTER 17
THE ILLUSION OF CROSS-PLATFORM

Illusions are never entirely false; their power lies in a part of the truth.

The expansion of an empire often accelerates because of the image of an oasis, while the oasis itself hides saline soil.

Complexity always begins with an illusion.

The reason illusions are alluring is not because they are completely false, but because they capture a part of the truth.

The story of React Native and Flutter is such an illusion.

Airbnb's empire, in its early rise, faced the enemy of time.

Their users were spread across the globe, and the iOS and Android markets were each independent and huge.

In a board report, the engineering leadership was asked:

"Why do we need twice the team to complete a feature?

Why is our speed not as fast as those small companies that only have one platform?"

The question was sharp and cruel.

It revealed the empire's pain point: the duplication and inefficiency of dual-platform development.

The emergence of React Native was like an oasis in the desert.

It promised:

- One codebase, usable on both ends.
- Implement once, available on both platforms.
- Front-end engineers can also participate in mobile development.

This promise was not an empty slogan, but a tangible benefit.

When Airbnb's tech team tried React Native for the first time, they did feel the speed gains.

A new feature module, in a native environment, might need to be implemented separately for iOS and Android.

Even with tight team collaboration, it often took weeks.

But in the React Native experiment, the same feature was completed by a single team.

The UIs on both sides were almost identical, logic was shared, and the development cycle was shortened by nearly half.

This efficiency, like a shot of strong liquor, quickly ignited the entire empire's enthusiasm.

The illusion of cross-platform became reality in that moment.

Illusions are powerful because they can break boundaries.

Airbnb's engineering team was large, and many of its members were front-end developers proficient in JavaScript. Before React Native, their value was concentrated mainly on the web. But React Native gave them the key to enter the mobile world.

Overnight, mobile development was no longer the domain of a few native engineers. Front-end developers began to join, team size expanded, and apparent output seemed to double. The previously separated front-end and mobile teams seemed to reunite on the same map.

This cross-disciplinary fusion excited management. They saw costs falling, manpower being flexibly reallocated, and the future of the "full-stack engineer."

The power of the illusion was not just a technical promise but an organizational mirage. It made people believe that the original divisions were being bridged.

The short-term gains were real.

With React Native's boost, Airbnb's teams did indeed ship multiple features in a short time. For example, they attempted to rapidly iterate the property listing flow. That process involved complex forms, real-time validation, and multi-language support. In native development, this would have been a long campaign. But in React Native, they quickly completed an MVP and rolled it out for fast global testing.

That speed was astonishing. Product managers began to praise the approach, believing that all future features should go the cross-platform route. Senior leaders emphasized in meetings: "This is Airbnb's future; we must fully embrace cross-platform."

In that moment, the illusion completely shrouded the empire. The short-term gains concealed the long-term costs.

However, the illusion was not a fabricated lie. Their power lay in the truth.

Airbnb's engineers did save time, did consolidate teams, and did achieve results in the short term. All of this was fact. It was precisely because of this that the illusion was more tempting.

Like an empire's army gathering at the edge of an oasis, drinking the clear water and eating the plentiful food, everyone believed the future would be better. No one asked: was the oasis's water source stable, was the soil fit for cultivation. They only saw the prosperity before them.

The promise of React Native and Flutter was exactly such an oasis.

What they offered was not a fabricated hope, but real short-term gains.

But precisely because of that, they were more dangerous.

Short-term victories often make people overlook long-term risks.

In Airbnb's records there is a passage that reads:

"In the initial phase, we did feel the speed and flexibility brought by React Native. Team morale was high, management was pleased, and users quickly received new features. We thought we had found the Holy Grail."

The Holy Grail.

This is the highest form of illusion.

It makes people believe that complexity has been conquered and the future will be a smooth road.

But complexity is never conquered; it only returns in another form.

Airbnb's short-term gains were like a lit torch.

It illuminated the road ahead, yet also caused people to ignore the shadows in the dark.

Complexity was gathering strength in the dark.

Short-term victories are the most dangerous; they make people think complexity has been defeated.

Yet complexity never surrenders; it only accumulates interest in silence.

The sweetness of the gains always fades quickly.

Airbnb's React Native experiment did indeed deliver exciting results in the first year.

However, complexity never disappears; it only waits.

As the short-term cheers gradually died down, the shadows behind the illusion began to surface.

Problems first appeared in the details.

Airbnb's app needed to run globally.

Different markets differed in language, currency, regulations, and payment methods.

In native development, these differences are often handled properly by system APIs.

In the React Native cross-platform layer, these differences had to be implemented via bridges.

Thus, the bridge layer gradually became a new quagmire.

Every currency symbol display, every tax calculation, every input validation had to cross the boundary between React Native and native.

This boundary appeared unified on the surface but was actually divided.

For example:

In the Japanese market, users are accustomed to entering the year first in a date picker, then the month and day.

In the U.S. market, it's month / day / year.

In native systems, these differences are handled automatically by the platform.

In React Native, the team had to write additional logic in the bridge layer to ensure consistency.

A seemingly simple date input consumed weeks of manpower.

This local duplicated work piled up like grains of sand.

Each detail can be explained as a "special case," but when special cases are everywhere in the system, the illusion begins to crumble.

The backlash of complexity also shows up in performance.

Airbnb's app has a core scenario: scrolling and loading the listing feed.

Users search for listings in the app, swipe the screen, and browse dozens of images, maps, and price tags.

This should be a smooth experience.

However, in the React Native implementation, performance bottlenecks kept appearing.

Image loading required frequent crossings of the bridge layer;

map interactions required synchronization between native and JavaScript;

list scrolling involved a large amount of rendering.

The result was: on iOS, occasional dropped frames during scrolling;

On Android, even noticeable stutters.

User complaints followed:

"Why isn't Airbnb's app as smooth as the native app?"

The danger of performance problems is that they hit the user experience directly.

A dropped frame, a sluggish animation, is enough to destroy a user's patience.

And when users' patience is exhausted, the advantages brought by short-term gains are completely offset.

The shadow of complexity also extended to team communication.

At first, React Native was seen as a symbol of unification.

Front-end engineers could take part in mobile development, and teams seemed to merge.

However, as complexity grew, this fusion instead brought division.

Front-end engineers excelled at JavaScript but were unfamiliar with native platform details.

Native engineers knew Swift and Kotlin but were impatient with cross-platform runtime mechanisms.

A gulf gradually formed between the two bodies of knowledge.

A simple bug fix often required collaboration between engineers from two different backgrounds. But the result of collaboration was not acceleration, but argument. The front-end team thought the problem lay in the native module; the native team thought the problem lay in the cross-platform logic. The debugging process became a process of passing the blame.

This cultural rift was more fatal than the technical problems. Because technology can be fixed, but culture is hard to mend. The team gradually split into two camps: one the believers in cross-platform, the other the guardians of native. They lived in the same empire, yet spoke different languages and held different beliefs.

The deepest trap of complexity is that it robs you of a sense of control.

Engineers at Airbnb, under the React Native system, increasingly felt powerless. When a bug appeared, they had to shuttle back and forth across a three-layer architecture: the React Native JavaScript layer, the bridge layer, and the native layer. Any layer could be the source of the problem, and each had its own debugging tools.

This debugging process was not exploration but a maze. Engineers were no longer masters; they were lost in complexity.

At one internal sharing session, an engineer said: "I spent a week just to locate a memory leak. The ultimate cause was React Native's caching mechanism in the bridge layer. But to find it, I had to switch repeatedly between Swift, JavaScript, and Kotlin. I wasn't developing — I was translating."

Translating. This was the new identity brought by complexity. Engineers were no longer creators but translators. They ran themselves ragged between three languages and three systems, only to maintain the illusion of unity.

The unraveling of the illusion did not happen in an instant. It was a gradual process.

Airbnb's team gradually discovered that their iteration speed did not continue to improve. The initial gains were offset while the later costs kept rising. Every new feature's development was accompanied by long periods of testing and debugging. Every system upgrade triggered a series of compatibility issues.

They found themselves trapped in a paradox:

- If the cross-platform path was maintained, problems would multiply and complexity would increase;
- If they returned to native, all the prior investment would be wasted.

This was the cruelest part of the illusion.

It made it hard to extract oneself.

Like an army of an empire marching deep into the desert, having reached an oasis only to find the water undrinkable.

Turning back meant losses; pressing on meant even greater danger.

The power of complexity lies in its ability to make people hesitate.

Hesitation itself is a form of consumption.

When a team spends every meeting, every planning session, every decision in hesitation, their morale is gradually drained.

Airbnb's records contain voices like this:

"We knew React Native could no longer meet our needs.

But it was hard to convince ourselves to give it up.

Because giving up meant admitting we were wrong, meant losing three years of effort.

We were trapped between illusion and reality."

This is the cruelest truth of complexity.

It consumes not only technology, but will.

It makes people afraid to decide and traps them in a painful cycle.

The most dangerous thing is not an external invasion, but internal hesitation.

When the senate keeps arguing without taking any action, the empire has already begun to decline.

Airbnb's team also reached a turning point amid such hesitation.

Their illusion had begun to fracture.

The short-term gains had dissipated.

Complexity was demanding repayment with compound interest.

The end of the illusion was not its shattering, but a return.

Because the law of complexity is written in time: whatever bypasses it will eventually be reclaimed.

The debt of complexity will always come due.

In Airbnb's experiment, that day did not arrive suddenly.

It was not a big explosion, not a systemic catastrophe, but a series of seemingly minor events that accumulated until they could no longer be ignored.

It was an ordinary spring.

The team was preparing for the summer travel season.

The product manager proposed a new requirement:

When users searched for listings, prices should be displayed on the map in real time, and multiple currencies should be supported for switching.

The requirement was reasonable and urgent.

Users had complained that they could not intuitively compare prices in different currencies while searching, leading to a poor experience.

However, when this requirement landed in the React Native system, it acted like a seed that quickly revealed the system's cracks.

Currency conversion is a complex domain in itself. Different markets have different tax rates, different exchange rates, and different rounding rules. In native development, these details are handled by platform-provided APIs. In React Native, they must cross the bridge and span three layers: the React Native layer, the bridge layer, and the native layer.

The team quickly found that performance became the biggest obstacle. Every price refresh required a large amount of computation and rendering. When users zoomed the map quickly, hundreds of listings updated prices simultaneously. On iOS, the map began to stutter; on Android, the app crashed outright.

The debugging process was extremely painful. Engineers switched repeatedly between Swift, Kotlin, and JavaScript, tracing performance bottlenecks in the bridge layer. They spent a full three weeks just to barely get the feature deployed. Even then, the experience remained unsatisfactory.

This incident made management realize: the short-term gains were gone. They had assumed React Native would help the team iterate faster and more stably, but in reality, complexity made velocity slow down and quality harder to guarantee.

Voices within began to shift. More and more engineers openly expressed disappointment: "We wanted unification, but we created more division." "We wanted to be faster, but we're slower than before." "We tried to save cognitive load, but were forced to learn three systems."

These voices, like rebels in the empire, no longer whispered but marched into the square to shout.

In the boardroom the atmosphere turned heavy. Management produced the data:

- Bug-fix times with React Native were more than 30% longer than native;
- Communication costs in the team were double what they had been in the native era;
- User experience complaints were frequent, and performance issues had become the norm;
- Native engineers gradually left because they no longer believed in the vision.

Data does not lie. It was like a cold inscription that completely shattered the illusion.

In that moment, everyone understood: the empire had to change course.

In 2018, Airbnb officially announced: they would gradually abandon React Native and fully return to native.

This was a strategic retreat. It meant that three years of investment were almost entirely voided. It meant that hundreds of thousands of lines of code would be gradually deprecated. It meant that management would have to publicly admit: they were wrong.

But it was the only option. Because complexity had proven its power.

The process of retreat was no easier than expansion.

The team needed to progressively migrate features, rewriting the parts that had depended on React Native back to native. This meant a lot of duplicated work and more time investment. But this time the team's mindset was different. They were no longer driven by an illusion; they had returned to sober reality.

Engineers regained control of the system. They no longer needed to switch between three layers or translate among three languages. They returned to familiar ground: Swift, Kotlin, UIKit, and native APIs.

Complexity still existed, but it had returned to manageable bounds.

Historians say the greatness of an empire lies not in how far it can expand, but in whether it can turn back in time when it errs. Airbnb's return was such greatness. They gave up the illusion and chose clarity. They admitted their mistake, and thereby won the future.

Airbnb's public announcement became a turning point for the whole industry. Many companies that had been waiting on the sidelines re-evaluated their cross-platform strategies. They began to realize that the short-term gains of cross-platform could not offset long-term complexity. They began to understand that the illusion of unification often hides more division.

The lesson of complexity is not an isolated one but a universal rule.

From Airbnb's story we see not just a company's choice, but a general law.

Complexity will not be defeated by shortcuts. It will not be reduced by the promise of "develop once, run everywhere." It will not dissipate because of new toolchains.

The only enemy of complexity is clear boundaries. The value of native is not that it is more "trendy," but that it is in sync with the platform's rhythm and aligned with the cognitive load. It frees developers from running between three layers so they can focus on true value.

Airbnb's retreat was a warning.

- Short-term gains are not enough to sustain long-term complexity;
- The true parts of an illusion cannot hide its false parts;
- Strategic courage lies not in expansion, but in admitting mistakes;
- The essence of software design is not speed, but clarity.

The history of software is the history of complexity. Airbnb's cross-platform experiment is only one page of that history, yet enough to become a fable. The fable tells us:

Complexity is like a desert; it will not disappear because of the mirage of an oasis;

Complexity is like gravity; it will not stop because of a single leap;

Complexity is like the fate of an empire; it will not be reversed by a single meeting.

The only thing to do is to respect it.

The only thing to do is to make peace with it.

The only thing to do is to remain clear-eyed in the face of illusions.

Airbnb's story draws the curtain here.

But the story of complexity continues.

In the world of SwiftUI, in the practice of TCA, in future collaborations with AI, complexity remains that silent force.

And we, as developers, as designers, the only thing we can do is remember this story when illusions arrive.

Remember: illusions are never entirely false; they seize a part of the truth.

But illusions can never overcome complexity.

The greatest courage is not chasing illusions, but admitting them.
The greatest wisdom is not to conquer complexity, but to respect it.

CHAPTER 18
CROSS-PLATFORM LESSONS FROM AIRBNB AND DROPBOX

History does not repeat, but it rhymes.

The fall of empires always has different excuses, but only one cause: the crushing weight of complexity.

Wind sweeps over the ruins, the desert swallows the remains.

People stand among broken columns and hear not the shouts of the past, but similar echoes in the wind.

This is the echo of history.

It reminds us: different dynasties may rise in different forms, but often decline in similar ways.

In the history of software, the stories of Airbnb and Dropbox are such echoes.

The story of Dropbox goes back to the early days of the mobile Internet.

The world then was still chaotic.

The iPhone had already changed what people held in their hands, and the App Store was giving rise to a new order.

In that era, Dropbox was like a bolt of lightning cutting through the night:

"Access your files anytime, anywhere" — the simplest yet most stunning promise.

Dropbox's users grew wildly, and in just a few years it became one of the most influential cloud storage services in the world.

However, grand visions come with great complexity.

They had to provide a consistent experience on both iOS and Android.

At that time resources were limited, and the team was not large enough to support two completely independent native codebases.

The illusion of cross-platform development resurfaced.

Dropbox's leadership chose a shortcut that seemed clever:

An HTML5 app shell.

Using web technologies, they could build the UI once and run it on multiple platforms.

This choice was praised as "forward-looking" because it promised:

A unified development experience, faster iteration, and cross-platform consistency.

Dreams always sound reasonable.

They thought they could, like a loom, weave a single cloth that would cover the whole market.

But history was bound to rhyme.

At first, everything seemed to go smoothly.

Dropbox's web technology team developed rapidly, and a prototype of the mobile app went online quickly.

Users downloading the app on different platforms saw similar interfaces and unified logic.

In the short term, iteration speed did improve.

They seemed to be getting huge output from very little manpower.

However, complexity began to grow in the shadows.

The HTML5 app shell could not hide the underlying differences.

iOS and Android have different system behaviors, different hardware optimizations, different interaction habits.

Dropbox's app gradually revealed fatal cracks in use:

- Scrolling was not smooth, touch responsiveness was delayed, making users feel the app was "laggy."
- Offline functionality was unstable; caching mechanisms behaved differently across platforms.
- File previews loaded slowly, especially images and large documents.
- Integration with the system file manager lagged far behind native apps.

These issues were not one-off bugs, but the root of complexity.

Because HTML5 could not perfectly embrace both worlds, the team had to constantly write "patches," filling gaps between the shell and the system.

Each patch added to the thickness of complexity.

And each added layer of thickness would erupt one day in the future.

User feedback became the harshest alarm.

Dropbox's ratings on the App Store and Play Store gradually declined.

Reviews were filled with comments like:

"Why is it so laggy?"

"Why do previews never load?"

"Why is the experience inconsistent with the system?"

The erosion of complexity was not felt first by developers, but first complained about by users.

When users' experience is damaged, the empire's frontiers begin to wobble.

Engineers inside Dropbox also gradually lost patience.

They were used to building clean systems, yet had to bury themselves in patching the cross-platform shell.

Their mental energy was consumed by trivial compatibility issues instead of creative design.

They gradually realized:

They were not building a product, they were building patches.

The shadow of complexity slowly pressed down on the decision-makers.

Dropbox's leadership held meeting after meeting.

In those meetings they discussed not features, but complexity:

"Should we continue to invest in HTML5?

Or should we fully return to Native?"

This was a difficult choice.

Returning to Native meant massive refactoring costs, meant overturning years of investment.

But continuing with HTML5 meant that the debt of complexity would continue to accumulate until it was uncontrollable.

Historians would say this is the crossroads of an empire.

You either admit the mistake and choose to contract;

Or you cling to the illusion until collapse.

Dropbox ultimately chose the former.

They announced they would abandon the HTML5 shell and rebuild the Native apps.

Their public statement was candid and calm:

"HTML5 made us move faster, but it did not take us farther.

User experience is our core, and user experience can only be realized through Native."

This decision put Dropbox back on the right battlefield.

They allocated more engineers to the Native teams and painstakingly refined the experience.

App smoothness, stability, and system integration improved rapidly.

User ratings gradually recovered, and their reputation was rebuilt.

Dropbox's turning point and Airbnb's turning point were separated by years in history, but were identical in logic.

Two different empires walked similar paths:

From the fantasy of cross-platform, to the quagmire of complexity, and finally to the sobriety of returning to Native.

The laws of complexity do not change with time, nor do they change with different technology names.

They are like gravity: in any era, they operate the same way.

The wrong path does not collapse immediately.
It lets you feel confident in short-term success and sober up at the cost of long-term consequences.
True wisdom is not in never making mistakes, but in daring to turn back.

Wind blows through the cracks in the ruins; the sound is like a warning.

Dropbox's HTML5 dream shone brightly before it collapsed.

That light illuminated their initial path, but it also blinded them with illusion.

When the meeting that decided to abandon HTML5 and fully return to Native concluded, the whole team fell silent.

The silence was not failure, but the weight of the cost.

They knew this meant years of investment would be discarded;

they also knew it meant harder years ahead.

The cost of complexity is not just technical debt, but the erosion of conviction.

Any team that overturns its own choices will go through a rebuilding of civilization.

Dropbox's reconstruction began with a comprehensive technical inventory.

They found that the HTML5 app shell and its internal logic had become deeply embedded throughout the system.

Removing it was like rebuilding the pipes in a city that was still in use:

Every bit of construction affected residents' lives;

Every change brought unintended consequences.

So Dropbox decided to replace it gradually.

They started with the most painful features: file browsing and previews.

This area had been the biggest weakness of HTML5 and the source of the most user complaints.

In the new Native implementation, engineers painstakingly restored the experience:

scrolling had to be smooth, zooming natural, previews fast.

They used the operating system's low-level optimizations to keep the app in sync with the platform itself.

Every detail was a battle against complexity.

However, complexity never disappears simply by turning around.

Removing HTML5 was only the first step; the real challenge was how to prevent falling back into illusion in the future.

Team fragmentation was the most obvious hidden danger during the rebuild.

The failure of HTML5 left some people despondent.

They had once been evangelists for cross-platform development, pouring themselves into the dream of unification.

Now they had to face reality: the path they had chosen had proven to be wrong.

This was not only a technical failure but a psychological wound.

Some people chose to leave the team and seek other opportunities;

Others stayed but were demoralized and full of doubts.

In meetings they would say coldly, "We have to write two codebases again? Didn't we just get rid of this burden?"

Management understood that such wounds had to heal, or the new path would be corroded as well.

They began to emphasize a new slogan: user experience first.

This was not a simple catchphrase, but a way to reestablish order.

Only when everyone stopped arguing about "cross-platform efficiency" and reached consensus around "user experience" did the team find a common direction again.

Complexity exists not only in code but also in communication.

If a team's cognitive boundaries are confused, complexity will breed within the discussions.

Dropbox's shift was a cultural return:

From pursuing the illusion of unity to pursuing the clarity of reality.

That echo was also heard at Airbnb, thousands of miles away.

While Dropbox was struggling to rebuild its Native architecture, Airbnb's React Native experiment continued.

They faced similar dilemmas:

Bugs were hard to track down, user experience was unstable, and the team was badly fractured.

Only their illusions differed.

Dropbox's illusion was HTML5's "write once, run everywhere";

Airbnb's illusion was React Native's "native experience, unified development."

But the laws of complexity do not change because of a name.

Both teams, at different points in time, took similar wrong turns.

They both discovered that the dream of unification only produced deeper division.

They both learned that the promise of cross-platform development ultimately trapped developers in a cognitive maze.

History has a way of rhyming.

Dropbox's voice became Airbnb's echo.

And in that echo, all who came after could hear the warning: complexity is not eliminated by unification; it is only amplified by it.

Dropbox's reconstruction was not without obstacles.

During the full return to Native, they encountered new challenges:

The team had to relearn the best practices for different platforms;

They had to reestablish sync mechanisms with Apple and Google;

They had to recruit native developers again to fill the gaps.

It was a hard road, but it was a clear one.

They knew complexity still existed, but at least it was within an understandable scope.

Native's complexity is complexity that keeps pace with the platform's rhythm;

HTML5's complexity is complexity that fights against the platform's rhythm.

The result of resistance can only be failure.

Only by adapting can something endure.

Dropbox's decision also sent shockwaves through the industry.

Their public statement became a profound reflection:

Cross-platform development is not impossible, but it can never replace Native's foundation.

Native is not a short-term shortcut, but a long-term safeguard.

Airbnb's engineers, in private discussions, also repeatedly referenced Dropbox's case.

They had seen the other's failures, yet still chose to try.

This is humanity's fate: each generation believes it can break the laws.

The echoes of history, however, keep reminding us:

The laws have never changed — only the names have.

Dropbox's story continued to spread in those echoes.

Users gradually returned to their embrace, and experience regained trust.

Team morale recovered, and they once again became an industry benchmark.

But they also left an internal warning:

"Do not fight complexity with illusions."

That warning was carved into their technical archives and became a textbook for those who came after.

Yet history tells us that even with warnings, illusions will reappear.

Because humans always hope to exchange less cost for greater gain.

That desire is complexity's most faithful ally.

Between Dropbox's rebuilding and Airbnb's struggle, we see a mirror.

What is reflected in the mirror is not a specific framework, but the essence of complexity.

It is not about languages, platforms, or tools.

It exists only in the boundaries of human cognition and the choices of teams.

The echoes of complexity reverberate between the two empires, reminding all who follow:

Technological illusions can change their names, but the laws of complexity do not change.

The same wind stirs similar sands in different eras.

The same complexity leaves similar cracks in different empires.

The home is not in illusion, but in clear boundaries.

The sound of the wind echoes among the ruins like an invisible chorus.

The stories of Dropbox and Airbnb, separated by years, sound like two movements of the same melody.

Different eras, different frameworks, different teams — yet the endings rhyme.

Dropbox's return was a moment of clarity.

They realized that the HTML5 shell had only delayed the emergence of complexity, while making the cost heavier.

When they finally abandoned the illusion and returned to Native's embrace, they regained the initiative.

Their team found confidence again, user experience was once more respected, and the system's evolution resumed keeping pace with the platform's rhythm.

Airbnb's struggle was a different kind of fate.

They lingered longer in the illusion of React Native.

They invested more resources, trying to sustain the illusion with stronger toolchains and more experts.

They hoped to tame complexity through systems and processes.

But complexity was never tamed.

It merely waited quietly, revealing its weight at critical moments.

When Airbnb too had to admit failure and gradually return to Native, they discovered that Dropbox's lesson had already been clearly echoed in history.

History is never short of warnings.

But humans have never truly learned to listen.

Dropbox's team had candidly written in a public post: "HTML5 made us move faster, but it didn't make us go further."

Their experience should have become a signpost for the whole industry.

Yet Airbnb still went down a similar path.

This was not because they were foolish, but because they believed they could break the laws.

Humans are always like this: each generation thinks itself smarter than the last; each team believes it can solve the fate of complexity.

But complexity is not a bug, not an algorithmic issue, not merely an engineering problem.

Complexity is a law, gravity, an ally of time.

Any illusion that fights it will ultimately be swallowed by it.

The stories of Dropbox and Airbnb read like two mutually echoing chronologies.

One took place in the era of HTML5, the other in the era of React Native.

Two different technologies, yet they point to the same truth:

The dream of unification ultimately produces deeper division.

The promise of cross-platform development ultimately creates a heavier Cognitive Load.

Complexity does not disappear; it only shifts and amplifies in the process.

We must step into the team's day-to-day to feel the true weight of complexity.

In Dropbox's era, engineers spent weeks debugging a file preview bug, only to find the problem was a conflict between HTML5's rendering mechanism and the system cache.

They fixed the bug, but knew similar problems would keep appearing.

In Airbnb's era, engineers stayed up late handling jitter in map zooming, only to find it was caused by thread scheduling in the bridge layer.

They fixed the bug, but understood such problems were everywhere.

This is the truth about complexity.

It will not destroy you, but it will consume you.

It will not knock you down, but it will wear you out day after day until your confidence is eroded.

The real destructive force of complexity lies not in the code, but in the human heart.

Only after abandoning HTML5 did Dropbox's engineers regain their confidence.

They were able to refocus on user experience instead of compatibility issues.

They were able to create again, instead of being exhausted by patches.

Only after abandoning React Native did Airbnb's engineers finally escape the black box of the bridge layer.

They once more became masters of the system instead of slaves to an illusion.

They regained rhythm, instead of being driven by complexity.

Complexity exhausts the heart; clarity revives it. This is the power of boundaries.

Why is Native the best long-term choice?

The answer is not about technical superiority, but about the laws of complexity.

Native's complexity is the platform's complexity.

It keeps pace with Apple's and Google's rhythms; its evolution is synchronized with the system.

This complexity is inevitable, predictable, and governable.

Cross-platform complexity is additional complexity.

It stacks a third world atop two others.

It creates bridge layers, compatibility layers, and testing layers.

This complexity is accidental, unpredictable, and uncontrollable.

Faced with inevitable complexity, humans can still govern it through boundaries and processes.

Faced with accidental complexity, humans can only passively endure it until they are exhausted.

This is Native's philosophical advantage.

The arrival of SwiftUI is another step in that historical evolution.

It is not a new illusion, but a reinforcement of Native's essence.

SwiftUI abstracts UI complexity into state, making the interface a mirror of state.

It concentrates logic that was previously dispersed across many places into a single source of truth.

It is not creating new bridges, but reducing old ones.

It is not manufacturing new illusions, but clarifying old confusion.

The philosophy of SwiftUI reminds us: the true path is not to avoid complexity, but to respect it, face it head-on, and stay in sync with it.

The echoes of history linger long among the ruins.

The epitaph of Dropbox reads:

"We abandoned HTML5 because user experience can only be achieved through Native."

Airbnb's records state:

"We abandoned React Native because the debt of complexity ultimately crushed us."

These two statements are like the last words of different empires, and also a common footnote for the whole industry.

They tell all who come after:

Do not be deceived by illusions; do not try to bypass complexity.

Complexity is a law, and the only way is to negotiate with it, not to try to fool it.

Developers in the SwiftUI era stand on this field of ruins.

They still face temptations: new cross-platform frameworks, new promises of unification, new illusions.

In the wind, the two empires' whispers echo:

"Do not repeat the same mistakes.

Do not lose yourselves in illusions.

Complexity will not be erased; it will only wait."

The cross-platform lessons of Airbnb and Dropbox are not isolated cases, but an inevitable manifestation of the laws of complexity.

They are like two echoes of history, reminding every developer:

- The enemy of software is not a lack of features, but the expansion of complexity.
- The allure of illusions is always sensible in the short term and fatal in the long term.
- Native is not a creed, but the only choice that aligns with the laws of complexity.
- SwiftUI is not a shortcut, but the result of optimizing cognitive load.

This is the answer history leaves us.

Not a list of new technologies, but an ancient truth: the goal of architecture is to reduce complexity.

When you pursue speed within illusions, remember the echoes of history.

It will tell you: only clarity and boundaries can traverse the sands of time.

CHAPTER 19
PERFORMANCE, ECOSYSTEM, AND PLATFORM RHYTHM

Fate does not come from divine will, but from the pulse of the system.

When the platform's heartbeat reverberates across the whole, any outlier will ultimately dance to its rhythm.

The story of complexity can be found as a footnote in the history of every great application.

If Airbnb's experience reminds us how the illusion of cross-platform breaks apart, then Instagram's story tells us: Native is not a choice, but fate.

Instagram's beginnings were far more humble than its glory.

In the autumn of 2010, a small team in a San Francisco apartment tried to answer a simple question:

In the early days of the mobile internet, how could people share photos faster and more naturally?

At that time mobile networks were still unstable, device performance limited, and the App Store was still young.

Developers did not have many established paradigms to rely on.

They had to create a smooth experience in an extremely constrained environment.

The early versions of Instagram did not intend to rely entirely on Native.

The team tried HTML5, hoping to leverage the convenience of cross-platform development to iterate features quickly.

It was an ideal: build once, run everywhere; update once, everyone benefits.

With limited resources, this seemed like the logical choice.

But the shadow of complexity was there from the start.

The promise of HTML5 quickly revealed cracks.

Instagram's core experience is images: quick capture, quick loading, quick sharing.

HTML5's performance was far from meeting this.

In users' hands, photo loading delays, stuttering scrolling, and unresponsive gestures were magnified into a disjointed experience.

The team recorded in a post-mortem:

"We originally thought HTML5 would let us save manpower and cover more platforms.

But the result was that we spent most of our time solving performance problems, not building the experience."

This is another form of complexity.

It is not branching logic, not chaotic architecture, but a fracture between performance and experience.

When one user must wait two seconds to see a photo, while another can do so instantly, those two seconds can be enough to decide the product's survival.

Complexity is the accumulation of such gaps.

It is not a single technical problem, but a breach of trust between people and technology.

Users will not forgive sluggishness, and the market will not wait for remediation.

The Instagram team soon realized that the HTML5 path could not sustain their ambition.

They had to commit to Native.

This was not a preference, but fate.

Native means syncing with the platform's heartbeat.

iOS's animations, rendering, and memory management; Android's thread scheduling and hardware optimizations—these are not things that can be mimicked from the outside; they are the platform's essential rhythm.

Only by going Native can you touch that rhythm.

It's like the laws of an empire: you can make your own customs on the frontier, but once you enter the capital you must submit to its tempo.

Instagram had to make a choice: either cling to the illusion and continue struggling in the HTML5 quagmire, or accept fate and embrace Native.

Choosing did not mean complexity disappeared.

On the contrary, it made complexity appear in another form.

Native development requires specialized skills, a deep understanding of the platform's evolution, and staying in step with Apple's cadence.

At that time, iOS's ecosystem was still evolving rapidly.

New APIs, new devices, new interaction patterns flowed in like a tide.

Each system update was a shock.

Developers had to remain constantly vigilant to catch the changes, or be left behind.

Instagram accepted this fate.

They knew complexity was unavoidable, but they could choose the battlefield.

On the HTML5 battlefield they would always be behind;

On the Native battlefield, at least they could stand alongside the platform.

The shift produced a qualitative leap.

Instagram reconstructed the experience natively, optimizing

capture and rendering so users felt almost instantaneous feedback.

Photos scrolled smoothly, filters loaded quickly, sharing became seamless.

The improvement in user experience directly drove user growth.

Complexity still existed: multithreaded scheduling, memory management, animation optimization.

But these complexities were, at least, transparent, controllable, and symbiotic with the platform.

They were like the institutions of an empire: unavoidable, but ones you can learn, follow, and master.

Historians would say this was a surrender to fate. But more accurately, it was a sober choice. Instagram was not defeated by complexity; rather, it chose to find a stable foothold amid the waves of complexity.

They accepted the cost of Native and embraced Native's rewards. These costs and rewards are things the cross-platform illusion can never provide.

This is only the beginning of the story. Complexity did not end; it merely changed its face. Instagram would next face new challenges: how to maintain balance between ever-expanding user demands and the platform's rhythm? How to preserve the purity of the experience amid the tug-of-war between performance and features? How to avoid repeating Airbnb's mistakes as the team grew and the architecture evolved?

Complexity will not stop; it is merely waiting for the next opportunity. And Instagram must be prepared to weather a bigger storm.

When an empire accepts the constraints of its institutions, it also accepts their tempo.

The platform's heartbeat is law; the developer's fate is to move with its pulse.

Instagram's acceptance of Native was not an end but a beginning. After the illusion of HTML5 was shattered, they entered a new battlefield. It was more real, harder, and also more brutal. Because here, complexity does not disappear; it appears in another form.

The complexity of the Native world begins with performance.

Instagram's core experience is photos. Photos mean data, rendering, scroll smoothness, and a user's craving for immediate feedback. Users will not tolerate waiting. In the mobile era, a one-second wait can mean losing a chunk of users.

Instagram's team rebuilt the experience natively and achieved massive performance gains. They optimized the rendering pipeline, leveraged iOS's animation system to reduce dropped frames and improve fluidity. Photo loading became nearly instantaneous, and applying filters felt light and natural. Those improvements translated directly into user growth.

However, the battlefield of performance never ends. As the user base expanded, Instagram had to handle massive volumes of photos, comments, and likes. Every data request, every scroll, every tap is a test of performance.

Performance optimization is not merely a numbers game but a struggle over cognitive load.

Engineers must constantly make trade-offs in code: how to avoid runaway memory growth while guaranteeing a smooth experience?

How to maintain stability while also enabling rapid iteration?

How to keep animations graceful rather than forced on limited hardware?

Complexity becomes visible through these trade-offs.

The complexity of the native world also comes from the ecosystem.

iOS is a rapidly evolving platform.

Every year, Apple releases new APIs, new devices, and new system features.

These updates are the platform's heartbeat.

For developers, each beat is a new pressure.

Instagram had to keep up.

When Apple introduced Retina displays, they had to update all image assets to ensure clarity.

When Apple introduced new animation frameworks, they had to adjust rendering logic to fit the new performance optimizations.

When Apple introduced background tasks, they had to rethink upload and sync strategies.

These changes are not optional.

They are like imperial decrees; once issued, everyone must comply.

If Instagram failed to keep up, their experience would fall behind and users would churn.

Keeping up means accumulated complexity.

The team not only had to maintain existing features but continually adapt to new system capabilities.

They had to commit manpower, refactor architecture, and redraw boundaries.

The cost of complexity ceased to be a one-time expense and became ongoing.

The native world's complexity also stems from user growth.

Instagram's user base surpassed ten million in just two years.

This meant:

- A surge in data volume, bringing more network requests and cache management;
- A diversity of devices, bringing more compatibility issues;
- A global user base, bringing more localization requirements.

Each new user was an added layer of complexity.

Each new market was a new frontier.

Instagram had to confront this exponential growth while their team size lagged far behind the pace of user expansion.

This asymmetry made complexity even heavier.

Engineers had to accomplish impossible tasks in limited time.

They had to make hard choices between iteration and maintenance.

Instagram's story here reveals a deeper destiny.

Native is not a universal cure.

It cannot eradicate complexity; it only transforms complexity into another form.

In the Native world, complexity manifests as:

- The limits of performance: every dropped frame can provoke user dissatisfaction.
- The platform's tempo: every system update is a new test.
- User growth: every million new users is a new source of pressure.

These complexities are not external but endogenous.

They are the Native world's fate—the cost of coexisting with the platform.

The team began to feel the weight of that cost.

In the early days, Instagram's team was very small.

They iterated at great speed, achieving the most with the least amount of code.

That small-and-fast rhythm allowed them to stand out in the market.

However, as the user base grew, the team had to expand.

New engineers joined, new groups formed, new processes appeared.

Complexity grew along with them.

A simple feature update might require coordination across multiple groups.

Fixing a bug might require multiple reviewers.

A system upgrade might require the whole team to refactor.

Complexity exists not only in code but also in organization.

As the team grew, communication costs rose and cognitive load increased.

Code complexity and organizational complexity echoed and amplified each other.

Instagram's team realized they had to find a new balance.

They could no longer rely solely on individual talent and effort as before.

They had to build institutions, set boundaries, and control the expansion of complexity.

These institutions are not cold, rigid rules but mechanisms for distributing cognitive load.

Every module must have clear boundaries;

every team must have explicit responsibilities;

every process must aim to reduce cognitive load, not add to it.

This institutional framework is the "law" of the Native world.

It enables teams to survive the flood of complexity rather than be drowned by it.

Complexity has never been the enemy.

It is fate.

It will not disappear; it only shifts.

In the illusion of HTML5, it manifested as performance shortcomings and fractured experiences;

in the reality of Native, it manifests as performance limits, the rhythm of the ecosystem, and user growth.

Instagram accepted this fate.

They knew the only thing to do was to dance with complexity.

Not to eliminate it, but to manage it;

Not to reject it, but to keep pace with it.

This is the truth of Native.

It is not a shortcut; it is a long road.

It is not a simple choice, but another form of complexity.

It requires developers to dance to the platform's heartbeat and requires teams to build levees against the flood of complexity.

Instagram's team is moving forward on this long road.

They accepted Native's costs and embraced Native's rewards.

They know that complexity will not stop, but they have learned how to confront it.

The next wave of complexity is still on the horizon.

With the introduction of video features, expansion into more markets, and the platform's continuing evolution, Instagram will face greater challenges.

And in these challenges, complexity will appear in new forms.

The empire's story is not yet over.

The arc of destiny continues to unfold.

Great empire does not endure because of vast territory, but because it can stay in rhythm.

Great software does not last because it has many features, but because it can remain clear-headed amid waves of complexity.

Instagram reestablished its footing in the embrace of Native, but complexity did not recede.

It was merely waiting for a larger wave.

The first crest of that wave came from video.

Originally, Instagram was an empire built of photos.

Users communicated through square images, created aesthetics with filters, and let narratives flow through scrolling.

The loading, rendering, and display of photos had already demanded tremendous effort from the team.

Yet the market did not stop.

In 2013, the demand for video swept in.

Users wanted to share short videos on Instagram, not just photos.

This was an inevitable trend, because visual storytelling does not remain in still images; it inevitably moves toward motion.

However, the complexity that video brought far exceeded that of photos.

Photos are instantaneous loads, while video is continuous flow.

Photos can load slowly, but video must play smoothly in real time.

Photo storage is relatively simple, whereas video storage must account for codecs, bandwidth, and caching.

Instagram's team once again faced performance limits.

In the Native world they had to redesign the rendering pipeline, heavily optimize the player, and tightly align with hardware capabilities.

Cross-platform solutions could hardly bear all of this.

Only Native could resonate in sync with the GPU, decoders, and system APIs.

The team went through countless crashes and failures while iterating on video features.

Memory leaks, frame drops, audio-video desynchronization, black screens after backgrounding... these issues repeatedly destroyed the user experience.

But they had no way back, because this was the rhythm of the market.

They had to dance to it, or be eliminated.

The second crest of the wave came from globalization.

Instagram's users were no longer limited to the United States.

They expanded into Europe, Asia, Latin America, and Africa.

Each market brought new complexity.

Linguistic diversity meant the interface had to adapt to countless localizations.

Cultural differences meant interaction habits had to be adjusted.

Network disparities meant the experience had to remain usable in the U.S. with fast 4G and in India with slow 2G.

This complexity could not be solved by a single unified solution.

It required finely tuned integration with system capabilities in the Native world.

How to cache video in poor network conditions?

How to ensure the interface doesn't overflow in different language environments?

How to guarantee consistent input experiences with different input methods?

Each question was a fragment of complexity.

When these fragments aggregated, they formed an insurmountable cognitive load.

Instagram's team had to build institutions to bear this burden.

They decomposed features into different teams through modularization.

They designed boundaries so each team only had to understand a portion of the complexity, rather than shoulder the whole weight.

This system was not a luxury; it was a matter of survival.

The third crest of the wave came from the platform's tempo.

Apple's and Google's system updates are like imperial edicts —issued once a year with thunderous force.

Each update can change underlying APIs and affect performance and experience.

When Apple introduced 64-bit architecture, Instagram had to complete the adaptation in a short time.

When Apple introduced Auto Layout, Instagram had to adjust its UI rendering logic.

When Apple introduced new hardware (the iPhone X's edge-to-edge display), Instagram had to redesign the UI.

These changes cannot be refused.

Any delay will be noticed by users.

Any lag will be exploited by competitors.

In this continual pursuit, Instagram felt the fate of Native.

Native's advantages are performance, ecosystem, and experience.

Native's cost is that you must forever follow the platform's tempo.

This following is painful.

But it is precisely this pain that kept Instagram in step with the times.

They were not eliminated or left behind; they remained at the forefront.

Complexity did not disappear through all of this.

It still existed like an undercurrent.

But Instagram's team learned how to coexist with it.

They understood:

Complexity cannot be eradicated, but it can be isolated.

Complexity cannot be avoided, but it can be managed.

Complexity cannot be defeated, but it can be allocated to appropriate places through boundaries.

They isolated the complexity of different modules through Native boundaries;

They shared the Cognitive Load of different functions through team boundaries;

They maintained overall order through institutional boundaries.

These boundaries are civilization.

Complexity without boundaries will consume everything.

Complexity with boundaries can be mastered by humans.

"Instagram's greatness does not lie in having many features, but in remaining clear-headed in the face of complexity.

It accepted Native's fate, accepted the platform's laws, accepted the existence of complexity.

It did not try to defeat complexity with illusions, but tamed complexity with boundaries and institutions."

Performance is its sword.

Ecosystem is its soil.
Platform tempo is its law.
Complexity is its enemy and its constant companion.
Instagram's story tells us:

- The illusion of cross-platform solutions will always be shattered by complexity.
- The cost of Native is continuously keeping pace with the platform's rhythm.
- True strength does not lie in eliminating complexity, but in coexisting with it.

The civilization of software is not made of miracles, but of restraint.

The greatest architecture does not conquer complexity; it reduces cognitive load.

The greatest code is not perfect, but understandable.

Fate will not change because of resistance, and complexity will not disappear because of illusions.
Being in sync with the platform and dancing with complexity is the enduring way of software.

CHAPTER 20
SHORT-TERM CONVENIENCE VS LONG-TERM CLARITY

The morning of an empire always begins with shortcuts.

Farmland is quickly reclaimed, roads are roughly laid, walls are hastily built.

This lets the empire rise fast, but it also buries cracks in the foundation.

Complexity is like a shadow, existing alongside choices everywhere.

Every technical decision is a balance between convenience and clarity.

Convenience is like a swift wind that can push a ship forward; clarity is like a lighthouse that guards the course on a long voyage.

And the fate of most empires often swings between the two.

Twitter's story is such a swing.

In its early years, Twitter was not the vast empire we see today.

It was just a small experiment, an idea born from hacker culture.

"Why can't people use short text to tell the world what they're doing anytime, anywhere?"

140 characters, as short as a whisper, yet it spread quickly because of its simplicity.

The early Twitter app was built like a temporary shack.

It used the simplest tools and the most direct paths to turn the idea into reality.

The shack had no grand design, no carefully considered structure.

Its only goal was: speed.

Fast enough to ship a new feature after a meeting, fast enough to attract a batch of new users after a talk.

That speed was a startup's most precious weapon.

And the cost of speed was buried complexity.

Before mobile apps became mainstream, Twitter's main battleground was the web and SMS.

When iOS and Android rose, they had to enter the mobile world quickly.

Users were no longer satisfied with a browser entry; they wanted native experiences, apps they could open anytime, anywhere.

So Twitter made its first major trade-off:

They did not build a fully native app from scratch, but chose a hybrid path.

Some features were handled by WebView, some interactions were implemented in native code.

This let them get the product to users in the shortest possible time.

The short-term convenience was obvious:

The team didn't have to write two sets of logic for iOS and Android;

They could quickly validate the product and rapidly gather feedback.

Users got the apps they wanted, and investors saw the growth they expected.

But complexity had already settled into the foundation.

The split between Web and Native was destined to bring contradictions in performance, experience, and architecture.

As user numbers surged, Twitter was no longer a shack but a city in expansion.

And the city's growth exposed the shack's fragility.

The hybrid architecture's flaws gradually became apparent:

- WebView's performance could not satisfy the fast-scrolling timeline.
- Communication between Native and Web suffered latency.
- UI consistency was hard to guarantee; animations behaved differently across platforms.
- Development teams had to master two systems and switch between them repeatedly.

Engineers were like the city's craftsmen, patching cracks every day.

They put patches at the seams between Web and Native and applied expedients for performance issues.

Each repair solved the immediate problem, but deepened the complexity.

Complexity never explodes immediately; it settles like dust.

It accumulates until one day you realize: no one can fully understand the system as a whole.

The real contradiction surfaced at the strategic level.

Twitter wanted more than a "usable" app; it wanted a "scalable" platform.

Their vision was to let people around the world share thoughts anytime, anywhere, to make this information stream the nervous system of modern society.

However, when the app itself was being held back by complexity, such a vision became out of reach.

In the conference room, arguments grew more heated.

Some argued a full switch to Native was necessary to resolve performance and experience issues.

Others insisted the hybrid route was the only way to maintain iteration speed.

Both sides had merit, yet both overlooked one fact: complexity had already become the true arbiter.

Complexity's verdict is never black and white.

It is not a sudden explosion but a gradual erosion.

In one release, Twitter's Android app suffered severe performance problems.

The timeline scrolled with stutter; user experience declined; complaints flooded in.

Engineers worked day and night trying to fix the issue, but found the root of the bugs hard to trace:

Was it poor WebView rendering? Was it a bottleneck in the native bridge? Or limitations of the Android system?

Weeks passed before the problems were barely alleviated.

But the team's morale had been exhausted.

They realized that short-term convenience was devouring long-term clarity.

This is the cruelty of trade-offs.

In the short term, convenience brings speed;

In the long term, complexity forces you to pay a higher price.

Twitter would continue to struggle along this path for years to come, until it made a decisive shift.

And in this first phase, complexity had quietly written a prophecy:

If the course wasn't changed, the city would eventually be brought down by the cracks it kept patching.

Short-term convenience is like strong liquor, filling an empire with fervor for a short while; but when the liquor fades, what remains is grogginess and decline.

Long-term clarity is like clear water: bland at first, yet able to nourish for a thousand years.

Complexity does not tear a city apart immediately; it clings like vines, quietly climbing every wall.

By the time Twitter's app entered the mainstream, user numbers surged, advertisers joined, and feature demands multiplied, those vines had already wrapped around the entire city.

It was 2012.

Twitter's mobile traffic surpassed the web for the first time.

This meant the empire's main battleground had fully shifted to the worlds of iOS and Android.

Yet their architecture remained that patched hybrid: some features ran in WebView, some ran natively, and more logic was scattered in the bridging layer.

Such patchwork could function at small scale;

But when user numbers reached the hundreds of millions, it became a monster that consumed energy.

Performance problems surfaced first.

Stuttering while users scrolled the timeline became the norm.

Ads loaded slowly, images displayed with delay, and the retweet button occasionally failed to respond.

For ordinary users these were infuriating details;

For advertisers, they were naked losses.

The team responded urgently; engineers debugged day and night.

They tried to optimize WebView rendering, reduce the number of bridge communications, and even implemented some key features separately on the native side.

Each remedial measure was like a temporary support beam, keeping the rattling house standing for a while.

But complexity had already decided: every support beam would bring new cracks.

The problems were not only technical but also organizational and cultural.

Twitter's team gradually split into three forces:

- Native camp: insist that iOS and Android should each be developed in their native languages to ensure performance and experience.
- Hybrid camp: believe that continuing to rely on web technologies is the only way to maintain iteration speed.
- Neutral camp: busy shuttling between hybrid and native, acting as translators who reconcile the contradictions.

These three forces were like different factions within the empire.

They shared a common goal—to make the app better—but their paths were opposed.

In the conference room, arguments erupted again and again.

Someone said, "If we move to fully native, the user experience will improve."

Someone retorted, "Then we will lose iteration speed, and competitors will seize the opportunity."

Others fell silent; they were tired of arguing and just wanted to finish the patches at hand.

The power of complexity lies in its ability to turn "technical choices" into "organizational rifts."

When a team spends massive energy arguing over tools and frameworks, they have already lost the real focus: users and long-term value.

And complexity loves that internal friction.

It knows that as long as people are busy fighting internally, it can continue to breed in the shadows.

One day, Twitter's iOS app crashed widely because of a caching bug.

Users could not load their timelines; the world fell into brief chaos.

Engineers investigated quickly but found the root cause was not singular.

Caching logic had been implemented redundantly between Web and Native, and the bridge layer introduced unexpected races.

The repair process was like unraveling a tangled web.

Every strand of that web was a legacy left behind by past efforts to "ship quickly."

By the time the issue was finally resolved, the team was exhausted.

In the retrospective they admitted:

"We spent 80% of our time understanding the problem and only 20% actually fixing it."

This is the true cost of complexity: it doesn't make problems unsolvable, it exhausts you before you can solve them.

Instability at the strategic level followed.

Management began to receive more and more warnings:

- Users complained about app stutter.
- Advertisers complained about slow ad loading.
- Engineer turnover rose; many no longer wanted to struggle within the hybrid architecture.

Complexity was no longer just an engineers' dilemma but a crisis for the entire empire.

It drove users away, hurt revenue, and exhausted talent.

Management had to rethink:

Continue chasing short-term convenience, or turn toward long-term clarity?

However, turning was not easy.

Any strategic shift is an act of self-negation.

Twitter's management understood: if they abandoned the hybrid architecture and chose fully native development, it would mean admitting that years of prior investment had been a mistake.

This was not only a technical challenge but a cultural rupture.

Many engineers were deeply embedded in the hybrid system; switching to fully native meant relearning and rebuilding.

And that transition period could allow competitors to gain the upper hand.

Complexity sneered at that moment.

It knew humans fear not mistakes but admitting mistakes.

As long as people were unwilling to give up past investments, it could continue to expand.

The empire's story is always cruelest at such moments.

When the Roman Empire realized its roads had rotted, they no longer had the strength to repair them.

When the Qing realized their institutions were backward, they had already lost the time to reform.

Twitter faced the same predicament:

They knew the hybrid architecture was the problem, yet hesitated to let it go.

So complexity kept growing.

Teams continued to split, users continued to complain, and bugs continued to accumulate.

The empire struggled in the mud; each step was heavier than the last.

The real turning point does not come from some grand declaration but from repeated, seemingly trivial defeats.

One engineer spent a full two weeks fixing a bug related to embedded videos in tweets.

The issue was that the video playback logic was tangled

between Web and Native, memory management ran amok, causing frequent crashes.

After fixing it, he wrote in an internal email:

"I can fix the bug, but I cannot fix the direction we've taken."

That sentence pierced management's self-comfort like a sword.

They realized complexity was no longer a technical issue but a strategic one.

In the empire's records, a footnote for the future has already been written:

If no choice is made, short-term convenience will devour long-term clarity;

If dependence on the hybrid architecture continues, complexity will utterly destroy the empire's foundations.

The real turning point is not in glorious battles but in silent choices.

Only when the empire finally admitted that short-term victories had become long-term shackles did it have a chance to regain clarity.

The force of complexity always appears in the form of compound interest.

It won't make you collapse on the first day; on the hundredth day, the thousandth day, it will make you realize that every decision you make has been shackled by ever heavier chains.

Twitter's experiment with a hybrid architecture was exactly such a chain.

It once helped them rise quickly and achieve short-term wins.

But when user volume and feature complexity reached their limits, they found this chain tightening around the throat of the entire empire.

True awakening often comes from repeated failures that cannot be ignored.

In 2015, after a major update, Twitter's mobile app experienced widespread crashes and stuttering.

Users frequently encountered white screens while scrolling the timeline, ads loaded with delay, and tweet videos failed to play properly.

Social media is supposed to be a stage of real-time interaction, but at that moment the stage lights flickered and complaints rose from the audience.

The engineering team scrambled to fix things.

They searched for the root cause between Web and Native but kept hitting dead ends.

The complexity of the problem had exceeded any single engineer's cognitive capacity.

In the end, they had to urgently roll back the release and keep things running in the clumsiest way.

This crisis made management fully realize:

short-term convenience had already devoured long-term clarity.

Continuing to rely on the hybrid architecture would not only fail to support the future, it would keep creating crises.

Discussions about shifting officially began in the conference room.

Some people still resisted.

They worried that a full move to Native would sharply reduce iteration speed and let competitors catch up.

They produced cost analyses, pointing out that rebuilding would consume massive manpower and time.

But others argued:

"Maintaining the status quo will only make the cost higher.

We are no longer building new features; we are fighting complexity.

If we don't choose clarity, convenience will eventually kill us."

The debate went on for months, and finally, at a high-level strategic meeting, a decision was made:

Twitter would gradually abandon the hybrid architecture and fully shift to Native.

This was a painful decision.

It meant denying years of prior investment;

It meant overturning existing systems;

It meant admitting that the empire's path had gone the wrong way.

But it was also a necessary decision.

Only clarity can sustain the future in the long run.

The process of shifting was not instantaneous.

Engineering teams rewrote key modules in batches.

Timeline, messages, notifications, search—these core features were migrated back to native implementations one by one.

The bridge layer was gradually dismantled, and the proportion of WebViews steadily decreased.

Engineers rediscovered their rhythm in the worlds of Swift and Kotlin.

The process took years.

During that time, development speed did slow and user complaints persisted.

But with each iteration, system stability improved, bug triage accelerated, and team morale recovered.

Complexity finally began to recede.

The cultural shift was deeper than the technical one.

Engineers who had once been running frantically, reduced to patch artisans, now became designers again, able to make long-term judgments within clear boundaries.

Teams that had been torn between hybrid and native camps reconverged under a common language.

There were no more "translators," no more "factions"—only one goal: keep the system clear.

This cultural transformation was like rebuilding an empire.

It was not an overnight cheer but a silent accumulation.

Every clean API, every stable feature, every reduced bug was a new brick.

Rebuilding a city from ruins is harder than expanding on sand, but it is also more solid.

Looking back at Twitter's journey, we can see the cruelty of trade-offs.

In the early days, short-term convenience was the only choice.

Without convenience there was no speed; without speed there was no survival.

A startup empire must trade convenience for life.

But in the long run, convenience becomes a trap.

It allows complexity to accumulate, causing the system to lose clarity.

It drags teams into internal friction and gradually rips apart culture.

It ultimately forces management to admit: without choosing long-term clarity, there is no future.

Philosophical answers have not changed.

Convenience is hard liquor; it can fill you with strength in the short term;

Clarity is clear water; it can keep you alive in the long term.

Convenience lets you win a battle; clarity lets you win a war.

The ledger of complexity always compounds.

You think every minute you save will ultimately have to be paid back many times over in the future.

You think every choice you avoid will eventually return to you in a heavier form.

Twitter's story is merely a page in the long river of complexity's history.

But it tells us an eternal truth:

In the world of software, the only thing worth holding on to is long-term clarity.

A Twitter engineer, while rewriting a module, left a simple note:

"We once took shortcuts, but the shortcuts did not shorten the road.

The true road is clarity."

That note was preserved by the team and became the opening of an internal document.

It was not just a technical summary but a philosophical inscription.

The survival of software does not depend on how many features it has, but on whether complexity can be tamed.
Short-term convenience is an illusion; long-term clarity is the truth.
Those who choose illusion will inevitably be trapped by complexity;
Those who choose truth will be able to stand their ground in the sea of complexity.

CHAPTER 21
THE LEDGER OF COMPLEXITY

Empires do not perish because of expansion, but rot because their ledgers are unbalanced.
The empires of technology are no different; complexity is that ledger that can never be forged.

Complexity is like interest.

It does not demand payment immediately, but quietly accumulates until one morning people find that all their freedoms have been mortgaged by it.

Every technology choice is a loan from complexity: you gain speed and convenience, but must repay the costs in cognition and maintenance in the future.

This ledger does not change with the strength of power, nor does it forgive based on wealth.

It is the only constant law in the software world.

The story of Slack is a footnote to that ledger.

When Stewart Butterfield and his team launched Slack in 2013, their goal was not technical elegance but survival.

The company had previously been a game studio; after failure they pivoted and the team needed to find a new direction.

As an enterprise communication tool, Slack was not novel—IRC, HipChat, Campfire already existed on the market.

But Slack's advantage lay in their ability to iterate faster, ship faster, and probe the market faster.

Thus, technology selection became a strategic issue.

They needed to build a cross-platform app in the shortest possible time:

- Desktop (Windows, macOS, Linux);
- Mobile (iOS, Android);
- Web.

Any traditional "write native from scratch" solution would mean huge team and financial investment.

They did not have that luxury.

At that time, Electron appeared on their radar.

Electron is a "shell-style" cross-platform solution: use web technologies (HTML, CSS, JavaScript) to build the UI, then wrap it in a shell so it can run on the desktop.

It promises "one codebase, run everywhere", allowing the team to quickly unify development.

- No need to separately hire Windows, macOS, and Linux specialists;
- Able to cover desktop and web with the same tech stack;
- Able to concentrate limited manpower on product iteration and user experience.

This was almost a perfect temptation.

Speed, cost, cross-platform consistency — at a startup's life-or-death moment, these are the overriding considerations.

So Slack embraced Electron without hesitation.

Their first-generation client was a palace built on Electron.

At first, everything went smoothly.

Slack updated features frequently; the team could ship new features within weeks.

Channels, direct messages, file sharing, the notification system — all these features went live at an astonishing pace.

Users kept pouring in, and word of mouth gradually spread.

The media began to call Slack "the app that kills email," and investors saw a unicorn taking off.

At that stage, Electron's disadvantages had not yet surfaced.

User numbers weren't large enough, data volumes weren't big enough, demands weren't complex enough.

At small scale, Electron's performance bottlenecks had not become a disaster.

Like an empire's ledger, it was still roomy in the early days.

People, intoxicated by the thrill of expansion, didn't check that ledger of complexity.

But the ledger of complexity never stays absent.

It simply waits silently.

Slack's architecture was essentially using web technologies to emulate a desktop app.

This meant:

- Higher memory consumption than native;
- Heavier CPU usage;
- Lower system integration;
- Every seemingly simple desktop feature (for example, file drag-and-drop, system shortcuts, offline support) required extra bridging and adaptation.

These problems were masked by speed in the early days.

Like when an empire expands, shortages in taxation are filled by spoils and institutional gaps are hidden by military glory.

But as the number of users grew, the cracks inevitably showed.

Slack's user base quickly surpassed a million, entering the enterprise application realm.

At that point, the ledger of complexity began to be turned.

Users began to complain:

"Slack uses too much memory."

"After opening a few channels, my computer's fan starts roaring."

"Notifications are delayed; sometimes it takes a few seconds for them to appear."

Engineers also felt the heavy burden:

- Every platform-specific bug required diving into Electron's black box;
- Compatibility issues in the bridging layer multiplied debugging costs;
- Performance bottlenecks often couldn't be solved by conventional means and could only be addressed by continuously stacking patches.

The interest on complexity was being collected bit by bit.

And the most terrifying thing about interest is that it's compound.

The longer you delay, the higher the cost.

Discussions inside Slack began to split.

Some insisted on Electron, believing it was still the most efficient solution.

They emphasized:

"If it weren't for Electron, we wouldn't have today's user scale. Speed is our moat."

Others began to question:

"We fix performance problems every day. We spend more time on patches than on new features. If this continues, we will be dragged down by our own complexity."

This was not a technical dispute but a philosophical one.

It was the struggle between "short-term efficiency" and "long-term clarity."

It was the other side of the ledger.

The ledger of complexity never allows escape.

It forced Slack's team to face one fact:

The essence of technology choice is not which language to write in, but how to allocate a limited cognitive budget.

Electron's speed was bought at the expense of future Cognitive Load.

Each performance bug, each black-box debugging session, each stacking of patches were interest on the debt.

And interest always has to be repaid.

Slack was still expanding, users were still growing, and the team was still struggling.

The ledger of complexity was already on the table, but they had not decided how to turn the page.

The real storm was still ahead.

When interest exceeded the principal, the debt would backfire.

When complexity exceeded cognition, the system would suffocate.

Complexity doesn't seize order overnight.

It is more like the water level in a reservoir, rising day after day until one day the dam suddenly loses support.

Slack's ledger was slowly filled in this way.

At first, users' complaints were like scattered noise.

"Slack uses too much memory."

"Notifications are sometimes delayed."

These voices were not enough to shake conviction.

The product still expanded, and the team still iterated.

Management treated these issues as "the cost of growth."

But the power of complexity never relies on a single burst.

It depends on accumulation and frequency.

When countless small problems stack up, they can engulf an entire empire like a sandstorm.

The problems first centered on performance.

At its core, Electron runs a browser shell inside the desktop operating system.

Slack's client was essentially a gigantic web page.

In enterprise teams of thousands, a Slack workspace can have tens of thousands of channels and millions of messages.

Electron was not built for that scale.

The result was:

- Startup times of tens of seconds;
- Message lists took a long time to load while scrolling, and CPU usage spiked;
- Memory consumption easily exceeded 1 GB, and in some scenarios approached 2 GB;
- Opening several workspaces would instantly send the computer's fans into overdrive.

Users began joking on social media:

"Slack is the heaviest game on my computer."

"Chrome + Slack = my laptop takes off."

Those jokes slowly turned into complaints, complaints into accusations.

And accusations eventually translate into loss of trust.

At the same time, the engineers' mental bandwidth was being drained.

In the world of Electron, any seemingly simple feature can become a maze.

Take file drag-and-drop: users expect to drag a file from the desktop directly into Slack.

In a native app that's just a few system calls, but in Electron it requires bridging, listening, forwarding, and finally handing it back to the OS.

Every detail can fail because of platform differences.

Another example is the notification system.

Slack had to ensure message notifications were real-time and reliable.

On iOS and Android, notifications rely on their respective push services;

In Electron, notifications must emulate native behavior, and as a result they frequently break across systems:

Windows notifications couldn't reliably wake the app, and macOS notifications would vanish in multi-desktop environments.

Each bug-fixing session is a journey through:

- Engineers had to dive into Electron's source code to understand how it called system APIs;
- Then go deeper into the Node.js runtime to confirm how events were dispatched;
- Finally return to Slack's own logic to see if the problem lay in the application layer.

Three-layer jumps pulled their minds back and forth.

Each context switch left them exhausted.

The ledger of complexity recorded not only technical burdens but also cultural rifts.

Slack's team gradually split into two voices.

One voice was "speed-first."

They emphasized:

"If it weren't for Electron, we wouldn't have today's market position. These problems exist, but as long as we keep optimizing, we'll find a way."

The other voice was "sustainability."

They questioned:

"We spend more and more time on remediation instead of innovation. Have we already sunk into a swamp of debt?"

This split appeared in meetings.

Some people brought charts showing user growth curves to prove Slack's momentum was still strong;

others brought performance monitoring data, pointing out that client startup time had become one of the reasons for user churn.

This was no longer a purely engineering discussion but a philosophical confrontation:

Is future speed worth today's pain?

Is short-term expansion worth long-term debt?

In Slack's corridors, the echoes of complexity grew louder.

Engineers were often woken in the middle of the night to handle client performance crises.

They filled whiteboards with diagrams, trying to trace the source of memory leaks.

Again and again they discovered the problem was not in Slack's business logic but deep in Electron's black box.

One engineer wrote an internal document:

"We are paying an increasingly high cognitive cost for Electron. We need weeks to understand an issue before we can write a line of fix. Our cognitive budget is being mercilessly consumed."

That sentence was like a stone thrown into a reservoir, creating ripples.

More and more people began to realize: the real ledger was not money, but cognitive capacity.

Every choice was an allocation of limited cognitive resources.

The outbreak of complexity was also reflected in user behavior.

In some large enterprises, IT departments had to restrict the use of Slack. Because it was so resource-hungry, employees' computers noticeably slowed down when running Slack. Some companies even began trying alternatives, or required employees to use only the web version.

Slack's reputation began to wobble. The once "email killer" was now criticized as "a new burden." This was not a failure of features, but the cost of complexity manifesting on the user side.

When the ledger of complexity extended to user experience, it could no longer be ignored.

The empire's decline did not come from enemies breaching the walls, but from losing the people's hearts. Software's decline is not from lacking features, but from complexity crushing the experience.

Slack's leadership was forced to reexamine. They found:

- Product teams were eager to launch new features, but development teams were held back by performance problems;
- Users craved a smoother experience, but Electron's architectural ceiling could not be breached;
- Investors wanted larger growth, but the interest on complexity had already eaten the dividend of speed.

This was another page in the ledger:

Any decision that seemed to "save" would ultimately be repaid in another form.

The power of complexity was not only to slow speed, but also to erode confidence.

Slack's engineers gradually fell into a state of fatigue. They were no longer excited about shipping new features, but feared the next performance report. They no longer celebrated user growth, but worried that more users meant more complaints. Their conversations were no longer "what can we do," but "how much longer can we hold on."

This cultural shadow was more frightening than any bug. When a team loses confidence, complexity has truly won.

When interest exceeds principal, debt devours the future. When Cognitive Load exceeds mental capacity, complexity devours the team.

Slack's ledger was already full. The only question was: when would they be willing to turn to a new page.

The greatness of an empire lies not in the breadth of its territory, but in the moment it acknowledges the ledger.

The wisdom of software lies not in boastful expansion, but in the clarity of contraction.

The water level of complexity had already overflowed the dam. The Slack team could no longer ignore the ledger. Complaints about performance had shifted from users' whispers to media reports, and cognitive exhaustion had moved from silence in meetings to attrition on the team. In a crucial strategic meeting, leadership finally admitted: Electron had fulfilled its mission, but the future of Slack would require a new path.

The decision to turn was not easy. Abandoning Electron meant giving up past speed, giving up past unification, giving up a former moat. It was like an empire that must admit it had overexpanded, must retract its borders, must rebuild its institutions. Such contraction would not win applause, only doubt.

Yet true wisdom is often hidden in doubt.

Slack's leadership announced: they would gradually rewrite the clients and return to native. iOS and Android would be taken over by their respective native teams; the desktop would undergo deeper optimization to gradually shed its dependence on Electron.

The news rippled like a stone dropped into a lake. The engineers' first reaction was not surprise, but relief. For they had long known that continuing to struggle in the swamp of debt would only exhaust all mental resources. Returning to native, though difficult, was the only hope.

The rewrite would be a long war.

On the iOS team, they embraced Swift and UIKit anew. On the Android team, they reorganized around Kotlin and Jetpack.

Every module needed to be rebuilt; every feature needed to be rewritten; every piece of logic needed to be redesigned.

This was not a simple migration, but a comprehensive philosophical shift: from "quick unification" to "long-term sustainability"; from "stacking patches" to "defining deep boundaries"; from "short-term expansion" to "cognitive restraint."

The ledger of complexity was opened again in that moment.

The team no longer fantasized about "write once, run everywhere," but acknowledged: every platform has its own particularities, and each experience requires dedicated cognitive investment. Rather than covering differences with bridges and patches, it was better to face them and design clear boundaries.

This choice was not wasteful, but saving. It saved future mental effort, saved pointless debugging, and saved the interest on complexity.

Slack's users gradually felt the change. Startup became faster, memory usage decreased, notifications became more reliable. These improvements were not miracles but inevitable. When complexity is redistributed and the cognitive budget is used sensibly, the system naturally regains clarity.

Users stopped complaining that Slack was "the heaviest game on the computer," and began to trust its value as a communication tool again. That trust is more important than any feature.

"Slack's rebuilding is not a technological victory but a cognitive one. It proves that the essence of technology choices is not a matter of syntax, but of allocating cognitive budget."

Cognitive budget—this concept needs to be remembered.

Every team's attention is limited, just as every empire's finances are limited. If you spend all your budget on bridges and patches, you will have no budget left for innovation. If you exhaust all your attention on black boxes and compatibility, you will have no attention left to improve the user experience.

The essence of technology selection is asking: Where are we willing to spend our limited cognitive budget?

Choosing Electron let Slack win speed early on, and that was the right decision. But continuing to rely on it caused Slack to lose clarity later on, and that was the wrong decision. This is not a question of technological right or wrong, but of budget imbalance.

Therefore, a truly mature technology choice must possess a kind of sobriety: short-term and long-term, speed and clarity, must be balanced on the ledger. Any expansion that ignores the ledger will ultimately be repaid in the form of debt.

Slack's story leaves us with three lessons engraved on a stone:

First, complexity does not disappear; it only moves. Cross-platform unification did not reduce complexity, it moved it to the bridging layer. You cannot fool the ledger.

Second, cognitive budget is the real currency. Teams are not infinite, attention is not free. Every choice must consider the mental cost.

Third, the hardest thing is not expansion but contraction. Admitting the illusions of the past, returning to native, and rebuilding boundaries — this is the hardest choice, and also the bravest.

The greatness of an empire does not lie in how much land it has conquered, but in whether it can acknowledge its own limits. The wisdom of software does not lie in how many new technologies it adopts, but in whether it can remain clear-headed in the face of complexity.

Slack's pivot is that kind of clarity. It tells us: the ledger of complexity cannot be escaped. The only thing we can do is allocate cognitive budget sensibly, place complexity with those who understand it best, and leave clarity for future readers.

Complexity is the only currency.
The essence of technology selection is cognitive accounting.
Every expansion is a loan;
Every contraction is a repayment.

May future engineers learn to budget carefully.

PART FIVE
ENGINEERING PRACTICE

CHAPTER 22
SWIFTUI REDRAWS, STATE TRAPS, AND INSTRUMENTS

Speed is not everything for an empire; stability is the cornerstone of its domain.

If a camel caravan in the desert tries to hurry, it will only sink into quicksand.

Complexity is a silent enemy, and performance is its most covert battlefield.

In the era of SwiftUI, this battle is particularly cunning.

Because SwiftUI's promise is that everything can be declared, everything can update automatically.

It is like a new decree from the empire: concise, elegant, seemingly flawless.

But beneath the decree, you still need supply lines, soldiers, and bureaucratic transmission.

Performance issues lurk in these invisible transmissions.

Spotify's iOS team deeply felt this lurking problem when they tried to introduce SwiftUI into core interfaces.

Their app is the empire's marketplace, with tens of millions of users streaming in at once; music, playlists, recommendations, and ads all interweave on the interface.

SwiftUI gave them new hope: the ability to build complex UIs faster, replacing verbose manual logic with declarative code.

They saw an oasis in the future — cleaner code, faster development, and more unified features.

However, the flood of complexity does not retreat because of a new tool.

It only takes a different form, waiting for new cracks.

The first cracks appeared in redraws.

SwiftUI's philosophy is to keep the UI consistent with state.

When state changes, the UI refreshes automatically.

This is wonderfully miraculous in small-scale interfaces.

The Spotify team initially built a small music detail page showing the album cover, play button, and song list.

Everything ran smoothly, updates were quick, and the development experience was unparalleled.

But when they applied this philosophy to the "home recommendation feed," things changed.

The home recommendation feed is Spotify's gateway; each user sees different recommendation cards: new song recommendations, featured podcasts, and top charts.

These cards scroll continuously, and each swipe could trigger dozens of state updates.

The result was frequent interface redraws.

Even if only some cards changed, the entire list could still trigger a refresh.

What users saw was not smooth scrolling but subtle stutters.

For ordinary people this was only a brief discomfort;

For a giant like Spotify, it was a crack threatening the empire's reputation.

Performance issues have never been about whether something can "run," but whether it can "run stably."

An empire's roads do not fear traffic passing through; they fear traffic repeatedly clogging at the same spot.

SwiftUI's redraw mechanism is like a road with no rate limiting — as state increases, the probability of congestion rises sharply.

The crack extended further into state.

Spotify's engineers discovered: state is everywhere in SwiftUI.

Playback state, download state, flags returned by recommendation algorithms, user-clicked preferences...

Every piece of state can trigger a UI refresh.

And these states are not completely independent.

A small toggle can set off a chain reaction.

Once, they tested a new feature: showing a song's playback progress in real time on home cards.

The intent was simple: let users see the progress bar without entering the playback screen.

However, this progress bar updated every second.

Each update triggered a redraw.

The redraw didn't just affect the progress bar; it rippled through the whole card.

As users scrolled up and down, these updates and redraws compounded, eventually creating noticeable performance problems.

Developers found themselves in a dilemma.

What they wanted was a more intuitive user experience;

What they paid with was a sacrifice of global performance.

This was not a technical failure but a clash of philosophies:

The beauty of declarative design colliding head-on with the cost of performance.

The crack was finally revealed in the tools.

Spotify's team decided to use Instruments to track down the problem.

They hoped to find the root cause of the performance bottlenecks through precise analysis.

- Redraws exceeded expectations, yet it was hard to determine which state triggered them;
- Memory consumption kept rising, but there were no obvious leak points;
- CPU spikes appeared occasionally, but could not be reproduced in every test.

Instruments gave them a map, but not a direction.

They saw the desert, but didn't know where the oasis was.

The power of complexity was on full display here:

The problem was not a localized failure, but the coordination cost of the whole.

Like an imperial bureaucracy, no single official was at fault, yet the entire system had slipped into sluggishness and waste.

SwiftUI's automatic refresh was intended to lighten developers' burden;

But in large-scale applications, it instead made developers lose their sense of control.

Spotify's case is a prime example of performance optimization.

It tells us: performance problems do not appear suddenly, but accumulate with complexity.

It also reminds us: tools cannot directly solve the problem; they can only reveal the shape of complexity.

Spotify's team did not give up; they began exploring new strategies:

How to limit unnecessary redraws, how to separate critical state, and how to make Instruments a true ally.

This was their next battle with complexity.

An empire's tax revenue does not collapse from a single famine, but from countless tiny erosions.

Software performance is not destroyed by a single bug, but by innumerable silent drains.

Instruments are merely accountants; they can record the numbers but cannot eliminate the burden.

Once the shadow of complexity appears, it does not recede.

Spotify's team realized they had to deeply understand SwiftUI's performance mechanisms, or this desert would swallow their oasis.

They decided to dissect the problems one by one under the guidance of Instruments.

In their first experiment, they chose the most intuitive metric: redraw count.

They hoped to confirm which views were being repeatedly redrawn and which states were causing needless refreshes.

However, the reports Instruments produced were not as clear as they had expected.

The reports were full of function call stacks, drawing paths, and thread switches.

The numbers were dense, like an ancient ledger, yet had not been translated into any directly actionable steps.

"We're like the empire's chroniclers," one engineer said at an internal sharing session, "recording everything, but we don't know the true direction of history."

In the second experiment they narrowed the scope. They picked a specific scenario: scrolling through a playlist. This is one of Spotify's core experiences; as users scroll they need to see information for hundreds of tracks, each row potentially containing a play button, a download state, and a recommendation badge. They suspected the performance bottleneck was hiding here.

The result was not surprising:

With every scroll, SwiftUI was redrawing frequently. Even a change to a single download badge could cause an entire row, or even the whole screen, to refresh. Instruments' flame charts burned like a volcanic crater, as if the entire system were forced to participate in a tiny event.

This "pull one hair and the whole body moves" phenomenon left the team feeling powerless. They seemed to see the empire's roads: because of a tax adjustment in a small town, the entire imperial bureaucracy had to re-sign documents. The cost of complexity is this kind of global waste.

In the third experiment, they decided to test memory. They found that as users switched back and forth between the home screen and playlists, memory usage gradually rose. There were no obvious leaks; the system's garbage collection mechanism was still functioning; but memory accumulated like drifts of sand in the desert—slow, continuous, and hard to eradicate. Over time devices began to heat up and battery drained rapidly.

Users complained in the comments:

"Why does my phone feel like it ran a marathon after only an hour of listening to music?"

This was the empire's granary quietly leaking away. Not because of thieves, but because of countless tiny fissures. SwiftUI's automatic memory management was not as perfect as promised; in complex scenarios it caused unpredictable buildup.

Facing these problems, the team fell into debate. Some insisted these were merely growing pains, and that as SwiftUI matured, Apple would gradually fix these issues. They cited history: when UIKit first appeared, it too went through countless optimizations to become the pillar it is today. They believed that, with patience, the problems would eventually disappear.

Others no longer harbored illusions.

They believed waiting was not a solution.

Performance optimization is not a sprint, but a long-term governance.

If you don't proactively establish a methodology and set boundaries, complexity will continue to accumulate and eventually crush the entire system.

The debate went on for weeks, until one day a user complaint was brought into the meeting room by the product manager.

It was an apparently ordinary piece of feedback:

"Why is Spotify still lagging on my new phone?

I changed devices — shouldn't it be faster?"

That sentence pierced the team's core like a sword.

Performance problems were no longer just engineers' headaches; they were a direct harm to user experience.

This meant complexity had moved from behind the scenes onto the stage.

So Spotify's team began looking for a new philosophy.

They stopped treating Instruments as merely a debugging tool and started treating it as a map.

A map won't tell you where the oasis is, but it will show the shape of the dunes.

They decided to treat complexity as a natural force that can be governed, rather than an occasional enemy.

The first step was learning how to separate state.

They found that, in many cases, not all state needs to drive UI refreshes.

A background download's progress doesn't need to update the UI in real time;

The state of a play button doesn't require redrawing the entire card every second.

They began to establish rules: which states are critical and which are secondary.

Critical states must drive the UI; secondary states are delayed or merged into batched updates.

This separation was like the empire establishing priorities for tax collection.

Not every village's grain needs to be reported immediately; instead, it is gathered at key nodes and transmitted together.

The system thus became stable.

The second step was learning how to limit redraws.

They discovered that although SwiftUI's philosophy is "state-driven," it doesn't mean you must unconditionally accept its global refreshes.

Through analysis, they gradually broke large views into smaller ones, confining local changes to local scope.

That way, even if a progress bar updates, it won't ripple across the entire card.

This approach was like setting up checkpoints along the empire's roads.

Traffic could circulate locally without having to run to the capital for permission every time.

The empire's efficiency was thereby restored, and the software's smoothness rebuilt.

The third step was learning how to use Instruments' results.

They no longer expected the tool to give them answers, but treated it as evidence.

For every test they recorded redraw counts, memory changes, and CPU peaks.

They established their own baselines: what kinds of redraws are acceptable, what levels of memory growth are reasonable.

They used these baselines to constrain their development cadence.

This was not a tactical victory, but the establishment of a strategy.

They shifted from "firefighting" to "governance," from "waiting for fixes" to "active defense."

However, complexity does not vanish because of new rules.

It is only temporarily suppressed.

Spotify's team understood that SwiftUI is still evolving and Apple's ecosystem is still changing.

Performance optimization cannot be solved once and for all; it can only be a long-term vigil.

At a retrospective meeting, a senior engineer said,

"We must accept one fact: SwiftUI is the future, but performance optimization is the present.

Future promises will not automatically solve today's problems.

If we do not set boundaries ourselves, we will be overwhelmed by complexity."

The phrase became the team's motto.

They posted it on the office wall and wrote it into the internal wiki.

They no longer passively accepted performance problems; they began to proactively establish processes.

But the cost of processes is a slowdown in speed.

Every development effort must pass benchmarking;

Every new feature must evaluate its impact on state.

This plunged the team into another tension:

how to find a balance between stability and innovation?

The power of complexity lies in its ability to constantly create new contradictions.

When you solve performance problems, it will make you face efficiency issues.

When you establish boundaries, it will make you confront the loss of flexibility.

"Governance is not victory, but the art of delaying decline."

Spotify's team stood at this crossroads of that art.

The limit of speed is an illusion.

Stable order is the long-lasting foundation of an empire.

The way of software is not about chasing the fastest, but about preserving clarity.

The shadow of complexity was like the desert wind.

It would not dissipate because of a single fix, nor retreat after a single victory.

Spotify's team soon understood that what they were really

facing was not an isolated bug, but a long-term mental exhaustion.

Performance optimization was no longer a single technical task, but an ongoing civilizational effort.

The turning point of the story came with a failed release.

They introduced a new recommendation mechanism on the home screen: recommendation cards that refreshed in real time based on users' listening habits.

The algorithms team was brimming with confidence, claiming this was a key feature to boost retention.

The design team supplied flashy interaction animations, making the recommendation cards switch as smoothly as shifting sand.

The engineering team completed the integration, and all tests appeared to pass.

However, when the feature went live, problems emerged.

Users frequently experienced stutters while scrolling the home screen.

Worse, some older devices crashed outright, and the app was forcibly terminated by the system.

The comment section erupted instantly:

"Why has Spotify become so laggy?

I just want to listen to music, not watch a PowerPoint."

This failed release was like a sandstorm, knocking everyone back to reality.

They realized they were still repeating old mistakes.

They chased peak performance while neglecting the foundations of stability.

The postmortem dragged on.

The algorithms team defended themselves: the recommendation mechanism itself didn't consume that many resources; it was the frontend implementation that was at fault.

The design team insisted the animations were an indispensable part of the user experience.

The engineering team replied bitterly: SwiftUI's state updates caused chain redraws, and they had done everything they could to avoid it.

The debate reached an impasse—until a senior architect spoke up:

"We need to admit one fact. Performance optimization is not a miracle cure; it is the institution of order.

If the institution itself lacks stability, no number of patches can prevent the next disaster."

The room fell silent.

They finally understood that performance optimization could no longer be treated as temporary firefighting but must be elevated to part of the team's culture.

So they began an unprecedented reform.

First, they established performance budgets.

Like an empire allocating rations for its army, they set performance limits for each feature.

- Scrolling frame rates must not fall below a certain standard;
- Memory growth must not exceed preset thresholds;
- Battery consumption must remain within an acceptable range.

Any feature that exceeds these limits, no matter how flashy, cannot go live.

This iron rule made many unhappy, but it gradually established order.

The second step was introducing performance guardians.

In every development team, one engineer would take on responsibility for performance.

His duty was not to write more code, but to be the team's sober voice.

When everyone else was immersed in feature iterations and design aesthetics, he would ask:

"Will this cause unnecessary redraws?"

"Does this state need to drive the UI in real time?"

"Is this animation worth sacrificing smoothness?"

This role was like an inspector in the empire, not participating in expansion but responsible for reminding of boundaries.

Their presence kept the team from blindly chasing speed and maintained a reverence for complexity.

The third step was reshaping the testing culture.

In the past, tests only focused on whether features worked;

now tests had to also check whether performance remained stable.

They added automated performance tests into the CI pipeline, so every commit would trigger benchmark measurements.

Any commit that caused a performance regression would be marked as high risk.

This was not punishment, but a reminder.

It made every developer understand:

performance optimization is not the responsibility of one team, but a covenant of the whole civilization.

Reform was not easy.

At first, many complained about reduced efficiency.

New features took longer to launch, designers' ideas were often rejected, and algorithmic innovations were required to sacrifice real-time behavior.

Some even said this would make Spotify lose its competitiveness.

But over time, results showed.

Users began saying in the comments:

"Spotify is finally smooth."

"My phone no longer heats up."

"The experience is much better than a few months ago."

These pieces of feedback boosted confidence more than any flashy feature.

The team gradually accepted: performance optimization is not an obstacle, but a moat.

Through this process they gradually realized a deeper truth:

The true meaning of performance optimization is not to make the system run fastest, but to keep the system stable.

Chasing the extreme of speed may bring momentary cheers, but it also lets complexity slip in through the cracks.

Only stability can resist the erosion of time.

It was like the army of an empire.

The lifespan of an empire is not decided by the fastest cavalry, but by the most stable supply lines.

Cavalry can win a battle, but supply lines sustain territories for a hundred years.

Spotify's team eventually wrote an internal document titled:

"The Philosophy of Performance Optimization."

The document opened with:

"The goal of performance optimization is not showmanship, but stability.

Do not chase extremes, but pursue clarity.

Do not worship miracles, but build institutions.

We do not compete over whose animations are cooler; we make users trust that every click is predictable.

This is the value of our existence."

This document circulated within the company and was regarded as the team's constitution.

It changed developers' mindsets and the team's culture.

"Spotify's turning point was not because SwiftUI's flaws were fixed, but because they learned to coexist with complexity.

They understood: performance optimization is not a one-time victory, but a long-term restraint."

Here we can see a larger truth:

The opponent of complexity has never been speed, but stability.

The enemy of Cognitive Load has never been features, but disorder.

True performance optimization is not the accumulation of tricks, but the establishment of a culture.

SwiftUI is only a tool: it provides declarative power, but it also brings the pitfalls of redraws and state.

Instruments is only a map: it reveals the shape of the maze, but it does not provide the exit.

In the end, the true answer lies not in technology, but in people.

It was the team that chose restraint, the culture that chose clarity, the developers that chose boundaries.

The longevity of an empire lies not in the speed of its cavalry but in the stability of its supply lines.
The longevity of software lies not in dazzling extremes but in clear moderation.
Complexity cannot be conquered, but it can be tamed;
Humans cannot be surpassed, but they can exercise restraint.
This is the true meaning of performance optimization.

CHAPTER 23
THE PHILOSOPHY OF OPTIMIZATION

Empires that chase extremes often collapse at their peak.

Only civilizations that hold onto stability have a chance to span centuries.

Complexity is a kind of weight.

At first it is so light you hardly notice it.

But as a system expands, as users grow, as dependencies stack exponentially, complexity becomes heavy like accumulated snow.

Faced with it, engineers are often tempted:

To chase extremes, to prove they can run at the pinnacle of performance.

Yet history repeatedly shows: enduring empires are never built on extremes, but on stability.

Netflix's story is a true illustration of this rule.

It was a moment to be remembered.

Netflix was no longer a DVD-by-mail company, but the synonym for global video streaming.

Their users were spread across the world, and their app appeared on every platform:

From iOS to Android, from TVs to set-top boxes, from browsers to game consoles.

Any slight tremor would be magnified into a global experience difference.

For Netflix, performance was a belief.

They had to ensure video played smoothly under any network condition,

To ensure the UI kept consistent interaction logic across devices,

To ensure every tap and every swipe did not betray users' expectations.

So the temptation of extreme optimization appeared.

Engineers saw countless opportunities:

on iOS, they could use the lowest-level APIs to squeeze the GPU's potential;

In the player, they could tune caching strategies to pursue millisecond-level responses;

In the recommendation system, they could leverage new machine learning frameworks to compress ranking time to the extreme.

These attempts were exhilarating, as if the empire were building a tower to the sky.

However, complexity never applauds ambition.

It only buries new risks in each extreme optimization.

The first crack appeared in the player.

To pursue millisecond-level startup speed, engineers radically optimized the caching logic.

They had the app preload videos users might play in the background, even trying to predict before a user clicked.

In the lab, the effect of this optimization was stunning: videos started almost instantly, and latency was reduced to the point of being imperceptible.

However, when this logic was rolled out to global users, problems erupted.

On some low-end devices, preloading caused memory usage to skyrocket and the app to crash frequently.

Under certain network conditions, background downloads triggered additional bandwidth consumption, prompting user complaints.

The achievements of extremes vanished in the face of reality.

Complexity laughed.

It knew that the cost of extreme optimization does not appear immediately, but is magnified at global scale.

Every device difference, every network fluctuation, is its ally.

Engineers' pride, in its eyes, was merely a new crack.

The second crack appeared at the UI layer.

To make browsing smoother for users, the team tried replacing system-native components with a self-developed rendering engine.

In test environments, scrolling speed doubled and animation frame drops almost disappeared.

It was a moment of glory for the engineers; they proved they could surpass the platform's limits.

But in the real world, this custom engine quickly exposed problems.

After system upgrades, some APIs were deprecated, causing rendering anomalies;

screen adaptation issues across different devices multiplied testing costs;

and worst of all, the team maintaining this engine gradually sank into a quagmire.

They had to follow every platform update, fix countless edge bugs, and in the end the result differed little from native.

This is the trap of extreme optimization.

You think you control the future, but in reality you have only taken on another debt.

The platform evolves, while you are trapped by your own pride.

The third crack appeared in the recommendation system.

Recommendation is Netflix's soul.

Engineers hoped to use the latest machine learning frameworks to compress ranking time to the millisecond.

They built massive models, optimized distributed computation, and even designed a lightweight inference engine specifically for mobile.

In papers and reports, it was all brilliant and dazzling.

But in actual user experience, the difference was hardly noticeable.

Users rarely notice differences in recommendation latency; they care more about:

Whether the app is stable, whether playback is smooth, whether interactions are intuitive.

When the team poured vast resources into extreme optimization but neglected stability, they lost the most precious thing: users' patience.

Netflix's engineers gradually realized:

Chasing extremes is like an empire pursuing the maximal expansion of its territory.

The farther the territory extends, the more fragile the supply lines become, and the more likely frontier generals are to lose control.

What truly determines an empire's lifespan has never been the breadth of its territory, but the stability of its institutions.

In the world of software, what truly determines a system's life is not extreme performance, but a stable experience.

Users won't stay because startup is 50 milliseconds faster, but they will leave forever because of a single crash.

Users won't be moved because recommendation ranking is a bit faster, but they will be furious because playback stutters.

The first lesson complexity teaches humanity is to distinguish illusion from essence.

Extremes are an illusion; stability is the essence.

Netflix's transformation did not happen overnight.

It formed through countless failed optimizations, through repeated crash reports, through stacks of user complaint emails.

They began to redefine their goals:

Not "push performance to the extreme," but "keep the experience stable."

They cut back excessive preloading logic and shifted focus to robust memory management.

They abandoned the custom rendering engine, returned to native components, and aligned with the platform's evolution.

They reduced extreme compression in the recommendation system and allocated more resources to testing and monitoring.

All of this was not because they stopped pursuing progress, but because they understood:

the longevity of a civilization relies not on extremes, but on restraint.

On this path, SwiftUI's philosophy becomes especially clear.

It does not chase extreme performance, but clear declarative logic.

It tells developers: UI is a projection of state, not a machine to be endlessly squeezed.

It reminds us: true optimization is not making machines run faster, but making things easier for humans to understand.

Stability over extremes is not only an engineering choice, but a wisdom of cognition.

Because human attention is limited, wasting it on extreme optimization is a betrayal of the future.

Empires once expanded their territories to the limit, but what remains in the end is not glorious land, but clear institutions.

Netflix's story is like an inscription in the desert, reminding us:

Chasing extremes often means collapse;

Holding onto stability is what endures.

Kingdoms that chase speed often forget to repair their roads.

Teams that pursue extremes often forget the limits of their mental capacity.

Stability is time's true ally.

The flood of complexity never reveals itself immediately.

It is like a dormant seismic fault line, quietly accumulating energy.

As engineers continue down the road of extreme optimization, they think they are building a tower to the sky.

But deep in the foundation, cracks have already spread.

Over years of exploration, Netflix gradually understood: extremes are not the goal; stability is what defines a civilization.

The turning point came with a global incident.

It was an ordinary weekend night.

North American users were preparing to watch the premiere of a new series, and European viewers were waiting for the subtitled version to go live.

Server traffic peaked and all systems were running at full capacity.

At that moment, the player's new caching strategy suddenly triggered unexpected behavior.

It misallocated memory under high concurrency, causing some devices to crash.

Millions of users worldwide were affected.

On social media, angry voices flooded in.

Engineers stayed up through the night; teams scattered across the globe worked around the clock to fix it.

They left countless screenshots, logs, and postmortem analyses in Slack channels.

Finally, when everything was restored, leadership had to face one question:

"Why are we risking things at the limit instead of investing in stability?"

After the incident, Netflix began to reassess its philosophy.

They found that many past optimizations, while dazzling in the lab, were fragile in the real world.

Meanwhile, those choices that seemed conservative often held the line when it mattered most.

So they established a new principle:

Stability takes precedence over extremes.

This principle was not a slogan on the wall, but something that permeated every line of design, every meeting, every test.

The first thing to change was the team's culture.

In the past, engineers were incentivized to chase performance breakthroughs.

Whoever could shave another 20 milliseconds off startup time was a hero;

Whoever could make the recommendation system a bit faster earned the stage.

But this culture cultivated short-term pride and indulged complexity.

Because each extreme optimization is like digging a new well in the desert:

At first fresh water gushes forth, but over time the surface becomes riddled with cracks.

In the new culture, stability became the primary value.

Discussions in meetings were no longer "can we be faster?" but "can we be more stable?"

The focus in reviews shifted from "how clever is this optimization?" to "will this logic still be understandable three years from now?"

Teams stopped worshiping short-term miracles and learned restraint and clarity.

This cultural shift was not easy.

Many engineers were used to proving themselves with

"breakthroughs" and were reluctant to accept praise for "boring" code.

But history kept reminding them: the most powerful systems are often the most ordinary.

An empire's longevity depends not on frequent miracles but on clear institutions.

The second change was the boundaries of the architecture.

Netflix's engineers reexamined the core logic of the player.

They found that many bugs did not stem from technical difficulty but from ambiguous boundaries.

Cache logic and rendering logic were tangled; preloading and memory management lacked isolation; the result was that any single change could trigger chain reactions.

So they decided to redraw the boundaries.

Every module of the player was given clear responsibilities, clear inputs and outputs.

Complex logic was hidden inside deep modules;

The interfaces exposed to the outside remained simple and stable.

This architectural shift was like an empire redrawing its provinces:

no longer letting local generals expand at will, but making institutions define the borders.

Complexity was contained within controllable bounds instead of being scattered into every corner.

In the process, they abandoned many of the "black magic" tricks they once took pride in.

Techniques that improved performance by 5% were judged not worth the cost;

Logic that only a few experts could understand was decisively refactored.

They learned that true optimization is not making machines faster, but making the team more resilient.

The third change was the testing and monitoring system.

Past testing focused more on extreme scenarios:

Can video play under the worst network conditions?

Can recommendations return under peak concurrency?

Those tests were important, but incomplete.

Because what truly affects user experience is not extreme scenarios, but everyday ones.

Users won't always be on the worst network, nor will they always encounter the highest concurrency.

They just want to be able to open Netflix smoothly every day and finish watching the shows they want.

Therefore, the testing system was rebuilt.

Engineers assigned a higher weight to stability.

They not only paid attention to extreme cases, but focused more on the 99% everyday scenarios.

Monitoring systems were also strengthened, reporting not only crash rates but also minor performance fluctuations.

This shift was like an empire beginning to prioritize road maintenance over border expansion.

The smoothness of the roads is the key to whether caravans can travel for the long term.

Behind all of this lies a deeper philosophy:

Stability is not stagnation; stability is restraint.

Restraint means:

When you have the chance to squeeze out the last 5% of performance, you choose to stop.

When you face a "clever" optimization, you choose to be skeptical.

When you could see a miracle in three months, you choose clarity three years from now.

This philosophy is not unique to Netflix.

In the iOS world, SwiftUI embodies the same spirit.

SwiftUI's declarative syntax does not chase extreme performance.

It pursues consistency, comprehensibility, and stability.

You describe state; the system is responsible for rendering.

You define boundaries; the platform takes care of optimization.

The core of this philosophy is not "how to be faster," but "how to be more stable."

In this sense, Netflix's transformation is in harmony with SwiftUI's spirit.

They both tell developers:

The end point of optimization is not extremes, but stability.

An empire's territory can be expanded to the limit, but it will ultimately decline when supply lines break.

The power of a civilization lies not in moments of miracle but in sustained stability.

After the incident, Netflix chose stability first.

They did not abandon optimization, but they redefined its boundaries.

They learned that extremes are an illusion; stability is the cornerstone.

Great civilizations are not famed for speed but endure by stamina.

At the peak of speed there is only the sound of wind; in the depths of stability there is order.

The story of complexity is never ended by a single incident.

It will reappear in every choice.

And Netflix's decisions were gradually clarified through one choice after another.

Once they established the "stability-first" philosophy, the fate of the entire team changed.

This was not a slogan on paper, but a culture that penetrated to the marrow, an order deeply embedded in the architecture.

The first payoff was global resilience.

In the age of chasing extremes, Netflix was often troubled by localized problems.

An optimization might succeed for North American users but completely fail in the India market;

A trick might perform perfectly on the latest iPhone but become a disaster on low-end devices.

When stability became the core, their perspective changed.

Optimizations were no longer aimed at being "the fastest" but measured by "the most stable."

They ran large numbers of experiments globally to ensure any change would behave consistently across different networks, devices, and markets.

The result was:

Even in bandwidth-starved countryside, Netflix still ran smoothly;

Even on old devices, the app remained responsive;

Even during sudden traffic surges, the system could still maintain service.

This resilience became Netflix's moat.

Other competitors might beat them on a particular performance metric, but none could maintain that kind of global stability.

The second payoff was team cohesion.

In the era of extremes, teams often fractured.

Some people chased performance breakthroughs while others were worn out fixing bugs.

Cross-platform coordination, expert bottlenecks, and the risks of "black magic" continuously drained the team's mental resources.

In the era of stability, restraint replaced recklessness.

The goal of code was no longer showmanship but understandability.

The goal of architecture was no longer extraction but clear division of responsibility.

The team's goal was no longer "faster" but "more stable."

This consensus reunited the team as a whole.

Reviews were no longer about poking holes in each other but about jointly maintaining stability boundaries;

Meetings were no longer debates about extremes but consensus on stability;

Culture no longer idolized heroes but praised patience.

Engineers began to understand:

True pride was not in shaving 10 milliseconds off latency, but in making the logic still readable to a newcomer three years later.

The third payoff was the industry's lesson.

When Netflix publicly shared their transformation, the whole industry was shaken.

They wrote plainly in their tech blog:

"We lost stability while chasing extremes; and when we held on to stability, we gained a real advantage."

This sentence was quoted by countless teams.

It became a mirror that made every developer reflect:

What exactly are we chasing?

Are we proving the power of technology, or protecting the user experience?

Are we showcasing the engineer's glory, or ensuring the longevity of civilization?

In the iOS community, the emergence of SwiftUI resonated with this trend.

SwiftUI's philosophy is, itself, "stability first."

It gave up UIKit's unlimited flexibility in exchange for declarative consistency;

It rejected flashy performance extremes in exchange for reduced Cognitive Load;

It tells developers: you don't have to control everything — the platform will guard stability for you.

The longevity of a civilization does not lie in short-term brilliance, but in the continuation of institutions.

The longevity of software does not lie in extreme performance, but in a stable experience.

Netflix's story is merely a contemporary annotation of this rule.

They made a choice between extremes and stability; their choice not only saved themselves but also inspired countless followers.

Here, complexity is redefined.

It is no longer simply bugs, nor just chaotic code.

It is the tension between human cognition and technical ambition.

When ambition is excessive, complexity will turn on you;

When cognition is limited, stability is the only line of defense.

In this sense, "stability first" is not a retreat but the highest form of wisdom.

It acknowledges human limits and protects humanity's future.

The wind blows over the sea of sand, whipping up the remnants of old civilizations.

The empires that once chased extremes have long since turned to dust;

Those that understood how to protect stability still persist through time.

Netflix's transformation is a monument in the desert.

It tells us:

- Extremes are an illusion.
- Stability is the truth.
- The philosophy of optimization is not how to run the fastest, but how to walk the longest.

For iOS developers, this philosophy offers a more direct lesson.

In SwiftUI, you may be tempted to chase performance extremes:

Trying complex tricks to reduce redraws, trying black magic to circumvent the rules of state management.

These techniques may work in the short term, but will become technical debt in the future.

And when you follow the principles of stability:

Maintain a single source of truth, preserve a clear flow of state, and avoid excessive abstraction and clever tricks, your code may not be the fastest, but it will be the most stable.

Your future self will thank the restraint you exercise today.

This is the philosophy of stability.

It is not abandoning optimization, but choosing boundaries;

It is not rejecting progress, but embracing restraint;

It is not compromise, but clear-headedness.

True optimization is not about making the system faster, but about making civilization last longer.
True strength is not in conquering extremes, but in safeguarding stability.

CHAPTER 24
THE F.I.R.S.T. PRINCIPLES

The laws of an empire are not written for today's judgments, but established for stability a hundred years from now.

Software testing is the same. It is not to prove that you are correct now, but to guard the order of the future.

The wind does not stop because of walls, but walls can change the wind's direction. Complexity does not disappear because of wishes, but contracts can slow its erosion. The history of software civilization proves: systems without tests, like empires without laws, will eventually fall into chaos.

In the era when GitHub rose, they were not the first code hosting platform. Before them, SourceForge once enjoyed great glory; Bitbucket also offered seemingly powerful tools. But GitHub became an empire. Not only because of their product, but because they built a civilization behind it: a covenant of testing and continuous integration.

When the number of repositories grew from thousands to millions, when users were spread across the globe, when Pull Requests became the everyday form of communication, GitHub faced the fate any empire meets: exponential growth of complexity. They could not rely on manual checks to confirm every merge was safe; nor could they expect teams to judge by memory which features would be broken by new changes. Thus, tests became a covenant, the foundation by which civilization could continue.

Complexity first showed its edge in GitHub's history when they expanded their notification system. At first, notifications were just simple email alerts. Later, users needed browser notifications, mobile push, and Slack integration. Each new channel meant new state machines and new boundary conditions. If testing relied only on manual tests, any small change could cause tens of thousands of users to receive incorrect notifications.

Historians would say: this is an empire without a covenant, orders cannot be properly conveyed, borders will be chaotic. So GitHub then established strict testing guidelines. They realized that tests are not to find bugs, but to define boundaries. They are like law, telling future developers: this must not be crossed, this must remain clear.

The power of the covenant is distilled in the F.I.R.S.T. principles. Fast, Independent, Repeatable, Self-validating, Timely. These five words are not a slogan, but the cornerstones of civilization.

Fast, because an empire needs to maintain its tempo in every iteration. If tests are like sluggish relay stations, orders cannot reach the front line. For that reason, GitHub's engineering teams emphasized early on that tests must finish within minutes; no one should have to wait half a day to learn the result. This is not for comfort, but for the civilized rhythm.

Independent, because an empire's laws cannot depend on chance. Tests must run in isolated environments, must not rely on external networks, must not depend on some lucky state.

That means any engineer, on any machine, at any time, can reach the same conclusion. Otherwise law becomes oral promise, not written covenant.

Repeatable, because civilization must be auditable. If the same code passes tests today and fails tomorrow, the team cannot build trust. Trust is the currency of civilization. GitHub knew that only repeatable tests could make thousands of engineers believe they were working under the same order.

Self-validating, because civilization cannot rely on interpretation. Test results must be unambiguous: pass or fail, not require engineers to interpret logs or infer meaning. On a platform with millions of users, ambiguous signals rapidly turn into disaster.

Timely, because civilization must hold the threshold of the present. Tests must be completed before merging, not remedied after deployment. Laws that arrive late are not laws, but epitaphs.

In GitHub's practice, these five principles are more than words in a document. They are woven into the entire workflow. When a Pull Request is opened, automated tests start immediately; results return within minutes, clearly telling reviewers whether it is safe; any failing tests must be fixed before merging; the team does not allow crossing the covenant on the pretext of "merge first, fix later."

This severity does not constrain creativity; it protects it. Because of the covenant, engineers can safely try new features without worrying about inadvertently breaking old ones. Because of the covenant, reviewers can focus on architecture and design instead of wasting effort verifying boundary conditions.

What complexity fears most is the covenant. Because the covenant robs it of the space to spread silently. When GitHub makes testing the covenant, the growth of complexity is confined within clear boundaries. Every new feature is accompanied by new tests; every bug fix leaves law-like annotations to ensure the mistake is not repeated.

An empire's territory can expand, but its system of laws

keeps it from descending into chaos. Software functionality can increase, but the covenant of tests keeps it from becoming incomprehensible.

Yet complexity never gives up easily. It will look for new breaches. In GitHub's story, it chose the tests themselves.

As the system grew, the number of tests exploded. From the initial dozens, to hundreds, then thousands. Test run times began to lengthen; processes that once completed in minutes gradually took ten or fifteen minutes. Developers began to complain about waiting, and CI queues during peak hours sometimes took half an hour to return results.

Complexity smiled in the dark. It knew the covenant itself would become a burden. If the covenant is too heavy, the empire will slow.

This became GitHub's second fate: how to find a new balance between covenant and speed.

The weight of law can shelter an empire, but it can also drag it down.

When the volumes of law become too heavy for anyone to carry, people begin to forget their meaning.

Complexity's counterattack is always silent. After GitHub established tests as the civilizational covenant, in the short term they did achieve order: developers could iterate with confidence, reviewers could focus on design, and the rate of bug recurrence fell. Everything seemed to enter a golden age.

Yet behind that prosperity, complexity had not disappeared. It chose another path: it no longer lurked in the feature logic, but in the tests themselves.

In GitHub's infrastructure, the number of tests began to grow exponentially. Each feature expansion meant dozens of new test cases. Each system integration meant hundreds of new contractual boundaries. At a certain scale, their test suite already contained tens of thousands of tests.

The empire's volumes were expanding. Each test was a law, and every law had to be enforced. As a result, CI processes that once completed in minutes gradually took ten or fifteen minutes, even half an hour. At peak times, an engineer submitting a Pull Request had to wait up to an hour to get feedback.

Rhythm lost its speed. And rhythm is the pulse of civilization.

Waiting became the new enemy.

While waiting, engineers' attention was divided; while waiting, they turned to other tasks; by the time results came back, they had forgotten the context of their submission. Thus, bug fixes were delayed, discussion momentum was interrupted, and the pace of iteration gradually slowed.

This is complexity's trick: it makes the covenant itself a burden, turning the laws that guard civilization into shackles that drag it down.

GitHub's engineers realized that if things continued this way, they would fall into a "covenant paradox":

The more tests, the stronger the trust;

The more tests, the slower the speed;

When speed slows to the point the team cannot bear it, trust collapses.

It's like an empire's laws. If laws are too cumbersome and the judicial process becomes suffocatingly long, citizens will choose to bypass the law. If test execution takes too long, engineers will tend to bypass tests and look for shortcuts. And once shortcuts become the norm, civilization begins to crumble.

To counter this trend, GitHub began to seek a new order. They had to find a balance between covenant and speed.

The first step was layered testing.

GitHub's testing system was reorganized:

- The most basic unit tests, which run fastest and cover the core logic.
- A higher layer of integration tests, covering critical module interactions.
- The top layer of end-to-end tests, covering the system's critical paths.

This layered logic is like an empire's administrative system.
Not every matter needs the emperor's personal judgment;
Not every dispute needs the highest court.
Most matters can be resolved locally.

Unit tests are the local rulings. Integration tests are the regional governors. End-to-end tests are the empire's highest law.

Through layering, GitHub concentrated the vast majority of tests at the fast layer, so engineers receive feedback within minutes; the more complex integration and end-to-end tests run on longer cycles to ensure thoroughness.

This is not loosening the law, but stratifying it, allowing the pulse of civilization to regain its rhythm.

The second step was parallel execution.

As GitHub's user base exploded, their testing infrastructure had to bear enormous load. Running tests single-threaded was like a narrow post road where only one caravan can move slowly through. The empire needed multiple roads to carry information and goods simultaneously.

So GitHub invested in large-scale parallel infrastructure. They distributed test cases across hundreds of machines to run concurrently, cutting processes that once took an hour down to under ten minutes.

This power of parallelism made waiting bearable again. Engineers were no longer forced to pace anxiously in conference rooms; they could maintain their iteration rhythm. The pulse of civilization beat again.

The third step was shaping culture.

A covenant is not only a tool but a culture. If tests are merely automated commands without cultural buy-in, they will eventually be avoided, bypassed, or reduced to formality.

GitHub's culture emphasized "tests as covenant." Pull Request reviewers cared not only whether the code was elegant but also whether sufficient tests were included. If a submission lacked tests, reviewers would explicitly require them to be added. This was not nitpicking, but guarding the covenant of civilization.

GitHub's engineers gradually reached a consensus: writing tests is not a burden, but leaves clear boundaries for future engineers. Tests are not constraints on creativity, but the moat that protects it.

When cultural buy-in and tooling combine, the covenant truly takes effect.

However, the war with complexity never ends.

GitHub solved test layering and parallelization and restored rhythm; but complexity kept seeking new breaches. This time, it chose test quality.

When the number of tests becomes vast, redundancy and fragility inevitably appear. Some tests cover the same logic and waste time; some tests over-rely on implementation details, causing small changes to trigger large-scale failures. These fragile tests are like corrupt officials of the empire—seeming to perform duties while actually consuming resources.

Complexity whispered in the dark: "You think quantity is safety, but quantity is also chaos."

This is the next challenge GitHub must face in the covenant of civilization: how to ensure tests not only exist, but are reliable, clear, and maintainable over the long term.

The number of tests is already sufficient; the problem is quality. The volumes of law are already vast; the problem is how to make them truly enforced.

The empire's prosperity still hung in the shadow of complexity. The turning point had not yet come.

If laws are not cleaned, they will be covered in dust;

If covenants are not maintained, they will become empty words.

The longevity of civilization depends on continually mending its own covenants.

Complexity's second counterattack was silent. When GitHub's engineers solved the speed problem of testing through layering and parallelism, they thought they had won stability. They found, however, that new cracks were already spreading from within.

Redundancy is like wildfire in the grass. In GitHub's testing system, as teams expanded and features accumulated, more and more tests began to cover the same logic. Different engineers, at different times and out of different concerns, wrote similar tests. These redundant tests did not immediately show harm; but within a system of tens of thousands of cases, they gradually slowed feedback and increased maintenance costs.

Fragility is like cracks in the city walls. Some tests depend too much on implementation details rather than behavioral boundaries. When underlying code is tweaked, tests can fail en masse even though external behavior remains correct. The red failure lights flash on the CI dashboard, creating false panic. Engineers have to waste hours fixing these spurious failures, and over time their trust in the tests is eroded.

What complexity does best is destroy trust. When the results of the covenant are questioned, when the authority of the law is weakened, civilization begins to decay.

GitHub's engineers convened a special internal meeting. The topic was not new features, not architectural evolution, but — testing.

At that meeting, a senior engineer said, "We have been held

hostage by our tests. They were once protectors; now they have become drains."

The remark stunned those present. It revealed a truth: tests themselves accumulate complexity. If left unguided, tests will, like production code, become a new burden.

So GitHub launched their third round of governance—the revolution in test quality.

Step one: remove redundancy.

The team carried out a large-scale audit of the test suite. They used tools to scan for overlapping coverage and analyze which tests were logically equivalent. The results were startling: among tens of thousands of cases, a substantial portion was duplicate work. These tests did not increase trust but lengthened waits.

So GitHub decisively deleted redundancies. Like an empire clearing redundant officials and soldiers, they removed tests that "appeared to guard but actually consumed." This cleanup was not a weakening but a strengthening. Trust's value lies not in quantity but in clarity.

Step two: strengthen resilience.

They established new guidelines: tests must rely on behavior, not implementation. In other words, tests should focus on "whether the result meets expectations," not "how the code achieves it."

For example, for a search feature, the test's focus is on correct results, not which sorting algorithm is used. Algorithms may evolve, but behavior must remain stable.

This shift made tests less fragile. Implementation details can change without causing mass failures; tests only alarm when behavior truly deviates.

The laws of civilization must be grounded in behavior, not process. Otherwise laws will be overturned by trivial details and ultimately lose credibility.

Step three: build a guardianship culture.

GitHub changed not only tools and guidelines but also culture. They emphasized: tests are not an accumulation of numbers, but an accumulation of trust. Every test must answer one question: "Does it guard a critical cognitive boundary for the future?"

This culture avoids the trap of blindly chasing coverage. Coverage can be quantified, but trust cannot. Trust comes from tests genuinely reducing Cognitive Load, not generating new noise.

Complexity was forced back again in this revolution. GitHub's testing system became leaner, more resilient, and more trustworthy. Redundancy was removed, fragility was repaired, and the culture was strengthened.

Pull Request reviewers regained their sense of trust. When they saw the green light, they knew it meant real safety; when red lights flashed, they knew it signaled real problems.

This trust is the currency of civilization. Without it, teams fall into chaos; with it, teams can stand unfazed before the flood of complexity.

Yet complexity still waits in the distance, biding its time. It will not disappear; it will only wait. It knows that human minds are limited, tools have boundaries, and cultural transmission is finite. But in GitHub's history of civilization, this time it was temporarily contained.

The F.I.R.S.T. principles, in this chapter of history, revealed their true meaning.

Fast—not for comfort, but for the preservation of rhythm;

Independent—not for isolation, but to eliminate flakiness;

Repeatable—not for mechanical repetition, but for the continuation of trust;

Self-validating—not to save effort, but for clear adjudication;

Timely—not to rush schedules, but to defend boundaries.

These five principles are not only engineering rules but a covenant of civilization. They allow thousands of engineers distributed around the world to collaborate under the same order; they allow millions of users relying on the same platform to continually receive a consistent experience.

GitHub's story tells us: tests are not "accessories"; they are the foundation of civilization. Without tests, complexity will breed in the dark; when tests run out of control, complexity will strike back within the covenant. Only by treating tests as a civic covenant and continually mending them can they truly guard the future.

In a broader history, the F.I.R.S.T. principles are not merely technical guidelines but a response to cognitive load. Human minds are limited; complexity is infinite. Tests are the levee raised between the finite and the infinite. They are not perfect; they leak, they age; but as long as people keep repairing them, they can protect the city of civilization from being swallowed by floods.

Ultimately, the meaning of tests is not to "prove correctness" but to reduce the future cost of understanding. It is mercy toward the future, compassion for the team, and a fight against complexity.

Tests are not the language of machines, but a covenant of humans.
They let your future self still understand your present self;
They keep the team's memory from being swallowed by complexity;
They allow the civilization of software to continue.

CHAPTER 25
SWIFTUI'S TESTING

An unverified system is not a system, but an illusion.

An empire can exist on a map, yet may collapse in reality.

The wind does not need strength; it only needs patience.

A grain of sand can easily be overlooked, but when countless sand and dust accumulate over the years, a city can be buried.

Testing is to software what a dam is to a flood. It is not decoration, but a barrier.

Without a barrier, the water will not immediately swallow the land, but it will slowly erode it until the empire collapses.

Lyft's engineering team has long understood this.

Their app is more than just a map plus a payment button.

Behind it is a vast ecosystem: real-time matching, dynamic pricing, route planning, two-way coordination between drivers and passengers.

Any small error can trigger a chain reaction: drivers unable to accept rides, passengers unable to pay, the city's traffic network thrown into chaos.

In such an environment, testing is no longer a luxury; it is a matter of life and death.

Without testing, it's as if an empire has lost the accounting of its granaries, the patrols on its roads, and the watchtowers at its ports.

Everything may seem prosperous, but is actually precarious.

In its early expansion, Lyft also underestimated the value of testing.

Their goal was speed, rapid iteration, and covering more cities in the shortest time.

In the first few years, engineers devoted almost all their energy to feature development and market expansion.

Testing existed, but it was fragmented, fragile, and unsystematic.

In a major update, this fragility was completely exposed.

It was an apparently ordinary feature: allowing passengers to choose "ride-sharing along the way" when placing an order; the system would automatically match them with passengers heading in the same direction.

The logic of this feature was extremely complex:

- It required real-time calculation of each driver's route deviation;
- It required dynamic adjustment of fares;
- It required instantly updating passengers' waiting times in the interface.

The team launched the feature but underestimated its risks.

They relied on manual testing during development and neglected systematic verification.

On the night it launched, many users reported that carpool prices were calculated incorrectly; some people paid more than the cost of a single-person ride.

Meanwhile, a bug on the driver side caused route planning confusion, forcing drivers to take detours.

Complexity erupted like a flood. In just a few hours, Lyft's customer support system was overwhelmed, social media was filled with complaints, and the pressure of public opinion forced senior management to hold an emergency meeting through the night. In the end, they had to urgently take the feature offline and calm the anger with compensation.

The incident was internally dubbed "Carpool Night." It made the whole team realize: speed can bring short-term victories, but speed without tests is just running on quicksand. Complexity will not disappear because of your ambition; it will quietly expand wherever things are unverified until it swallows your system.

From that night on, Lyft's team entered a new era. They decided to build a systematic testing framework, using tests as the empire's laws and covenants to restrain the flood of complexity. They adopted a simple principle: any feature not covered by tests is not a real feature.

Unit tests are the empire's tax records. They are not grand, but they are indispensable. Every piece of logic, every calculation must have explicit verification. Engineers began to add fine-grained unit tests into SwiftUI's view logic. Not to chase coverage numbers, but to ensure every branch and every state remained within a controllable range.

Snapshot tests are the empire's map. SwiftUI's declarative UI brings convenience but also risk: a tiny change can unintentionally alter the entire layout. In one update, Lyft's team once introduced a minor change that caused buttons on the passenger interface to overlap the map, preventing users from placing orders. The introduction of snapshot testing allowed them to quickly detect these potential deviations on every UI change. Just as a map makes an empire's territory visible, snapshot tests make the state of the UI immediately clear.

UI tests are the empire's patrols. They don't focus on single details but verify the overall flow: from opening the app, to selecting a destination, to completing payment. After the carpool incident, Lyft's team established end-to-end UI tests to ensure all critical paths could connect seamlessly. They even run these tests in every CI build, like posting patrols on every road to ensure order does not collapse.

Contract tests are the empire's treaties. Lyft's system depends on countless microservices: payments, maps, pricing, notifications. Any change in a single service can trigger an avalanche. Contract tests ensure clear boundaries between different services: as long as the contracts are not broken, the system can run stably. They are the arbiters of complexity, the covenants between competing forces.

But building a testing practice is not accomplished in one go. It requires a cultural shift, requiring the team to move from "feature-first" to "verification-first." In this process, Lyft's engineers went through countless debates and adjustments.

Some questioned: tests will slow down development. Some insisted: without tests, speed is just an illusion. This argument persisted across multiple quarters, until one real incident after another forced the skeptics to admit: tests are not a burden, but a liberation.

Complexity never disappears; it only chooses weak points to attack. The presence of tests prevents complexity from finding a breakthrough. They let your future self quickly understand and verify the choices made today.

None of this immediately changed Lyft's fate. But after "Carpool Night," they were no longer the same team. They began using the testing taxonomy to build an invisible wall for themselves. Unit, snapshot, UI, contract—each link a brick, each piece a barrier.

Complexity still lurked, but it no longer seeped in silently. The empire learned to keep watch.

An empire's territory is secured not by expansion but by the system's ability to self-heal.

Without systems, even the most splendid cities will crumble over time.

The wind has no shape, the water has no memory. The seepage of complexity is neither noisy nor violent. It is like the desert wind, blowing day after day, slowly wearing down stone pillars. If "Carpool Night" was a storm, then the years that followed were silent erosion.

Lyft's team learned their first lesson through pain: features can fail, speed can falter, but tests cannot be absent. From then on, they launched a reform at the organizational level. This was not a short-lived campaign, but the rebuilding of institutions.

The first transformation was in the toolchain.

Lyft pushed CI/CD to the extreme. After every commit, the system automatically runs hundreds or thousands of test cases. From the smallest unit tests to the most complex UI flows and contract verifications, every stage is included in the automation. Test results are no longer a developer's "conscience" but the system's "law."

One engineer once said, "Committing code is not writing a promise, but signing a contract." Because once a commit enters the pipeline, it must submit to the judgment of tests. Those who pass enter the mainline; those who fail are sent back for changes. No one can bypass the system, and no one can rely on personal luck to take shortcuts.

In this setup, complexity can no longer sneak in at will. It is forced to reveal itself, forced to be exposed. Every attempt to break a contract is intercepted on the pipeline.

It is like the checkpoints the empire sets up: every caravan and carriage must be inspected, every pedestrian must show a pass. The system does not rely on a general's memory but on the enforcement of law.

The second transformation was cultural.

No matter how tight the rules, people must follow them. If engineers still treat tests as a burden, the system will ultimately become ceremonial. Therefore, after "Carpool Night," Lyft's leadership elevated testing to a cultural principle.

They introduced an internal slogan: "Tests first, features second." This is not an empty slogan but a philosophy of survival. Features can be delayed, but a feature without tests cannot exist.

At first, the slogan met considerable resistance. Some engineers complained that writing tests wasted time and delayed releases. They were used to solving problems with experience and intuition and saw tests as an extra burden.

But after one real incident after another, that resistance gradually disappeared. They discovered that tests did not slow down speed but made speed real. Speed without tests is false speed—running on sand. Speed with tests is real speed—traveling on solid ground.

Cultural change is not achieved in a day. It requires countless failures, countless verifications, until the team realizes: tests are not for machines but for people. They are your future self's demand of your present self.

The third transformation appears in the context of SwiftUI.

Lyft's team quickly realized that SwiftUI's state-driven model introduced new challenges. In the world of UIKit, tests often relied on manual event-driven interactions and UI verification. But in SwiftUI, the interface is driven entirely by state. This means:

- Any omission of state can cause UI anomalies.
- Any improper state transition can trigger logical chaos.
- Any uncovered combination can become a breeding ground for complexity.

In one iteration they encountered this problem: when a rider switched payment methods during booking, the interface would occasionally freeze. Engineers initially suspected an animation bug, but later discovered it was a lapse in state management. A boolean wasn't being reset correctly, causing the UI to fail to respond to new input.

After the bug was discovered, the team held heated internal discussions. Some said it was a problem of insufficient test coverage; others said it was an architectural design issue. Ultimately, they reached a consensus: in the world of SwiftUI, tests must be bound to state.

So the team began to build a new testing strategy: not only testing the UI itself, but testing every change of state. They made state-machine-ification a core idea, bringing every state combination into the test suite. In the process they discovered: tests are not just guarantees, but an extension of the architecture.

Complexity still existed; it would not be eliminated by policy, only take another form. Lyft's engineers found that as the testing system gradually improved, complexity no longer concentrated on "functional defects" but shifted to "the tests themselves."

They began to encounter new problems:

- Tests ran too slowly, causing CI queues to back up.
- Snapshot tests were too sensitive; an insignificant change could cause widespread failures.
- UI tests occasionally produced "false positives," wasting the team's time chasing non-existent bugs.
- Contract tests required coordination across teams, increasing communication overhead.

At this point, complexity seemed to wear a different face. It no longer disguised itself as bugs, but as "test noise." Engineers grew tired: they found they were spending almost as much time fixing tests as developing features.

This is the shadow of complexity. It is never destroyed; it

only transfers. You think you have built a dam, but it seeps through the dam's cracks.

At an internal sharing session, a senior engineer said:

"Testing is not an endpoint, but a new starting point.

We have built a testing system, but complexity still approaches on another level.

We need a higher level of clarity, otherwise the tests themselves will become a burden."

The remark triggered a long silence.

Everyone understood: testing is not a panacea.

It can defend against complexity, but it can also create new complexity.

True wisdom is not in building tests, but in balancing them.

At this moment, Lyft's story entered a new phase.

They were no longer satisfied with mere coverage and began to pursue "cognitive optimization" of tests.

They wanted to reduce noise, reduce context switching, and make testing a natural part of development.

They began to explore:

- How to make tests faster so CI can complete verification in minutes;
- How to make snapshot tests smarter, filtering out irrelevant differences;
- How to make UI tests more stable, reducing false positives;
- How to make contract tests more transparent so cross-team communication is no longer a burden.

This was a more difficult battle.

Because it was no longer just a matter of process, but a matter of philosophy:

The goal of testing is not to validate machines, but to reduce human cognitive load.

When the first line of defense is built, the enemy does not disappear but looks for new breaches.

Complexity is such an enemy.

It shifts from bugs to tests, from features to systems, from explicit problems to hidden costs.

At this moment, Lyft's team stood at a new threshold.

They had a solid dam, but they had to learn how to maintain the dam, not be trapped by it.

The flood of complexity still flows in the dark.

The walls of tests are rising, but the systems and culture inside those walls still need new order.

The real test has only just begun.

The continuation of civilization does not lie in a single great victory, but in long-term self-restraint.

Testing is not a weapon to conquer complexity, but a system to coexist with it.

The wind kept blowing, the sand kept piling up. Complexity did not stop; it merely regrouped in new corners. Lyft's team knew they had already passed through two stages:

The first stage was the chaos without tests, where complexity erupted as bugs;

The second stage was the establishment of testing systems, where complexity shifted into test noise.

Now they had to enter a third stage: make tests reduce burden, not add to it.

The transformation began with snapshot tests.

SwiftUI interfaces are declarative—changing any single property can alter the entire layout. Snapshot tests were meant to guard interface stability, but they were too sensitive. A one-pixel shift, a tweak to a shadow, or an animation change unrelated to the business could trigger hundreds of test failures.

Engineers grew weary of dealing with these irrelevant differences. In meetings they complained:

"We're not protecting user experience; we're protecting pixels."

So the team began to overhaul snapshot testing. They introduced a diff-filtering mechanism to let tests ignore changes that don't affect functionality or readability. They established layered verification: strict checks for critical paths, lenient checks for non-critical paths. They turned snapshots from a "harsh judge" into a "measured gatekeeper."

This layering was like the evolution of an empire's laws. Early laws treated all offenses the same and punished them equally. The result was courts overwhelmed and the system rigid. Later, the law learned to distinguish: leniency for minor offenses, severity for major ones. Only then could the empire achieve lasting stability.

Next came the dilemma of UI tests.

End-to-end UI tests are the closest validation to real users, but they are also the most fragile. A network hiccup or an unrelated system notification could cause a test to fail. In Lyft's CI queue, false positives from UI tests became commonplace. Engineers spent hours investigating, only to find the "error" didn't exist.

The shadow of complexity reappeared:

It made people doubt the system, lose patience, and question the value of tests.

The team did not give up.

- Core flows must be covered, with secondary flows supplemented by unit and contract tests.
- UI tests should only verify key interactions, not exhaustively cover every detail.
- Test results allow retries to filter out flaky failures.

UI tests transformed from an "omnipresent police force" into "sentries at critical nodes." They no longer disrupt the daily development rhythm but stand guard where it truly matters.

The evolution of contract testing felt more like a diplomatic revolution.

Lyft's system depends on countless microservices: payments, maps, pricing, push notifications. These services belong to different teams, and the boundaries of complexity are often blurred. The original intent of contract tests was to ensure each service adhered to its contract, but they also brought huge communication costs.

In early practice, changing an interface required coordination among multiple teams, and tests often became the cause of delays. Someone complained: "We're not writing code; we're drafting diplomatic documents."

But the enemy of complexity is the blurring of boundaries. Without contracts, dependencies between services wind like vines until responsibilities cannot be distinguished.

Lyft's team gradually realized that the value of contract testing lies not in enforcement but in transparency. It makes boundaries clear and responsibilities traceable. So they built a shared platform for contract documents, allowing all teams to view dependencies in real time. They stopped treating contracts as a burden and started treating them as a map. A map does not hinder travel; a map makes travel safer.

In the process, Lyft's culture was quietly shifting.

At first, tests were seen as a burden; later, as law; and now, as language.

Engineers no longer argued about "whether to write tests"; they discussed "which tests are appropriate." They no longer saw testing as an extra task but integrated it into the design process. When a new feature is proposed, the team's first reaction is not "how to implement it" but "how to verify it."

This shift made tests no longer a patch applied afterward but a constraint up front. It brought complexity into the light at its inception rather than scrambling to address it when it later erupted.

The particularities of SwiftUI further elevated this culture.

SwiftUI's state-driven nature means everything stems from state. Therefore, the philosophy of testing must also revolve around state. Lyft's team said in an internal sharing:

"If we can cover all states, we can cover all possibilities."

They began to build a testing matrix based on state enumerations. Every state combination was listed, and every possible transition was verified. This approach fused testing with architecture and merged verification with design.

Complexity still existed, but it was brought into a controllable framework. This was not to eliminate complexity, but to tame it.

In the end, Lyft found its balance.

They no longer pursued 100% coverage, nor did they blindly believe in any single test's omnipotence. They established a lineage:

- Unit tests guard logic, like tax records;
- Snapshot tests guard the UI, like territorial maps;
- UI tests guard flows, like patrolling sentries;
- Contract tests guard boundaries, like diplomatic treaties.

The four are not isolated but complementary. They form an organic whole, like an empire's civil and military system: taxation, maps, patrols, and diplomacy—none can be lacking.

Complexity was never defeated. It still lurked in the corners of the system, waiting for new opportunities. But in Lyft's world, it was no longer an invisible storm but a tide that could be perceived. The tide still rises and falls, but the dam had been built.

This journey leaves us three lessons:

First, testing is not a machine's need but a human need. Its purpose is not to make code run faster, but to allow humans to understand and maintain the system. Its essence is to reduce future Cognitive Load.

Second, testing does not eliminate complexity but manages it. Complexity will not disappear because of tests, but it will be brought into an institutional framework. It still exists, but it is no longer out of control.

Third, testing is not a single tool but a lineage. Unit, snapshot, UI, and contract tests are like institutions, laws, culture, and diplomacy—they depend on and complement one another.

Only a lineage can withstand complexity's multi-faceted onslaught.

Lyft's story is not an ending but a footnote. It tells us: testing is not cold, impersonal technology, but the language of software civilization. In the world of SwiftUI, this language is especially important. Because the state-driven model brings unprecedented possibilities, it also brings unprecedented complexity.

The testing lineage is our contract with complexity. It allows our future selves, in a world of winds and shifting sands, to still see a clear path.

The greatest defense is not the height of the walls, but the clarity of institutions.
The greatest testing is not about sheer numbers, but about lightening the burden.

CHAPTER 26
CONTINUOUS INTEGRATION AND GUARDRAILS

An empire's territory is not maintained by land, but by roads and waystations.

The civilization of software is not maintained by features, but by processes and guardrails.

An empire without roads will crumble in silence; software without guardrails will rot in silence.

The real danger of complexity is not its sudden outbreak, but its subtle, insidious erosion.

Code decay does not happen overnight, but accumulates through one commit after another, one "we'll do it later" after another, one quick patch after another.

A human mind will not collapse because of a single bug, but will be gradually drained by hundreds of small problems.

For this reason, great teams establish processes to negotiate with complexity.

In ancient empires, those processes were roads, waystations, and taxes;

In the modern software world, those processes are continuous integration and static checks.

Google's story is enough to serve as a footnote to this civilization.

Inside Google, code is not merely an individual's expression, but the empire's archive.

Their entire codebase is called the "Monorepo"—a massive repository containing billions of lines of code.

This repository is not a free wilderness, but a city with strict rules.

Every street has guards, every door has locks, and everyone who enters must obey the law.

Google's engineers know clearly:

Without processes, this repository would collapse under its own weight.

They need a guardrail that prevents complexity from spreading at will.

Thus, continuous integration became their road system.

Every commit is automatically built, automatically tested, automatically analyzed.

Static checks act like the city's patrols; SwiftLint, Clang-Tidy, and custom static analyzers all look for possible cracks.

Once an anomaly is found, the build fails immediately, like a checkpoint on the road that stops a faulty caravan from entering the empire's core.

This is not about being harsh.

This is an act of mercy.

Imagine a world without guardrails:

- Engineers write code that contains potential memory leaks and merge it smoothly;
- Weeks later, a bug erupts in some corner, and the team spends days tracing it back to the source;
- The cost of explanation and the cost of fixing are magnified indefinitely.

This is the stealthy breach of the Cognitive Load threshold.

Human mental capacity is limited; once the threshold is exceeded, chaos quickly follows.

Teams without processes distribute all complexity evenly among everyone;

Teams with processes concentrate and digest complexity on the guardrail.

Google's CI system is not meant to restrict engineers, but to protect them.

It keeps complexity outside the gate, so every line of code that enters carries order.

However, processes are never naturally accepted.

When Google first introduced Gerrit code review, many engineers complained that it was too cumbersome:

"Why does the code I wrote need someone else's approval?"

"Why can't I submit if the build fails?"

"This slows us down."

Just as when an empire sets up checkpoints, there will always be complaints that the roads are no longer smooth.

But true wisdom lies in trading short-term inconvenience for long-term order.

Years later, those complaints gradually faded.

Engineers realized that without those processes they would spend more time struggling in chaos.

Processes are not shackles, but liberation.

They free human attention from trivial details and let people focus on the designs that truly matter.

Static checks are precisely this kind of process in action.

In the Swift world, static analysis can find many potential problems: inconsistent naming, unused variables, possible crash points.

Google's internal Swift team even customized rules for their projects to keep the team's code style consistent.

This consistency is not an aesthetic issue but a cognitive one.

When everyone follows the same rules, reading code is like reading the same language.

No one needs to worry about differences in indentation, chaotic naming, or arbitrary styles.

The burden of those details is borne by the process, preserving developers' mental capacity for understanding the real logic.

But complexity will not withdraw easily.

It will seek new entry points.

In Google's history, complexity was not thoroughly eradicated by processes.

It migrated into the processes themselves.

When there are too many rules, checks are too strict, and procedures too cumbersome, the processes themselves can become a Cognitive Load.

This is "process complexity."

If an empire's checkpoints are too numerous, caravans will collapse from the frequent stops.

If CI guardrails are too harsh, engineers will lose patience because of frequent failures.

So Google had to find a balance between process and flexibility.

They began to set different rules for different projects, give experimental features more freedom, and impose more constraints on core modules.

This is the true meaning of the Cognitive Load threshold:

Not to make complexity disappear, but to keep complexity stable within a range humans can bear.

Continuous integration and static checks are not merely technical tools, but the cornerstones of civilization.

They are like roads, checkpoints, and laws, maintaining the empire's order.

Without them, complexity would sweep everything like a sandstorm;

With them, complexity still exists, but is concentrated before the guardrails, allowing developers' minds to survive.

An empire without processes will collapse into chaos;
An empire overloaded with processes will suffocate under red tape.
True wisdom lies in finding the balance.
Complexity will not disappear; it will only migrate.

The original purpose of continuous integration is to keep complexity from crossing the guardrails.

The meaning of static checks is to catch errors at their bud.

Like an empire's border defenses, they initially played a tremendous role.

However, as in historical empires, once fortifications are built they tend to be continually reinforced;

once rules are established they tend to expand.

When guardrails become increasingly dense, they themselves become a form of complexity.

Google's Monorepo once faced such a dilemma.

At first, continuous integration was only simple compilation and unit testing.

- Every commit must pass the complete test suite;
- Every module must comply with static analysis rules;
- Every change must go through code review;
- Every comment must conform to the documentation generator's format.

Viewed individually, these rules are all reasonable.

But when they stack up, it's like an empire's checkpoints

multiplying—caravans must stop, be inspected, and pay tolls at every station.

In the end, engineers found that the cost of committing a single line of code exceeded their patience.

A story circulates in Google's internal archives.

An engineer needed to fix a tiny typo.

It was a copy bug in the user interface and required changing only one string.

He submitted the change on Gerrit.

The CI system started running and triggered thousands of tests.

Static analysis tools began checking and reported dozens of warnings unrelated to the change.

Code reviewers asked for additional comments, even though the change had nothing to do with logic.

In the end, fixing that typo took three days.

The story became a joke among engineers, but the laughter carried resignation.

Complexity had migrated from the code into the processes.

The guardrails that were meant to reduce Cognitive Load sometimes magnified it instead.

The emergence of process complexity is not unique to Google.

Throughout history, every organization that relied on processes to maintain order faced the same dilemma.

In the late Roman Empire, the tax system grew so complex that the levies farmers had to pay left land fallow;

In the Ming Dynasty of China, the bureaucracy became bloated, memorials were passed up and down in layers, and decision-making lagged far behind the battlefield.

These examples tell us: processes are necessary, but excessive process is equally lethal.

The software world is just an extension of this rule.

Continuous integration and static checks are the institutions of engineering civilization.

But without restraint, they too become fences that hinder progress.

Google's teams recognized this.

They began to reflect: the purpose of guardrails is not to create more rules, but to control Cognitive Load.

So a reform began.

They tiered the tests:

- Fast tests, used to catch the most obvious bugs, take only a few minutes to complete;
- Full tests, used to verify system consistency, can run overnight;
- Experimental tests, used to explore new features, can be executed selectively.

This way, when engineers submit a fix for a typo, they do not have to wait hours for the full test suite; passing the fast tests is sufficient.

Full tests still exist, but are deferred and no longer block every commit.

They tiered static analysis rules:

- Mandatory rules: directly cause build failures and must be fixed;
- Advisory rules: suggest improvements but do not block commits;
- Experimental rules: enabled only for specific projects for exploration.

This way, engineers do not have to be frustrated by warnings unrelated to their changes.

Only errors that truly affect maintainability become guardrails.

They even introduced a "lightweight review" mechanism in Gerrit.

For low-risk changes, a single approval is sufficient;

For core modules, multiple layers of review are required.

The essence of these reforms was not to weaken the process, but to realign the process with Cognitive Load.

The essence of complexity has never been quantity, but whether it can be understood.

When processes cause the human mind to collapse, they themselves become part of the complexity.

Google's reforms were precisely to bring process complexity below the threshold.

This philosophy applies equally in the Swift world.

SwiftLint can be configured with countless rules, but if too many are enabled, the team will be drowned in irrelevant warnings.

True wisdom is to choose a few key rules and focus attention on the parts that truly affect comprehension.

Continuous integration can run countless tasks, but if every commit requires hours of waiting, engineers' creativity will be worn down.

True wisdom is to distinguish quick feedback from comprehensive verification.

Google's story continued to circulate.

Once, a team developing a new feature for Android needed to iterate prototypes quickly.

They decided to bypass some CI checks in order to validate ideas rapidly.

A few days later, they brought their results to the review meeting.

The reviewers pointed out:

"You violated the process, but your results prove that flexibility is necessary."

This did not become a reason for punishment, but an opportunity for reform.

Google began to provide "sandbox branches" for prototype design and experimental features.

In this branch, rules were simplified and engineers could experiment quickly.

Only once a prototype matured would it be brought under the formal guardrails.

This is the wisdom of process: processes are not rigid slabs, but dynamic balances.

The migration of complexity is like the cycle of history.

It migrates from code to process, and then from process back to flexibility.

True victory is not annihilating complexity once and for all, but remaining clear-headed during its migrations.

Google engineers wrote in an internal document:

"Our task is not to build a perfect process, but to build a process aligned with the human mind.

The purpose of process is not to satisfy machines, but to be understood by humans."

This sentence, like a key, reveals the relationship between process and complexity.

It makes us understand: continuous integration and static checks are not technical problems, but cognitive ones.

Their goal is not to cover every possibility, but to guard the boundaries of the human mind.

The wisdom of an empire lies in knowing when to expand and when to contract.

The wisdom of process lies in knowing when to be strict and when to be lenient.

Google's story is a warning about process complexity and proof of the Cognitive Load threshold.

Guardrails are not there to stop humans, but to stop chaos.

The meaning of law is not to instill fear, but to maintain understanding.

When process and mind align, complexity can be tamed;

when process and mind diverge, complexity will bite back.

Google's story did not end when the reforms concluded.

Process complexity was alleviated, but complexity did not disappear.

It still existed like an undercurrent, only taking a different form.

A real turning point came after a major organizational change.

That year, Google launched an initiative codenamed "Unified Frontend."

The goal was to unify the development experience for Android, iOS, and the Web as much as possible under a single continuous integration system and set of guardrails.

- A unified build system,
- A unified code review process,
- A unified set of static analysis rules.

In the meeting room, the plan looked flawless.

It was like the elders of an empire deciding to promulgate a new code, making every territory obey the same laws.

However, the ideal was once again tested by complexity.

The problem first appeared with the iOS team.

The SwiftUI ecosystem was still evolving, and many features were in rapid iteration.

Google engineers frequently had to switch to beta versions of Xcode to test new capabilities.

However, the unified continuous integration system did not offer sufficient flexibility for these experimental needs.

As a result, whenever the iOS team tried new APIs, builds

often failed and static analysis reported a large number of unrelated errors.

At the same time, the Android team encountered similar issues when dealing with new Jetpack Compose features.

Compose's syntax and structure differ significantly from traditional Android, and the unified rules could not fully accommodate them.

Engineers were repeatedly blocked by CI when submitting code.

Google's ideal was "unification," but the reality was "fracture."

Each team was fighting the guardrails rather than relying on them.

This situation made management aware of a deeper problem:

Unified rules do not equal a unified Cognitive Load.

Different platforms, different technologies, and different teams each have different complexity curves.

Forcing everyone into the same system is equivalent to pushing everyone toward the same cognitive threshold.

This kind of "egalitarian" system will ultimately overwhelm the teams that most need flexibility.

So Google began a more thorough rethinking.

They wrote in an internal document:

"Continuous integration is not for creating uniformity, but for maintaining clarity.

Static checks are not for eradicating errors, but for reducing Cognitive Load.

What we really need is not a set of rules, but a philosophy."

This philosophy has three cores:

First, processes must be aligned with complexity.

In stable modules, rules can be strict;

In experimental modules, rules must be lenient.

Processes are not one-size-fits-all; they should be like water, varying by context.

Second, the goal of processes is to protect the human mind.

Whether a rule is necessary should not be judged by whether it can find errors, but by whether it reduces the cognitive cost of understanding.

If a rule causes engineers to spend a lot of time explaining why they were blocked, then it is harmful.

Third, processes must be able to evolve.

Complexity migrates, and processes must follow.

Today's critical rules may become tomorrow's burdens.

Today's advisory rules may become tomorrow's core.

The life of a process is not fixed; it evolves.

The result of this reflection was a philosophy of the "Cognitive Load threshold."

Google no longer emphasized the number of rules, but their alignment with human cognition.

Engineers began to use this as a guideline to decide whether to add a rule or modify a process.

In the iOS team, this philosophy brought significant changes.

SwiftUI's rapid iteration required the team to frequently try new features.

Thus, the CI system provided a "gray channel" for SwiftUI modules:

Experimental commits could bypass some rules as long as they passed basic builds and critical tests.

This flexibility allowed the team to explore faster while still being protected by basic guardrails.

In the core payment module, rules remained strict:

Every commit had to pass full tests and strict review; no detail could be compromised.

This differentiated system kept teams within the Cognitive Load threshold across different scenarios.

Historians would say this is the maturation of systems.

The empire's laws were no longer cold, rigid statutes, but contracts aligned with reality.

Software processes were no longer obstacles, but protection.

This philosophy did not belong only to Google.

Across the software world, more and more teams began to realize:

Continuous integration and static checks are not about pursuing perfect rules, but about guarding limited mental capacity.

In the iOS community, the use of SwiftLint also shifted from "as many as possible" to "as few as possible."

Excellent teams no longer enable hundreds of rules; they select the dozens that most reduce Cognitive Load.

They understand:

The meaning of rules lies not in their quantity, but in their direction.

In large applications' continuous integration, teams began to adopt layered testing and differentiated builds.

Critical modules require strict validation; secondary modules only need quick checks.

They understand:

The meaning of testing lies not in covering every possibility, but in protecting the most fragile boundaries.

At the end of the story, Google engineers wrote in a public talk:

"We no longer treat continuous integration as a set of tools, but as a culture.

Its goal is not to block humans, but to protect humans.

Its existence is not to make code perfect, but to make code understandable."

This sentence reads like a declaration of civilization.

Looking back over the whole story, we see:

Continuous integration and static checks were initially guardrails against complexity;

Later, they themselves became a source of complexity;

Ultimately, they evolved into a philosophy aligned with the boundaries of the human mind.

This path is so similar to the history of empires.

An empire's institutions move from initial simplicity, to later complexity, and finally to maturity;

Software guardrails move from initial purity, to later over-concentration, and finally to balance.

This is the inevitable curve of civilization.

Therefore, we can draw these conclusions:

Complexity cannot be eradicated, only governed.

Guardrails must not ossify, they must evolve.

Cognitive Load cannot be ignored, it must be managed.

Continuous integration and static checks are not cold, impersonal technologies, but gentle covenants.

Their goal is not to create fear, but to safeguard understanding.

When institutions align with the mind, software civilization can endure.

Great code is not about how clever it is, but how easy it is to understand.
Great institutions are not about how complex they are, but how close they are to humanity.
The war on complexity will not end.
But when humans and institutions resonate, civilization is sustained.

PART SIX
AI AND THE FUTURE

CHAPTER 27
AI CAN WRITE CODE, BUT CANNOT DO DESIGN

Water can carry a boat, but it can also capsize it.

Machines can produce code, but cannot give it meaning.

Meaning belongs to the designer, not the copyist.

The wind comes from the void, carrying indifferent algorithms.

It does not understand intent, trade-offs, or the fragility of civilization.

It only knows how to, within the trajectory of its training, output the most likely answer.

This is the essence of AI: it can write code, but cannot do design.

On a spring morning, a mid-sized iOS team experienced their turning point.

The team wasn't large—about twenty-some engineers—yet they were responsible for all of a fast-growing company's mobile business.

Their app, in just two years, grew from an initial prototype into a tool with millions of users, and demands surged like a tide.

The team was exhausted, bugs were rampant, and the balance between speed and quality was teetering.

Then news of GitHub Copilot arrived.

AI assists with writing code, autocompletes functions, generates test cases.

Its slogan was like a shot in the arm: "Let developers focus on creation, not repetitive work."

The team's leaders decided to try it.

They saw hope:

Perhaps AI could lighten engineers' burdens, reduce mechanical repetitive tasks, and allow humans to do more important design and decision-making.

It was an enticing vision.

After all, who wouldn't want to be freed from tedium?

The initial experience was exhilarating.

Engineers typed a few comments into a SwiftUI view file, and Copilot produced the complete view structure.

When they needed to handle network requests, the AI almost immediately generated an asynchronous function, even considering error handling.

Even more surprising, when someone wrote a test case title, the AI automatically generated mock scenarios and assertions.

The team felt unprecedented efficiency.

A feature that used to take half a day to complete now took only an hour.

Some junior engineers could even write code close to senior level with the help of AI.

They cheered in their internal Slack channel:

"The future is here!"

"This is the second Industrial Revolution!"

But complexity is never absent; it is only waiting.

Soon, problems began to surface. The code Copilot generated, though runnable, often did not align with the team's design principles. Some code used incorrect abstractions, making simple problems more complicated; some introduced patterns the team had long since abandoned, leading to inconsistent styles; worse still, some code hid performance traps that only became apparent after going live.

The most typical example appeared in a feature related to SwiftUI state management. Engineers asked Copilot to generate a view showing the user's message list. The AI-written code ran, but caused the entire interface to redraw on each state update, leading to a severe performance decline. Fixing the bug took days before the team realized: the AI did not understand SwiftUI's "minimal redraw" philosophy. It was merely stitching together seemingly reasonable answers from its training data based on probability.

The team's atmosphere began to change. The initial excitement gradually turned into confusion and anxiety. They asked themselves: "Are we accelerating, or taking a detour?"

The danger of complexity lies not in the errors themselves, but in their distribution. AI-generated code is not obvious bugs, but subtle deviations. It does not crash immediately; instead it quietly increases future cognitive load.

When engineers on the team reviewed AI-written code in code review, they found themselves spending more time understanding intent. Some variable names were vague, some logic looked reasonable yet conflicted with the overall architecture. Each review became a battle against complexity. Engineers began to wonder: was AI truly saving time?

This doubt was fully ignited by a single incident.

One night, the team's app experienced a severe crash in production. While users were making payments, the app failed to handle error responses correctly, causing transactions to be charged multiple times. Angry users denounced the company on social media, and the customer support team descended into chaos.

Engineers worked through the night to investigate and eventually discovered that the function handling payments had been generated by Copilot. It appeared sound, but had hidden flaws in its exception-catching logic. These flaws never triggered in the test environment, but were exposed under the large-scale requests in production.

The incident came at a painful cost. The company not only compensated users for their losses, but also suffered a heavy blow in the court of public opinion.

At the postmortem, someone said:

"We can no longer blindly rely on AI. The code it writes has not been designed."

Design.

That is the key.

AI can write code, but it does not do design. Design means understanding the whole, weighing trade-offs, and considering future evolution. AI can only, based on past patterns, generate the most likely answer. It has no memory and no responsibility. It cannot understand why a particular architecture was chosen, nor can it predict the cost of a design for the team ten years from now.

Design is a philosophy, an active governance of complexity.

AI, on the other hand, only creates new complexity.

The team fell into a new dilemma. They were unwilling to abandon Copilot because it did improve productivity. But they also could not fully trust it, because the complexity it introduced was devouring the future.

So they began seeking a new balance. They established new rules:

AI may generate boilerplate code, but architectural decisions must be made by humans.

AI may offer suggestions, but naming and boundaries must be defined by humans.

AI may assist with tests, but the coverage and trade-offs of test cases must be overseen by humans.

This was not an easy path.

Because every choice is a negotiation with complexity.

The power of AI is like an imperial cavalry. It can sweep across great distances in the short term, but it cannot govern territory. Governance requires institutions, boundaries, and carefully considered design. Without design, AI will convert short-term speed into long-term debt.

This iOS team, between trial and reflection, gradually came to see reality more clearly. AI is a tool, not a designer. They must learn restraint, learn to distinguish oases from mirages in the sea of complexity.

The relationship between the team and AI is shifting from euphoria to skepticism. They have not yet found the final answer. The shadow of complexity still quietly accumulates in their code repository.

Machines can give you answers, but they cannot give you questions.

Machines can replicate structure, but they cannot give it a soul.

The gaps in architecture are not something speed can fill, but meaning and boundaries.

Storms do not reveal themselves at first.

They always change course quietly when humans think they have everything under control.

In that iOS team, AI's presence was initially only a tool, like an improvement to the typewriter or an accelerator for the assembly line.

However, when the tool was mistaken for the designer, the storm had already begun.

One year after Copilot was introduced, the team's codebase underwent changes visible to the naked eye.

The number of features doubled, lines of code surged, and development cycles shortened dramatically.

To outsiders, this looked like a miracle of efficiency.

Company executives even wrote in the quarterly report: "Our development team has significantly increased productivity thanks to AI assistance."

But the truth deep within the codebase was known only to the engineers.

Cracks in the architecture had quietly appeared.

The cracks first showed up as a split in style.

In the world of SwiftUI, consistent patterns and conventions are key to reducing complexity.

But Copilot did not understand the team's conventions.

It generated different implementations in different scenarios.

Some views used state bindings, others used environment objects;

Some features used async/await to manage asynchrony, while others mixed in Combine publishers.

Engineers found themselves confused again and again during code reviews:

"Why is this logic completely different from how we implemented it before?"

"Who wrote this? Oh, it was AI."

The differences spread like cracks.

Two attitudes gradually formed within the team:

Some people thought they should accept AI's diversity, since it worked as long as it ran;

others insisted on manually fixing things to unify the code style.

This divergence was not just a technical choice, but a cultural conflict.

It made the team argue endlessly in meetings and made collaboration difficult.

And complexity grew precisely in this invisible erosion.

The cracks also showed up in architectural consistency.

SwiftUI's philosophy is a single source of truth.

Yet AI-generated code often broke that principle.

It would store the same state in multiple places and introduce new global variables where they didn't belong.

It may seem convenient in the short term, but in the long run it means potential disaster.

Once, the team needed to refactor a piece of logic related to user authentication.

They discovered the user's login state was stored separately in three places:

Once in the app's root view, once in a distinct service layer, and once in a seemingly unrelated component.

These states had been generated by AI for different requirements and were never unified.

When a user logged out and then logged back in, contradictions arose between the three states.

Some screens showed the user as logged in, while others remained in guest mode.

Bug reports flooded in, and users left angry reviews on the App Store.

Engineers spent weeks before they could reconcile those scattered states.

In the internal postmortem, someone sighed, "This isn't a bug; it's an architectural collapse. AI only knows how to generate, not how to guard."

Deeper cracks lay in the relationship between testing and trust.

AI could generate test cases, which initially amazed the team.

They only had to write the test descriptions, and Copilot would autocomplete the assertions.

But as features increased, the test suite also ballooned.

Many tests appeared to exist, but lacked real coverage value.

Once, the team released a new version that crashed in production.

They were baffled: why didn't the test suite catch this?

They later discovered that the AI-generated tests only repeated the most common scenarios; true edge cases were never covered.

The number of tests increased, but their quality declined.

This plunged the team into a "false sense of security."

"We were blinded by AI," a test engineer said. "It made us think we were doing enough, when in reality it was just building form over substance."

This false sense of security is more dangerous than having no tests at all.

Because it relaxes human vigilance and hands trust over to a machine that does not understand design.

The cracks were not only technical but also in the team's mindset.

The arrival of AI narrowed the gap between newcomers and veterans.

Newcomers relying on Copilot could complete tasks quickly; veterans felt their years of accumulated experience had become less important.

"If AI can generate code, then what is the meaning of our existence?"

This sentiment quietly spread through the corridors and the break room.

The pride of senior engineers gradually faded, and they began to question their own value. Newcomers grew increasingly dependent on AI and were unwilling to spend time understanding the underlying principles. This cultural rift plunged the team into a strange state: on the surface things were faster, but in reality their cognitive reserves were declining.

The true killer of complexity is this collective incapacitation. When a team stops accumulating experience, stops guarding the architecture, and stops caring about boundaries, complexity will sweep everything away.

The cracks eventually reached the decision-making level.

Company leaders were initially excited by the sense of speed

AI brought. They showed growth curves to investors, claiming they had found a "weapon of the future." However, as incidents became frequent, user experience declined, and developer morale sank, doubts began to emerge.

Investors asked, "If AI is so powerful, why is our product experience getting worse?"

Users complained, "There are more and more features, but stability is getting worse."

Inside the team they argued in meetings, "Are we developers, or caretakers of AI?"

This multiplicity of pressures forced management to rethink. They realized that AI was not a universal answer but a new variable. Left unchecked, it would not reduce complexity; it would create more.

At a strategy meeting, a senior architect said, "AI is like an army: it can fight wars, but it cannot govern a country. Governing requires institutions, boundaries, and design. If we hand everything over to AI, we are abandoning governance."

Those words plunged the meeting into a long silence.

The power of complexity lies in how it silently alters human choices. AI seduces people with speed and makes them neglect design; it leads people to believe in the illusion of uniformity while ignoring the limits of cognition. When the cracks spread through the entire organization, complexity ceases to be merely a technical issue and becomes a civilizational one.

This iOS team had reached a crossroads. They had to choose: continue blindly relying on AI, or redefine the relationship between humans and AI?

The team was torn across cultural, architectural, and cognitive lines, and the shadow of complexity hung over the entire organization. The real choice had not yet arrived.

If an empire hands its scepter to the cavalry,

it will surely see the cavalry destroy its own city.

If design is handed over to machines, one will surely see machines destroy its intent.

Meaning has never belonged to indifferent algorithms.

Night cloaked the office; light refracted across the glass curtain wall like a sea of anxiety.

That iOS team once again faced an unexpected incident.

This time, the problem occurred in the core booking flow.

Users reported that when selecting dates and listings, the system would sometimes return unavailable results:

Rooms that were clearly fully booked still showed as selectable; after payment succeeded, orders were stuck in processing.

Angry users launched boycotts on social media, customer support was forced to work overtime, and the brand's reputation suffered again.

The engineers immediately began investigating.

This time they found no obvious bug.

All the code looked correct, and all the tests passed.

Only when they reviewed the logic line by line did they find the root cause.

The booking flow code had been generated by Copilot months earlier.

When faced with complex business logic, the AI had stitched together multiple implementations:

Some logic relied on state bindings, some relied on environment objects, and some called an old, unmaintained service.

These cobbled pieces could run in the short term, but they accumulated into huge hidden dangers over the long term.

Eventually, as the business scaled and user concurrency increased, these hazards converged into a disaster.

The debt of complexity erupted in that moment.

After the incident, the team convened a crisis meeting.

The air in the conference room was heavy; everyone knew this was a moment they had to face.

Someone angrily accused, "We handed critical logic to AI, and it gave us cobbled garbage."

Someone asked in frustration, "But without AI, we simply couldn't have completed iterations this fast."

Someone calmly summarized, "AI can generate code, but it cannot do design. The problem is not AI, but that we misused it."

Those words were like a stone dropped into a lake, stirring long echoes.

The meeting fell into a long silence.

This was the question they had to answer: What is AI's role on the team?

If AI is treated as a developer, they will inevitably fall back into the mire of complexity.

Because AI will not take responsibility for the architecture, will not fortify boundaries, and will not pay the bill for cognitive budget.

It will only write "possibly correct" fragments, but cannot guarantee a whole that is "understandable in the long term."

If AI is treated as a tool, then humans must resume responsibility for design.

Design means defining boundaries, choosing patterns, and anticipating future extensions.

This is the work of the human mind, and the only way to govern complexity.

The team finally understood: they had to change course.

The process of changing course was full of pain.

They decided to refactor the booking flow and completely remove the cobbled-together logic generated by AI.

The work took a full two months.

They rebuilt state management using TCA, unifying the scattered state into a single source of truth.

They reexamined data flows, clarified boundaries, and removed redundant bridges.

Every change signified remorse for their past reliance on AI.

Someone wrote in the refactor log: "We are not fixing bugs; we are redeeming the future."

That line spread throughout the team and became their new creed.

As the refactor progressed, the team began to redefine the rules for using AI.

They established three iron laws:

- AI can write boilerplate, but it cannot write architecture.

Small UI components, repetitive tests, and formatted documentation can be handed to AI;

But module design, state management, and dependency boundaries must be decided by humans.

- AI can provide candidates, but it cannot provide answers.

Engineers must proactively ask questions and review and modify AI's suggestions.

They learned to apply their own judgment to AI's outputs instead of trusting them blindly.

- AI can reduce labor, but it cannot reduce understanding.

Any code generated by AI must be understandable and explainable by the team, and documented.

If a piece of logic cannot be explained, it must be rewritten.

These three iron laws, like an empire's new edict, became the team's defense against complexity.

The shift was not merely a technical change, but a cultural awakening.

Senior engineers reclaimed their value.

They no longer competed with AI over who could code faster; instead they used experience to guard boundaries and judgment to choose paths.

Newcomers were also taught: AI is not a mentor, but a tool.

You must understand the architecture to use AI.

You must know the cost of complexity to tame the machine's speed.

The team gradually formed a new tacit understanding:

AI is the scribe, humans are the designers.

AI is responsible for speed; humans are responsible for meaning.

This division of labor put them back on track.

A few months later, they entered a new release cycle.

This time, the app went live with almost no major bugs.

User complaints decreased, and team morale recovered.

They finally realized: it wasn't because AI disappeared, but because they had learned how to use AI.

Complexity still existed.

It was like the winds of the desert, never stopping.

But this time, they learned to build barriers, to find direction in the sandstorms.

They no longer handed the scepter to machines; instead they used machines as aids to defend their civilization.

"The arrival of AI is not the end of civilization, but a new beginning.

It makes humanity see clearly: speed is not everything; meaning is fundamental.

Machines can generate answers, but they cannot create questions;

Machines can imitate structures, but they cannot establish institutions.

Institutions and boundaries must be designed by humans."

This iOS team ultimately gained new wisdom through their adjustment with AI:

They understood that AI can write code, but it cannot do design.

They realized design is the art of cognition, the governance of complexity.

They came to believe that in the sea of complexity, the only ones who can plant a flag are humans.

AI's power will only grow stronger, and code generation will become ever faster.

But true civilization will not be built by speed; it will endure through restraint.

Let AI write code,

Let humans do the design.

The greatest architectures are not machine-generated, but human-tempered.
The greatest future is not created by speed, but safeguarded by understanding.

CHAPTER 28
ADVANTAGES AND BOUNDARIES

A machine can carry stones across the desert, but it cannot decide where the city walls should be built.

It can write a thousand lines of regulations, but it cannot legislate.

The human task is not speed, but choice.

The shadow of complexity stretches into the new era once again.

If Airbnb's cross-platform experiment was an illusion of empire, then the rise of artificial intelligence is a temptation of a different scale.

Its promise is greater, its call is louder, its illusion deeper.

Shopify, the e-commerce empire that supports millions of merchants, began large-scale trials of GitHub Copilot after 2022.

Their teams publicly shared data: more than 30% of new code snippets were automatically generated by AI, and engineers' day-to-day development speed increased significantly.

At first, this boost in efficiency excited everyone.

Engineers seemed to suddenly have countless assistants: boilerplate code no longer had to be written by hand, test cases could be generated in moments, and even inspiration for function names was provided for them.

This was a new oasis.

In the desert of complexity, AI is like a tireless waterwheel, carrying mundane buckets of water for humans.

It does not tire, does not get bored, does not question.

Its speed far exceeds that of humans, its memory far surpasses that of humans.

But complexity does not retreat because of new tools.

It only changes form and reappears at the boundaries.

Within Shopify's teams, the place where AI first demonstrated value was boilerplate.

E-commerce systems are full of repetition:

- API call wrappers;
- Serialization of data models;
- Standardized UI components;
- Templates for logging and instrumentation.

These tasks used to take up a lot of engineers' time.

And the introduction of Copilot made this repetitive work almost disappear instantly.

A single prompt could generate the required wrappers;

A comment could yield complete test cases;

even error messages could be auto-completed.

For the first time, engineers felt that the cloak of complexity had been stripped away, and they could finally focus their attention on higher-level thinking.

They were no longer trapped in the quagmire of boilerplate but freed to think about more valuable problems.

However, complexity did not dissipate as a result.

It only retreated to a deeper level.

The problem began with testing.

Copilot can quickly generate test cases from comments, covering common edge conditions.

At first, this was seen as a tremendous boon.

Test coverage rose rapidly, and the green lights on reports were reassuring.

But not long after, engineers discovered:

although these tests appeared to cover many scenarios, they lacked true "design intent."

The essence of testing is not coverage but validating assumptions.

Humans design tests not to collect more green checkmarks, but to confirm whether a system's behavior matches expectations.

AI does not understand "expectations."

It can only generate tests in a statistical sense and cannot capture the constraints that truly matter at the architectural level.

One of Shopify's payment modules was blind-sided for weeks by AI-generated tests.

All tests passed; coverage reached 95%.

Yet in the real world, some transactions still failed under extreme network conditions.

Engineers eventually discovered that the AI's tests had ignored timing issues in the distributed system.

It never understood that "timing" is critical for a payment system; it only produced assertions that "looked reasonable."

Complexity speaks here:

tools can help you carry stones, but they cannot decide where the city walls should be built.

Another crack appeared in search.

AI-assisted search capabilities let engineers quickly locate functions, classes, and interfaces in a massive codebase.

They could ask questions in natural language and get immediate answers.

This dramatically lowered the barrier to entering unfamiliar modules.

But a problem followed:

Search gave them answers, but not understanding.

When a newcomer finds a call chain via AI, they know "where" but not "why."

Architectural intent is hidden in the team's history of decisions, and AI cannot comprehend that history.

It can provide a path, but it cannot convey the philosophy.

So engineers grew more reliant on search and progressively lost holistic grasp.

It's like a mapping app that can show you the shortest route but cannot explain a city's cultural fabric.

The shadow of complexity reappears: when humans hand understanding over to tools, the ability to understand begins to atrophy.

This atrophy is not immediately visible.

It lurks in daily work like an undercurrent.

It only became fully apparent when a real architectural decision arrived.

When Shopify's team was discussing the architecture for a new checkout flow, disagreements emerged.

AI produced several viable implementations; each was syntactically correct and each would work.

But the team could not decide which one to pick.

Because the key to the choice was not syntax but trade-offs.

Prioritize performance or prioritize scalability?

Centralized state management or a distributed event stream?

Pursue short-term rapid delivery or long-term maintainability?

These are questions AI cannot answer.

It can only generate candidates, not make value judgments.

The real burden falls on human shoulders.

Complexity reappears here:

tools can extend your hands, but they cannot extend your mind.

The true boundary is not what machines can do, but what humans should give up.

Shopify's engineers gradually realized:

AI's advantages lie in boilerplate, tests, and search;

But its boundaries lie in architecture, trade-offs, and Cognitive Load.

AI can help them write thousands of lines of code, but it cannot answer for them "which line should be written."

Speed is an illusion.

If the direction is wrong, running faster only takes you further from the goal.

True strength is not how many stones are moved, but whether the wall built from them is solid.

Shopify's engineers felt an unprecedented lightness for the first time.

The quagmire of boilerplate disappeared, repetitive labor was replaced, and code commits surged.

Statistics showed the team's productivity rose by 40%.

Product managers excitedly presented the curves in meetings, as if the empire's tax revenue had suddenly doubled.

AI had indeed delivered on its promises:

- API wrappers no longer required line-by-line copy-and-paste;
- Data models no longer needed to be defined by hand;
- Logging and instrumentation could be automatically generated;
- Unit tests could be almost instantly completed.

Developers' fingertips grew light; they were no longer trapped in tedious labor.

They even began to wonder whether the years of struggle they'd endured were merely a wait for this moment's arrival.

But complexity never retreats because of increased speed.

It only changed its posture, quietly lying in ambush at a deeper level.

The introduction of AI into Shopify's payment system produced an unexpected result: the volume of code swelled dramatically within just a few months.

Because generation became so easy, engineers tended to produce more wrappers, more tests, more utility functions.

The sea of code grew ever wider, but clear channels no longer existed.

In the past, writing code itself was a kind of "friction" that forced humans to reflect on "whether this layer of abstraction is necessary."

When the friction disappeared, so did that reflection.

AI was like an endless loom, rapidly weaving a huge web that enveloped the entire system.

But the loom did not understand "structure"; it only understood "continuation."

What it wove was not architecture but a cobweb.

Complexity revealed itself here: the dividend of speed often comes at the cost of structure.

The problem first appeared in testing.

AI-generated tests pushed coverage to unprecedented heights.

The team cheered; reports were full of green lights and the numbers were reassuring.

But behind the green lights hid a cognitive void.

On one occasion, after a payment module went live, users discovered in real usage that transactions were being charged multiple times under network jitter.

This was a serious issue that affected merchants' and users' trust.

The team pulled the logs and found that all tests had covered this scenario.

So why did it still fail?

Eventually they found that AI-generated test cases only verified input-to-output matching; they did not verify the system's intent.

It did not know that "idempotency is a core principle of payment systems."

It mindlessly generated assertions without understanding the philosophy behind them.

This time, complexity reminded humans in an indifferent way: testing is not form, but thought.

Tests without thought are just the illusion of green lights.

Another crack appeared in search and understanding.

AI natural-language search let newcomers get up to speed quickly.

One question, one prompt, and they could immediately find the relevant functions and call chains.

Newcomers marveled: "The learning curve has dropped dramatically."

But months later, problems began to surface.

They knew where functions lived, but not why they existed.

They could quickly find an entry point but could not grasp the meaning of the exits.

Architectural intent was drowned in thousands upon thousands of search results.

A senior engineer sighed in a meeting: "We are cultivating a development habit that only knows how to 'query' but not how to 'understand.'"

Complexity disguised itself again. It makes people feel relieved in the short term, yet lose sight of the whole in the long term. Like imperial officials who can quickly find statutes but don't know why those laws were made. When the system needs reform, they can only recite, not judge.

The real crisis appears in the absence of architectural decisions.

Shopify's team was discussing the architecture for a new checkout flow. AI was integrated and generated multiple possible implementations. They were all superficially correct, logically feasible, and even came with complete code examples. But the team became deadlocked when choosing.

Because the key issue is not "whether it can be implemented" but "how to weigh the trade-offs."

Should they pursue centralized state management or adopt event-driven decoupling? Prioritize smooth user experience or system scalability? Meet short-term business goals or preserve room for long-term evolution?

These questions have no single answer. They require human value judgments, experience, intuition, and historical reference. AI can only generate code; it cannot generate values.

The meeting fell silent. Engineers stared at the candidate solutions listed on the screen, feeling a strange emptiness. In the past they had to wrestle with complexity; now they had to make choices within an illusion. Complexity no longer presented itself as code but pressed on human shoulders as the weight of choice.

An imperial historian wrote: "When an empire's army becomes too large, victory in battle no longer depends on the number of warriors but on the generals' choices. When a system's code becomes too convoluted, solving problems no longer depends on the number of functions but on architectural trade-offs."

Shopify's team began to feel this pressure. They had countless candidate solutions but lacked a clear direction. They had countless tools but lacked real boundaries.

AI unleashed tremendous energy in boilerplate, testing, and search, but left a vast vacuum in architecture, trade-offs, and cognition.

Complexity grows in that vacuum. It no longer manifests as

repetitive labor but as uncertainty. It no longer appears as bugs but as hesitation and wavering.

Time is the best revealer.

A few months later, the team discovered: development speed had indeed increased, but the cost of fixing bugs was higher. Features went live faster, but the system evolved more slowly. There was more code, but fewer people who understood it.

This is the paradox of complexity: it gives you short-term gains but makes you pay in the long term. It lets you see speed on the surface while eroding clarity beneath.

The empire's archives reminded them once again: "Speed is an illusion; choices are real. Humanity's task is not to run, but to decide the direction to run."

Shopify's story had not yet reached its end. They were caught between illusion and reality; they were facing a new face of complexity: the boundaries of AI.

The more powerful the tools, the blurrier the boundaries.

But if boundaries are abandoned, civilization will collapse.

Tools are not rulers; tools are merely servants.

In Shopify's offices, lights still burned bright, keyboards still clicked, and code continued to be submitted in torrents. But the air was heavy with an ineffable weight. The introduction of AI made speed soar, boilerplate vanish, testing flourish, and search agile. Yet beneath this flourishing, the shadow of complexity had quietly gathered.

The team finally realized: they had to reexamine the relationship between tools and boundaries.

The first true awakening came from a catastrophic failure.

It was a global promotion day, with millions of users flooding Shopify's checkout system simultaneously. At first everything went smoothly—transactions flowed and orders surged. But soon after, the payment service began experiencing widespread latency. Logs showed some nodes' state had been locked, causing requests to pile up and transactions to fail.

Engineers immediately began investigating. They were surprised to find that the problem did not stem from a traditional performance bottleneck but from AI-generated redundant logic. A seemingly harmless utility function had been generated three times by AI prompts and used in different modules. Under high concurrency, these redundant pieces of logic entangled one another, causing a deadlock.

All tests had passed, searches could locate the functions, and all the boilerplate was impeccably tidy. Yet the system still collapsed.

"This is not AI's fault," a senior engineer said in the postmortem. "This is our mistake for abandoning boundaries."

That failure became a turning point.

Managers, architects, and developers regrouped. They began to ask the most fundamental question: what should AI do, and what should it not do?

The answer gradually became clear: AI's strengths lie in repetition, in speed, in scale. It can generate boilerplate, fill in tests, and aid search. It can free human fingertips, but it cannot replace the human mind.

AI's boundaries lie in choice, in architecture, in trade-offs. It cannot determine the shape of the system, weigh short term against long term, or understand the weight of Cognitive Load. It can generate ten answers, but it cannot tell which one suits the team or the future.

So Shopify established a new principle: AI is an assistant, not a designer.

This principle was written into the team's engineering charter. It means:

- All architectural decisions must be discussed and made by the human team; they must not rely on AI-generated conclusions.
- The boundaries of all critical modules must be defined by humans; AI may only fill in internal details.
- All test cases must explicitly verify "the system's intent," rather than chase the illusion of coverage.
- All onboarding for new hires must emphasize understanding architectural philosophy, not relying on search shortcuts.

This is not a denial of AI, but a clarification of AI's role. They took AI down from the "throne of kings" and returned it to the "seat of servants." Complexity was thereby reframed within the limits of human cognition.

A young engineer wrote in a journal:

"AI is a mirror; it amplifies our speed and it amplifies our chaos. When we blindly chase its power, we only accelerate our fall. Only when we clearly define boundaries can AI become a true assistant. Boundaries are not restrictions, they are protection."

This sentence was widely circulated within the team and even posted on the office whiteboard.

The story of complexity has never been about tools winning or losing, but about human restraint.

Shopify's team finally understood: AI can carry stones, but it cannot decide where the walls should be built.

The form of the walls determines the empire's boundaries;

the form of the architecture determines the fate of the software.

So they brought AI within boundaries, rather than handing boundaries over. They used it to speed up boilerplate, but did not let it decide structure. They used it to supplement tests, but did not let it define intent. They used it for search, but did not let it substitute for understanding.

An imperial historian wrote: "Tools are an extension of civilization, but if civilization abandons its boundaries, the tools will turn against their masters."

Complexity was not brought by AI; it has always existed. AI only makes complexity appear in a new guise:

It turns the problem from "how to write" into "how to choose";

It turns the risk from "insufficient speed" into "lack of understanding."

But when humans reclaim boundaries, complexity is no longer a flood but a river. Floods destroy everything; rivers nourish civilization.

Shopify's experience tells us:

- AI's strengths: boilerplate, testing, search. It can accelerate, scale, and augment.
- AI's boundaries: architecture, trade-offs, cognition. It cannot understand, cannot choose, cannot exercise restraint.
- Human responsibility: guard boundaries, make choices, shoulder complexity.

This is the true meaning of cognitive engineering:

Not to let machines think for you, but to let machines free up space so you can think better.

History will remember this moment:

Humanity introduced AI to write code at scale for the first time, yet soberly realized:

True wisdom is not in machines, but in boundaries.

True power is not in speed, but in restraint.

Complexity still exists, but humans now know how to live with it. This is the key to whether software civilization can endure.

Boilerplate can be replaced by machines, tests can be augmented by machines, search can be accelerated by machines.
But architecture must be designed by humans, trade-offs must be borne by humans, complexity must be faced by humans.
AI is a waterwheel, not a legislator.
The future of code is not automation, but clarity.

CHAPTER 29
THE PHILOSOPHY OF HUMAN–AI COLLABORATION

Machines can replace the hand, not the heart.

Design belongs to humans, because design is about trade-offs.

Machines can offer shadows, not names.

Naming belongs to humans, because naming creates meaning.

The wind has no weight, yet it can move sand dunes.

AI has no thought, yet it can produce answers.

In the sea of complexity, the arrival of AI is like a fresh breeze.

It can bring coolness, but it can also whip up new storms.

When GitHub Copilot was introduced, the entire software world was shaken.

Engineers saw for the first time that the editor was no longer just a silent container, but a companion that "completes thoughts."

All it took was writing a few lines of comments, and candidate implementations would automatically appear.

All of this seemed to herald a new era: programming would no longer be human solitary labor, but a collaboration between humans and machines.

However, historians remind us:

Every time a new technology is born, it is a double-edged sword.

The steam engine brought speed, and also crowded smoke;

Electricity brought light, and also new dependencies;

AI brings productivity, and also illusions of cognition.

One spring, the Orion team decided to introduce GitHub Copilot.

They were the iOS group at a medium-sized tech company, developing a complex social app with SwiftUI.

The app's structure was large: state management relied on TCA, the network layer had hundreds if not thousands of requests, and the UI layer had hundreds of views.

The pressure of complexity had already worn them out.

Thus, Copilot's arrival was seen as salvation.

The team's engineers were amazed on their first try:

A comment, a candidate;

A function name, an implementation.

They seemed to have an invisible auxiliary force clearing the way for them in the night.

The product manager, hearing this, brightened:

"This means we can ship faster, right?"

The engineering manager nodded:

"At least, it can reduce our repetitive work."

But as the lessons of history tell us: complexity will not disappear because of a new weapon; it will only take another form.

In the first few weeks, Copilot really worked wonders.

Orion's engineers no longer needed to hand-write lengthy boilerplate when composing network requests.

AI could auto-complete the request structure, parameters, and parsing logic.

They cheered:

"This saves at least a third of the time!"

The UI portion was also easily handled by Copilot.

Engineers only needed to write "create a card view with an avatar and a display name," and Copilot would generate candidates.

Although some tweaks were still required, it was much faster than starting from scratch.

However, problems began to appear in subtle ways.

When the team tried to merge branches, they found that the candidate code from different engineers differed greatly.

The implementations AI produced were not unique.

Some generated simplified logic, some produced over-abstractions, and some even hid potential performance problems.

On the surface everything ran; but in the details, the pieces felt like fragments from different civilizations, hard to fit together.

Complexity reemerged.

It no longer appeared as repetitive work, but lurked in the form of inconsistent candidates.

A unified style and clear boundaries were struck by AI's diversity.

Debate arose within the team.

Someone said:

"We can just pick the most appropriate candidate and not worry."

Someone retorted:

"But how do we judge which candidate is the most appropriate? AI won't tell you its reasons."

The discussion grew heated.

The product manager listened uneasily; they had expected AI to make the team faster, but instead it had created new hesitation.

The engineering manager thought for a long time and then spoke the crucial line:

"AI can write code, but design still needs humans.

The real problem is not the candidates, but how we define the problem.

Only when the problem is clearly defined do candidates become meaningful.

And the final naming must be done by humans."

Naming.

This is the core of all software design.

Naming is not merely giving variables names; it is giving logic meaning, building a bridge between human understanding and the machine's implementation.

Naming is an interpretation; it is a commitment.

It tells future readers: what the intention of this logic is, what responsibility this boundary has, what choices this history represents.

No matter how powerful AI becomes, it cannot truly understand "intent."

It can predict common patterns, but it cannot grasp a specific philosophy.

It can reuse tens of thousands of training samples, but it cannot feel the team's unique context.

Therefore, naming must be done by humans.

To verify this, the Orion team decided to run an experiment.

They had Copilot generate ten different candidate implementations to fulfill the same requirement:

A state-driven view for displaying a user's friend requests.

These candidates differed in details:

Some emphasized performance optimizations;

Some over-abstracted into generic components;

Some were blunt and simple, with almost no boundaries.

Then they asked the team's engineers to read each candidate in turn and describe its "intent" in one sentence.

The result was obvious:

No candidate reached consensus in naming.

AI provided implementations, but it could not tell you which one better aligned with the team's philosophy.

The real decisions still needed to be made by humans.

The engineering manager summarized in the meeting:

"AI can give us candidates, but it cannot replace our definition of meaning.

Candidates are only shadows; naming is the soul.

If we let candidates dominate, we will be consumed by complexity;

if we let naming dominate, we can truly master the candidates."

This experiment made the team realize the true philosophy of collaboration.

The relationship between humans and AI is not substitution, but division of labor.

AI's role is to provide many candidates and reduce the burden of repetitive work.

The human role is to define the problem, select candidates, and give meaning through naming.

This is a new civilizational pact.

Just as an empire needs clerks and armies, generals and craftsmen, the new era of software also needs designers standing shoulder to shoulder with AI.

AI is an auxiliary force, but the general will always be human.

However, complexity will not stop because of this awakening.

It only takes another form, waiting for new cracks to appear.

In the use of Copilot, new problems gradually surfaced:

The team began to rely on candidates, and their habit of thinking began to weaken.

Some young engineers even only waited for AI to provide answers, no longer reasoning themselves.

This is a new danger.

"When an empire depends on mercenaries, its core strength begins to dissipate.

When a team depends on AI candidates, their mental boundaries are being eroded."

The Orion team introduced Copilot and went through surprise, confusion, experiments, and an initial awakening. But the real test was yet to come: AI is not just a tool; it is a new source of complexity.

When a civilization begins to rely on prophets, it is already on the road to decline.

When a team begins to rely on automation, it has already overdrawn its cognitive reserves.

AI's candidates are like prophecies in an empire. They appear omniscient but are actually echoes of the past. In the Orion team's office, the voice of prophecy gradually became routine: the cursor pauses for a moment, and an answer appears on the screen. The young engineers laughed: "Why write it yourself? Let Copilot do it."

At first, this ease felt like a gift. Repetitive boilerplate no longer needed to be handwritten; common patterns no longer needed to be memorized. The team's output seemed to improve. The numbers in the meeting notes looked bright: more commits, faster feature launches.

But the shadow of complexity always lurks behind the joy.

The first sign came from a code review.

A senior engineer noticed that a certain module's logic was unusually messy. Different functions had wildly different styles; some were long and verbose, others over-simplified. Comments were sparse, naming inconsistent. They looked as if written by different hands, as if fragments from different civilizations had been pieced together.

When he asked the author, the young engineer laughed:

"Copilot gave this; I thought it worked, so I didn't change much."

Silence spread through the air. The code runs, but will your future self understand it? If the future reader is you, are you willing to bear such a Cognitive Load?

This is not a technical problem but a cultural turning point. The convenience of AI is quietly eroding human caution.

The second sign came from an online outage.

The app's messaging system suddenly crashed and users couldn't receive notifications. An emergency investigation found the source in an extremely small error: inconsistent timestamp formats, which caused discrepancies when passed between services.

The erroneous implementation came from a Copilot candidate. It referenced common examples but did not take the team's special conventions into account. The engineer accepted the candidate in haste, without deep thought.

The outage was fixed, but at a great cost.

Not just user complaints, but the team's trust.

Copilot provided candidates, but it cannot understand "why."

Humans did not clearly define the problem, so AI naturally could not provide the correct answer.

The empire's roads will not become smoother simply by building more of them.

If the institutions are unclear, the more roads there are, the greater the chaos.

AI's candidates are like roads; only under human institutions will they not descend into disorder.

The third sign was more subtle.

The young engineers gradually developed a new habit:

They no longer started from the problem but filtered from the candidates.

They waited for Copilot to produce several options, then picked one that seemed suitable.

They began to lose the ability to reason through solutions and the courage to design independently.

Senior engineers felt uneasy.

They knew this was a cognitive degradation.

Just as an empire that relies on mercenaries sees its soldiers' courage gradually dissipate;

When a team relies on AI candidates, the muscles of design will likewise atrophy.

One day, during an internal training session, a young engineer even said:

"Why should we still learn architecture? Copilot can write it anyway."

That sentence rang like an alarm.

If such thinking spreads, the team will no longer be designers but merely selectors.

Complexity will seize everything, because no one will proactively take precautions.

The engineering manager decided to intervene.

He called a meeting whose title consisted of only four words: Boundaries and Responsibility.

In the meeting room, he presented no numbers and did not discuss specific bugs.

He told a parable:

"In ancient times there was an empire.

They hired large numbers of mercenaries to guard the frontiers in place of their own soldiers.

At first, this system made the empire appear stronger.

The borders were stable and enemies were repelled.

But over time, the nation's soldiers lost their training and their courage.

When the mercenaries betrayed them, the empire collapsed in an instant.

AI is our mercenary.

We can use it, but we cannot rely on it.

The true guardians must be ourselves.

Defining problems is our responsibility.

Naming meaning is our responsibility.

If we hand these over to AI, we will be like that empire and will eventually collapse."

The meeting room fell silent for a moment, then someone nodded slightly.

They felt that this was not merely a technical discussion, but a declaration of civilization.

However, boundaries cannot be drawn in a single sentence. The convenience of AI is so great that it seeps into daily life like running water. Even if the team reaches consensus, usage habits continue to change subtly.

Senior engineers began to establish new rules:

- Each candidate must be confirmed with a human-assigned name;
- Each candidate must include an "intent" comment explaining the reason for choosing it;
- Each candidate must pass a double verification in code review.

These rules were like new laws, attempting to constrain the empire's behavior. But enforcing laws requires cultural support. If the young engineers do not truly embrace them, they will ultimately be mere words on paper.

Months later, new problems resurfaced.

The product manager found that the team's speed had not significantly improved. AI was supposed to make them faster, but the rules and reviews made the process slower. They began to worry: "Are we heading to the opposite extreme? Are we fighting complexity with complexity?"

The engineering manager shook his head: "No, this is not a confrontation, but protection. Complexity will always exist; what we can do is ensure it remains within understandable boundaries."

This did not entirely dispel the doubts. Under the pressure of KPIs, speed remained the top priority. The convenience of AI and the rigor of the rules formed a new tension. The team's culture was being pulled by this tension.

The shadow of complexity reappeared. This time it came not from technical fissures, but from cultural rifts. Some engineers wanted to increase reliance on AI to gain speed; others insisted on guarding boundaries to protect future understandability. The two voices rose and fell like tides.

"An empire's split often occurs not because of external enemies, but because of differences in internal beliefs." The Orion team was standing at such a crossroads.

AI had already deeply integrated into the team; convenience and risk coexisted, and culture and rules conflicted. The shadow of complexity was spreading through the cracks in the culture.

Machine's power lies in its ability to offer countless possibilities.

Human power lies in their ability to decide which possibility becomes reality.

Naming is the imprint of civilization.

Candidates are shadows, names are the soul.

The shadow of complexity had already spread to every corner of the Orion team. AI's candidates brought convenience, but also created rifts. Some pursued speed, others insisted on boundaries. They were like two groups of travelers standing at a fork in the road: one longing to run, the other longing to survive.

The turning point came in a crisis.

One summer night, the app's core functionality suddenly collapsed. The app frequently crashed when users uploaded photos. The problem quickly escalated, and social media was full of complaints. Management urgently called everyone together and demanded an immediate fix.

The engineers were frantic. They found that the problem originated from a Copilot-generated candidate. When handling large file uploads it had chosen a blunt, simple approach: load the entire file into memory first, then encode it. For small files this posed no problem; for large files it directly caused an out-of-memory.

This was a typical AI trap. The candidate could run, but it had not considered boundaries. AI does not understand "we are a social app and users will upload hundreds of megabytes of photos and videos." It can only offer the statistically most common implementation.

The crisis lasted several days. The engineers worked overnight to fix it and ultimately solved the problem using native streaming processing. User complaints gradually subsided, but the internal impact on the team was greater.

In a postmortem meeting, the engineering manager spoke: "This outage reminded us that AI is not the designer. It is merely a provider of candidates. Our mistake was not accepting the candidate, but failing to define the problem clearly. If we had specified during the requirements phase that large file uploads must be supported, the AI candidate would have been filtered out. If we had clearly required during review that implementations must adhere to streaming principles, the candidate would not have been merged into the main branch. The fault is not AI's; the fault is ours."

The meeting room fell silent in thought. Everyone realized: AI is not the enemy, but it needs boundaries. Without boundaries, AI's convenience can turn into a trap.

From then on, the Orion team embarked on a profound reform. They proposed a new collaboration model:

First, define the problem. Every requirement, before development, must undergo rigorous definition. Not only describe the functionality, but also the boundary conditions, performance constraints, and long-term maintainability. Requirement documents are no longer vague descriptions, but clear cognitive boundaries.

Second, AI provides candidates. Copilot is allowed to freely generate solutions, but those solutions are only "candidates." They must be screened by humans and must pass the test of the team's philosophy.

Third, humans name. The final implementation must be named by people. Naming is not just giving a label; it is conferring meaning. It represents the team's choice and a promise to future readers.

These three rules, like a new constitution, were gradually written into the team's culture.

In one development task, the team needed to implement a complex filter: recommending appropriate events based on users' interests, geographic location, and time. They first defined the problem in the requirements document: it must be scalable, support future event types, and guarantee performance. Then they allowed Copilot to generate candidates. There were many candidates, with various styles coexisting. Finally, they sat together and discussed each candidate's intent one by one. They gave the final selected solution a name: EventFilterEngine.

The naming process was not merely formal. It forced the team to think: what is this module's responsibility? Where are its boundaries? What is its future direction?

At the moment of naming, a candidate truly became part of civilization.

As this model spread, the team's culture gradually changed.

Young engineers no longer blindly relied on AI candidates. They learned to define the problem before candidates appeared. They wrote clear boundaries during the requirements phase and used naming during implementation to guard those boundaries.

Senior engineers rediscovered their value. They no longer only fixed flaws in candidates but guided the team in defining problems and naming boundaries. Their experience was transformed into the team's culture rather than a personal burden.

Product managers also began to understand the balance between speed and quality. They found that although this model slightly slowed development, the failure rate dropped significantly. In the long run, overall efficiency improved.

Complexity still existed, but it had been tamed. It was no longer a flood but guided into channels. AI was no longer an illusion but had become a real tool.

The team gradually formed a new tacit understanding: when Copilot provides candidates, everyone knows this is only a starting point, not the answer. When a name is given, everyone knows it is a commitment, not a casual choice.

This is the collaboration philosophy between humans and AI. Not replacement, not blind obedience, but division of labor. AI offers countless possibilities; humans decide which possibility becomes reality.

"Complexity will not be eliminated; it can only be understood. AI will not bring wisdom; it only amplifies habits. If habits are clear, AI will make clarity faster. If habits are chaotic, AI will deepen the chaos. The ultimate outcome depends on whether humans are willing to take on the responsibility of defining and naming."

This story is not just a team's practice. It is an allegory of the entire software civilization.

In the future, AI will become ever more powerful, and candidates ever more precise. Even so, the core of design will not change. Because the core of design is not generating answers but choosing answers. Not implementing logic, but naming meaning.

Complexity still churns in that sea of sand. It waits to drown lazy teams and waits for awake teams to build levees. AI is wind: it can push you forward or scatter you. The key is whether you have sufficiently clear boundaries to decide the wind's direction.

- AI can write code, but it cannot design.
- Candidates are shadows; naming is the soul.
- Humans' responsibility is to define problems and name boundaries; AI's responsibility is to provide candidates.
- If humans abandon defining and naming, complexity will instantly devour everything.
- If humans hold fast to defining and naming, AI will become the most powerful auxiliary force.

This is the collaboration philosophy between humans and AI. It is not a shortcut, but a discipline. It is not an illusion, but a covenant.

In the end, code is not written for machines, but for humans.
AI can generate countless answers, but only humans can give names.
And the name is civilization.

CHAPTER 30
AVOID THE BLACK BOX

When knowledge can be summoned easily, people forget the value of understanding.

When complexity is temporarily hidden, it doesn't disappear but accumulates in the black box, waiting for the right moment.

The most cunning disguise of complexity is not chaos, but clarity.

It can sometimes make everything look neat, even faster, smoother, and more efficient than before.

But it is precisely beneath this illusion that complexity quietly grows.

The birth of GitHub Copilot is the perfect embodiment of this illusion.

It promises: the moment you write a function name, it can auto-complete the implementation; when you write comments, it can infer the logic; when you're tired, it can continue writing code for you.

It sounds like magic, like the long-held dream of developers.

One spring, a startup decided to fully adopt Copilot.

Their app was a SwiftUI application aimed at travelers, helping users quickly find hotels, restaurants, and activities.

The team was small, just over ten engineers, but the growing demand had worn them out.

They had argued in meetings about whether to hire more people or cut features.

And then AI's promise appeared.

"We don't need more engineers," a leader said, "we need smarter tools."

So Copilot was introduced to the project, as if a silent newcomer had joined the team.

The initial experience was euphoric.

The engineers found: they only needed to write a comment, and Copilot could generate a complete piece of logic.

They only needed to type a few keywords, and the UI layout would automatically appear.

Boilerplate that used to require effort seemed to be completed by an invisible hand.

A feature that used to take two days now took only one.

A previously tedious test was now almost auto-completed.

The team's speed increased severalfold within just a few weeks.

At the sprint retrospective, everyone cheered.

"This is the future."

"We can finally spend our time on what really matters."

"AI is our new teammate."

This joy was real.

On the surface, Copilot did relieve their burden.

Complexity seemed to have been eliminated, at least in their daily work.

But complexity never truly disappears.

It only takes another form, waiting to return.

Another illusion brought by speed is the loss of a sense of control.

Most of Copilot's suggestions are reasonable, but not all are correct.

Some logic looks perfect yet buries traps in edge cases.

Some implementations seem concise but hide invisible dependencies.

The engineers' initial euphoria was gradually replaced by a subtle unease.

They began to ask:

"Why is this logic written this way?"

"What was the basis for choosing this API?"

"If there's a bug, can we find its root cause?"

AI did not answer.

It just silently kept generating, as if no explanation were needed.

The silence of the black box is more frightening than mistakes.

One concrete incident amplified this unease.

The team needed to implement a hotel booking flow.

The logic wasn't complicated: pick dates, confirm guest count, calculate the price, submit the order.

An engineer wrote a few lines of comments, and Copilot quickly generated a complete implementation.

The code was clean and elegant, seemingly flawless.

However, after going live, users began to complain.

In some cases, the price calculation was wrong.

Some users saw a total that was a few dollars less than the amount due; others were charged an extra service fee.

The issue was marked urgent.

The team immediately began investigating.

They combed through logs, reproduced the flow, and dug into the code step by step.

They eventually discovered the problem lay in a subtle conditional check.

When generating the logic, Copilot had omitted an edge case for a certain tax rate.

The bug wasn't fatal, but it revealed a larger problem:

The team could no longer fully understand where the code had come from.

They didn't know who had written that line of logic.

They didn't know whether that line of logic had been given sufficient thought.

They only knew that the line had been automatically generated by AI.

The fear of the black box arrived for the first time.

The essence of complexity has never been technical difficulty, but the cost of understanding.

When you don't understand a system, you cannot control it.

When you cannot control it, you can only be dragged along by it.

The black box of Copilot stripped the team of the initiative to understand. They thought they were reducing cognitive load, but in reality they were merely deferring it. And the price of deferral is paid back many times over when bugs appear.

That repayment is not merely a fix, but a collapse of the mind. The engineers began to feel frustrated:

"I don't know whether I really understand this logic."

"I don't know whether the AI's choice is correct."

"I don't know where the next bug will appear."

Complexity transformed into a fog.

It was no longer visible branches, inheritance, or abstractions, but invisible generated logic.

Under the fog, the team's speed remained high, but their sense of direction gradually vanished.

"When a civilization relies too much on oracles, it loses the ability to reason.

When truth comes from a black box rather than logic, the seeds of decline have already been sown."

This is the danger of AI.

It brings speed, but it also brings a black box.

It reduces the burden of the present, but increases the debt of the future.

The team had not yet realized they were walking a dangerous path.

They were still intoxicated by the thrill of speed, still believing they controlled everything.

But the sands of complexity had already piled up under their feet.

When humans lose the habit of reasoning, the machine's suggestions become law.

But if law cannot be questioned, it is not order, but a disguise of chaos.

The power of the black box lies not in causing a one-time disaster, but in making disasters hard to locate.

The weight of complexity is imposed on the human mind in this way.

That small team felt unprecedented speed in the initial phase of adopting Copilot.

But months later they entered a new cycle: the number of bugs didn't decrease, while the difficulty of fixing them multiplied.

Each problem was like searching for a lost crystal in a sea of sand.

The first crisis appeared in the payment system.

During a promotional campaign, the app needed to support a time-limited discount.

An engineer wrote the logic in a comment, and Copilot quickly generated an apparently reasonable implementation: multiply the order amount by a discount factor, then round to two decimal places.

This logic was accepted, and the tests also passed.

But after going live, problems appeared.

For some users, the order amount was one cent less than expected.

Though the discrepancy was small, it affected thousands of orders.

The accounting team discovered a shortfall in the total amount and had to trace it.

The issue was submitted to the development team.

They began investigating: was it a backend problem? Floating-point calculations in the database? Or client-side rounding?

Three days later, they finally found that the problem lay in the logic automatically generated by Copilot: it used the wrong rounding mode, which in some cases led to undercounting the amount.

The error seemed simple, but it cost the team huge effort.

Because they hadn't fully understood the AI-generated logic at the start and had simply accepted it.

When the bug appeared, they were forced to trace its origin.

This is the cost of the black box: you save understanding in the moment, but must pay it back many times over in the future.

The second crisis occurred in performance optimization.

SwiftUI's UI rendering requires careful handling of state changes.

The team had previously optimized carefully, but after adopting Copilot they found that much of the boilerplate logic could be handled by AI.

So they gradually relied on Copilot to generate parts of the state-management implementation.

At first everything went smoothly.

But weeks later, users began to complain: certain screen transitions were noticeably laggy, animations were not smooth. The problem was especially pronounced on lower-end devices.

The team spent weeks analyzing performance.

They tracked memory with Instruments, logged state changes, and stepped through with breakpoints.

They eventually discovered the root cause was certain state-update logic generated by Copilot: it triggered redraws when unnecessary, causing performance degradation.

These pieces of logic weren't errors, but "reasonable yet inefficient."

The engineers didn't notice at first because they worked correctly on the surface.

But as the app scaled, the problem was amplified.

The second cost of the black box became apparent: it can not only generate mistakes, but also hidden inefficiencies.

Such inefficiencies are invisible at small scale but become disastrous at large scale.

The third crisis arose in the team's collaborative culture.

Two attitudes gradually formed within the team. One group were the proponents of reliance: they embraced Copilot, believing it could save time and that any defects could be fixed later. The other group were the skeptics: they doubted Copilot's reliability and believed every line of generated logic must be carefully reviewed.

The proponents argued that speed is a competitive advantage and excessive questioning only slows progress. The skeptics argued that understanding is the key to survival and blind reliance only accumulates debt.

The debate gradually turned into a rift. During code reviews, the proponents often submitted large amounts of AI-generated logic, while the skeptics raised objections. The atmosphere in the meeting room grew increasingly tense. Some complained, "You're always nitpicking AI's problems but not looking at the time it has saved us." Others retorted, "You're just pushing problems onto our future selves—who will take responsibility then?"

The third cost of complexity appeared: it not only increased the technical burden, but also tore the team's culture apart.

The decline of an empire is not just broken roads and rotting warehouses, but also a split in belief. The decline of a software team is not only more bugs and worse performance, but also the disintegration of its culture.

"When the black box becomes the norm, reason is replaced. When explanations are ignored, trust collapses. Complexity not only devours systems, it devours civilization."

The engineers of the small team gradually felt their daily work had turned into a gamble. They were gambling whether the AI-generated logic was reliable; they were gambling whether bugs would be exposed before going live; they were gambling whether future maintenance could still be traced.

This uncertainty enveloped the team like a fog. They still moved quickly, but no longer knew the direction. Speed became an illusion, understanding a luxury.

At an internal sharing session, a senior engineer said, "We introduced Copilot to lighten the load. But now I feel we've only shifted the burden onto our future selves. We're not reducing complexity; we're creating new complexity."

Those words fell heavily on everyone. They reminded people of a warning from the history of empires: when rulers think they can control the future, the future is already laughing at them in the dark.

The black box of AI is such a future. On the surface it is a gift, but in truth it is a debt. It reduces the labor before us, but increases an invisible cognitive load.

The team began to struggle. They still needed speed, because the market waits for no one. They also yearned for clarity, because complexity was devouring them. They stood at a crossroads, uncertain which way to go.

The value of a tool lies not in how much it can do for people, but in how much it helps people understand.

If a black box is not tamed, it becomes a tyrant; if it is tamed, it becomes a servant.

But at certain moments, a civilization chooses to face its own illusions. For that SwiftUI team, the turning point did not come from a catastrophic bug, nor from an external failure, but from a quiet internal reflection.

It was an unassuming retro meeting. A young engineer presented his week's work log. On the screen, red bug tags scattered across the schedule like meteors. He pointed to a comment and said, "This piece of logic was generated by Copilot. It looked fine at the time, but it took me three days to confirm why it was wrong. During those three days I barely wrote any new code—I was just tracing back a line of logic I should have understood from the start."

The room fell silent. No one argued, no one defended themselves. In that moment they realized: the problem was not AI itself, but the way they used AI.

They recalled a historian's adage: "The black box is not the demon; blind faith is."

So the team began to establish new rituals.

The first ritual was a covenant of explanation. They required that any AI-generated logic be accompanied by an explanation. If an engineer could not, in the review, explain in one sentence the origin and purpose of that logic, they could not submit it. This rule was not meant as punishment, but to ensure understanding. Because understanding is the true currency of cognitive load.

At first, this rule slowed their pace. Many engineers found they could not quickly explain the AI's choices, so they had to go back and reread the logic, even rewrite parts of the implementation. But over time they found that the number of bugs noticeably decreased. Complexity remained, but it no longer lurked in the form of fog. It was revealed, understood, controlled.

The second ritual was a covenant of boundaries. They clearly specified which scenarios could use AI and which had to be implemented by humans.

For example:

- Boilerplate logic, test stubs, repetitive UI: AI generation allowed.
- Core business logic, state management, payments and security: must be designed by humans.

This agreement was like the borders of an empire. It acknowledged AI's value, but also human responsibility. It allowed complexity to be governed in zones, rather than being thrown into a chaotic black box.

This division of labor restored a sense of control to the team. They were no longer slaves to the black box, but masters of it. They knew which areas could be entrusted to tools and which they had to bear themselves.

The third ritual was transparent review. They added a special step to code reviews: mark AI-generated parts with symbols or comments to distinguish them. When reviewers saw the marks, they paid extra attention and demanded explanation and verification.

This transparency changed the team's atmosphere. The skeptics were no longer opposed to the proponents, because everyone could clearly see which code was AI-generated and which was written by humans. Fewer arguments, more understanding. AI was no longer a mysterious colleague, but an explicit assistant.

The empire's archives recorded: "The greatness of an institution lies not in its elimination of problems, but in making problems visible." This is precisely the meaning of transparency.

These three rituals did not eliminate complexity. But they made complexity visible and allowed cognitive load to be allocated reasonably. They turned AI from a maker of fog into a sharer of burdens.

A few months later, the team's metrics changed noticeably: bug counts fell, fix times shortened, and development speed remained steady. More importantly, the team's confidence was restored. They no longer feared the black box; they knew how to use it.

Historians would say this was a civilization's act of self-rescue. When humanity learns to set boundaries for oracles, the oracles truly become tools rather than rulers. When a team learns to make AI serve understanding rather than replace it, AI becomes a partner instead of a threat.

After this turning point, the team coined a maxim: "AI should reduce cognitive load, not create fog."

The sentence was written on the whiteboard in the meeting room and put into the repository's documentation. It was not a slogan, but a line of defense. It reminded everyone: speed is not value, understanding is the essence.

This story did not belong only to that small team. Around the world, thousands of teams were going through a similar process. They were first intoxicated by AI's speed, then troubled by the black box, and ultimately forced to establish boundaries and policies.

Airbnb's experience with React Native has already proven the illusion of cross-platform solutions. The SwiftUI team's experience with Copilot once again proved the danger of black boxes. Different technologies, the same lesson: complexity will not be eliminated by promises; it will only be deferred. True wisdom lies in governing within boundaries, not indulging in illusions.

AI is not a savior, but a tool. The meaning of a tool is not to think for you, but to help you save the cost of understanding. The black box is unavoidable, but it must be made transparent. Complexity cannot be eradicated, but it must be governed by partition. Cognitive load cannot be destroyed, but it must be reasonably allocated.

The greatest tools do not replace understanding; they amplify it.
The greatest engineering is not the pursuit of speed, but the safeguarding of clarity.

If the black box is revealed, it is a friend; if it is indulged in, it is an enemy.

PART SEVEN
BATTLEFIELD NOTES ON COMPLEXITY

CHAPTER 31
FROM COMPLEX IF-ELSE TO STATE MACHINE ENUMERATION

The empire's gates are not destroyed by siege, but by the gatekeeper's hesitation.

A software login is not destroyed by attacks, but by confused logic.

The wind does not blow from the border, but seeps through the cracks of the city gate.

The invasion of complexity often doesn't begin with grand architecture, but with the most everyday feature—the login.

Early Twitter was like a newborn city-state.

The city-state longed to expand, to let more citizens in.

So they built the first gate: username and password.

At first, this seemed sufficient. Users entered credentials, the system verified them, the gate opened.

However, an empire never stays at its original size.

The number of users kept expanding, attackers' methods became increasingly complex, and product managers kept coming up with new requirements.

They needed password recovery, email binding, SMS verification, third-party login, OAuth, two-step verification.

Each requirement was a new brick embedded in the gate.

But no one stopped to rebuild the gate's structure; they just kept adding locks to the existing latch.

This is how complexity arises: not from a single explosion, but from one addition after another.

The original Twitter login system was meant to be clear:

check username → verify password → login successful.

But as features were added, the logic began to deform:

If the user hasn't bound an email, go into email verification;

If they've bound an email but not confirmed it, go into a confirmation flow;

If there are too many attempts, go into a verification-code flow;

If two-step verification is enabled, go into SMS or app verification;

If the user comes from a third-party platform, go to an OAuth redirect;

If OAuth fails, fall back to password login.

This is not a map, but a maze.

Developers wander through it like gatekeepers, asking each time:

"If this condition holds, then what? If it doesn't, then what?"

if-else is like a branching road; at first there are only two or three branches, and it's not difficult to navigate.

But as branches increase, each path may lead to new forks.

In the end, you stand at a crossroads, facing countless possibilities, not knowing which path leads to the exit.

The essence of complexity is not the amount of code, but the number of branches.

The human brain can only track a limited number of states at once.

In the sea of if-else statements in a login system, every condition is a new state, every exception a new world.

Twitter's engineers soon found they could no longer quickly understand the system.

A single bug investigation could take weeks.

When a user reported a login failure, engineers had to trace dozens of branches to find the real root cause.

Worse, even if one bug was fixed, a new one would appear in another branch.

Complexity is like a desert, if-else like sand dunes.

When there are only a few dunes, you can easily cross them.

When the dunes form mountain ranges, you can only get lost among them.

This is not just a technical problem, but a cognitive one.

A newly joined engineer needs weeks to understand the entire login flow.

They must remember:

- The order between email verification and two-step verification;
- The fallback logic when OAuth fails;
- The conditions that trigger a verification code after multiple failures;
- The differences among SMS providers in different countries;
- The different user experiences across platforms.

They are no longer engineers but gatekeeping priests.

They have mastered a complex ritual that can only be performed correctly after long study.

If someone forgets a detail, the system will have a vulnerability.

Cognitive load became a new tax.

Every new developer must pay weeks of learning before they can start contributing.

Every team's decisions must take countless exceptions into account to avoid disaster.

The empire's gate should be clear.

Citizens should know how to enter, guards should know how to check.

But when too many mechanisms are added to the gate, even the guards forget the order.

Thus the gate ceases to be protection and becomes an obstacle.

Twitter's login system is such a gate.

It was originally designed for security and convenience, but in the end it became a maze of complexity.

Every user's entry is a gamble; every developer's change is an adventure.

The shadow of complexity grew ever darker.

Users began to complain: why is logging in so cumbersome?

Engineers began to complain: why is fixing bugs so difficult?

Management began to complain: why are iterations so slow?

Complexity does not answer; it only keeps accumulating.

It blankets the entire team like a dust storm, making it hard to breathe.

The most dangerous enemy is not the besieging army, but the gatekeepers crushed by their own rules.

The heaviest lock is not iron, but memory.

Complexity is not a battle, but a climate.

It does not begin at a single moment, but accumulates from countless small changes.

By the midlife of Twitter's login system, it was no longer a gate but a maze.

A maze has an entrance, but no clear exit.

Every branch is like a forked road, every condition like a hidden door.

Users who enter the maze often wander within it.

Engineers who enter the maze often lose their way.

That was the most humiliating moment for the user experience team.

A user played a video in a meeting:

He tried to log into Twitter, entered his password, and the system required him to bind an email;

After binding the email, it required SMS verification;

SMS verification failed, and it required entering a verification code;

The verification code was correct, but it then said email confirmation was needed;

After confirming the email, it asked for the password again.

At the end of the video, the user laughed, but the smile was full of irony.

"I want to post a Tweet, not play a maze game."

The conference room fell silent.

Everyone understood this was not an isolated incident, but a microcosm of the whole system.

Complexity had spread from an engineering problem into a user-experience problem.

Complexity always does this: it turns internal Cognitive Load into external friction.

When internal engineers cannot understand the system, external users cannot use it smoothly.

When a system's logic exceeds the limits of human cognition, disaster begins to spill over.

Twitter's team fell into a new dilemma:

They fixed bugs, yet introduced new ones;

They simplified flows, yet created more exceptions;

They added security, yet made the experience more tedious.

The empire's gatekeepers stayed up late at night, trying to rearrange the order of the latches.

But every adjustment caused another door to jam.

They were no longer guards, but prisoners.

The loss of control over complexity also manifested in team communication.

In a requirement review, the product manager proposed a seemingly reasonable feature:

"We want the system to automatically trigger a security alert after a user fails to log in three times and require additional verification."

It sounds like merely adding a condition.

However, when engineers put this condition into the if-else maze, they found it spawned a new whirlpool.

What if the user logged in via OAuth?

What if the user has bound an email but it is unconfirmed?

What if the user is overseas and SMS is delayed?

What if the user's device doesn't support rendering verification codes?

Each "what if" is not a philosophical question but an engineering nightmare.

The team argued for hours in meetings but could not reach a clear answer.

"This is like building a castle on a pile of sand," an engineer said helplessly.

"You think adding one brick will make the castle more stable, but it ends up making the whole castle more fragile."

Complexity also devoured time.

An iteration for a new feature often takes two or even three times as long.

Because developers must not only implement the new feature but also carefully avoid triggering traps in the old logic.

The testing team's workload multiplies; they must cover all possible combinations.

A test-case document can be hundreds of pages thick.

It records various states:

- User has bound an email but not confirmed it;
- User has bound a phone but the SMS never arrived;

- User's password is correct but OAuth fails;
- User passed verification by code but the email is invalid.

Testers acted like copyists, repeating these scenarios word for word.

They knew this document could never truly cover every situation.

Because the combinations of if-else are far greater than they imagine.

Complexity makes time itself an enemy.

Engineers are consumed by time, users disappointed while waiting, management anxious over delays.

The ledger of time becomes complexity's sharpest weapon.

The runaway complexity also brought security risks.

During a security review, the team discovered a serious issue:

A logical flaw in one branch allowed attackers to bypass two-step verification.

The vulnerability was not due to a lack of security measures, but because the branching combinations were too complex.

An inconspicuous path inadvertently skipped a critical check.

The security team wrote in their report:

"We were not defeated by attackers, but by our own complexity."

This is the empire's most terrible nightmare:

the gate did not break because of the enemy's battering ram, but because the guards themselves forgot the order of the keys.

Team morale began to collapse.

Young engineers felt frustrated: they discovered their time was spent not on innovation but on fixing stale logic.

Senior engineers felt exhausted: they found they could no longer master the whole.

Even the team leaders began to feel powerless.

They held countless meetings and proposed various plans:

Simplify flows, cut features, refactor logic.

But every attempt was like digging channels in the dunes, soon filled again by new winds and sand.

Complexity is a kind of despair.

It makes you realize that even if you give your all, you cannot change the overall situation.

"The empire's gatekeepers have added too many locks to the gate.

Locks should symbolize security, but when the number of locks exceeds the capacity of human memory, the locks become new vulnerabilities."

Twitter's login system was such a gate.

The gatekeepers added countless locks but forgot whether they could remember all the keys.

In the end, complexity turned locks into burdens and security into an illusion.

Yet crisis also breeds opportunity.

In an all-hands retrospective, a senior engineer raised a question:

"Why are we using if-else to simulate states?

Why don't we treat login as a state machine?"

The question was a spark that ignited long-dormant thought.

The team began to rethink:

Login is not a combination of conditions, but transitions between a finite set of states.

A user is either logged out, logged in, in verification, or failed.

All logic should not be branching crossroads, but flows of state.

This was a new perspective.

It does not evade complexity, but acknowledges it and organizes it more clearly.

Complexity will not disappear, but the Cognitive Load can be redistributed.

The idea of a state machine became a new hope.

When the gate's locks are so many that no one remembers their order, the polity is in peril.

When the gatekeepers put down the keys and embrace order, the polity truly has a gate.

Complexity is not the enemy; it is a natural force.

The if-else maze is not an evil creation, but the result of human groping in chaos.

The real mistake is not building the maze, but forgetting that a maze needs a map.

Twitter's team, after countless failures and setbacks, finally began to rethink: what would happen if the login flow were not a pile of conditions, but a series of finite states?

The turning point came in a seemingly ordinary incident.

One weekend, a large number of users reported they could not log in.

Monitoring showed: server load normal, database fine, network traffic stable.

The team was baffled.

After more than ten hours of investigation, they found the problem lay in an unremarkable conditional branch:

When a user had two-step verification enabled, the email unconfirmed, and OAuth login failed, the logic fell into a loop and the system kept asking the user to re-enter their password.

This was a path that seemed almost impossible, but in the real world it happened.

A tiny if-else kept tens of thousands of users shut out.

The engineers, exhausted, realized: the problem was not a single bug, but the structure of the whole system.

As long as logic was stacked in if-else chains, new traps would keep being created.

So a new idea emerged:

"We need a finite state machine."

A finite state machine is not a new invention.

It appears in the classics of mathematics, in compiler parsing, in the logic gates of circuits.

But in the world of application logic it is often ignored.

Because people are more accustomed to thinking in terms of conditions rather than modeling in terms of states.

A state machine requires us to view the world as a finite set of states and the transitions between them.

It does not rely on branching forks, but on rules of order.

Its power lies not in reducing complexity, but in making complexity orderly.

Twitter's team began to experiment.

They drew a diagram.

On the diagram there were only a few nodes:

- Not logged in
- Logging in
- Logged in
- Login failed
- Verifying

All logic had to be reduced to transitions between these states.

For example:

user enters password → transition from Not logged in to Logging in.

Password correct → transition to Logged in.

Password incorrect → transition to Login failed.

Two-step verification required → transition to Verifying, then decide whether to enter Logged in or Login failed.

This diagram was not code, but order.

It made everyone see for the first time: the essence of login is not a stacking of conditions, but the flow of states.

Engineers began to discuss issues in meetings using state diagrams.

In the past they would say: "If the user has bound an email

but not confirmed it, and has two-step verification enabled, and OAuth login fails..."

Now they would say: "If a transition from Verifying fails, enter the Login Failed state."

The change in language brought a change in thinking.

The change in thinking brought a change in culture.

Complexity did not disappear, but it was contained within boundaries.

Boundaries are not walls, but order.

The state machine is that boundary; it confines chaotic possibilities within a finite order.

The team advanced the refactor incrementally.

They did not tear everything down at once, but replaced modules one by one.

First password login, then email verification, then two-step verification, and finally OAuth.

Each module was redefined as part of the state machine, and each state machine followed the same principles.

In the process they discovered more bugs.

Vulnerabilities that had been hidden in the sea of if-else statements now stood clearly on the state diagram.

They could plainly see which state transitions were illegal and which paths should never exist.

The state machine was like a mirror that reflected the truth of complexity.

It did not make complexity vanish, but it made complexity transparent.

The most notable change happened in cognitive load.

New engineers no longer had to memorize hundreds of branching rules.

They only needed to understand the state diagram to get up to speed quickly.

The testing team no longer needed to write thick test-case manuals.

They only needed to cover transitions between states to ensure logical completeness.

Complexity still existed, but it was no longer an unordered sandstorm; it was a controllable river.

The human brain could finally grasp the whole system within its limited capacity.

This shift also changed the team's culture.

Previously, meetings were full of arguments:

"What if this happens? What if it fails? What if verification times out?"

Now meetings became concise:

"Is this a new state? Is this a legal transition?"

Culture shifted from debating exceptions to debating order.

Complexity transformed from an individual burden into a shared map.

Historians call it "the awakening of gatekeeping order."

The empire's gate no longer depends on the gatekeepers' memory.

Gatekeepers no longer have to memorize every key; they only need to follow order.

Order outweighs memory; systems outweigh craft.

Twitter's login system, after years of refactoring, finally regained clarity.

Users no longer complained about hassles, engineers no longer felt lost, and security vulnerabilities dropped significantly.

Complexity was not eradicated, but it was brought into order and tamed within boundaries.

This story leaves us with three profound lessons:

First, complexity will not disappear; it only moves.

If-else is not a mistake; it is the most instinctive human response to complexity.

But when complexity exceeds mental capacity, if-else becomes a trap.

Second, the real solution is not to eliminate complexity, but to reorganize it.

State machines do not reduce the amount of logic, but they present logic in an orderly way.

They do not remove sand; they compact sand into bricks.

Third, boundaries are the essence of civilization.

Without boundaries, complexity will spread like a sandstorm;

With boundaries, complexity can be tamed and become an understandable, maintainable order.

The history of software civilization is the history of complexity.

Twitter's login system is only one chapter of it, yet it is enough to serve as a fable.

The fable tells us:

Complexity is not a demon, but a flood.

If-else is the primitive levee; the state machine is the formalized reservoir.

A levee can resist a temporary flood, but a reservoir is what sustains long-term civilization.

The goal of software architecture is not showmanship, but order.
The most powerful code is not a miracle, but the ordinary that future people can understand.

CHAPTER 32
UIKIT'S LEGACY AND SWIFTUI'S PHILOSOPHY OF COMPOSITION

The trunk grows upward, inevitably bringing the weight of branches.

Vines intertwine; though chaotic, they survive through flexibility.

Inheritance is the genealogy of an empire, composition is the alliance of nomads.

The story of complexity always begins with a seemingly harmless choice.

In the era of UIKit, inheritance was the starting point of everything.

Apple's documentation encouraged you to inherit view controllers, to inherit buttons, to inherit scroll views.

Developers at the time seemed to be given a sacred key: just inherit, and you could obtain everything.

However, inheritance is also a contract.

What it promises is not only power, but also chains.

Once you choose inheritance, you are bound to the fate of the superclass and cannot easily disentangle yourself.

The superclass's bloat must be borne by the subclasses; the superclass's constraints must not be defied by the subclasses.

LinkedIn's iOS team built their empire on exactly this kind of legacy.

Their app rapidly expanded in the early 2010s, with user growth and a surge in features.

Messages, jobs, feeds, contacts — each feature took root in the app.

To move faster, they relied on UIKit's inheritance system:

A huge base view controller that spawned countless subclasses, each feature finding its place on this family tree.

At first, such a design seemed flawless.

Code reuse was high, and the team could iterate quickly.

The convenience brought by inheritance was like the passing down of an imperial bloodline, allowing a newborn module to possess full authority and functionality from birth.

However, the corrosion of complexity began here as well.

LinkedIn's base view controller was hailed as the "universal controller."

It contained thousands of lines of code, encompassing network requests, data binding, UI layout, error prompts, and logging.

Every subclass naturally inherited from it.

Over time, the number of subclasses kept increasing and branching logic kept accumulating.

One day, the team discovered:

changing a single line of logic in the base class could affect the behavior of dozens of subclasses.

A seemingly harmless optimization could cause the entire app to crash in different corners.

The convenience of inheritance turned into fragility.

This is the fate of inheritance: it lets you move fast at first, but the burden grows heavier the further you go.

The larger the empire's genealogy, the more complex the bloodlines, and the higher the risk of internal turmoil.

The team began to feel fear. They dared not modify the base class at will, nor introduce new features lightly. They seemed to stand before an ancient temple, aware that it was precarious, yet afraid to touch any of its stones.

The problem with inheritance was not only technical, but cognitive.

When new engineers joined LinkedIn's team, it took weeks or even months to grasp the full scope of the "universal controller." They had to trace complex call chains and understand countless conditional branches to make safe changes in subclasses. This was not learning code but entering a maze.

The Cognitive Load was laid bare. The layers of inheritance were like successive walls, trapping newcomers. To find your way out of the maze you had to understand all the hidden passages left by predecessors. And these passages often had no map.

Complexity here seemed cold and impartial: it didn't care about your talent, only your patience. It wouldn't spare you because you were a genius; it demanded you pay the full cognitive cost.

The corrosion of inheritance ultimately manifested as a slowdown in velocity.

LinkedIn's app update speed began to decline. Each feature iteration had to be tested cautiously, fearing changes would trigger chain reactions. Bug fixes took longer and release cycles grew slower. The team's anxiety and exhaustion increased day by day.

At this point, inheritance was no longer a blessing but a shackle. It prevented the team from acting freely; they could only move forward in fear.

Against this backdrop, voices advocating composition began to emerge.

Some engineers started to question: "Why are we piling everything onto a single base class? Why can't we break functionality into independent modules and assemble them through composition?"

At first those voices were faint, dismissed as "idealist." Because composition meant overthrowing the existing genealogical system and redesigning module boundaries. That required courage and time.

But the force of complexity was forcing them to change. The empire of inheritance was already teetering. They had to find a new path.

The arrival of SwiftUI was like a gust of wind blowing into this collapsing empire.

SwiftUI's philosophy was not inheritance but composition. A user interface was no longer a relationship of base classes and subclasses but a stitching together of small components. These components are independent and clear, can be composed freely, and do not bring the chains of hierarchy.

LinkedIn's engineers saw hope. They began experimenting with introducing a compositional architecture for some new features, replacing the huge base class with small components. At first, it was only an experiment, like a small well in the desert. But soon they discovered: this well could truly quench their thirst.

The philosophy of composition stood in stark contrast to the fate of inheritance.

Inheritance is like an empire's bloodline: once determined, it cannot be changed. Composition is like a nomadic alliance: it can be dismantled and reassembled at any time. Inheritance intoxicates people with the concentration of power; composition lets people breathe freely again.

LinkedIn's team stood on the edge of this choice. They knew that continuing to rely on inheritance meant the empire would eventually collapse. Turning to composition meant overthrowing the old order and rebuilding structure.

This was a choice about destiny.

Inheritance makes people believe everything is already arranged; composition teaches that everything must be chosen.

An empire's flourishing depends on the transmission of bloodlines; a civilization's continuation depends on the reformation of alliances.

Complexity is not a sudden disaster but a slow quicksand. After struggling for years within UIKit's inheritance system, LinkedIn's team finally understood: this quicksand would not stop by itself. They had to act.

Their first attempt was on a marginal feature.

It was a "job recommendation" interface. In the past, such a feature would naturally fall into a subclass of the "universal controller," inheriting all the common logic. But one engineer proposed, "Why don't we try composition?"

So they didn't create a new subclass; instead they broke the interface into several small view units: job cards, company information, apply button, recommendation reasons. Each unit existed independently and could be developed, tested, and reused on its own.

When these units were stitched together, a new interface was born. It didn't rely on a huge base class or require inheriting complex logic; it came together like a puzzle.

The results were astonishing. Development moved faster than expected, there were fewer bugs, and testing was easier. More importantly, new team members only needed to understand a few small components to contribute, rather than become familiar with the maze of the "universal controller."

This was the first victory of composition. It gave the team hope.

However, complexity will not give up easily.

When the team tried to extend the compositional approach to

more features, they quickly met resistance. The old inheritance system remained, and the massive base classes still governed much of the app's functionality. New compositional modules had to coexist with legacy inherited modules, with blurred boundaries and chaotic interfaces.

Engineers felt as if they were living at the boundary between two eras. On one side was the ancient empire—strict bloodlines and intricate systems; on the other, emerging tribes—flexible and free, yet lacking unified order.

They had to maintain both worlds at once. In meeting rooms they argued, "Should we overthrow the old system all at once?" "If we migrate incrementally, will complexity become worse during the transition?"

This was a real test. Any architectural migration is a tug-of-war between real-world pressures and the pursuit of ideals.

In that tug-of-war, the team gradually realized a truth: composition is not merely a technical approach; it is a philosophy, a culture.

The culture of inheritance is dependency and obedience. Once you inherit, you must accept the rules of the superclass. The culture of composition is contract and collaboration. Each component has clear boundaries, takes on only its own responsibilities, and coordinates through explicit interfaces.

The conflict between these two cultures is not just a conflict of code, but a conflict of team mindset.

LinkedIn's team made a decisive choice: they formed a dedicated group responsible for defining standards for compositional components.

This group was not a traditional architecture committee, but a "components council." Their task was not to dictate every component's implementation, but to set boundaries and contracts. They defined:

- Components should be independent and not rely on global state.

- Components should be reusable and composable in different contexts.
- Components should be testable; each component must be verifiable on its own.
- Relationships between components are not parent-child, but equal collaboration.

The establishment of this system was the true beginning of the composition philosophy. It no longer depended on the enthusiasm of individual engineers but became a team consensus.

However, complexity still lurked in the shadows.

During one iteration, the team tried to refactor the messaging interface using composition. The messaging interface was one of the most complex parts of the LinkedIn app, encompassing conversations, attachments, emojis, read receipts, and push notifications. When the team broke these features into components, they quickly found that the dependencies between components were greater than they had imagined and the boundaries were more blurred.

For example, the emoji component needed to know the state of the input box, the attachment component needed to access the networking layer, and the push component needed to integrate with the notification system. These cross-dependencies made composition look less like a clear puzzle and more like a complex web.

The engineers felt frustrated for a time. They wondered: is composition really better than inheritance? Or is it just a different way of producing complexity?

In their confusion, they reexamined SwiftUI's ideas.

SwiftUI's philosophy is not merely "replace inheritance with composition" but "state-driven." A component does not directly depend on another component; instead it depends on shared state. Changes in state drive changes in the UI, rather than direct communication between components.

This idea gave the team a new direction. They began to

introduce the concept of a Single Source of Truth, centralizing all shared data at the state layer. Components no longer depended on each other directly but collaborated indirectly through state.

This made the web clearer. Each component only cared about state and no longer about the implementation of other components. Complexity did not disappear, but it was moved to a layer that was easier to manage.

The power of composition gradually revealed itself.

The LinkedIn team found that when they adhered to state-driven principles and clear boundaries, the advantages of a compositional architecture became increasingly apparent. New features could be developed independently without touching the legacy system. Locating bugs became faster because issues were usually confined to a single component. Test coverage improved because components could be tested in isolation without relying on the entire system.

More importantly, the team's culture began to shift. When new members joined, they no longer needed to understand the massive base class; they only needed to learn the contracts of a few components. Their learning curve shortened and their cognitive load decreased. The team's morale was rekindled.

However, the shadow of inheritance still remained.

The legacy system was still massive, and many features still depended on that "universal controller." It was like an ancient palace—ruined, yet still operating. The team could not overthrow it all at once; they could only move forward amid the transition between old and new.

This transition was the most painful phase. They had to endure double complexity: the shackles of inheritance and the challenges of composition. In each iteration they had to carefully migrate a portion of functionality into the compositional system. It was a long journey with no shortcuts.

A civilization does not transform from an empire to an alliance overnight. It must go through turmoil, conflict, and reconstruction. LinkedIn's team was also moving forward within such a fate.

They knew this road would not be short. But they had no way back. The empire of inheritance had already decayed; the alliance of composition was the future.

When the palace collapsed, the stones did not disappear—they would be re-laid as the walls of villages.

When an empire disintegrated, bloodlines did not end—they would continue to flow within new alliances.

The decline of a technology does not mean an end; it means the rewriting of order.

The empire of inheritance had reached its end, and the alliance of composition was beginning to emerge. LinkedIn's team stood at a historic turning point. They could neither completely abandon the old system nor indefinitely postpone the moment to rebuild. The crushing weight of complexity left them no choice: they had to undergo a complete transformation.

Transformation was not a single decision but a series of compromises. They first picked the most vulnerable feature modules. Job recommendations, company profile displays, and resume rendering—these features frequently failed and generated constant user complaints. If these modules failed, the damage to the entire app would be enormous.

The team decided to use these features as the entry point for refactoring. They rewrote the job recommendation page in a componentized way. They split the resume rendering logic into multiple small components: education history, work experience, skills list. Each component rendered independently and did not interfere with the others. When a bug appeared, they only needed to modify a single component without worrying about the collapse of the entire system.

This approach brought immediate benefits. Development speed increased, testing time shortened, and release risk decreased. More importantly, the team's confidence gradually recovered. They were no longer like tightrope walkers but like people walking on level ground.

But complexity never easily leaves the battlefield.

When the team tried to expand into larger features, problems resurfaced. The refactor of the messaging system gave them headaches. The messaging interface contained far more logic than the job recommendations: input box, push, attachments, emojis, read, unread, conversation management. Each feature was intertwined with the others. When they tried to decompose it component-wise, they found the dependency relationships were tangled.

Components were not isolated but shared state. The input box needed to know the conversation state, attachments needed network access, and push needed to notify the UI. The team briefly fell into chaos; the composition puzzle looked clear, but because of shared state it became a maze.

At that moment, SwiftUI's philosophy reappeared. SwiftUI's "state-driven" idea was not empty rhetoric but a form of order. LinkedIn's engineers realized that the problem was not the number of components but the boundaries of state.

They began to redesign the state layer. They established a Single Source of Truth, centralizing conversation state, message content, and push information. Components no longer communicated directly but collaborated indirectly through state. The input box cared about state, not attachments; attachments cared about state, not push.

This design made the system clear again. Complexity did not disappear, but it was consolidated in the state layer, where it could be understood and controlled by humans.

The team's culture also shifted through this practice.

The culture of the inheritance era was lineage and authority. New features had to inherit the old system and follow the base class's rules. Any deviation was seen as dangerous because it might break the existing order.

The culture of the composition era was contract and collaboration. Each component existed independently and was equal to the others. New features did not join a lineage but joined an alliance. They had to abide by contracts but did not have to bear the shackles of bloodlines.

This cultural shift was deeper than the technology. It moved the team from fear to freedom, from passivity to initiative. New members no longer needed to recite ancient family trees; they learned contracts and state. The learning curve shortened, cognitive load lightened, and creativity was unleashed.

The archives of history record such a moment:

At an internal sharing session, an engineer presented the interface they had refactored using a componentized approach. He showed how the job recommendation page was broken down into small components and how dynamic updates were achieved under a state-driven design. At the end of the demo, applause broke out. A senior engineer slowly stood up and said one sentence: "We are finally no longer afraid to change the code."

That sentence became a turning point for the team. It was not merely an expression of feeling but a declaration. The shadow of inheritance was receding, and the dawn of composition had arrived.

Of course, the road to transformation remained long. The legacy UIKit inheritance would not vanish overnight, and the massive base classes still existed. The team had to hover between the two systems and migrate gradually. This migration would take years and require sustained investment and persistence.

But they had found a direction. Complexity still existed, but it was no longer an uncontrollable flood. They built levees and carved channels to let the flood flow in an orderly way.

The emergence of SwiftUI gave them philosophical support. SwiftUI was not a mere technical framework but a way of thinking:

- The UI is a function of state;
- Composition over inheritance;
- State-driven over direct communication;
- Clear boundaries over convoluted abstractions.

The LinkedIn team, working in the world of UIKit, had already put these ideas into practice. Their experience validated SwiftUI's direction. SwiftUI did not appear out of nowhere; it was an answer to the inheritance dilemma and an affirmation of the composition philosophy.

Inheritance and composition are not just technical choices but also the fate of a civilization.

The benefits of inheritance are obvious at first. It lets you build quickly and reuse existing logic. But as the system grows, the complexity that comes with inheritance accumulates like debt. Eventually, it becomes an unbearable burden.

The benefits of composition are not obvious initially. It requires more design, stricter contracts, and clearer boundaries. But as the system evolves, the flexibility and maintainability brought by composition become the only remedy against complexity.

LinkedIn's story is precisely a microcosm of this fate. They began with inheritance, expanded rapidly, but fell into trouble. They turned to composition, endured pain, and yet found the future. This is not just the story of one company, but of the entire iOS development world.

The legacy of UIKit is an empire of inheritance. The philosophy of SwiftUI is an alliance of composition. We live at the boundary between these two worlds; we must learn from the predicaments of the past and draw strength from the philosophy of the future.

The truth about complexity is revealed here: it does not disappear because of inheritance or composition; it only changes form according to our choices. Inheritance concentrates complexity deep in the bloodline, making it hard to touch; composition exposes complexity at the boundaries, making it easier to govern.

The wisdom of software is not to eliminate complexity, but to choose the appropriate form to bear it.

Inheritance is the legacy of empires; composition is the future of alliances. UIKit left behind genealogies; SwiftUI brought contracts. We suffer in the shadow of inheritance and advance in the dawn of composition.

Great architecture is not about eliminating complexity, but about placing complexity in the right place.
Great teams do not inherit the old order; they compose the new.

CHAPTER 33
HELPER HELL

When an empire's bureaucrats outnumber its soldiers, when documents outnumber weapons, decline is already written into fate.

Wind has no shape, yet it can move sand.

Helpers have no shape either, yet they can change the course of software.

They are born in the name of "convenience", grow under the name of "reuse", and ultimately often turn into traps of complexity.

Twitter's mobile team once sank into such a trap.

In their history, there was a long period during which almost every problem was solved by adding a Helper.

At first, Helpers were created with good intentions.

In a rapidly growing product, time is always tight.

When two features needed to share logic, extracting that part and putting it into a Helper file seemed like the most natural choice.

It was the developer's intuition, and an engineering truism: don't repeat yourself.

In the early stages of Twitter's iOS app, this practice did yield benefits.

Whether it was date formatting or network request wrapping, the existence of Helpers reduced duplicated work.

They were like the empire's clerks, recording affairs and ensuring commands were conveyed consistently.

However, an empire's fate is never decided by one or two victories.

What truly decides fate is the long-term accumulation of systems.

The number of Helpers increased geometrically as the team size expanded.

At some point, they stopped being helpers and became rulers.

The formation of Helper hell is often silent.

In Twitter's codebase, there were only a few scattered utility classes at first.

But as requirements iterated, each team began adding its own Helpers.

Each thought it was just a small convenience.

However, when everyone did this, convenience turned into chaos.

In an internal review, engineers found:

The same logic existed in different Helper files, with similar names but not exactly the same behavior.

For example, the "string processing" Helper had more than a dozen different versions;

the "date conversion" Helper was repeatedly implemented in different modules.

Each team believed they were avoiding duplication, but from a global perspective, they created even greater duplication.

This is the trick of complexity: local optimizations can lead to the collapse of the whole. Each Helper is like a newly established office in the empire: it solves a local problem but increases the cost of communication. When there are enough such offices, the transmission of orders falls into a maze.

Signs of the maze gradually appeared in Twitter's app.

An engineer debugging a crash traced down the call chain: from the UI layer to the logic layer, then to a Helper, that Helper calling another Helper, and so on, nested layer upon layer. Almost no one could tell the root cause at a glance. Each Helper file contained only a few dozen lines of code, but they intertwined to form a network that was hard to understand.

This is the essence of Helper hell: complexity is fragmented and hidden in countless small files, causing the cost of understanding to rise sharply. If complexity were a great river, at least people could see its course; but when it is divided into countless hidden channels, you can only get lost in a maze.

This situation has far-reaching effects on the team.

First is the sharp increase in cognitive load. A newly joined engineer often needs weeks to understand the Helper system behind a feature. They must jump between dozens of Helper files and remember the behavior and differences of each small function. Working memory capacity is limited, and Twitter's Helper network far exceeds it.

Second is the fragmentation of team collaboration. Different groups maintain their own Helpers, and few people truly understand the global picture. Bug fixes require cross-team communication, but different teams' Helper naming and design approaches are completely different. It's like provinces of an empire each making their own laws, making central decrees hard to enforce.

Worst of all is the disaster of debugging and maintenance. When a bug occurs, no one can immediately determine which Helper it is in. Fixing one problem can trigger another because there are too many implicit dependencies between Helpers. Every fix is a gamble.

The weight of complexity began to overwhelm developers' minds.

Twitter's mobile app, as global users grew, bore ever-increasing pressure.

Every release meant hundreds of millions of users might encounter problems immediately.

And in Helper hell, engineers grew increasingly unconfident.

They knew that any small change could unintentionally trigger a chain reaction.

Once, the team needed to optimize the loading performance of the tweet list.

They found that some of the list rendering latency came from a string-processing Helper.

But when they tried to modify that logic, they discovered the Helper was called from multiple modules.

Some calls depended on the old logic, some on the new logic.

Changing it meant having to consider the application's behavior as a whole.

In the end, they had to compromise and write a new Helper to address the immediate need.

And this is the loop of complexity:

Each fix comes at the cost of a new Helper.

Helpers did not reduce problems; they merely pushed them into the future.

When the bureaucratic system balloons, efficiency falls;

when there are too many laws, people are left bewildered.

The fate of Helpers is so similar to the fate of an empire:

They were meant to liberate productivity, but ultimately became shackles.

By this period, Twitter's mobile team had already fallen into trouble.

Their app still ran, users still used it, and outsiders could see no issue.

But in the developers' hearts, the shadow of complexity already loomed over everything.

The wind continued to blow, the sand continued to fall.

Helper hell was not formed overnight; it was the accumulation of countless "clever little moves."

Each "this logic can be extracted," each "write a Helper for reuse," was a grain of sand.

Those grains piled into dunes that eventually pressed down on the team's minds.

When the number of Helpers exceeded the limits of human memory, when abstraction obscured understanding, when reuse became a maze, the empire had already lost its way.

When archives are so numerous no one can consult them, when regulations are so complex no one can follow them, the empire exists in name only.

Complexity will not destroy a city; it merely makes everyone lose their way.

Helpers were not born of malice. Their appearance often sprang from a desire for efficiency. But in Twitter's codebase, that desire was amplified without limit and ultimately became shackles.

The first attempt to govern Helpers was launched during an ordinary sprint.

At that time, engineering managers noticed: code reviews were getting slower, bug fixes took longer, and the pace of new feature iteration had clearly declined. The product team complained, "Why does a change to a button take two weeks to ship?" And the engineers' answer was often, "Because we have to confirm this logic doesn't affect other Helpers."

So a new plan was proposed: establish a Helper registry. All newly created Helpers would have to be approved and recorded. Meanwhile, existing Helpers would be gradually classified to avoid duplication.

On the surface, this looked like a return to order. The

empire's archives had finally established a unified catalog, and the chaotic laws seemed to have a chance to be reorganized.

However, the inertia of complexity was far stronger than imagined.

First, maintaining the registry itself became a new burden. For every feature development, engineers had to search the registry first to confirm whether an appropriate Helper already existed. But because Helper naming was chaotic, many pieces of logic were not easy to discover. So some engineers, to meet deadlines, created a new Helper and only added the record afterward. Before long, the registry became a lengthy checklist rather than a practical tool.

Second, the classification process exposed bigger problems. Take the same "date handling": the differences between Helpers were not just implementation details but business logic. Some Helpers handled UTC, some local time, some server offsets. They had dependencies in different scenarios and could not be easily merged. The classification team tried to establish a unified standard, but every attempt sparked team debates. In the end they could only compromise: keep all versions and add annotations to them.

Annotations became a new maze. "Only used in the Feed module." "Only used in the Notifications module." "Only used in experimental features." Annotations were supposed to clarify meaning, but when they were too numerous they created new confusion.

The most cunning thing about complexity is this: every attempt to govern it instead creates new complexity.

The registry slowed down approval processes; classification plunged teams into arguments; annotations increased the cost of understanding.

The empire's bureaucracy did not decrease; it merely took another form.

The second attempt was through refactoring.

Some senior engineers believed the problem lay not in

management but in structure. They proposed using a unified "core library" to replace the scattered Helpers. All common logic should be centralized in this core library as the single implementation.

The proposal gained brief support. A small team was formed to build the core library. They started with the most fundamental functions: string handling, date conversion, network requests. Each piece of logic was redesigned to try to cover all needed scenarios.

However, new conflicts soon emerged.

First was the migration cost. There were hundreds of existing Helpers spread across different modules. To migrate to the core library, each one would have to be replaced and tested individually. That meant enormous work, and the product team was unwilling to delay feature development for it.

Second was divergence of scenarios. The core library had to cover all requirements, but different modules had different needs. The Notifications module needed one date format, Messaging another, Ads a third. The core library tried to accommodate all cases and became extraordinarily complex. A single date function might take a dozen parameters to handle different calling styles. And this, in essence, was a new Helper—only in different packaging.

Worse, concentrating complexity in the core library made any change dangerous. Once modified, the impact radius was huge and testing effort multiplied. Engineers began to fear touching the core library; it gradually became a sacred, untouchable territory.

The empire's code was supposed to be unified, but when the code became so complex that no one dared modify it, it ceased to be law and became a burden.

The shadow of complexity did not dissipate under governance; it only grew denser.

Team morale began to suffer. Some engineers complained, "We spend more time managing Helpers than implementing features." Others mocked themselves, "We are not developers, we are archivists."

Even more seriously, the team's sense of trust began to crumble. When collaborating across groups, people no longer assumed each other's Helpers were reliable. Everyone worried that calling someone else's Helper might trigger new problems. So they chose to write new Helpers to ensure safety. This mistrust further accelerated the expansion of Helpers.

The empire's provinces no longer shared laws; each made its own rules. Complexity was no longer accidental but inevitable.

The real crisis appeared in a systemic bug.

It was a winter night when Twitter's global service suddenly malfunctioned. Large numbers of users reported that their timelines were out of order and tweet timestamps were incorrect. Some complained that tweets they had just posted were appearing days earlier; others were surprised to see unsent drafts showing future dates.

This was not only a user-experience issue; it struck at the platform's core trust. Twitter's timeline must strictly reflect the real order. Once order is disrupted, the credibility of information falters.

Engineers worked through the night and found the problem lay in date-handling logic — precisely the hardest-hit area of Helper hell.

Different modules used different date Helpers. Some calculated by UTC, some by local time, some included server offsets, some had experimental parameters. One configuration error caused the logic of multiple Helpers to conflict, ultimately leading to timeline chaos.

Debugging was extraordinarily difficult because no one could precisely point to which Helper was the authoritative version. Each module insisted its Helper was correct; each team defended its logic. It took the developers an entire week to gradually restore order.

A week on a stage of hundreds of millions of global users

meant countless complaints and doubts. The cost of complexity was laid bare.

When institutional chaos threatened the empire's core order, reform was no longer a choice but a necessity.

Twitter's leadership finally realized: Helpers were no longer a small problem but a systemic risk. They had to take more drastic measures, or the empire would collapse.

So a new refactoring plan was proposed. This time, it was no longer a local governance effort but a comprehensive reform. The goal was: to thoroughly clean up Helpers, establish clear module boundaries, and replace fragmented abstractions with deep modules.

However, this path was destined to be difficult. Because the inertia of complexity, like the winds of the desert, cannot be eliminated with a single effort. It required a long struggle, sacrifice, and patience.

The flames of Helper hell had already been ignited. They burned not only code but the team's trust and the foundations of its culture. Twitter's developers stood at a turning point. They had to decide whether to continue wandering the maze or embark on a painful but necessary path of refactoring.

Winds rose, sand fell.

Complexity remained silent, yet it hung over everyone.

When the empire was on the brink of collapse, only rebuilding order could prevent ruin.

The cost would inevitably be heavy, but this was the only way for civilization to survive.

After the chaotic timeline crisis, Twitter's leadership finally made up their minds: the Helper problem was no longer an engineers' gripe but a hidden risk threatening the credibility of the entire product. This meant reform; it meant refactoring.

Refactoring began with a symbolic ceremony.

At an all-hands engineering meeting, the tech lead displayed a slide: it listed the total number of Helper files in the codebase at the time. The number was huge and shocking. Each module had contributed its own "convenience," which ultimately added up to hundreds of Helpers scattered everywhere.

"This is debt," the lead said calmly. "This is debt we have all created together. Now it is time to pay it back."

The room fell silent. No one argued because everyone understood: this was a war that could not be avoided.

The first step was to establish boundaries.

The team decided to abandon the concept of "global Helpers." They introduced the idea of "deep modules": each module must have its own clear boundaries; logic must be concentrated rather than scattered.

For example, all date-handling logic must belong to a "Time module." This module can be complex internally but should expose only a simple interface externally. Other modules must not directly write new date Helpers but must depend on the Time module.

This approach was not novel, but at the time it felt especially important. Because it was not just an adjustment of code but a shift in culture: from "personal convenience" to "collective order," from "short-term speed" to "long-term clarity."

However, refactoring is never a smooth path.

First is the cost. Existing Helpers are scattered throughout the codebase; migrating them into deep modules means massive replacement work. It's not just rewriting code but rewriting tests, revalidating, and redeploying. Every replacement can introduce new bugs, and every bug can affect hundreds of millions of users.

So the team had to adopt a gradual strategy. They grouped Helpers by priority, migrating the most critical parts first and then expanding step by step. This was a war of attrition, not a swift victory.

Second is resistance. Some engineers were used to writing

Helpers. They felt refactoring was too tedious and slowed feature development. Under pressure, some secretly kept creating new Helpers to deal with urgent needs. This was like provinces of the empire secretly preserving the old system during reform.

Management had to establish strict review mechanisms. Any new Helper submission would be rejected unless there was a compelling reason. This made short-term development harder but was key to whether the reform would succeed.

The inertia of complexity made reform extraordinarily difficult.

Once, the Ads team urgently needed to ship a new feature. They found the existing Time module inadequate and proposed changes. The modification process triggered weeks of discussion: Would the logic needed by Ads affect Notifications? Would new parameters break existing conventions? In the end, they were forced to accept: not to add a new Helper, but to collaborate with the maintainers of the Time module to jointly extend it.

This mode of collaboration was inefficient at first but gradually cultivated new trust. When module boundaries were clear, communication—though frequent—was no longer chaotic. The empire finally began to build a new order.

Refactoring also brought psychological pain.

Some senior engineers felt attached to their Helpers. After all, many Helpers were written by their own hands and had solved countless problems over the years. Now, these Helpers were treated as debt and gradually phased out, and they felt their work was being invalidated.

To ease these feelings, leadership emphasized: refactoring is not a denial of the past, but a way to make the future sustainable. Helpers were once necessary tools; they simply no longer apply today. The evolution of civilization always requires letting go of old systems at the right time.

This message was gradually accepted by the team. They learned to see refactoring as inheritance, not negation.

As time passed, the results of the refactor began to show.

The most typical example still concerned date logic. Once all handling belonged to the Time module, the number of bugs dropped significantly. Engineers no longer needed to search through a dozen Helper files for answers; they only had to consult a single module. The cognitive cost fell sharply, and newcomers ramped up noticeably faster.

Similar results gradually appeared in areas like string processing and network requests. The establishment of deep modules concentrated system complexity in a few places rather than scattering it across pervasive Helpers. This meant that although modules could be complex internally, their external usage was simple. The Cognitive Load was compressed to a manageable range.

The empire finally saw the dawn.

Helper hell did not disappear entirely, but it was brought under control. The team learned to refuse short-term convenience and instead pursue long-term clarity. They no longer reused for the sake of reuse, but designed for understanding.

This change went far beyond code. It transformed the team's culture. People began to proactively discuss boundaries rather than casually writing Helpers. In reviews they stopped asking, "Can this logic be extracted?" and started asking, "Is this logic worth becoming a deep module?"

Complexity remained, but it was respected and managed rather than an uncontrolled dust storm.

The fate of Helpers is a microcosm of software civilization. When abstractions are abused, they hide complexity instead of dissolving it. When reuse becomes a slogan, it creates new burdens instead of reducing them.

Twitter's story tells us:

- Abstraction is not the goal; reducing cognitive load is.
- Reuse is not a virtue; clarity is.

- Deep modules are closer to the essence of civilization than countless Helpers.

For iOS developers, this story has a more direct lesson:

In the world of SwiftUI, the temptation of abstraction is everywhere. We can keep breaking view logic into smaller components, and we can abstract state handling into countless little utilities. But without clear boundaries, those small components and utilities will eventually turn into a new Helper hell.

The true philosophy of SwiftUI is not infinite decomposition, but a single source of truth and clear boundaries. It asks us to concentrate complexity rather than disperse it. It asks us to use deep modules to encapsulate complexity, not to shred it into Helpers.

The story of Helper hell begins in pain and ends with refactoring. It reminds us: convenience is not free, abstraction is not harmless. Every "we might reuse this later" thought is a grain of sand. When enough grains accumulate, they form dunes that will crush future developers.

The responsibility of civilization is to establish order before the dunes have swallowed us. To draw clear boundaries before complexity devours us. Before Helpers proliferate, ask yourself: "Is this a necessary deep module, or a superfluous fragment?"

The beauty of abstraction lies not in quantity but in clarity.
The power of boundaries lies not in isolation but in understanding.
The greatest code is not a clever maze, but plain, understandable code.

CHAPTER 34
COMBINE'S BLACK BOX VS ASYNC/AWAIT'S CLARITY

Magic always tempts people to set out at a low cost.

But when the cost is truly exacted, people remember: clarity is the only talisman.

The wind swirled in the hall, the curtain outside fell. At WWDC 2019, millions of eyes worldwide were fixed on the same screen. An engineer on stage announced a name — Combine.

Its arrival felt like a newly issued imperial code, declaring that developers were entering a new era.

Apple defined it succinctly and enticingly:

A declarative, reactive framework that can chain data streams like rivers and make asynchronous programming as natural as snapping LEGO together.

When developers heard these words, they seemed to see the future: a world with fewer callbacks, less boilerplate, and more elegance.

Combine's demo was astonishing.

On stage, a few lines of chained calls could complete data processing and UI updates.

Like magic, complex asynchronous logic was compressed into brief expressions.

Applause erupted in the audience, and social media quickly filled with posts.

Combine looked not like a framework, but like a new language.

The temptation of magic lies in making people think complexity has disappeared.

At that moment, iOS developers worldwide seemed to see the illusion of complexity being melted away.

However, complexity never disappears.

It merely puts on a different coat.

When the WWDC heat faded, when developers actually introduced Combine into projects, cracks began to appear.

Combine's concepts are numerous. Publisher, Subscriber, Operator, Scheduler — these names were like offices in a new empire, each needing to be understood one by one.

Every operator was like a decree: map, flatMap, switchToLatest, debounce… a vast number, complex in their combinations.

When beginners learn, they always feel as if they are standing before a maze.

Even worse, Combine's internal mechanisms were encapsulated like a black box.

A Publisher would emit data, pass through a dozen Operators, and then arrive at a Subscriber.

What exactly happened in the middle? How did the data flow? Which link was stuck?

Developers soon discovered: debugging Combine's data flow was like tracking the traces of wind in a desert — you can see the sand but you cannot touch the wind.

Complexity had not disappeared; it had merely shifted to a new dimension:

From explicit callbacks to implicit flows.

From visible code to an invisible black box.

In Silicon Valley, a startup decided to build their brand-new app on Combine.

It was a health-tracking app focused on monitoring users' heart rate, steps, and sleep, and providing real-time feedback to the UI.

The team was young and full of enthusiasm; they believed they were using Apple's "framework of the future," at the forefront of the times.

Early development was full of excitement.

Combine made it easy for them to chain together multiple data sources:

- Heart rate coming from Bluetooth devices;
- Steps provided by system APIs;
- Personalized recommendations returned from the cloud.

All the data seemed to converge like rivers into one stream, flowing effortlessly to the UI.

They cheered for this "magic."

Compared to the callback hell of the past, Combine was like a tidy palace.

Data flowed smoothly, logic was compact, and the app went live quickly.

But the cost of magic never asks for payment at the beginning.

The first problem appeared after the user base grew.

More and more feedback pointed out that the app would become choppy after running for a long time, and even crash for no apparent reason.

The team began to investigate, but found the issue elusive.

Crash logs were vague, and stack traces seemed veiled.

They suspected that some Publisher wasn't being released properly.

They suspected that some Operator behaved abnormally under multithreading.

But Combine's internal workings were like a black box.

Data flowed inside it, yet could not be tracked with the naked eye.

Developers could only, like fortune-tellers, blindly insert print statements into the chain of Operators, hoping to catch a clue.

Complexity now revealed its true power.

It was no longer obvious logic, but an invisible Cognitive Load.

Developers' work was no longer writing new features, but explaining why existing ones stopped working.

Deeper pain came from communication within the team.

The startup's members had diverse backgrounds.

Some were well-versed in functional programming and comfortable with the concept of streams.

Others came from the UIKit era and were more accustomed to callbacks and delegates.

Combine's black box created a rift between the two.

When discussing a bug, the former would say, "You need to use flatMap here."

The latter would be puzzled, not understanding why the problem was there.

Team meetings often devolved into semantic arguments rather than problem solving.

This is the essence of complexity: it raises human communication costs above the cost of technical implementation.

When a team needs two hours to explain a data flow, they have already lost to complexity.

The magic Apple showcased on the WWDC stage became a daily burden for the team.

Combine had promised "elegance," but ended up producing "opacity."

Complexity is like an imperial tax: at first it seems reasonable, but in the end it crushes the people.

Engineers at the startup began to wonder:

"Should we continue using Combine?

Or revert to the familiar but verbose callbacks?

Do we choose magic, or do we choose clarity?"

There was no answer yet.

But the shadow of complexity had already quietly fallen.

At Apple's headquarters, similar doubts were also brewing.

Internal teams using Combine encountered the same difficulties with debugging and steep learning curves.

They knew the cost of a black box would reveal itself sooner or later.

And an empire cannot rely on magic to maintain order indefinitely.

In some corridors, discussions about a new asynchronous model quietly began.

A way closer to human thinking, an expression clearer than a black box.

Its name was not yet public, but it was already being nurtured in the labs.

A black box does not hide the truth; it merely delays it.

The truth has not disappeared; it is only waiting to appear at the most inopportune moment.

In the first few months, the health-tracking startup still basked in Combine's halo.

They thought they owned the future, that they had mastered the magic.

But as user numbers surpassed one million, reality began to show its face.

Complexity does not charge at dawn; it quietly falls in the afternoon.

It does not attack under the banner of an enemy army, but seeps in through the minutiae of daily work.

The first cracks came from the invisibility of the data flow.

User data did not come from a single source.

They were like an interlaced web: heart rate from Bluetooth devices, steps from HealthKit, personalized recommendations pushed from the cloud, sleep reminders from the push service.

In Combine's world, these data were elegantly "combined" into Publishers, then routed through chains to the UI.

Developers felt exhilaration as they wrote those chains.

Seemingly verbose logic was condensed into concise expressions.

But when bugs appeared, they discovered:

The chain was like an underground river — you could hear the water but it was hard to trace.

Once, a user reported that heart rate readings jumped erratically while wearing the band at night.

The team tried to reproduce it, only to find the issue occurred under certain specific conditions.

They traced the data flow and inserted logs, but the logs were like falling into a deep well, receiving no reply.

A Publisher emitted data, but it never reached the Subscriber.

Or the data arrived, but the order had been scrambled.

The whole process became a black box that swallowed their inquiries.

Complexity showed its coldest face at that moment:

Not that the logic was hard to write, but that the logic could not be explained.

A more serious challenge came from performance and memory consumption.

Combine's designers intended to simplify asynchronous logic through declarative, chained calls.

However, in real-world usage, complex chains often led to unpredictable performance issues.

The startup's engineers discovered:

When multiple Publishers ran simultaneously, the system's performance degraded.

Especially during long runs, memory usage grew slowly and eventually triggered crashes.

They suspected that "subscriptions were not being released."

So they inspected each sink and assign one by one, trying to find the runaway subscription.

But Combine's internals were over-encapsulated, and developers couldn't clearly see the lifecycle of subscriptions.

They were like doctors facing a blurry X-ray — aware of a lesion but unable to pinpoint its location.

They tried tracing memory in the debugger, but all they saw were hundreds or thousands of anonymous closures.

These closures were like nameless heads in an imperial tax register: numerous, but impossible to identify.

Developers wasted time in confusion while complexity quietly accumulated strength.

The cultural rift deepened further.

Two camps gradually formed within the team:

One was the "believers in the magic," well-versed in the mysteries of functional programming and convinced Combine was the future — any difficulty was just a learning curve;

The other was the "realists and skeptics," who felt Combine was overly complex, opaque, and unsuitable for the team's long-term prospects.

The two sides argued constantly in meetings.

The believers said, "This is a break-in period we must go through; once mastered, we'll be faster than any team."

The skeptics said, "We spend more time explaining the framework than solving business problems."

Meetings repeatedly reached deadlock.

On the surface they still cooperated; in reality each had already built their own psychological boundaries.

This split was another form of complexity: it not only consumed minds but also tore the culture apart.

The real crisis appeared in an apparently routine update.

The team planned to ship a major update before the Spring Festival, adding a "Family Sharing" feature:

Parents could view their children's health data, and children could remotely monitor their parents' sleep.

This feature meant more data streams.

New Publishers needed to handle multiple users' data simultaneously and synchronize across multiple devices.

They tried to use Combine to manage these streams.

The result was disastrous.

When family members used it simultaneously, data streams became entangled and the logic grew beyond control.

When heart rate updated, step counts were lost; when sleep data arrived, the parents' app crashed.

Developers felt as if trapped in a chaotic web: data trembled in every direction, but they could not trace its path.

The QA team ran themselves ragged; bug reports piled up.

The release plan was forced to be postponed, and investors began to question the team's execution.

Complexity had now become fully visible: it was no longer an abstract concept but an iron wall blocking the business.

What made it more despairing was the impotence of the debugging tools.

Developers tried using Instruments to analyze memory, but were overwhelmed by countless closures and subscriptions.

They tried to reconstruct the data flow from logs, only to find the output too massive and disordered to make sense of.

They felt like hunters searching for an enemy in the night: their torches were weak, and the wind muffled the footsteps.

Complexity not only created problems but also a sense of powerlessness.

It made people feel that all efforts were in vain.

One developer wrote on Slack: "I no longer believe I can explain this logic. It doesn't belong to me; it belongs to Combine."

This was the most terrifying moment of complexity: when developers felt they were no longer masters but slaves to the framework.

Meanwhile, the outside world was changing.

Inside Apple, experiments with async/await were gradually maturing.

Its goal was clear: to simplify asynchronous programming in a way closer to human thinking.

No complex chained calls, no obscure Operators.

Only natural sequential logic, like telling a story.

This was a completely different philosophy: not hiding complexity with magic, but facing it with clarity.

However, the startup knew nothing of this.

They were still struggling inside the black box, still expending mental energy in the fog of magic.

They did not know that a turning point was brewing in distant corridors.

Black boxes inspire fear; clarity brings calm.

Magic creates illusion; sequence creates understanding.

Humans are not creatures who chase illusions; humans yearn to understand.

The story of complexity reached a turning point at the black box's darkest hour.

In 2021, at WWDC, Apple unveiled a new paradigm—async/await.

This was not mere syntactic sugar but a new order.

It liberated asynchronous logic from the black box and let developers once again express it in the natural sequential order of language.

The onstage demos were concise and brisk: developers no longer needed endless chained calls, nor to be trapped in the maze of Operators.

They could describe the flow of data as if telling a story.

Waiting was simply waiting; returning was simply returning.

Logic was no longer hidden; it was laid bare again on the path of human understanding.

Developers around the world looked at the demo screen and felt a long-lost sensation: this was not magic, this was understanding.

The startup saw the scene too. In their office, several engineers gathered to watch the live stream. When the presenter showed an async/await example, they looked at each other. One engineer whispered, "This is what we've been looking for."

At that moment, the exhaustion that had been weighing on them seemed to find an outlet.

The migration process was not easy. The team's code was already covered in traces of Combine. Publisher, Subscriber, and Operator chains crisscrossed like a vast bureaucracy. Migrating them to async/await one by one was like rebuilding an empire.

But this time, they did not hesitate.

They decided to start from the most painful spot: the heart-rate monitoring data stream.

In the past, that logic had given them the most headaches. Publishers were composed layer upon layer; if any link failed, debugging fell into a bottomless pit. They rewrote it using async/await. The logic became direct, errors could be caught step by step, and the path of the data flow was immediately clear.

During the first test, everyone fell silent. The silence was not because of problems, but because they had seen clarity again.

Clarity is a kind of power.

In the weeks that followed, they gradually migrated key modules to async/await. Each migration was like walking a straight road out of a maze. With each code review, discussion time shrank and communication became more efficient. Developers no longer needed to explain the meaning of Operators; they described logic in natural language.

The team's atmosphere quietly changed. The skeptics were no longer angry, and the believers were no longer obstinate. They rediscovered a common language.

This is the truth about complexity: it is not only a technical problem but a communication problem. When the way of expressing things is clear, the team can unite again.

During the migration, they also confronted a reality: not every scenario is suitable for async/await. Some highly dynamic data streams still require Combine's capabilities. But by then, their attitude had changed.

They no longer treated Combine as magic, but as a tool. They understood clearly that any black box must be used with caution. They wrote detailed documentation for every piece of Combine logic, explaining the direction of the data flow. They no longer indulged in the glamour of Operators, and instead focused on understandability.

Magic abdicated; clarity ascended.

At an all-hands meeting, the CTO said, "What we truly need is not tools that let us write less code, but tools that help us better understand our code."

Everyone nodded.

In the past they thought complexity could be made to disappear by the magic of a framework. Now they understood that complexity can only be tamed through clear expression.

The echoes from the outside world confirmed their choice.

Apple itself, in its official documentation and new APIs, gradually replaced most Combine use cases with async/await. Frameworks such as URLSession, Core Data, and SwiftUI introduced async/await-based interfaces. Community discussion among developers was lively, and more and more people migrated to the new model.

Combine did not disappear, but its status quietly declined. It retreated from the empire's canon back to a tool for specific scenarios. Async/await became the new standard.

Historians wrote, "The rise and fall of magic is not a failure, but a reminder to humanity: complexity should not be hidden, it should be faced."

After completing the migration, the startup reached a critical moment. They tried the "Family Sharing" feature again.

This time the logic was no longer a black box but a clear path. Developers could debug step by step and accurately capture the data flow in logs. The number of bugs dropped significantly, and the testing cycle was cut in half. The feature was finally launched smoothly, and user feedback was positive.

At the celebration someone raised a glass and said, "This was not a victory of technology, but a victory of understanding."

Everyone laughed. Their smiles carried both relief and renewal.

Looking back on the journey, they came to a deep realization:

Magic brings brief excitement but long-term fatigue. Clarity brings short-term effort but long-term peace of mind.

The essence of complexity is not the amount of logic, but the difficulty of understanding. When understanding becomes easy, complexity is reduced. When understanding is blocked, complexity swells.

The black box of Combine is a symbol of obstructed understanding. The sequential order of async/await is a symbol of understanding being restored.

Do not be seduced by the illusion of magic. The price of magic is always paid by your future self.

What is truly worth pursuing is not "writing less code," but "having less code to explain." Because your future self, your future team, and future readers do not truly need magic, they need clarity.

The civilization of software is built on clarity.
Magic is fleeting; clarity is eternal.

CHAPTER 35
THE RIGHTS AND WRONGS OF MANAGING STATE IN SWIFTUI

An empire does not perish in its territory, but in the distortion of command transmission.

State does not rot in logic, but in the fog of synchronization.

State is like water in the desert.

Invisible, yet decisive.

When it is properly preserved, cities can prosper; when it leaks or disperses, the empire will dry up.

In the software world, state is the most fragile wealth. It does not appear on the screen, yet it flows through every click, every refresh, every collaboration.

The favorite soil of complexity is the chaos of state.

The branches and leaves of logic can be pruned, the bricks of architecture can be replaced, but once state is scattered, it is like a sandstorm that obscures everything.

The story of Trello is a parable about state.

The early days of Trello were like an emerging frontier town.

Its features seemed simple: a board, some cards, a group of users.

Users could create tasks, drag cards from "To Do" to "In Progress," then to "Done."

At first glance, this was just a copy of an electronic whiteboard.

However, the real complexity was not on the surface.

Trello's magic lay in its real-time collaboration.

Multiple users could operate the same board simultaneously.

You move a card in New York, and your colleague in London can see it immediately.

This real-time aspect was its attraction and its trap.

Because state must always be consistent.

Once there is a difference, users' trust collapses.

If I see a card in the left column while you see it in the right column, the system's value instantly drops to zero.

Early Trello did not have unified state management.

Each client maintained its own local state.

The mobile client had one state, the web had one state, and the server had one state.

They synchronized through events and APIs, but synchronization was not instantaneous; delays, losses, and conflicts could occur at any time.

Thus, cracks appeared.

- Some users dragged a card and saw it instantly snap back to its original position.
- Some users clearly created a task, but it disappeared after a refresh.
- Some teams, during meetings, had the board displayed on the screen out of sync with real operations, and confusion spread like a plague.

The root of these problems was not in the features, but in state.

State was scattered across multiple places, each of which thought it was the master.

In the end, no one was the master.

The dark side of complexity reveals itself here.

Engineers tried to fix it.

They added more event listeners, more callbacks, more patch logic.

They hoped to hide the fundamental chaos with "faster synchronization."

But the result was that the logic became more complex and bugs harder to locate.

A single bug investigation might require searching the client, the server, and the network logs simultaneously.

Some bugs only appear under poor network conditions; others are only exposed when multiple people edit at the same time.

Developers, like archaeologists, piece together the truth from countless fragments.

The darkness of state is not just feature failure, but an expansion of Cognitive Load.

Every engineer must simultaneously understand the differences among three layers of state.

They are no longer just coders, but tired translators, translating the subtle differences of three languages.

SwiftUI developers will find this familiar.

SwiftUI brought a revolutionary state-driven model.

The UI is no longer updated imperatively but is a direct mapping of data.

When state changes, the UI refreshes automatically.

This makes the code concise and the logic clear, as if dispelling a fog that had lingered for years.

But SwiftUI also has its dark side.

If state is managed in a scattered way, if multiple places can modify the same data, if refreshes have no boundaries, complexity will return.

The UI may redraw after an unintended state change, degrading performance;

Different Views may keep state in different scopes, causing inconsistencies;

"ghost copies" of state may quietly appear without engineers noticing.

SwiftUI's magic, like Trello's real-time collaboration, is both power and trap.

Once it gets out of control, complexity resurrects itself within state.

Trello's users felt this loss of control.

They complained in the community:

"Why is the card position I see always different from my colleague's?"

"Why did the task I just added disappear?"

"Why is the board's refresh always delayed?"

The users' voices, like rumors on the empire's frontier, quickly reached the capital.

Trello's team had to admit: their fundamental problem was not a lack of features, but disorder in state.

The dark side of complexity is not that some feature cannot be implemented, but that the whole system loses trust.

When state cannot be guaranteed consistent, users stop trusting the system.

And a system that has lost trust is like a city that has lost its spring—left with only dust.

All of this is the metaphor SwiftUI developers must face head-on.

SwiftUI's state model offers a bright promise: data-driven, automatic refreshes, declarative syntax.

But if developers do not understand the nature of state, if they casually store state in different components, if they lack a unified single source of truth, they will fall into the same predicament Trello faced in its early days.

The light and dark of state hang in a thin line.

Once scattered, it is darkness;

Once centralized, there is light.

The greatness of a system is not in forbidding chaos, but in putting boundaries around it.

The order of state does not lie in absolute correctness, but in a single voice.

"Chaos cannot be eliminated, but it can be brought under control."

When Trello's team realized the dark side of state was devouring everything, they recognized:

The only way out was to establish a single source of truth.

They began to refactor.

This was not a minor patch, but a systemic reconstruction.

They decided to stop letting every client maintain its own truth and instead gather the truth into a central place.

The server became the final fact; clients were merely mirrors.

Thus, a new data flow gradually took shape:

Clients emitted intents, the server validated and updated state, and all clients then synchronized the new truth.

Moving a card was no longer "each client interpreting on its own," but adjudicated centrally.

Conflicts were no longer individual chaos, but resolved by the system.

This was Trello's turning point.

They moved from "distributed truths" toward a "centralized truth."

The shift was extremely difficult.

Because the previous logic had been implemented locally.

Clients were accustomed to assuming they "knew the truth" and directly mutating the UI.

Now they had to give up control and wait for the server's result.

This introduced latency, discomfort, and initial user dissatisfaction.

But as the system gradually stabilized, the benefits became apparent:

- Users no longer saw states that were out of sync with one another.
- Cards no longer disappeared after a refresh.
- Conflicts were explicitly resolved, and trust in the system was restored.

Centralizing state tamed the chaos. Darkness receded, and light emerged.

SwiftUI developers will find a familiar brightness here.

SwiftUI's philosophy is "state-driven UI."

It tells developers: the UI should not operate independently, nor be manually mutated.

The UI is merely a mirror reflecting state.

If the state is correct, the UI will naturally be correct.

This idea is strikingly consistent with Trello's reconstruction.

It gathers the truth into state, rather than scattering it across logic and views.

It strips the UI of autonomy, but in doing so gains consistency.

However, light always brings new pitfalls.

Trello's centralization did not completely eliminate complexity. New problems emerged:

- When there is network latency, users must wait for the server to confirm before seeing results.
- When multiple people act simultaneously, the order of state updates can produce differences in experience.
- When the volume of data is large, the cost of centralization is performance bottlenecks.

These problems were no longer "inconsistent truths," but "truth that is too centralized."

The empire's capital can issue uniform decrees, but the roads' capacity and transmission speed are limited.

Thus, a new dilemma arose: the correctness of the system began to conflict with the smoothness of the user experience.

SwiftUI's state management faces a similar contradiction.

When developers put all data in one place and use a single state to drive all views, a bright consistency appears.

The UI updates automatically, logic is simplified, and cognitive load decreases.

But soon they will discover:

- Each state change can trigger too many UI refreshes.
- Performance problems surface, especially in complex views.
- Once state is centralized, the scope becomes too large, making local optimizations difficult.

Thus, SwiftUI's light turns into a new darkness.

Not "inconsistency," but "over-updating."

Not "chaotic copies," but "burdensome centralization."

Trello's engineers, in order to solve this problem, created new layers.

They introduced local caches and temporary state on the client.

User actions first apply locally, immediately reflecting in the UI.

Meanwhile, requests are sent to the server to ultimately confirm the truth.

If the confirmation succeeds, the local state and the central state merge;

If the confirmation fails, the local state rolls back and the user is notified.

This is a compromise.

It guarantees a smooth experience while preserving a unified truth.

It prevents the light from fading because of latency.

But this compromise itself introduces new complexity:

A precise synchronization mechanism is required between local state and central state.

Rollback logic needs rigorous design.

This is no longer a single truth, but a "tiered truth."

SwiftUI developers will encounter similar trade-offs.

In practice they found:

- Some state should be centrally managed, such as user login info and global configuration.
- Some state should be held locally, such as the temporary content of an input field.
- If all state is centralized, performance and flexibility suffer;
- If all state is dispersed, inconsistency will reappear.

Thus SwiftUI's state management moves toward a balance:

Global state and local state coexist, centralization and distribution intertwine.

Like Trello's central store and local cache, it is a hierarchical compromise.

Historians would say this is the inevitability of civilization.

There is no absolute centralization, and no absolute dispersion.

A true system is always layered and always compromised.

Trello's experience teaches us:

The clarity of state is not the absolutization of a single source of truth, but layered consistency.

SwiftUI's philosophy is the same.

It provides powerful tools, but how to use them, how to layer them, how to balance them, remains a matter of human wisdom.

However, new traps still lie in wait.

In Trello's system, engineers must always be careful:

Don't let local state lose contact with the central state.

Don't let temporary caches become the new truth.

Don't let patch logic erode the original clarity.

And in SwiftUI, developers face the same warnings:

Don't overuse local state and bury critical data in hard-to-track places.

Don't let multiple views modify the same piece of state at the same time.

Don't leave the design of state boundaries to chance; instead, impose institutional constraints.

Light can be blinding. In the light, people often forget that darkness still exists.

Although Trello's team welcomed order after centralization, they also found that unifying state was not an endpoint but a new starting point. They had to continuously govern, continuously adjust, and continuously seek new balances.

SwiftUI developers must accept the same. State management is not a one-time decision but an ongoing evolution. The light and dark of state will reappear with every iteration.

True order is not the permanence of light but the alternation of darkness and light.

State is the same: centralization and dispersion, light and dark, never cease.

When Trello's team completed the centralization reform, they did not achieve everlasting peace. What they gained was a new responsibility: to continuously manage and continuously reconcile. Because state does not stand still—it is like water and will always find new cracks.

It was a turbulent period.

Trello's user base rapidly expanded, from small teams trying it out to multinational companies adopting it fully. When hundreds of people operated on a board simultaneously, problems resurfaced. The central truth became enormous, and no matter how fast data flowed, latency could not be completely eliminated. Thus new complaints arose: "Why does moving a card sometimes lag?" "Why do the comments I see take a few seconds to appear?"

The central truth was right, but right too late. In this rapidly changing world, belated correctness is also a fault.

So Trello began a second evolution.

They overlaid layered governance on top of centralization. The central store remained the ultimate truth, but clients were allowed to play a more active role. Clients were not just passive waiters; they could "predict" results.

When a user dragged a card, the client immediately showed the movement locally. Meanwhile, a request was sent to the server. If the confirmation succeeded, the local state merged with the central state; if it failed, the client rolled back.

This mechanism was called "optimistic updates." It was an act of trust: the client was temporarily given authority, as if a frontier governor could issue orders in an emergency and then await the capital's approval.

The introduction of optimistic updates greatly improved the user experience. Actions became instantaneous, collaboration became smooth, and latency was no longer glaring.

But this mechanism also requires stricter governance:

- How to handle failed rollbacks to avoid confusing users?
- How to resolve conflicts when multiple people operate the same card simultaneously?
- How to ensure that the local prediction and the central truth eventually converge?

These questions are no longer technical details but questions of institutional design. Engineers are no longer merely writing logic; they are like legislators, setting rules for the boundaries.

SwiftUI developers can see a mirrored mapping here.

SwiftUI provides multiple ways to store state: global, local, temporary, environment. It requires developers, like Trello's team, to judge which parts of state belong to the central truth and which parts can be predicted locally.

The temporary text in an input field can be stored locally;

A global user login record must be managed centrally;

A complex form can be saved locally first and then update the global truth upon submission.

This layering is precisely the core wisdom of SwiftUI state management. It is not pure centralization, nor total dispersion, but an institutionalized hierarchy.

However, complexity refuses to be tamed.

Within Trello's team new divergences emerged. Some argued for further centralization, reducing the client's freedom to avoid potential inconsistencies. Others argued for further decentralization, making clients smarter to ease the burden on the central system. This debate is not a technical opposition but a philosophical split.

It is like two factions of an empire: central authority versus local autonomy. The former emphasizes unity; the latter emphasizes flexibility. Both are right, and both are dangerous.

In the end, Trello chose a middle way. They established strict boundaries: which data may be optimistically updated and which must wait for central confirmation. They established procedures: how conflicts are resolved and how failures are rolled back. They established a culture: engineers must explicitly state the ownership of state when designing.

Thus the light and dark of state were finally tamed within a framework. It was no longer arbitrary chaos but bounded chaos. It was no longer unknowable darkness but darkness confined within a container.

SwiftUI developers should do the same.

The light of SwiftUI can be intoxicating. UI refreshes automatically, logic is clear, and it feels as if all problems have disappeared. But true wisdom is not to revel in the light, but to be wary of the return of darkness.

Abusing state will make refreshes ubiquitous and bring back performance issues; dispersed state will let inconsistencies quietly revive; a lack of boundaries will leave engineers lost during future debugging.

SwiftUI state management is not magic, but a responsibility. It requires developers, like legislators, to make rules, define boundaries, and allocate authority. It requires teams, like civilizations, to have institutions, constraints, and a culture.

Trello's story has by now evolved into a chronicle of civilization.

It moved from chaos to centralization, from centralization to layering, from layering to institutionalization. Each step was met with the backlash of complexity; each step involved philosophical choices. In the end, they did not eliminate complexity, but learned to coexist with it.

This is precisely the wisdom SwiftUI developers must learn.

"The clarity of state is not eternal light, but darkness kept under control.

The darkness of state is not total failure, but a reminder that our institutions are incomplete."

The future of software is not in eradicating darkness, but in finding a balance between light and dark. The future of SwiftUI is not in providing perfect magic, but in whether developers can use it with clear heads.

To summarize this journey, we can say:

The clarity of state is the power of unity.

The darkness of state is the risk of dispersion.

True wisdom is, between light and dark, to establish institutions, define boundaries, and guard clarity.

Trello's story tells us: state management is not a technology, but a civilization.

SwiftUI's state model reminds us: light and dark always coexist.

And complexity is our eternal enemy.

The greatest achievement is not to make state always correct, but to make state's errors understandable and fixable.
The greatest design is not to eliminate darkness, but to prevent darkness from destroying the light.

PART EIGHT
TEAMS AND CULTURE

CHAPTER 36
COGNITIVE LOAD AND SCALE

The borders of an empire can still be measured, but the boundaries of the human heart are hard to draw.

Beyond architecture, there are systems; beyond code, there is culture.

Without these two, complexity will inevitably find cracks to creep through.

Winds rise over the sea of sand; dunes are not high because of the wind alone, but because winds cross directions.

Teams are the same.

When the number of people is small, everyone faces the same gust;

when the number swells, the wind becomes noisy, they collide, and the dunes split.

The story of Shopify is a parable about team size and architectural boundaries.

In the earliest days, Shopify's mobile team was only a dozen or so people.

They maintained a monolithic application: code centralized, logic compact, knowledge nearly shared in everyone's head.

They were like a group of explorers traveling together through the desert; every decision reached everyone instantly.

Code complexity had not yet become a disaster, and the Cognitive Load remained manageable.

At that stage, the monolith was not a burden but a strength.

Everyone could understand the whole picture; changing one piece of logic did not require worrying about rippling effects across the system.

Testing was simple, releases were controllable, and discussions were fast.

At that scale, deep modules naturally formed:

A network layer led by one engineer, whose boundaries everyone understood;

A UI component maintained by another engineer, whose domain others respected.

Cognitive depth was concentrated in individuals; team size did not dilute knowledge.

It was like an ancient tribe: few people, limited land, simple systems, and everyone knew each other's duties.

Complexity had not disappeared, but it was compressed into individual memory and collective tacit understanding.

However, as Shopify rose, all of this quietly changed.

User numbers increased, features expanded, demands grew.

The mobile team grew from ten people, to fifty, then to hundreds.

When headcount crossed a certain threshold, the shape of complexity changed with it.

In the era of the monolith, every line of code lived in the same repository.

At first this meant concentration and efficiency, but as the team scaled, it became a burden.

Different groups modified the same parts of the logic, merge conflicts became frequent, and impacts were hard to isolate.

CI build times grew longer and longer, and every commit felt like waiting for an imperial edict.

Worse still, knowledge sharing was no longer possible.

When the headcount exceeded thirty, no one could understand the whole picture.

When it exceeded fifty, there wasn't even anyone who could explain all the dependencies.

The monolith ceased to be a clear deep module and became a murky behemoth.

Its boundaries were no longer visible, and its Cognitive Load exceeded the limits of individuals.

At this stage, Shopify's teams encountered the typical "communication complexity inflation."

Psychohistory had long predicted:

When an organization's size grows linearly, communication paths increase exponentially.

A five-person team has ten possible communication paths, a ten-person team has forty-five, and a one-hundred-person team has nearly five thousand.

This means that any information must pass through many layers, and any decision must span multiple groups.

Time was consumed by communication; attention was consumed by alignment.

Complexity was no longer an attribute of the code, but of the team.

It was not in the files, but in the meeting rooms;

it was not in the logic, but in the Slack channels.

Shopify's engineers realized they needed new boundaries.

Not boundaries of code, but boundaries of teams.

Thus, modularization became inevitable.

They decided to split the large monolith into multiple Feature Modules, each module independently owned by a small team.

Swift Package Manager became the technical tool here, but more important was the organizational contract.

A module was not just a collection of code, but the cognitive territory of a team.

A module's API was the boundary between teams;

A module's dependencies were the roads between teams;

A module's tests were the contracts between teams.

Within such a system, small teams regained depth.

They could pursue clarity within their own modules without bearing the global complexity.

Large teams, meanwhile, limited the spread of complexity through module boundaries.

Complexity was not eliminated, but it was partitioned into different territories.

However, modularization was not a silver bullet.

It transformed complexity from "shared chaos" into "boundary governance."

If boundary design is not clear, complexity will strike back in the form of dependencies.

Shopify's team once made a mistake during a refactor:

They allowed a core module to depend on too many feature modules, which turned it into a "supermodule."

Every team's changes had to go through that module's build, and CI times grew long again.

Complexity was reborn in a new form.

This incident reminded them:

Module partitioning is not just a technical task but organizational design.

If organizational boundaries are unclear, module boundaries will fail.

If team responsibilities are vague, dependency relationships become chaotic.

Over this long evolution, Shopify's teams gradually understood:

Beyond architecture, there is culture;

Beyond code, there are governance and processes.

The strength of small teams lies in deep modules:

Everyone can understand the whole, and complexity is concentrated in individuals' minds.

The strength of large teams lies in boundary governance:

Each module is a city-state, teams are autonomous within it, and the empire's order is maintained through contracts.

This is not an abstract metaphor but a practical survival strategy.

In an empire without boundaries, complexity ravages like a sandstorm.

In an empire with boundaries, complexity still exists, but it's confined locally and cannot swallow the whole.

Shopify's teams had embarked on a new path, but the storm of complexity never vanished.

They had to learn to build culture on top of boundaries; to build processes beyond architecture.

Complexity would not dissipate; it would only change faces.

Once boundaries blur, chaos appears in the empire.

The rulebook is not measured by its thickness but by its clarity.

A team's architecture, if not sustained by culture, will eventually become a new maze.

The windblown sand does not stop because of borders.

At Shopify, modularization did not eliminate complexity; it only changed where complexity lived.

It transformed from a monolithic beast into the invisible tensions between modules.

That tension does not show up in the code; it echoes between teams.

The initial modularization brought brief relief.

Each group had its own territory and could be self-sufficient within its boundaries.

Build times shortened, merge conflicts decreased, and engineers regained their rhythm.

That period felt like a brief calm after the empire had reorganized its territories.

But complexity never left.

It merely disguised itself, waiting for a new entry.

The problem first appeared in the dependency chain.

During an annual refactor, Shopify's team split the order system into multiple modules: order details, payments, invoices, discounts, and shipping.

On the surface, these module boundaries were clear and each was independent.

But as business requirements increased, calls between modules became frequent:

The discounts module needed to call order details, the payments module depended on discount logic, and the shipping module needed to obtain payment status.

Soon, a new "supermodule" appeared.

It was no longer the beast of the monolith but a "hub" born from modularization.

All modules depended on it; it became the empire's checkpoint.

Engineers found during builds that whenever this module changed, the entire system had to be rebuilt.

CI build times lengthened again, and complexity was resurrected in a new form.

This is the nature of complexity: it does not disappear; it moves.

If you drive it out of the monolith, it hides deep in the dependency chain.

If you drive it out of the code, it seeps into organizational relationships.

The problem then manifested as blurred boundaries.

Shopify's team tried to use documentation to define module responsibilities.

However, business always moves faster than governance.

During one marketing campaign, the team needed to add new promotional logic into the checkout process.

Should this logic live in the orders module or the discounts module?

Both sides had reasonable arguments and both had urgent needs.

The argument lasted for days, and the final result was: the logic was split across the two modules.

In the short term the issue was resolved, but in the long run the boundary was broken.

At the next maintenance, engineers needed to understand the implementations of both modules, and the Cognitive Load multiplied.

Once boundaries blur, complexity seeps in like grains of sand.

It no longer concentrates in one place but scatters into every corner.

When the team tried to locate the complexity, they found it was everywhere.

Deeper cracks appeared in the cultural differences between teams.

After modularization, each group gained greater autonomy.

This was a good thing: they could decide their own implementations and independently set testing standards.

But as autonomy expanded without limits, differences gradually emerged.

One group was used to strict test-driven practices, with each module having comprehensive unit tests; another favored rapid iteration, with tests often lagging.

One team pursued abstraction, striving to reduce duplication;

the other leaned toward direct implementation, aiming for fast delivery.

In the monolith era, differences were forced into uniformity; in the modular era, differences are amplified into conflicts.

As a result, when two teams' modules need to collaborate, stylistic differences become obstacles. Tests are inconsistent, levels of abstraction differ, documentation habits vary. Engineers feel unfamiliar and resistant when reading code from another module.

Complexity is no longer a technical problem but a cultural one. When culture lacks cohesion, complexity breeds within differences.

At this point, Shopify's team began to ask: can modular boundaries endure without cultural maintenance?

So they tried to establish "guardrails." Guardrails are not a pile of rules, but red lines for Cognitive Load. For example:

- Each module must have a clear API; cross-layer calls are forbidden.
- Each module must minimize dependencies; hub modules are prohibited.
- Each module must provide documentation explaining its boundaries and responsibilities.

Guardrails are like the empire's code—not measured by thickness, but by clarity. They tell engineers what is allowed and what is not. They confine complexity within boundaries instead of letting it spread.

However, the guardrails themselves create tensions.

Some engineers feel they are overly restrictive and constrain creativity; some teams feel they add overhead and slow delivery.

At an internal discussion, a senior engineer said, "Guardrails are not meant to restrict you, but to protect you. They spare you from having to understand the entire system's complexity and let you focus within your own boundary."

That remark was like a light, illuminating the chaos. Complexity will not be reduced by guardrails, but it will be contained by them. Guardrails are not shackles, but safety rails.

Shopify's team gradually realized: beyond architecture, there must be culture; beyond modules, there must be governance.

Without culture and governance, modularization only creates new chaos. Complexity will revive in blurred boundaries, breed in divergent cultures, and spread in unclear processes.

Shopify's modularization has not reached perfection; it has only moved from a monolithic beast toward an archipelago of modules. The sea lanes between the islands need processes to be planned and culture to sustain them.

The empire has not yet collapsed, but the shadow of complexity still hangs over it.

The survival of an empire lies not in the breadth of its territory, but in the clarity of its code of law.

The survival of a team lies not in the number of its members, but in the clarity of its boundaries.

Complexity cannot be eliminated; it can only be managed.

The storm of complexity finally forced Shopify's team to stare into the abyss.

They found that mere modularization could not truly defeat chaos.

Modules are merely divisions of territory; without cultural support, they quickly become new sand dunes.

So they embarked on a long "governance reform."

The first step of this reform was to make boundaries truly visible.

In the past, boundaries lived in engineers' memories and in vague documentation.

Over time they faded.

Now the team decided to make boundaries first-class citizens.

They created "contract documents" for each module.

The documents are not long-winded explanations but boundary declarations:

- What is this module responsible for?
- What are its inputs and outputs?
- Which modules does it depend on?
- Which modules should it not depend on?

These contracts are not legal constraints but a way to reduce Cognitive Load.

When a new member joins, they don't need to understand the entire system; they only need to understand the contract of the module they belong to.

Complexity has not decreased, but it has been compressed into a clear map of boundaries.

The second step was to make the guardrails institutional.

Internally at Shopify, a new rule was widely accepted:

Guardrails are for future engineers, not for present convenience.

Therefore they added automated checks into the CI pipeline:

- Forbid cross-module calls to unpublished interfaces;
- Forbid certain modules from becoming hub dependencies;
- Forbid merging modules that lack boundary documentation.

This is not to punish, but to remind.

When CI blocks a commit, it whispers:

"You are trying to break a boundary; you are letting complexity spread freely."

Institutions make culture land. Guardrails moved from verbal commitments to barriers in code and process.

Complexity still exists, but it cannot easily cross boundaries.

The third step was to make culture a consensus.

Institutions can prevent mistakes, but they cannot generate buy-in.

If engineers see institutions as external shackles, they will look for ways around them.

Only when institutions become part of the culture do they truly take root.

Shopify's team began to convey culture through stories. They shared "failure cases" internally:

A chain of bugs caused by a boundary breach;

A release delay caused by tangled dependencies;

A newcomer lost because of missing documentation.

These stories became the empire's chronicles, reminding successors:

The disasters of complexity are not theoretical but firsthand.

Culture settles in stories and becomes shared memory.

At the same time, they also shared "success cases":

A module could be quickly refactored because its boundary was clear;

A team was self-sufficient in a crisis because its contract was explicit;

A system upgrade avoided disaster because guardrails were in place.

Stories are not boasting, but proof:

Boundaries are not only constraints, they are freedom.

The reform did not happen overnight but was a multi-year evolution.

There is no end to governing complexity; it must be reasserted in every iteration.

Every new module needs a contract;

Every architectural change needs guardrails;

Every cultural transmission needs stories.

In this long process, Shopify's team gradually formed a new mental model:

- Small teams survive by deep modules;
- Large teams survive by boundary governance;
- Boundary governance must be institutionalized;
- Institutions must be accepted by culture.

This is the wisdom they bought with countless failures.

In the end, Shopify's modular architecture stabilized.

It was no longer a fragile monolith, nor a chaotic archipelago.

It became like a federation:

Each module an autonomous city-state with its own boundaries and guardrails;

Culture and institutions were the empire's code, enabling harmonious coexistence between city-states.

Complexity still existed, but it was trapped locally.

It could not easily engulf the whole, nor quietly corrode culture.

The team finally learned to live with complexity instead of being enslaved by it.

"The empire endures not because its territory is vast, but because its institutions are clear.

The team endures not because its numbers are large, but because its boundaries are clear."

This sentence is the footnote to the Shopify story.

When we look back at all this, we can see three layers of lessons:

First, Cognitive Load determines the limit of scale.

Small teams can rely on shared memory to maintain a monolith, while large teams must rely on boundaries to limit complexity.

The larger the scale, the heavier the Cognitive Load, and the more important the boundaries.

Second, there must be culture beyond architecture. No matter how perfect the modularization, without cultural maintenance it will eventually degenerate into new chaos. Culture turns boundaries into consensus and makes institutions a matter of conscience.

Finally, complexity cannot be eliminated, only governed. It is like wind, like water, like sand—never disappearing. Human wisdom lies not in eradicating complexity but in confining it within finite boundaries.

From Shopify's story we see how complexity changes with scale, how it lurks in the monolith, is reborn in modules, and is ultimately tamed by culture and institutions. We also see that software architecture is not just the shape of code but the shape of the team. Culture and institutions are the architecture beyond architecture.

Make code friendly to humans; let boundaries navigate us into the future.
Complexity cannot be extinguished; only human clarity can govern it.

CHAPTER 37
MODULARITY AS ORGANIZATIONAL THEORY

When an empire's territory is vast, the central decrees cannot reach the frontier; only provinces and governors can maintain order.

When software grows large, the monolith's rules cannot bear the complexity; only modules and boundaries can prevent collapse.

The weight of complexity presses not only on the code but also on the organization.

When an application has only a few thousand lines, complexity is merely a memory challenge for an engineer.

When it balloons to a million lines and a team of a hundred, complexity transforms into a form of institutional pressure: communication, boundaries, and collaboration are all forced into its vortex.

LinkedIn's mobile empire was moving forward under this kind of heavy pressure.

Around 2010, their iOS app was still a monolith: a small team was responsible, the code was concentrated in a single repository, and although builds were slow, they were still tolerable.

At that time, the app's functionality was relatively simple, and the team size was only a few dozen people.

However, when LinkedIn's global expansion swept in, recruiting, the news feed, instant messaging, the ad engine, and search recommendations each joined like new territories.

The monolithic architecture became like an increasingly bloated capital: all traffic had to pass through it, and all decrees had to be issued by it.

Problems began to surface.

The first crack was compilation.

After one merge, the iOS app's build time exceeded an hour.

For a team that needed to iterate quickly, this was catastrophic.

Each engineer was like a merchant forced to wait for a travel permit, watching precious time be wasted in the lengthy build process.

They joked that they could go get coffee or even attend meetings in that time, but deep down they knew: this was no joke; it was a real collapse of productivity.

The second crack was merging.

Different functional teams developed within the same monolith, and frequent conflicts were like friction on the frontier.

The deployment of one requirement often accompanied the rollback of another feature; fixing one bug could accidentally break a module far away.

The larger the empire's territory, the more frequent the collateral damage.

The third crack was responsibility.

When the app crashed, who would bear it?

The crash log pointed to some corner of the monolithic code, and that code might have been written three years earlier by an engineer who had left.

Members of the current team had to spend days understanding the context before they could start fixing it.

A sense of responsibility was diluted in the monolith; complexity eroded ownership.

LinkedIn's leadership realized:

This was no longer a "technical optimization" problem, but an "organizational" problem.

The shape of the code was determining the shape of the teams.

They began to push for modular reform.

No longer would everyone be trapped inside the monolith; instead, functionality was split into modules, each module like a province of the empire, with its own boundaries and its own guardians.

In this way, build pressure could be dispersed, the risk of conflicts confined, and responsibility clearly assigned.

This was a strategic shift.

Just as an empire moves from centralization to a provincial system—not because it favors a more complex regime, but because a single system can no longer sustain a vast territory—software modularization is the same.

In LinkedIn's practice, modularization was not only a technical operation but a reshaping of cognitive boundaries.

They set one rule:

A module must be fully understood and owned by a single team.

If a module is so complex that it exceeds a team's cognitive capacity, it must be further split.

That splitting was not mechanical, but highly aligned with organizational boundaries.

The recruiting module was given to the recruiting team;

The feed to the content team;

Instant messaging to the social team.

Each module had clear boundaries; each team guarded its own province.

But complexity does not automatically diminish because of division.

It is merely transferred, from "global chaos" to "local autonomy."

If boundaries are unclear, modularization will degenerate into new chaos.

LinkedIn's engineers quickly realized:

The key to modularization is not quantity, but depth.

A deep and simple module can contain complexity;

Ten shallow, fragmented modules will only create more dependencies and friction.

They began to emphasize "contracts."

Between modules there would be not arbitrary calls but contract-style collaboration.

Like provinces of an empire that do not pillage one another at will but are held together by explicit systems of taxes and tributes.

The introduction of Swift Package Manager (SPM) provided tooling for this kind of contract.

Dependencies were explicitly defined, and boundaries clearly delineated.

This was not only a change at the build level but an organizational innovation as well.

However, modularization was not a victory won overnight.

It required refactoring, migration, and enduring short-term pain.

In practice, LinkedIn's teams encountered challenges that even exceeded expectations.

The first challenge was cultural.

In the monolith, anyone could change any part.

After modularization, boundaries meant constraints.

Some engineers felt uncomfortable and complained, "Why can't I just modify it directly?"

Constraints seemed to impede efficiency, but leadership insisted:

"Boundaries are not obstacles; they are protections."

The second challenge was technical debt.

Old code could not be split immediately; some legacy problems had to remain.

The push for modularization therefore met resistance.

LinkedIn chose a gradual migration: start with new features, then incrementally refactor old modules.

They accepted a fact: the debt of complexity cannot be cleared all at once; it can only be slowly reduced over time through rules and processes.

The third challenge was the toolchain.

SPM was not mature at the time, and the team had to develop custom tools to support large-scale modularization.

While awaiting official improvements, they built their own build-acceleration system.

This was a dual contest of technology and policy.

The battlefield of complexity is never single-front.

It exists in code, in teams, and in tools.

LinkedIn's modularization effort was like a multi-front operation:

On one hand reshaping the form of the code, on the other adjusting organizational boundaries, and at the same time building the right tools.

In the process, LinkedIn's engineers gradually realized:

Modularization is not merely a technical choice but an organizational philosophy.

Each module is a cognitive territory;

Each team is a province that guards it;

Each contract is a bridge spanning complexity.

Complexity did not disappear; it merely took another form.

LinkedIn's empire was rebuilding order under the new system.

The road ahead remained long and rugged.

When the frontier was divided into provinces, order could be temporarily maintained;

When contracts were ignored, the frontier fell into chaos again.

The world of software and the world of empires are no different.

Complexity doesn't retreat because of a single reform.

It only hides temporarily, waiting for new cracks to appear.

LinkedIn's modularization reforms initially yielded clear results: build times shortened, team responsibilities became clearer, and the scope of bugs was easier to locate.

But as modularization gradually penetrated the entire organization, complexity began to strike back in another form.

The first conflict appeared on the boundaries.

In the monolith era, any engineer could freely enter any part of the code, like merchants freely traversing territories.

After modularization, boundaries were set: certain teams had stewardship over a module, and external teams could only call through public interfaces.

This was logically clear, but culturally it sparked friction.

Some engineers asked in internal forums:

"Why do I have to submit a request to another team to change a small feature? Before I could do it in minutes; now I have to wait days."

This is the irony of complexity: the existence of boundaries reduces overall cognitive load but increases local communication cost.

Like an imperial provincial system: taxation is more orderly, but merchants crossing provinces must pay additional tariffs.

LinkedIn's leadership responded, "Boundaries are protection, not obstacles. Without boundaries, complexity would inundate everyone like a flood."

That statement is rationally indisputable, yet it could not immediately soothe engineers' anxiety.

They were used to the freedom to fix things at any time, and now had to rely on contracts and processes.

The conflict between freedom and order spread through the teams.

The second conflict appeared in dependencies.

The ideal of modularization is to make each module autonomous.

But in practice, the dependency relationships between modules were more complex than imagined.

The feed module depended on the user data module, the user data module depended on the authentication module, and the authentication module depended on the networking module.

When a low-level module is updated, the entire dependency chain must be re-verified.

The introduction of SPM became the key to resolving this chaos.

Dependencies were no longer invisible calls but explicit contracts.

For one module to call another, it had to be declared in the dependency manifest.

This made complexity visible instead of hidden, concrete instead of vague.

However, visible does not mean simple.

SPM exposed the dependency structure, and for the first time engineers could plainly see how their code affected the whole system.

Some teams discovered their module was depended on by more than twenty other modules.

That meant any change could trigger a global tremor.

They described themselves as bound by chains—move slightly and the whole body aches.

Here complexity revealed its cruellest aspect:

modularization clarified its form, but also made its weight inescapable.

The third conflict appeared between tools and people.

SPM, as rolled out at LinkedIn, was not a perfect tool.

Its performance, caching, and dependency resolution at large scale were far from mature.

Engineers had to endure instability in their day-to-day development.

Once, a team's build system was down for two days due to an SPM caching bug.

Engineers angrily asked in a meeting, "We introduced this to reduce complexity—why are we adding a new complexity?"

This is the perennial dilemma of reformers.

Before a new order is established, it is always more painful than the old one.

The imperfect toolchain led many to question the value of modularization.

Some even suggested returning to a monolith to make everything "simple" again.

LinkedIn's architects replied at an all-hands: "Modularization is not for today but for the future.

Today's pain is to buy tomorrow's clarity.

If we do not endure this pain, complexity will eventually consume the entire team."

This was not encouragement but a proclamation.

The architects were clear: complexity will not decrease by retreating; it will only rebound faster if we retreat.

The push for modularization gradually revealed a new organizational shape at LinkedIn.

In the past, team boundaries were fuzzy.

Anyone could touch any part of the code.

That freedom was an advantage in small teams but a disaster in large ones.

Now, boundaries have become clear.

One team corresponds to one module, with responsibility and cognitive scope closely aligned.

- When a bug occurs, responsibility is clear; no longer does everyone need to investigate.
- When a feature iterates, the number of contacts is limited; you no longer need to cross multiple departments.
- When an engineer joins, the learning scope narrows, and they can master the full picture of a module in a short time.

Complexity is no longer evenly distributed; it is digested locally.

This is the essence of modularization: aligning complexity with cognitive boundaries.

However, complexity still lurks in the dark.

Modularization is not a silver bullet.

It solves some problems but creates others.

The most typical case is "over-splitting."

In one architecture discussion, a team proposed breaking an existing module into ten submodules.

Their rationale was: this allows more fine-grained division of labor and increases reusability.

But the architects questioned, "Are you trying to increase real reuse, or are you creating new dependencies?"

As it turned out, that split made dependency relationships more complex and communication costs higher.

In the end, the team had to withdraw the plan.

This is another illusion of complexity:

It tempts you into believing that "more modules" equals "less complexity."

In reality, complexity does not decrease with more modules; it multiplies as dependencies increase.

LinkedIn's modularization reform gradually solidified amid pain and struggle.

SPM's role became increasingly clear: it was not merely a tool but a symbol of contract.

Dependency declarations were the covenant of boundaries;

module relationships were the map of the organization.

Engineers learned to read their position on the dependency graph.

They understood how the modules they owned affected the whole and how changes to their interfaces rippled to other teams.

Complexity was no longer a vague fear but a terrain that could be mapped.

Historians would say:

This is the empire entering a stage of institutionalization.

Before this, the frontier was held together by heroes, by individual generals and sages solving problems.

After this, the frontier was maintained by institutions, by provinces and contracts that sustained order.

LinkedIn's teams experienced the same turning point.

In the monolith era, they relied on individual heroism to solve complexity.

In the modular era, they managed complexity through contracts and institutions.

Complexity still existed, but its form had changed.

It was no longer a random flood but a river channeled into conduits.

It was no longer an intangible fog but mountains marked on a map.

LinkedIn's modularization reform is not yet complete.

The shadow of complexity still gathers in some corners.

But the embryo of order has already appeared.

A great empire is not built on the breadth of its territory, but on the clarity of its borders.

A great team is not built on the sacrifice of heroes, but on the solidity of its contracts.

The war against complexity yields only staged victories.

As LinkedIn's modularization entered its third year, teams gradually learned to breathe under the system.

SPM's dependency contracts stood like stone tablets at the organization's boundaries.

Module splits were no longer just code refactors but reconstructions of cognition.

However, the real turning point was not successive technical optimizations, but cultural maturity.

In the monolith era, heroism prevailed.

When a bug appeared, the engineer most familiar with the system would step forward;

When a feature was delayed, senior developers would pull all-nighters to fix it.

This heroism helped teams overcome crises time and again, but it also allowed complexity to be ignored repeatedly.

After modularization, heroism lost its efficacy.

A module's guardian could not make decisions for another module;

A cross-module bug required multiple teams to locate together.

The power of institutions replaced the halo of individuals.

At first, this left engineers feeling bereft.

They felt their value diluted, no longer the "saviors" who could rescue the whole.

But over time they began to understand:

this was not a devaluation of the individual, but a protection of the individual.

Institutions prevented complexity from weighing solely on

individual shoulders and instead dispersed it across team boundaries.

This shift was like an empire moving from an age of heroes to an age of codified law.

Individual bravery receded to the background;

The clarity of institutions became the true cornerstone.

SPM's contracts gradually permeated every aspect of the organization.

In the past, communication between teams often relied on oral agreements.

Whether an interface could be modified or a dependency introduced was often decided by a few engineers in a meeting.

The result was: decisions lacked transparency, and consequences lacked traceability.

SPM put all of this into contract.

Dependency declarations, like official documents, must be made explicit in the code;

Module versions, like decrees, must comply with the standards;

Interface changes must go through a Pull Request and be reviewed by the module guardians.

Complexity was no longer a vague oral transmission but a clear written agreement. This changed not only the code but also the team's behavior. Engineers no longer relied on memory and tacit understanding; they relied on systems and documentation.

This institutionalization produced two notable results.

First, the Cognitive Load decreased. In the past, a newly hired engineer needed to understand the logic of the entire monolith before they could safely modify code. That was almost impossible. Now, newcomers only need to master the boundaries of their own module to start contributing. Their cognitive scope is clear; the learning curve is steep but limited. This boundedness gives them a sense of control within a limited time.

Second, team collaboration stabilized. In the past, cross-team collaboration often came with disputes: who had the right to change something, who should take responsibility. Now, SPM's contracts provide an objective basis for those disputes. Dependency declarations are in the code, and responsibility boundaries are in the documentation. Arguments are no longer decided by who speaks the loudest but by the clarity of the contract.

Complexity has not disappeared, but its weight is borne by an institutional order.

Of course, the system is not perfect. LinkedIn's modularization also experienced new difficulties.

Once, a team, in order to accelerate iteration, bypassed SPM's dependency declarations and directly called another module's internal interface. In the short term they succeeded; the feature went live faster than expected. But months later, when another team refactored that module, the hidden dependency was exposed. The application crashed in the test environment, and it took weeks to trace the failure back to the original violation.

This incident triggered intense internal debate. Some complained the rules were too strict and hindered efficiency; others insisted the rules must be defended, otherwise modularization would become empty talk.

In the end, LinkedIn's leadership chose the latter. They reiterated internally: "Contracts are not constraints but flood defenses. One bypass may buy short-term smoothness; the long-term result is the collapse of the entire system."

From then on, the position of the rules became more secure. Engineers gradually accepted that true freedom is not the absence of boundaries but the clarity of boundaries.

The cultural shift is the key to the success of modularization.

LinkedIn's teams learned a new language:

They no longer say "I changed some place," but "we adjusted a module";

They no longer ask "who will fix this bug," but "which module's guardian will fix it";

They no longer rely on verbal promises, but on contractual dependency declarations.

This change of language symbolizes a change of cognition.

Teams gradually realized:

Modularization is not a code refactor but a cognitive reconstruction.

It prevents complexity from spreading and confines it within boundaries.

Historians would say this is a mark of an empire reaching maturity.

In the age of heroes, an empire was sustained by individual power;

In the age of institutions, an empire endures by contracts and laws.

LinkedIn's modularization is such an institutional history.

Complexity still exists, but it has been tamed by institutions and circumscribed by contracts.

Engineers no longer fear the unknown but face controllable risks.

The organization is no longer driven by complexity but uses boundaries to resist it.

At root this is a philosophy:

Modularization is organizational science.

Code boundaries are team boundaries;

Dependency declarations are declarations of responsibility;

SPM's contracts are the organization's contracts.

Complexity is not a technical problem but a cognitive one.

Modularization is not a compilation problem but an organizational one.

LinkedIn's story tells a lasting truth:

In the empire of software, complexity will never disappear.

What we can do is not fantasize about eliminating it, but, through institutions and contracts, make it operate within controllable boundaries.

SPM is not just a tool but a symbol.

It gives the torrents of complexity a levee, gives teams territorial borders, and gives the reservoir of cognition capacity.

Complexity is like the gravity of an empire.

A monolithic architecture makes everyone bear the whole and eventually crushes them;

Modularization localizes complexity and protects teams with boundaries;

SPM writes boundaries into contracts, allowing institutions to replace heroes.

LinkedIn's modularization reform ultimately changed not only the code but the culture.

It proves a profound fact:

The form of software determines the form of the organization.

When we discuss modularization in the world of SwiftUI and SPM, we are not discussing tools but philosophy.

It is a philosophy about boundaries, a philosophy about cognition, a philosophy about complexity and institutions.

Boundaries are contracts.
Contracts are order.
Order is civilization.
The future of software lies not in unlimited freedom but in clear boundaries.

CHAPTER 38
COMMUNICATION IS COMPLEXITY

Language is the river of an empire. If the river becomes muddy, the fleet runs aground;

If communication becomes chaotic, the system decays.

Complexity does not only exist in code.

It is like dust, not only covering branches of logic, but also permeating the team's conversations.

If bugs are local wounds in the system, then communication problems are a disorder of the blood.

Once the blood is in disorder, the whole body becomes unbalanced.

In the history of software, countless teams have fallen into quagmires because of communication failures.

They did not fail for lack of brilliant engineers, nor because they chose the wrong language, but because internal team communication became an amplifier of complexity.

Amazon's story is the clearest example.

In the late 1990s, Amazon was still just an online bookseller.

Their technical team was not large, and communication was relatively direct.

A new feature could be completed after a few meetings;

A problem could be solved by a conversation in the hallway.

However, when the business began expanding from books to music, electronics, and daily necessities, the situation changed.

Team size rapidly swelled.

Different groups were responsible for different product lines, and different markets required different customizations.

What should have been simple discussions turned into lengthy coordination.

Every new feature had to cross multiple groups; every change could affect different interests.

This was the moment communication complexity became visible.

Mathematicians have long pointed out that the number of communication relationships does not grow linearly but exponentially.

When there are 5 people on a team, there are at most 10 communication lines.

When the number increases to 12, the lines become 66.

When the team expands to 50 people, the communication relationships reach as many as 1,225.

Communication spreads like a spiderweb, eventually entangling everyone.

At Amazon, this communication complexity was especially evident.

Every product release involved a dozen or so teams.

They spent hours in meeting rooms yet still failed to reach consensus.

Sometimes, because of unclear definitions, two teams wrote two similar but incompatible pieces of code for the same feature.

The result was not increased efficiency but duplicated work.

The true face of complexity is this hidden cost of communication.

It does not appear in code metrics, yet it devours the life of every project.

In one internal project, Amazon planned to roll out a new feature: allowing users to see the estimated delivery time directly in the shopping cart. Seemingly simple, it affected many moving parts:

- The inventory system needed to update in real time;
- The logistics system needed to predict delivery times;
- The frontend needed to display an accurate interface;
- The customer service team needed to provide consistent explanations when users questioned it.

Project meetings dragged on for weeks with no conclusion. Different teams proposed different assumptions, used different data sources, and even had varying definitions of "estimated time." Some argued for displaying the most conservative estimate to reduce customer complaints; others argued for showing the fastest estimate to boost conversion rates. The result was prolonged debate, delayed decisions, and engineers left waiting.

The complexity of communication had replaced technical complexity. The real challenge was not how to calculate delivery time, but how to get dozens of teams to communicate within the same context.

At this point, Jeff Bezos proposed a now-widely-cited principle: the "two-pizza team" principle. A team should be small enough to be fed with two pizzas. Beyond that size, communication costs spiral out of control.

This was not a joke but a profound insight. Team size determines communication complexity; communication complexity determines system complexity. If a team is too large, even the clearest code will be swallowed by the friction of communication.

Behind this principle was an insight into cognitive load. Human working memory is limited. In meetings, we can retain no more than seven points at once. When a dozen or so teams speak at once and information floods in like a torrent, the mind's reservoir overflows quickly. The result of overflow is not "understand everything," but "lose most of it."

Amazon repeatedly encountered this kind of overflow in those meetings. Engineers entered meetings enthusiastic and left three hours later confused. They forgot details others had said, misinterpreted intentions, and the code they ultimately wrote drifted from its original intent. The limits of cognitive load became the ceiling for the project.

The shadow of complexity is not only present in cross-platform frameworks, nor only in deep inheritance chains. It also exists within human language and communication. When teams grow, language stops being clear and boundaries stop being defined; complexity then seeps into every conversation. Amazon's early struggles were a microcosm of this phenomenon.

They realized that if they could not control the complexity of communication, then any technical progress would be futile.

No architecture, no clever design pattern, could survive chaotic communication.

This lesson repeats itself throughout the history of software civilization.

Conway's Law long ago pointed out: the design of a system inevitably reflects the organization's communication structure.

If an organization's communication is chaotic, the system will be chaotic.

If an organization's communication is clear, the system will be clear.

Amazon's "two-pizza team" was not a joke but a civilizational choice.

It reminded all developers: complexity does not come only from technology; it largely comes from humans themselves.

This was only the beginning of the story.

Amazon's subsequent reforms were the real turning point.

They not only reduced team sizes but also redefined team boundaries.

They realized: reducing cross-team cognitive load required not only size control but also coordination in processes and architecture.

If a territory has no borders, the frontier will swallow the capital.

If a team has no boundaries, communication will drown creation.

Complexity is not a wave; it is more like seeping mud.

A wave may surge at a moment, but muddy water will silently soak every inch of land.

At Amazon, the two-pizza-team principle was only the first step; the real challenge was how to let these small teams collaborate without huge friction.

Two-pizza teams reduced internal communication friction.

Within a small team of fewer than ten people, information can be fully grasped by everyone and cognitive load won't overflow.

But a new problem arises: when the number of teams grows from a few to dozens or hundreds, a new communication complexity appears between teams.

Amazon soon discovered that they had avoided the pitfall of "large-team failure" but had fallen into the quagmire of "many-teams disorder."

Each small team was like a ship—nimble and efficient on its own.

But when they needed to form a fleet, those ships collided at sea.

Once, Amazon planned to launch an entirely new international payment system.

That system involved multiple two-pizza teams: payments,

settlements, risk control, currency conversion, and user experience.

Each team was independent and highly efficient.

But when they needed to complete a feature together, chaos reappeared.

The payments team said, "We only handle initiating transactions; we don't guarantee currency conversion."

The settlements team said, "We handle aggregating transactions; we don't guarantee consistency of the user experience."

The risk team said, "We only handle risk scoring; we don't guarantee latency performance."

No one was wrong, but everyone guarded only their own corner.

The result was that the pieces of the feature resembled fragments painted by different artists—when pieced together they looked uneven.

What users saw was not a smooth payment experience but a series of disjointed transitions.

Complexity reappeared, not inside the technology, but at the boundaries of communication.

At this point Bezos introduced another institutional iron rule:

"Anything a team builds must be exposed externally through a service interface; direct data access is forbidden."

This iron rule later became known as Amazon's "service mandate."

It required every team to be like an independent city, with its own walls and gates, and all communication had to go through the gate.

Any attempt to cross the walls or take shortcuts by accessing others directly was prohibited.

It was a harsh discipline.

Many engineers at first could not understand: why impose artificial barriers? Why not access another team's database directly?

They felt efficiency was hindered and development timelines were slowed.

However, in the long run, this "barrier" actually reduced complexity.

Because it made communication clear.

In the civilization of software, the scariest thing is not too many boundaries but blurred boundaries.

Blurred boundaries create endless context switching.

When one team must constantly guess another team's intentions and speculate about another system's implementation details, cognitive load multiplies.

Amazon used service-ification to turn blur into clarity.

Each team only needed to master the interfaces they provided, not the internal details of others.

Communication became like a protocol, not chit-chat; like a contract, not guesswork.

This is the true governance of cognitive load: not reducing information, but reducing useless information.

The far-reaching significance of this rule is that it shifts complexity onto boundary design.

A service with a clear boundary is like a deep module:

Complex internally but simple externally.

A service with a blurred boundary is like a shallow module:

superficially simple but exposing countless details outward.

The former concentrates cognitive load on a limited number of points; the latter lets cognitive load spread between teams.

The former is civilization; the latter is chaos.

In the world of SwiftUI, this principle holds as well. A small iOS team, without clear boundaries, will fall into the same predicament. The UI team and the networking team become interdependent, state is modified in multiple places, and anyone can directly access global variables. On the surface, this may seem fast; in reality, communication complexity has already seeped into the code.

A state change that goes from the UI, to being read by the

networking layer, and then synchronized to local storage involves three teams. Without clear boundaries, every discussion requires re-explaining "where exactly the state is." Developers fumble around in the dark, with no lighthouse to guide them.

But when teams define clear boundaries—

The UI only renders state and does not directly manage data;

The networking layer only exposes services and does not directly manipulate the UI;

The storage layer only guarantees consistency and does not interfere with business logic—

Communication complexity drops instantly. Each team becomes like Amazon's service interface, only required to honor its own contract.

Amazon's transformation was not accomplished overnight. In the early days of implementing service-orientation, many complained about decreased efficiency. They were used to taking shortcuts: directly calling another team's database, directly modifying another team's data structures. Service-orientation took those shortcuts away.

But time proved this to be a necessary price. Behind shortcuts lies endless complexity. Short-term convenience yields long-term chaos. When a system scales to millions of users worldwide, only clear boundaries can keep the empire running.

Communication complexity is not merely a problem of headcount; it is a problem of governance.

If a team's boundaries are blurred, every communication becomes a new burden. People must repeatedly confirm and speculate, ultimately descending into chaos. If a team's boundaries are clear, communication flows like water into channels, and everyone knows what they should do.

Amazon's "service mandate" is essentially a code of communication. It tells each team:

- You are independent; you are responsible for guarding your boundaries;

- You are open; you must communicate with others through clear interfaces;
- You are limited; you do not need to know the secrets behind others' walls.

This is a profound respect for human cognitive load.

From the outside, Amazon looked like a unified empire. From the inside, it resembled an alliance of countless city-states. Each city-state had its own laws but shared a set of communication covenants. It was this institutional arrangement that allowed the vast empire to avoid being destroyed by communication complexity.

In the software world, the fate of an organization is tightly linked to the fate of its systems. Conway's Law is validated here once again: systems inevitably grow to mirror an organization's communication patterns. If an organization's boundaries are clear, a system's boundaries will be clear; if an organization's communication is chaotic, a system's interfaces will be chaotic.

Amazon's case tells us: communication is complexity. The way to reduce complexity is not to eliminate communication, but to make communication obey clear boundaries.

In SwiftUI teams, this means:

- Do not let everyone modify global state;
- Do not let every feature span responsibilities across multiple teams;
- Do not let communication rely on memory and guesswork; rely on contracts and documentation instead.

Boundaries are tools to reduce communication burden.

However, complexity does not disappear entirely because of service-orientation. It reappears between boundaries. When boundary design is poor, dependencies between services can still explode. When protocols are overly complicated, communication will still be overwhelmed.

Amazon's story did not end with the "service mandate." They still had to face the next problem: how to get these countless services to truly coordinate without turning into new chaos.

When city-states proliferate, peace is maintained not by compromise but by covenants.

When systems proliferate, stability is maintained not by genius but by boundaries.

The enemy of complexity never truly leaves. After Amazon completed its service transformation, a new situation emerged: they were no longer one huge whole but hundreds of autonomous teams. Each team was like a city-state, owning its own interfaces and guarding its own boundaries.

But when there are too many city-states, complexity shifts from the inside to the outside. The original chaos came from "communication of large teams"; the current chaos comes from "coordination of many teams."

During a peak shopping season, Amazon's systems faced unprecedented pressure. Users initiated millions of order requests in a short period. In a traditional monolithic system, such requests would be routed through a single entry point. In a service-oriented architecture, those requests are split into countless call chains: from cart to payment, from payment to inventory, from inventory to logistics.

Each link is a team's responsibility, and each communicates via service interfaces. In the ideal case, this architecture can tolerate massive concurrency. In reality, any delay in one link can amplify like the flap of a butterfly's wings. A timeout on an inventory query can cause payment requests to pile up, which in turn can make the frontend display errors.

Ultimately, the whole system resembled an overcomplicated

mechanism, with every gear spinning at high speed and each gear potentially becoming a bottleneck.

Engineers discovered in the postmortem that the problem was not with any single team. Each team had fulfilled its responsibilities. The real problem was the resurgence of cross-team cognitive load.

When a system is composed of hundreds of services, no single engineer can understand the overall behavior. They can only understand their own service and cannot predict the entire call chain. Bugs are no longer local but span multiple services. Communication again becomes an amplifier of complexity:

- Investigating an issue requires contacting five or six teams;
- Each team provides logs, but there is no unified language;
- Every meeting turns into a tug-of-war over "whose responsibility it is."

The shadow of complexity returned, this time wearing the guise of "autonomy."

Bezos and the leadership soon realized: service-orientation was only the first step; true governance required a combination of culture and policy.

So they imposed new institutional requirements:

- Every service must have a clear API contract, documented, and not rely on verbal handoffs.
- Every service must be independently deployable and independently testable to avoid cross-team dependencies.
- Every call must have monitoring and logs to ensure issues can be traced across the call chain.

And at the cultural level, they promoted a more fundamental idea: teams are owners of the product, not merely providers of features.

This sense of ownership thoroughly changed Amazon's team culture.

In the past, teams were only responsible for a single functional module. For example, the "inventory team" only handled inventory, and the "payment team" only handled payments. Under the new culture, teams are responsible not just for modules but for the experience. If the inventory system causes an order to fail, the inventory team must be accountable for the user experience, not pass it to the payment team.

This culture avoids the blame-shifting mode of communication. Teams no longer offload complexity onto others; they proactively assume responsibility. Communication shifts from "splitting responsibilities" to "safeguarding the experience."

Governance of complexity is not only a matter of policy; it is fundamentally a cultural issue.

Without policy, teams will take shortcuts;

Without culture, policy becomes bureaucratic.

Amazon reduced cross-team cognitive load through a dual approach. Policy clarified boundaries; culture ensured those boundaries were respected. Thus complexity was constrained within boundaries, rather than spreading beyond them.

In the iOS world, this lesson applies as well.

A SwiftUI team without clear boundaries will fall into the same predicament:

- The UI team changes state, causing the networking layer to crash;
- The networking layer updates an API, causing the UI to render incorrectly;
- Every meeting becomes a place for explaining responsibilities instead of creating.

Institutional boundaries:

- The UI only renders state and does not alter business logic.

- The networking layer only provides data and does not decide UI presentation.
- State management has a single source of truth and is not altered everywhere.

Cultural boundaries:

- The UI team is not just "drawing interfaces" but the owner of the user experience.
- The networking team is not just "providing APIs" but the owner of data quality.
- The state management team is not just "writing tools" but the guardian of system consistency.

Only the combination of policy and culture truly reduces cognitive load.

"Complexity does not disappear because of boundaries; it is merely constrained by them."

Amazon's story is a parable of software civilization. They moved from the chaos of large teams to the autonomy of small teams; from blurred boundaries to clear service-orientation; from a culture of passing the buck to a sense of ownership.

All of this is for one goal: to reduce cross-team cognitive load, allowing limited human minds to be sustained over the long term.

This is the philosophy of communication.

Communication is not free; it consumes mental resources, just as computation consumes CPU. When communication is out of control, Cognitive Load overflows and complexity will 吞没 civilization. When communication is orderly, Cognitive Load is contained and complexity can be tamed.

In the end we understand: communication is complexity. The only way to reduce complexity is not to make people try harder, but to make institutions clearer and boundaries brighter.

In SwiftUI teams, this means:

- Do not make everyone bear the cognitive load of the entire system;
- Give each team clear boundaries so those boundaries bear the complexity;
- Make communication a contract, not a consumption;
- Let culture be a relief, not an added burden.

The strongest teams are not those that know everything about each other, but those that trust each other's boundaries.

CHAPTER 39
ACTIVE LISTENING

Empires do not perish because of silence, but because no one is willing to truly listen.

Listening is not waiting for an opportunity to speak; it is a ritual of understanding.

The wind comes from afar, sweeping over the dunes, carrying a voice not yet formed.

In a land of deserts, the distance between waystations determines an empire's lifespan; in the empire of software, the quality of communication determines the course of a system.

Without listening, architecture is nothing more than a castle built on sand.

In Atlassian's meeting rooms, complexity does not manifest as thousands upon thousands of lines of code.

It manifests as a question that goes unheard, a concern that is ignored, an explanation that is cut off mid-meeting.

The company is known for its collaboration tools; they built Jira, Confluence, and Bitbucket, systems that serve the boundaries of countless development teams.

Yet their own development teams face the same enemy: complexity.

And the most insidious breeding ground of complexity is not in code, but in communication.

The story's beginning is not dramatic.

An Atlassian mobile team is refactoring Jira's mobile experience.

They decide to adopt SwiftUI to shed the historical baggage of UIKit.

What was meant to be a technical innovation gradually evolved into a test of culture during the discussions.

The air in the meeting room is always tense.

The product manager anxiously stresses the users' pain points: slow load times, sluggish interactions, and outdated visuals.

The designer presents new interface proposals, hoping to take advantage of SwiftUI's animation and composition capabilities more naturally on iOS.

The engineers quietly warn that SwiftUI is still evolving, some controls' behaviors are unstable, and certain features will need to fall back to UIKit.

The problem is not a clash of opinions, but an absence of listening.

When the product manager reiterates the emphasis on speed, the engineers' concerns are ignored;

When the designer demonstrates new interactions, warnings about performance are drowned out;

When the engineers offer compromises, the meeting's focus has already shifted to release cadence.

They think they are communicating; in reality, they are merely waiting for their turn to speak.

Complexity is born in that silence.

Listening is not a gentle courtesy, but a technical practice.

In the world of SwiftUI, the state-driven philosophy requires each part to faithfully reflect changes in the whole.

Communication is the same: if a team cannot accurately listen to each other's state, the final product will inevitably be unbalanced.

Within Atlassian's Jira mobile team, this imbalance gradually became apparent.

Designers submitted increasingly bold proposals—layered animations, smooth transitions.

But the engineers' alarm bells grew louder: SwiftUI's redraw overhead, list performance bottlenecks, rendering pressure from complex interactions.

They tried to raise these issues in meetings, but were always quickly brushed past.

No one truly listened—only a string of nods and a push to move forward.

Weeks later, when the prototype reached internal testing, the problems erupted.

The animations were indeed elegant, but caused severe frame drops when scrolling lists;

the interface was indeed fresh, but memory usage spiked dramatically.

User experience did not improve; instead, it brought more complaints.

This was not SwiftUI's fault, nor the designers', nor the engineers'.

It was the result of absent listening.

An unheard concern ultimately turned into a real disaster.

Complexity sometimes shows up as technical debt, sometimes as architectural redundancy, but at a deeper level, it manifests as distortion in communication.

This was exactly the distortion Atlassian's team faced.

When an empire's waystations no longer pass along accurate intelligence, orders from the capital inevitably diverge from reality.

The software empire is no different: when teams stop truly listening, decisions inevitably diverge from feasibility.

After the storm, the team began to reflect.

They realized the real problem wasn't SwiftUI, nor feature planning, but the way they communicated.

Listening is not a soft courtesy, but a hard technique.

Like testing, like performance monitoring, like architecture reviews, it is a means of governing complexity.

Atlassian's team tried introducing a new ritual:

In every discussion, the person who raises an issue first states it fully, and others must paraphrase it in their own words to confirm before moving on.

The approach is clumsy, but effective.

It forces everyone to listen before speaking, and to think after listening.

This kind of listening makes communication a true synchronization of state, rather than talking to oneself.

The erosion of complexity does not come from clashes of opinion, but from deviations in understanding.

When a team is merely arguing rather than listening, they are sowing the seeds of future complexity.

Atlassian's Jira mobile team is learning this ancient wisdom:

Listening is not waiting for an opportunity to speak, but a responsibility to participate in design.

This is only the beginning of the story.

The real test lies deeper.

In cross-team collaboration, in the noise of remote work, in organizations of hundreds, can listening still become institutional?

Or will it once again disappear under the pressure of clamor and schedules?

When an empire's waystations are scattered thousands of miles apart, information no longer travels by speed alone, but by loyalty and accuracy.

Listening is the courier's only weapon.

The wind does not always blow nearby.

Sometimes it comes from a thousand miles away, passing through unfamiliar valleys and distant towns.

In the modern empire, that wind is called remote collaboration.

And at Atlassian, it became the second proving ground for listening practices.

After the Jira mobile team learned the listening practice of "full paraphrase," they briefly felt the tide of complexity slow.

The quality of team meetings improved, misunderstandings decreased, and decisions ceased to be overturned so often.

However, when this method was promoted to cross-team levels, new problems arose.

Atlassian's organization is extremely distributed.

Headquarters is in Sydney, R&D in San Francisco, design in Amsterdam, and support teams are scattered around the world.

This global layout brought commercial resilience, but it also made communication like intercontinental relay routes.

Email, Slack, Confluence, and Zoom became the new waystations.

Messages could be delivered, but whether they were truly understood was another matter.

Complexity here took on a different face.

It no longer manifested as bridging a three-tier architecture, but as the overlapping of time zones, languages, cultures, and tools.

When one team meets in the morning, another is already in the middle of the night.

A sentence that seems vague in English can be completely distorted in the minds of Dutch or Japanese speakers.

When meeting notes are uploaded to Confluence, hundreds of comments can cover the original intent like dust.

In such an environment, listening becomes harder and more important.

A real incident became the turning point.

The team was designing a new "offline mode" for Jira's mobile app.

Users could still edit tasks while on a plane or in areas with unstable signal, and changes would automatically sync when the network recovered.

This was a repeatedly requested feature and an important product improvement.

At the start of the discussion, the product manager in Sydney emphasized the importance of user experience:

"We want users not to notice the lack of network; everything should feel like it's done locally."

An engineer in San Francisco hesitated on Zoom and raised concerns:

"That means we need to design a full local caching system and handle complex conflict-resolution logic.

Sync delays, version conflicts, data loss... these will all become risks."

But because of time zone differences and unstable connections, some of these remarks were missed by parts of the team.

In the meeting notes, there was only a brief summary:

"The engineers said it's a bit difficult, but they can try."

Weeks later, when the designer completed a prototype based on that 'summary,' conflict erupted.

The engineering team angrily pointed out: this is not 'a bit difficult' but a massive systemic challenge.

They would need several more months of development, a new testing regimen, and might even have to refactor parts of the networking layer.

The product manager insisted, however: this is a strong user demand and cannot be postponed.

The root of all the conflict was simply that no one truly listened at the time.

A single ignored explanation became an interdepartmental conflict.

Complexity does not take root in code; it grows in the silence of being unheard.

Listening, in this environment, was forced to evolve.

Atlassian's team began experimenting with "mirrored listening."

That is, in every cross-time-zone meeting, any decision had to be paraphrased by the other side in different words and confirmed before it could be recorded.

It seemed inefficient, but it significantly reduced misunderstandings.

They also introduced a practice of "asynchronous listening."

On Confluence pages, any proposal had to include a "core concerns" section in which the author clearly listed the three points they cared about most.

This way, readers would not just look at the surface proposal, but understand the true intent behind it.

It's like SwiftUI's "single source of truth":

Not state scattered everywhere, but a clear declaration centralized in one place.

These attempts were not achieved overnight.

They required more time, more discipline, more patience.

But they changed the team invisibly:

From "how to speak" to "how to listen."

The essence of complexity is information asymmetry.

In software, it appears as inconsistent state;

In teams, it appears as inconsistent understanding.

Active Listening is the tool to resolve this asymmetry.

In the Jira mobile team's remote collaboration, this was repeatedly validated.

Once, the San Francisco team proposed an optimization on Confluence:

"To improve performance, we plan to reduce some animations in exchange for smoother list scrolling."

If this had been in the past, designers in Sydney might have immediately objected:

"Animation is core to the user experience; we can't sacrifice it."

But because of the "asynchronous listening" practice, the designers first read the three concerns engineers had written down:

- Frame drops caused by animations are especially noticeable on lower-end devices.
- Frame drops directly affect the user's input experience.
- Optimizing early can reduce future maintenance costs.

So the designers' response was no longer a flat rejection, but a compromise:

"Can we retain key transition animations but reduce decorative effects?"

This time, communication did not turn into conflict but into collaboration.

Listening changed the trajectory of complexity.

However, the real challenge is not in these specific practices.

The real challenge is whether listening can become culture as the organization scales.

Atlassian's headcount doubled in just a few years.

New hires brought fresh energy and new noise.

In a rapidly expanding empire, there are more waystations and intelligence grows more complex.

Without institutionalized listening, all attempts will be swallowed by scale.

So the team began to incorporate Active Listening into training.

In their first week, new employees did not just learn tools and processes; they learned listening skills.

They were required to practice paraphrasing and confirmation repeatedly in simulated meetings;

To explicitly extract others' concerns in documents;

To state the other party's point of view before expressing their own during conflicts.

This may seem like a "non-technical" training, but in fact it is the deepest technical practice.

Because it directly determines whether complexity can be controlled.

"When an empire's territory is vast enough, differences in language and time zones become inevitable.

What truly decides success or failure is not weapons, but whether intent can be transmitted accurately."

Atlassian's remote teams are using listening to mend the cracks.

But complexity never stops; it still lurks deeper.

In cross-department collaboration, in high-level strategy, in long-term evolution, it will continue to lie in wait.

An empire's survival does not depend on the grandest walls but on the clearest conversations.

Listening is the covert current that sustains institutions.

When that current is severed, the empire will sink.

In Atlassian's chronicles, 2019 was recorded as a turning point.

That year, remote collaboration had already become the norm and the ritual of listening had taken root in small teams.

However, an unexpected crisis made the whole company truly appreciate the significance of Active Listening as an institutional practice.

The crisis began with a seemingly harmless decision.

Product leaders proposed: Jira's mobile app needed a comprehensive performance overhaul.

The reason was simple — competitor Trello kept raising the bar on mobile experience, and users' patience was being worn thin.

Surveys showed: Jira's mobile app had a higher crash rate on low-end devices than the industry average, and list loading times were noticeably long.

This wasn't a single bug but a systemic bottleneck.

At an executive meeting, the decision was made: complete the full optimization within three months and ensure reputation is reversed in the next release.

When the message reached the frontline teams, the air went still.

Three months, for a globally collaborative team, is a brutal deadline.

They would have to optimize rendering flows on both iOS and Android, refactor parts of the caching mechanism, and still preserve the user experience.

If listening were absent, this goal would become a disaster.

And indeed, that is how it began.

At the first cross-department sync, tension erupted immediately.

The product manager repeatedly emphasized the goal: "We need to see results within three months."

A designer asked worriedly: "If we cut animations, will it harm the brand experience?"

An engineer was silent for a moment, then quietly said, "Do you know this means rewriting the entire rendering pipeline?"

The meeting hit an impasse.

Everyone was speaking, but no one was truly listening.

The shadow of complexity fell again.

Just then, an engineering manager proposed: "We've learned to use Active Listening within our small teams. Now let's scale it up. No one is allowed to state their position directly; first they must paraphrase the other person's concerns."

The meeting restarted. The product manager was asked to

first restate the engineers' viewpoint: "You believe that completing this in three months requires rewriting the rendering pipeline, which will introduce huge risks." The engineers nodded: "Yes, and if rushed, stability will suffer." Then it was the engineers' turn to restate the designers' viewpoint: "You're worried that cutting animations will damage the brand experience and consistency." The designers nodded: "Exactly."

As this "mirrored listening" proceeded, the atmosphere gradually loosened. For the first time they discovered they were not opponents but standing on different parts of the same boundary, trying to safeguard the same goal.

A real conversation finally took place.

The engineers proposed: "If we reduce animations by 30% and optimize the rendering pipeline in phases instead of rewriting it all at once, we can deliver staged results within three months." The designers responded: "If we keep the core transition animations and sacrifice decorative effects, I can accept that." The product manager added: "Then we can split the optimization into two phases: the first to address performance bottlenecks, the second to gradually restore animations."

The pressure of complexity did not disappear, but it was redistributed. Listening prevented conflicts from accumulating and instead turned them into compromise and collaboration.

The crisis was not over. The three-month deadline remained tight, and the team was still exhausted. But in the dozens of meetings that followed, Active Listening became mandatory.

Any decision had to first go through a "paraphrase confirmation"; any disagreement had to begin with the opposing side stating the other's viewpoint before rebutting; any document had to explicitly list three core concerns.

These rules were like SwiftUI's "single source of truth": they did not eliminate complexity, but they made it flow within visible boundaries. They did not guarantee perfection, but they guaranteed understanding.

Three months later, the Jira mobile app was released on schedule.

List loading speed improved by 40%, crash rate dropped by 25%, and user ratings gradually recovered. Animations were indeed reduced, but users cared more about smoothness. More importantly, the team did not collapse under the pressure; instead, they maintained trust through listening.

In the retrospective, someone wrote:

"This was not a mere optimization but an organizational drill.

We learned that complexity lives not only in code but also in silence.

Listening is our only solution."

"When an empire faces external enemies, swords are not the only defense.

When a software team faces complexity, code is not the only tool.

Listening is the overlooked weapon."

We must understand that Active Listening is not a little psychological trick.

It is a technical practice for governing complexity.

When state-driven UIs need a single source of truth;

When modular architectures need clear boundaries;

When tests need to be independent and repeatable;

Communication likewise requires institutional constraints.

Without listening, any architecture will crumble.

With listening, even in the flood of complexity, a team can find footholds.

Atlassian's story tells us:

The root of complexity lies not only in code but also in language.

Unheard concerns will become bugs;

Ununderstood compromises will become debt;

Unconfirmed intent will become cracks.

And Active Listening can turn these invisible complexities into explicit consensus.

It gives our limited human minds a chance to establish order amid chaos.

It brings teams from noise to clarity, from conflict to collaboration.

Beyond code, listening is the most important architecture.
Within boundaries, understanding is the strongest defense.
Complexity cannot be eliminated, but through listening we have learned to live with it.

CHAPTER 40
PSYCHOLOGICAL SAFETY AND CULTURE

When truth can only whisper, falsehood will sing loudly.

The collapse of an empire is not because of an invading army, but because no one dared to say: "The road is cut off."

In the history of the decline of all empires, the most frightening thing is not corruption or foreign enemies, but silence.

When soldiers no longer dare to question a general's orders, when scholars no longer dare to correct the emperor's misjudgments, when engineers choose to remain silent in the meeting room, complexity then gains its most loyal ally.

Complexity never fights alone.

Its most faithful partner is a culture of silence.

The archives of Pixar Animation Studios offer an unusual footnote.

The name is often associated in people's minds with art, creativity, and imagination.

Toy Story, Finding Nemo, Coco... These works made the whole world believe that animation is not just children's playthings, but an art form that can touch the deepest human emotions.

However, few people notice that behind these triumphs is a nearly stringent system: a culture that permits questioning.

Pixar's story is about art, but it is also about engineering.

Because in any field that requires collective intelligence—whether animation or software—psychological safety is the foundation of the architecture.

At Pixar, there is a meeting called the Braintrust.

It is not a review in the traditional sense, but a unique cultural practice.

In this meeting, directors present their not-yet-mature works to colleagues.

The film may be rough, the plot may be chaotic, the characters may be unappealing.

Then, team members will offer criticism without reservation, even saying bluntly, "This part doesn't work at all."

The key is:

All criticism is free of the threat of authority.

Whether senior directors or newly promoted screenwriters, everyone can question each other's judgments.

Criticism is not an order, but a suggestion; not a struggle of power, but a clash of wisdom.

Directors have the right to decide whether to adopt suggestions, but do not have the power to stop others from raising questions.

It is precisely this system that ensures Pixar's works can be continuously refined in the early stages.

They believe: if no one dares to question, then a bad film is the inevitable outcome.

And allowing questioning is the only soil in which clarity and greatness can be born.

In the software world, the situation is strikingly similar.

The evolution of a SwiftUI architecture often begins with a small design decision. For example, should state be stored in the View, or centralized in a Store? For example, should a Feature module be packaged independently as a Package, or kept in the Monolith? These questions seem technical but are actually organizational.

If in the meeting room no one dares to question the team leader's proposal, complexity will accumulate in the silence. Short-term decisions might bring quick satisfaction. But long-term architecture will inevitably become mired for lack of early correction.

The scenario complexity likes best is "no one speaks up." Because in that moment, it knows it has already won.

Pixar's Braintrust is essentially a ritual of psychological safety. It sends a signal to the team: here, you can question without fear of punishment. Here, your voice is not an affront to authority, but a contribution to the future.

This is precisely the culture most software teams lack. How many times have engineers clearly spotted architectural flaws during Code Review but chosen to remain silent? How many times have junior developers had doubts in meetings but stayed quiet for fear of "saying the wrong thing"? How many times has a team, out of fear of arguing, let a poor decision pass unchallenged?

Each instance of silence is a vote for complexity.

In Pixar's archives there is this story.

At one Braintrust meeting a director showed an early cut of a film. The footage was rough, the plot chaotic, and he himself felt uneasy. When the clip finished screening, the room fell into a brief silence. Then a young writer spoke up: "This sequence makes no sense. I can't understand why the character would make this choice."

In another company, that remark might have been considered offensive. But at Pixar, such questioning is encouraged. So others joined in, raising questions from different angles. By the end of the meeting, the director was not depressed but rather relieved. He knew this was the only way the film could become clear.

This story was later included in Pixar's internal training manual. They called it the "right to fail." Because only by allowing failure is true clarity possible.

The connection between psychological safety and clear architecture is not as distant as it may appear. In software development, the accumulation of complexity often stems from early hesitation and silence. When no one dares to say, "this path is too complex," it gets adopted. When no one dares to say, "this abstraction is meaningless," it stays. When no one dares to say, "we need to refactor," refactoring is postponed forever.

Thus, complexity wraps around like seaweed until the whole system can no longer breathe.

A team that allows questioning is like Pixar with its Braintrust mechanism. They dare, in the early stages, to call out problems, expose hidden risks, and resolve future pain in advance. That courage does not come from technology, but from culture.

Pixar's experience has been studied by countless Silicon Valley companies, including software teams. They found that when psychological safety is established, a team's code quality improves significantly; when psychological safety is undermined, complexity accumulates rapidly.

Google's "Project Aristotle" confirmed this as well. They surveyed hundreds of teams and found that the biggest factor affecting team performance was not the presence of geniuses, nor perfect processes, but psychological safety. When members dare to question, admit mistakes, and surface doubts, complexity will not grow in silence.

A software team's Braintrust is not a copy of Pixar's model, but a ritual suited to engineering. It might be an open architecture review; it might be an anonymous technical retrospective; it might be a blameless postmortem.

The key is: the team must clearly send a signal—here, you can question without being punished. Here, you can speak a different voice without being ostracized. Here, questioning is not destructive but constructive.

Complexity is an ally of silence, and psychological safety is its opponent. In Pixar's meeting rooms, the voice of questioning is the only guarantee that a film can become clear. In software meeting rooms, the voice of questioning is likewise the only guarantee that architecture can become clear.

We have seen the significance of psychological safety and the story of Pixar. But that is not enough. In software teams, how does psychological safety concretely affect SwiftUI architecture? How does it help us avoid Massive ViewModel, help us stick to a single source of truth, and help us delineate module boundaries?

These questions still need to be further uncovered. The shadow of complexity has not yet dissipated, and the power of questioning has only just begun to emerge.

The rise of complexity never depends on armies, but on silence.

Silence lets fragile decisions pass unchallenged until one day the empire finds it can no longer breathe.

An empire's territory is not always land on a map. In the software world, territory is the codebase, module boundaries, and the countless commits merged into the main branch. Every commit is a brick, every line of comment a whisper. When whispers fall silent, the bricks begin to lean.

Medium's iOS team once hovered on such a frontier.

It was the era when SwiftUI was just emerging. Apple showcased this brand-new framework at WWDC like a bolt of lightning illuminating the road ahead. Declarative UI, single source of truth, state-driven—these words lit hope in developers' eyes. Medium's team was no exception. They hoped to use

SwiftUI to completely shed the tedium and weight of the UIKit era.

At first, everything seemed to go smoothly. In small experimental projects, SwiftUI's simplicity and elegance were exhilarating. A few lines of declarations could achieve layouts that used to take dozens of lines. State bindings tied UI and logic closely together. Engineers felt as if they had regained the freedom to create.

However, complexity never appears at dawn. It prefers to quietly grow in the afternoon's shadows.

The problem arose in the ViewModel.

As features grew, SwiftUI Views were no longer just a few buttons and texts but began to carry full business logic. Medium's engineers soon found the ViewModel starting to bloat. It bore data requests, state management, navigation logic, and even some business rules. This is what people commonly call the Massive ViewModel.

At a team architecture discussion, a young engineer raised a question: "Our ViewModel is too large and hard to maintain. Should we consider architectures like TCA or Redux to make state management clearer?"

The room fell silent for a moment. Everyone understood that the question struck at the heart of the matter. The Massive ViewModel had already made their code hard to understand, and testing costs were rising. Yet the very act of asking the question suddenly made the air coagulate.

Because questioning often implies a challenge to the decisions of existing leadership. Without psychological safety, such questions would be covered by silence.

At that moment, Medium's team made a choice. They did not suppress the young engineer. The team's technical lead nodded and said, "This is a question worth discussing. We don't need to rush to a conclusion, but we must face it."

So a Braintrust-style architecture meeting was convened. Engineers from different levels gathered and engaged in intense discussion. Some worried that TCA's learning curve would be too steep and add burden to the team. Some worried that Redux's templating would be too verbose and violate SwiftUI's philosophy of simplicity. Others insisted that keeping the current pattern was safer and wouldn't incur major migration costs.

However, unlike most software teams, this meeting was not a struggle for power but an exchange of viewpoints. The young engineer's voice was not shut down, and the senior engineers' concerns were heard. Every question could be raised; every concern could be recorded.

Psychological safety played a decisive role here.

Without psychological safety, the discussion might have been entirely different. The young engineer would have stayed silent for fear of questioning, and the Massive ViewModel would have continued to bloat. By the time the problem fully erupted, the team would be forced to refactor and pay many times the cost. This is complexity's favorite path: it accumulates in silence and then demands interest in the future.

But in Medium's meeting room, psychological safety left no place for complexity to hide. It forced the team to face problems early, turning potential cracks into fixable gaps.

The meeting did not reach a conclusion immediately. But it produced a more important outcome: the team established a new cultural mechanism.

They decided to hold an open architecture review once a month, where anyone could raise questions. These reviews were not meant to overturn existing decisions but to expose problems and ensure complexity would not accumulate in silence. They also established a rule: questioning is not challenging authority, but taking responsibility for the future.

This rule was later written into the team's engineering handbook and became part of the onboarding that new members had to learn.

The power of psychological safety is not to make everyone

agree, but to make everyone dare to disagree. When a team loses dissenting opinions, it also loses a clear future.

Because of this culture, Medium's team gradually matured in their SwiftUI practice. They tried to introduce parts of TCA's ideas, using Reducers to manage complex state flows; they retained parts of MVVM's structure to keep simple modules lightweight. This hybrid architecture was not perfect, but it was clear. Because it was born out of open discussion, not silent compromise.

Historians would say this is the fate of empires. Some empires collapse because of silence; others are reborn because of questioning.

In the software world, complexity is that silent decay. Psychological safety is the only cure.

Although Medium's team established a culture of questioning, complexity would not stop there. It would breed in deeper places—within the testing system, at module boundaries, in cross-functional collaboration. Psychological safety is only the first line of defense, not the final victory.

When a king is afraid of being questioned, his kingdom has already lost a clear future.

When a team fears speaking up, their architecture has already begun to blur.

The wind blows through silent meeting rooms, bringing whispers of complexity. If the first crack appears in the silence of engineers, the second crack often appears at cross-functional boundaries.

Software is not the work of engineers alone. It is an empire woven together by the product manager's vision, the designer's drafts, the engineer's code, and the tester's guardianship. When this empire lacks psychological safety, complexity will grow rampant in the gaps at the boundaries.

Medium's team knew this well.

In the evolution of SwiftUI architecture, they needed not only engineers' consensus but also product and design understanding. Because SwiftUI's principles—state-driven, single source of truth, composition-first—are not just an engineering philosophy; they directly affect how the product iterates.

For example, when a product manager proposed a complex interaction requirement: "We want to add a dynamic recommendation card on the reading page that can change in real time based on the user's reading time and interests."

This is natural in the product vision, but in engineering implementation it can mean an explosion of state. The recommendation card needs to depend on reading time, user tags, network requests, cache state... If these states are not centrally managed but scattered across multiple ViewModels, complexity will grow like vines.

Engineers need to stand up and question: "Can we abstract these states into a single unified Store? Without a single source of truth, this requirement will quickly destabilize our architecture."

The problem is, if the team lacks psychological safety, who dares to say "no" in front of the product manager? "No" is often interpreted as blocking progress or rejecting innovation. But in the world of architecture, true clarity often arises from refusal. Refusal is not conservatism but restraint; it is not a denial of the vision but protection of the future.

Medium's team experienced such a scene in a cross-functional meeting. The product manager proposed a "multi-entry navigation" scheme, hoping to provide multiple jump paths on the reading page to accommodate different user habits. The designer showed a beautiful prototype—complex logic, fancy animations. In a team lacking psychological safety, engineers would likely accept it in silence. But here, a senior iOS engineer calmly said, "If we implement the prototype as-is, the ViewModel will immediately spiral out of control. We need to revisit the interaction design, or we'll pay a long-term cost for it."

The air briefly froze. The product manager and designer glanced at each other and then nodded. They reopened the discussion and ultimately decided to simplify the plan, consolidating the multiple entry points into a single clear path.

The crack of complexity was thus plugged—not by technology, but by questioning.

Psychological safety in cross-functional collaboration means more than just "daring to say no." Its deeper value lies in creating a shared language.

In Medium's team, product, design, and development gradually built a new vocabulary:

- They no longer say "the feature is cool," but instead ask "how much cognitive load will this feature add?"
- They no longer say "the design is flashy," but instead ask "will this design break the single source of truth?"
- They no longer say "ship it quickly," but instead ask "can we first keep the boundaries clear?"

This shift in language stemmed from psychological safety. Only when questioning is allowed will language be shared. And only shared language can resist complexity.

Historically, an empire's frontiers often collapsed because of poor communication. A frontier general who saw the enemy approaching dared not write an honest memorial; officials in the capital, afraid to speak plainly about damaged roads, only reported "everything is fine." The result: by the time the empire discovered the cracks, they were already beyond repair.

The fate of software teams is the same. When product managers don't dare question market illusions, when designers don't dare question the burden of aesthetics, when engineers don't dare question architectural collapse, complexity will break through the silent boundaries like an invading army.

Psychological safety exists not only in meeting rooms but also in code review.

Medium's team once encountered this scenario: a newly hired engineer submitted code that introduced a new state variable but didn't put it into the Store. If left unchecked, this would cause state to gradually disperse, undermining the single source of truth philosophy.

In a team lacking psychological safety, a senior engineer might silently fix it or perfunctorily comment "pay attention" during review. The new engineer would not truly understand, nor grow from it.

But in Medium's team, review comments were open and candid: "If we scatter state across multiple places, it will cause serious complexity problems in the future. Let's discuss together how to put it into a unified Store."

This comment did not make the new engineer feel humiliated; instead it made him feel included in a larger system. Because the team's culture had long been clear: criticism is not blame but construction.

The power of psychological safety also lies in its ability to make the team admit mistakes.

In their early SwiftUI practice, Medium's team also made mistakes. They once stuffed too much logic into the View layer, causing frequent redraws and degraded performance. When users reported noticeable lag, they had to carry out a large-scale refactor.

Without psychological safety, such mistakes might be concealed or blamed on individual engineers. But here, the team chose to discuss openly: "This is a shared mistake we made while exploring a new framework. We need to learn from it, not look for scapegoats."

This attitude turned mistakes into assets rather than burdens. Complexity fears being exposed and loves to be hidden. Psychological safety means complexity has nowhere to hide.

The story so far has revealed the meaning of psychological safety in cross-functional collaboration. It is not an abstract value but concrete practice:

- In meetings, allow engineers to question product;
- In design, allow developers to call for clear boundaries;
- In reviews, allow newcomers to make mistakes and learn from them;
- In retrospectives, allow the team to acknowledge shared responsibility.

These practices prevent complexity from growing through silence.

But we must look further. Psychological safety is not merely a tool for reducing complexity; it is the cornerstone of team culture.

Across the long history of software, technologies change and frameworks shift. Today it is SwiftUI; tomorrow it may be a new paradigm. Only culture endures. Only teams that allow questioning can remain clear amid the flood of complexity.

Summarizing this section, we can distill three philosophies:

First, silence is complexity's ally. When questioning is suppressed, complexity will grow in unknown corners.

Second, psychological safety is the moat that protects architecture. It allows teams to raise issues and face cracks early, repairing the system sooner.

Third, culture determines the lifespan of architecture. The best technology, if lacking psychological safety, will be devoured by complexity; the newest framework, if built on a culture of questioning, can remain clear over the long term.

True clarity does not come from tools but from culture.
When a team allows questioning, they truly own the future.
When a team loses dissent, they have handed their future over to complexity.

CHAPTER 41
THE TRUE MEANING OF CODE REVIEW

The laws of an empire are not for punishment, but for continuation.

Software reviews are not for finding faults, but to keep the future clear.

Complexity is like a forest.

When trees are young, they are straight and clear; as years pass, branches and leaves intertwine, and paths become blurred.

If no one regularly clears the dead branches, the forest will silently become impassable.

Code Review is the team that patrols the forest; their job is not to blame which tree grew crooked, but to ensure that future people can still walk through this forest.

In Pixar's world, film production and software development bear an astonishing similarity.

An animated feature usually takes five years or even longer.

In that process, countless ideas converge into a sea: characters, story, storyboards, lighting, rendering.

Every decision can affect the progress for years to come.

Complexity is not an abstract concept, but a reality that presses on the shoulders of directors and teams every day.

Pixar's most famous mechanism is called the Braintrust.

It is an advisory group made up of directors, writers, and producers.

At every stage of production, they regularly gather to review parts of the work and provide feedback.

Their discussions are candid and pointed, but the goal is never to find faults; it is to help creators see the complexities that may arise in the future.

During the early development of Toy Story, the existence of the Braintrust saved the entire project.

At the time, the team had portrayed Woody in the second draft of the script as sarcastic, sharp, and even somewhat cruel.

The result was that audiences in test screenings could not empathize at all.

If this problem had not been discovered, the whole film might have failed.

Members of the Braintrust pointed out in the review meeting:

"Woody cannot be a protagonist people dislike, or the entire narrative will collapse."

This was not about finding faults, but about seeing a potential explosion point of future complexity.

Once the audience cannot accept the protagonist, all subsequent efforts will be wasted.

So the team revised the script, keeping Woody's humor and wit, but giving him more warmth and a sense of responsibility.

It was this change that made Toy Story the first all-CG feature film in history, and ultimately changed the entire film industry.

Code Review in software development is essentially the same as the Braintrust.

Its purpose has never been to "find faults."

Finding faults is only the surface; the real task is to help the team avoid an explosion of future complexity.

When an engineer submits an implementation, on the surface it may work, tests pass, and the logic is self-consistent.

But the value of Code Review isn't to confirm whether it runs, but to judge:

- Will future developers be able to understand it?
- Will it become a shackle when requirements change?
- Does it hide Cognitive Load that will become an obstacle months later?

Complexity, like bad habits, doesn't explode immediately; it lies dormant.

The true meaning of Code Review is to unearth potential debt before it erupts.

Pixar's Braintrust provides a key insight: the tone and goals of reviews determine the success or failure of the system.

If reviews become a power game, creators will fear feedback and only go through the motions.

If reviews become petty finger-pointing, the team will be mired in details and ignore real complexity.

The secret of the Braintrust is that their feedback carries no authoritative compulsion.

Directors don't have to accept any advice, but they must listen and must take warnings about complexity into account.

This "strong recommendation + freedom of choice" makes feedback a true asset rather than a punishment.

In the software world, Code Review must be the same. It is not a tool for superiors to inspect subordinates, but an expression of collective wisdom.

Each comment is a reminder of future complexity, not a reproach for present mistakes.

Such a culture is what makes engineers willing to be open-minded and allows the team to truly benefit.

However, complexity does not yield easily.

Just as Pixar must repeatedly return to the Braintrust for each subsequent film, software teams must continually conduct Code Reviews.

One review won't change the future, but a sustained culture can change the direction.

During the development of Finding Nemo, the Braintrust played its part again.

In the original version of the story, Nemo's father Marlin was overly fearful and had almost no room to grow.

The Braintrust pointed out that if the protagonist doesn't grow, the audience's emotions won't be moved.

So the team rewrote large portions of the plot, allowing Marlin to gradually learn to let go during the journey.

This adjustment made the film not just an adventure, but a profound journey of a father and son.

Code Review is the same.

It is not a one-off bug fix, but a continuous exercise of the mind.

It lets the team, through repeated discussions, form a shared vigilance toward complexity.

That vigilance is the most valuable cultural asset.

In the archives of the software empire, Code Review should not be defined as "finding faults."

Finding faults is the job of testing.

The mission of Code Review is to warn of future dangers before complexity has manifested.

It is a form of "cognitive defense," a compassion for future readers.

Pixar's story teaches us:

A great film is not great because it has no mistakes, but because it avoided complexities that would make future audiences lose their way.

Likewise, great software is not great because it has no bugs, but because it avoided complexities that would make future developers lose their way.

In this forest, Code Review is the patrol, and the Braintrust is the prophet for the audience.

Their job is not to punish trees for leaning, but to ensure the forest remains passable in the future.

Complexity still lurks in the dark, but with such systems and cultures, it will not silently destroy civilization.

As teams expand, the voices of review become like a parliament.

If those voices are merely reproachful, the future will be swallowed by noise;

If those voices are warnings, the future will be clarified by order.

Complexity is like the tide.

It is gentle in small teams and turbulent in large ones.

When the number grows from ten to a hundred, from a hundred to a thousand, the force of complexity multiplies.

It is hidden not only in the code, but also in the gaps of communication, process, and culture.

Pixar's Braintrust began as a small-circle meeting, with a few directors and writers sitting around a table, exchanging candid opinions.

But as the studio succeeded, projects multiplied and team sizes swelled.

The Braintrust had to expand too, growing from a dozen or so people to dozens, then hundreds.

Along the way they encountered new challenges:

When there are too many voices, feedback becomes noise;

When opinions are too scattered, complexity increases instead;

When criticism carries the weight of power, creators go on the defensive and stop being open.

This is precisely the portrait of software teams in Code Review.

At a well-known Silicon Valley tech company (internal documents of which were later made public), a large team fell into an unexpected predicament because Code Review had been institutionalized.

The team numbered in the hundreds, distributed across time zones.

Every piece of code had to be approved by at least two reviewers before it could be merged.

The system's original intent was to guarantee quality.

However, the actual outcome was starkly different.

Reviewers were often exhausted, processing dozens of PRs a day.

Feedback became mechanical:

Some only checked superficial formatting and dared not dig into the logic;

Some picked at trivial naming issues while avoiding architectural discussions;

Some, to avoid responsibility, simply wrote "LGTM" (Looks Good To Me), allowing potential complexity to pass.

The result was:

- Genuinely critical architectural issues went unaddressed;
- Insignificant details were amplified into protracted debates;
- Engineers came to feel that Code Review was merely a formality and no longer believed it could deliver value.

The system became a shell while complexity quietly grew. This is what historians mean when they say:

"When the law becomes ritual rather than spirit, the empire is already corrupt."

When faced with similar challenges, Pixar's Braintrust made an important choice.

They insisted the Braintrust must always be advice, not command.

Any opinion must be won by persuasion, not imposed by authority.

This way, creators can genuinely listen without becoming defensive.

At a Braintrust meeting for Ratatouille, someone raised the concern: "Audiences might not accept a mouse freely operating in a kitchen."

This seemed like a fatal problem.

But director Brad Bird chose to keep the premise because it was core to the story.

He listened to the feedback but resolved the complexity in other ways: by crafting detailed character design so audiences would empathize with the little mouse Remy rather than feel disgust.

The result proved the director right.

The film ultimately won the Academy Award for Best Animated Feature.

The value of the Braintrust is not in "forcing change" but in "illuminating complexity early."

Code Review in software development needs the same culture.

If review comments are mandatory commands, teams become conservative and afraid to innovate.

If review comments are constructive suggestions, teams can genuinely incorporate complexity into their thinking and seek appropriate solutions.

The most dangerous aspect of complexity is not its explicit errors but its implicit compromises.

In software teams, review comments often slide to two extremes:

Either excessively harsh, nitpicking every unnecessary detail and wearing people down;

Or excessively lax, allowing potential complexity through and leaving debt for the future.

This is why many teams, despite having Code Review processes, are still overwhelmed by complexity.

They have forgotten the real goal.

The goal of Code Review is not zero defects but future understandability.

If future developers can quickly understand the logic, that is a successful review.

If the code can smoothly evolve when future requirements change, that is a successful review.

Everything else is just surface.

Pixar's experience offers another insight:

truly important problems are often not immediately visible.

During the development of Inside Out, the Braintrust once got into trouble.

The first half of the film had a tight pace, but the second half felt scattered.

Audiences could not clearly understand the rules of the "emotional world."

This problem was not any single concrete "error," but that the overall architecture's complexity was too high.

After many discussions, the Braintrust members finally made a key recommendation:

the number of "emotions" must be simplified so audiences can grasp the rules within their limited mental capacity.

Thus the film ultimately decided to keep only five core emotions: Joy, Sadness, Anger, Fear, and Disgust.

This decision made the film clear and accessible, and turned complex psychological ideas into something popular and moving.

This is the power of the Braintrust:

It helps the team identify future complexity hotspots and prune them ahead of time.

In software teams, Code Review must also have this kind of foresight.

It should not fixate on the immediate details, but anticipate future complexity.

An extra state, an ambiguous boundary, an excessive abstraction—any of these can become a nightmare later.

The duty of Code Review is to call out these risks today.

However, the enemy of managing complexity is not just code but human emotions as well.

In an iOS team, one scene played out like this:

A junior engineer submitted a PR.

A reviewer left a long critical comment, pointing out issues line by line.

The junior engineer fell silent for three days and then quietly requested a transfer.

His reason: "I don't want to be picked apart every day; what I want is to learn and grow."

The team later realized their review culture had gone off course.

Reviews had become a display of power rather than a safeguard for the future.

They lost a promising developer and allowed complexity to breed on another level: cultural complexity.

Pixar's Braintrust avoided this because they insist feedback be candid but always directed at the work, not the person.

They criticize a scene in the film, not the director's competence.

This boundary protects creators' psychological safety and lets feedback become a constructive force.

Software teams must learn this wisdom.

Code Review is not against people but against code.

It is not a contest of power but an act of compassion for the future.

Complexity is everywhere in an expanding empire.

If review culture is imbalanced, complexity will multiply.

If review culture is healthy, complexity will be pruned in advance.

Pixar's story tells us:

Review is an institution of civilization, not a ritual of punishment.

Its goal is not to make the present perfect, but to keep the future viable.

When an empire teeters on the brink of collapse, systems reveal their true meaning.

In chaos, only clear rules can point the way;

In storms of complexity, only the wisdom of review can safeguard the future.

Complexity sometimes seeps in like water, and other times strikes like a sudden storm.

It can quietly accumulate over years, or it can destroy years of work in an instant.

In Pixar's history, a storm of complexity nearly swallowed a film.

And that crisis precisely demonstrated the institutional value of the Braintrust.

The story of Toy Story 2 has almost become a parable in Pixar's history.

By 1998, Pixar had already established its position with Toy Story and A Bug's Life.

Disney asked them to produce a sequel to continue the commercial momentum.

At first the sequel was defined as a direct-to-VHS release, with a limited budget and a tight schedule.

The team cobbled together a version in an extremely short time; the plot was rough and the logic was confused.

After test screenings, everyone felt uneasy: the movie completely lacked the soul of the original.

Here complexity showed its cruelest face:

In the pursuit of speed they sacrificed clarity;

To meet short-term goals they accumulated debt the future could not bear.

The Braintrust was convened.

The meetings lasted for days, and all the directors and writers mercilessly pointed out the problems: the story structure was irrational, the characters lacked motivation, the audience could not engage.

This was no longer nitpicking, but a rescue of the future.

In the end the team made an almost insane decision:

They nearly tore the film apart, rewrote the script, and redid the animation.

Everyone worked day and night and completed the new version in 1999.

This time, the story of Woody, Buzz, and the new character Jessie was full of power and moved audiences.

The film became a major success, not only soaring at the box office but also receiving high praise from critics.

Without the Braintrust's candid feedback, Toy Story 2 might have become a failure and shaken Pixar's future.

This crisis proved:

The value of review is not in finding minor errors, but in saving overall clarity.

In the world of software, we can see similar stories.

An iOS team at a large tech company decided to introduce a new payment flow in a key release.

The design looked elegant, the functional logic was self-consistent, and early tests passed smoothly.

However, during Code Review a senior engineer raised a concern:

"This flow has too many states; if more payment methods are added in the future, complexity will quickly get out of control."

On the surface, this wasn't a bug.

The app could run and payments could complete successfully.

But what the engineer saw was a future flood of complexity.

If the architecture wasn't adjusted now, every additional payment method later would make the code more fragile.

The discussion lasted several days.

Some complained that progress was being delayed; others insisted it must ship.

In the end the team decided to refactor this logic and introduce clearer state modeling.

As a result, over the next two years' worth of iterations this part of the code supported multiple payment methods while remaining clear.

This is the power of Code Review.

It is not about nitpicking errors but about safeguarding the future.

It helps teams avoid latent debt so future complexity doesn't explode.

The real danger of complexity is that it always wears the cloak of "temporarily workable."

Like the first cut of Toy Story 2: it wasn't completely wrong, it just barely held together.

Like the initial payment-flow code: it didn't crash immediately, but it hid risks.

The shadow of complexity often grows in places that are "almost okay."

The existence of the Braintrust let Pixar see future crises in such "almost okay" situations.

The value of Code Review is likewise to warn of future danger in those "almost okay" moments.

The story of Brave provides another footnote to this philosophy.

During production the film went through a change of directors.

The original version was criticized in tests for loose plotting and insufficient character motivation.

The team fell into disarray and the direction wavered.

The Braintrust's intervention helped them rediscover the core: the conflict and reconciliation of the mother-daughter relationship.

Although the final film did not reach Pixar's highest peaks, it still rescued the project and won the Academy Award for Best Animated Feature.

This again shows:

the value of review is not in pursuing perfection, but in preventing complete loss.

Software development is the same.

The goal of Code Review is not to make the code absolutely perfect today, but to prevent it from descending into unmaintainable chaos in the future.

It is an institutional guardrail that keeps the team from getting completely lost in the maze of complexity.

If the Braintrust is Pixar's guardian, then Code Review is the software team's psychohistory.

The core of psychohistory is not to predict an individual's behavior, but to grasp the overall trends.

Code Review is the same.

It is not about correcting a single line of implementation, but about preserving the clarity of the whole.

Through countless discussions it shapes a collective intuition:

Seeing potential complexity, foreseeing future risks, and making trade-offs in advance.

This intuition is the team's most precious asset.

It is more important than any line of code.

Code can be rewritten, but a lost intuition takes years to rebuild.

In this vast sea of software, complexity is always present.

No institution can completely eliminate it.

But institutions can decide whether complexity accumulates in the dark or is pruned in the light.

Pixar's Braintrust tells us:

Review is not nitpicking, but illuminating clarity for the future.

Software's Code Review must also remember:

Its mission is not perfection but restraint;

Its value is not zero bugs but low complexity;

Its power is not authority but collective wisdom.

When you next leave a comment in a Code Review, remember:

You are not speaking for today's correctness, you are building bridges for future understandability.

Every sentence you write is not criticism, but compassion for future readers.

Your eyes are lighting the way for future developers.

Complexity does not destroy a system because of a single mistake;
It destroys systems because no one sounded the alarm ahead of time.
The true meaning of Code Review is not to find faults, but to leave clear order for the future.

CHAPTER 42
A CROSS-FUNCTIONAL UNIFIED LANGUAGE:

The collapse of a civilization is not caused by swords, but by language.

When people no longer share the same narrative, an empire heads toward division.

The deepest root of complexity is not in algorithms, nor in architecture, but in language.

Language is a boundary. Language is a protocol. Language is humanity's first tool for handling complexity.

When language fractures, complexity slips in through the gap.

Figma's history is, in this way, a history of language.

It was 2012.

At that time the design world still relied on Photoshop and Sketch.

Designers worked on islands, and exported files arrived in developers' hands like parchments carried by imperial waystations.

Developers had to reinterpret those parchments on another continent: translate colors into code, pixels into layout, and interactive animations into abstract logic.

Every translation introduces error.

Color deviations are like the fudged numbers in the imperial granary;

Differences in size are like small corruption in taxation;

Omissions in interaction are like frontier soldiers who never received the capital's orders.

This is not the fault of Photoshop or Sketch, but the inevitability of a language fracture.

Designers and developers did not share a common language.

They each spoke within their own contexts, yet had to converge in the product.

This convergence was bound to be full of complexity.

Dylan Field and Evan Wallace saw this rift.

They realized that the future of software was not just to make designers more efficient, nor just to make developers more efficient, but to give both a unified language.

If the capital and the frontier of an empire spoke the same tongue, orders would no longer need translation.

If design and development shared the same canvas, complexity could be dissolved in advance.

Thus, Figma's experiment began.

The initial reaction was skepticism.

Designers asked: Why give up the tools I'm familiar with?

Developers asked: Why make me step into the designer's canvas?

Product managers asked: Why in the cloud, not files?

Behind the skepticism was a mistrust of language.

Language is not only a medium of communication, it is also a symbol of power.

Designers use their own language to control aesthetics, developers use their own language to control logic, product managers use their own language to control requirements.

Who is willing to give up? Who is willing to compromise?

Figma's innovation was not a pile-up of lines of code, but an institutional invention: making language a common good rather than private territory.

It put design in the browser. It allowed developers to inspect parameters directly without waiting for handoffs. It let product managers participate in reviews without relying on verbal explanations.

This was not a change of tool, but a unification of language.

Complexity's favorite condition has always been "blurred boundaries." When the dimensions designers specify don't match the dimensions developers implement, when the interactions product managers imagine differ from the interactions actually presented, complexity quietly grows. It doesn't require conspicuous holes—only enough small errors. Those errors accumulate and can strip a product of its soul.

Figma dissolves such errors at their inception. Because it lets the three parties share one canvas and one language, complexity loses its fertile ground.

The power of unified language is vividly demonstrated in a concrete case.

In 2016, Figma's team faced a critical scenario: they needed to implement a new collaboration feature in the app that would allow multiple designers to work simultaneously in the same file. This was revolutionary at the time. But problems followed:

- Designers wanted the interaction to be smooth, with no latency, as if working on a local file.
- Developers worried about performance and had to handle synchronization and conflicts.
- Product managers cared about the experience and had to ensure users wouldn't be confused by version conflicts.

This could have been a prolonged tug-of-war. But on Figma's canvas, the three parties shared the same real-time view. Designers could see performance bottlenecks, developers could see breaks in the experience, product managers could see interaction chaos. They no longer needed to translate one another's language; instead they negotiated directly within a unified context.

In the end, they found a balance: a smooth experience + a tolerant synchronization mechanism + clear version cues. This wasn't a victory for any single party, but a victory for unified language.

The unification of language is not merely a revolution of tools; it is an evolution of civilization. It strips complexity of its dark hiding places. It makes communication no longer depend on translation, but happen directly on the same level. It turns cross-functional collaboration from consumption into creation.

But the evolution of civilization always exacts a price.

Figma's experiment did not proceed smoothly.

They hit performance bottlenecks, faced skeptical questioning, and confronted repeated "is this really necessary?" challenges.

The road to a unified language was destined to be long.

"When an empire possesses a unified language, only then can it truly govern vast territories.

When a team possesses a unified language, only then can they truly govern complexity."

Figma's unification of language had only just begun.

A unified language does not imply a unified will.

Just as under the same sky there will still be storms and lightning.

The art of negotiation is not to eliminate conflict, but to prevent conflict from destroying civilization.

Complexity will not vanish entirely because language is unified.

It only loses its disguise and reappears in a more direct form.

When Figma pulled product, design, and development onto the same canvas, contradictions no longer hid in emails, documents, or screenshots, but were exposed naked.

This is not a bad thing.

The evolution of civilization always begins by making conflict visible.

Hidden conflict is the breeding ground of complexity; visible conflict is what can be governed.

In 2017, Figma faced a critical scaling: they needed to extend real-time collaboration from single small-file scenarios to complex, large-scale design projects.

That meant files might contain hundreds of pages, thousands of layers, and countless images and vector objects.

This was the expansion of an empire's territory. The larger the territory, the harder the governance.

Designers' demand was crystal clear:

They still wanted smoothness.

No matter how massive the file, it had to feel as silky as local operations.

They were used to moving elements quickly, zooming the canvas, and dragging images, and did not want any delay to interrupt their flow.

Developers' demand was equally clear:

They worried about performance bottlenecks.

Browser limits, network latency, and memory consumption were real boundaries.

They knew real-time collaboration meant synchronization—every action must be broadcast, every change merged.

This is an algorithmic problem and a systemic burden.

Product managers' demand was grounded in the whole experience:

They had to satisfy designers' need for smoothness without letting engineering collapse.

More importantly, they had to consider users' tolerance.

Where can slight delays be acceptable? Where are they absolutely unacceptable?

This is a philosophical question, not just a technical one.

All three stood on the same canvas; the language was unified, yet their opinions diverged.

This was a new form of complexity.

The first battlefield of conflict was the definition of "real-time."

Designers believed real-time meant "zero latency."

They wanted every action to take effect immediately, as if working in a local file.

Any delay, even just 200 milliseconds, would break their train of thought.

Developers insisted that true zero latency was impossible.

Networks have transmission time, browsers have rendering overhead, and conflict merging has algorithmic complexity.

If zero latency were pursued at all costs, the system would inevitably collapse.

The product manager mediated:

"Can we redefine real-time?

Not zero latency, but perceptually near-zero.

Not every pixel movement synchronized, but sync in batches, layers, and by priority."

This was a reconstruction of language.

A unified language does not mean its meanings will not change.

The word "real-time" has different interpretations in different functions.

Complexity is hidden within those differences.

The second battlefield of conflict was the boundary of "file size."

Designers wanted files to expand without limit.

They did not want to be told, "Your file is too large to edit."

Their creative impulse, like an empire's expansion, always hoped for borderless territory.

Developers, however, had to face real technical limits.

Memory overflows, network congestion, and browser freezes do not disappear because of ideals.

They had to set an upper limit, or the entire system would lose stability.

Product managers stepped in again:

they proposed the concept of "progressive loading."

Files could be very large, but users would not need to load all content at once.

They would load only the parts they currently needed; the rest would be loaded lazily in the background.

This was an institutional invention.

It satisfied both designers' sense of boundlessness and developers' sense of limits.

Complexity was tamed, not eradicated.

The third battlefield of conflict was how to handle "version conflicts."

Designers wanted to operate simultaneously without restraint, like multiple people painting on the same canvas.

They did not want to lose the joy of collaboration because of "locks" or "waiting."

Developers, however, were clear that conflicts were inevitable.

When two people modify the same object at the same time, there must be rules to merge the changes, otherwise it will be chaos.

They worried that without a strict merging mechanism, the final result would be unpredictable.

The product manager proposed a compromise:

preserve the "freedom to act," but provide "traceability of history."

If conflicts arise, don't forcibly prevent them; allow rollbacks to previous states and manual adjustments.

This is a philosophy: freedom takes precedence over control, but freedom must be accompanied by responsibility for its consequences.

This approach became one of Figma's hallmarks.

It allowed multi-user collaboration to remain smooth while avoiding total chaos.

Complexity was not eliminated but was incorporated into the institutional framework of "history."

Through these conflicts and negotiations, the Figma team gradually developed a methodology:

a cross-functional unified language does not mean everyone speaks the same words, but that everyone understands the same meanings.

This is a huge distinction.

The former is homogenization; the latter is mutual translation and consensus.

Unifying language is not about erasing differences, but about enabling differences to be negotiated within a shared framework.

Complexity still lurks.

It will reappear in new features and return with new requirements.

But a unified language prevents it from secretly accumulating; it must be confronted center stage.

Real stories are sometimes more powerful than parables.

In an internal retrospective, the Figma team wrote:

"We found that the greatest value was not in reducing bugs, but in reducing misunderstandings.

Misunderstanding is the greatest complexity."

That sentence, like a bolt of lightning, illuminated the essence of cross-functional collaboration.

Bugs can be fixed; misunderstandings continually spawn new bugs.

If language is not unified, misunderstanding becomes the largest source of complexity.

Complexity hides in negotiation, but negotiation itself is the power of civilization.

An empire's territory cannot be without conflict.

Team collaboration cannot be without contradictions.

The important thing is not to eliminate conflict, but to let conflict occur in a unified language and be tamed within institutional boundaries.

Figma's story reaches this point.

It proved that unified language is not an illusion but a real weapon.

But it also reminded us: unified language is not the end, but the starting point of a new contest with complexity.

When an empire expands, language ceases to be merely a communication tool and becomes a tool of governance.

If language is unified, civilization endures; if language is divided, complexity transforms into civil strife.

The dilemma of civilization never happens just once.

Figma's early success did not end complexity; it only postponed its next assault.

As they moved onto a larger stage—enterprise customers, global markets, cross-time-zone teams—the test of language came again.

Complexity is like a river.

You build a dam and it finds a new outlet.

You guide it toward the plains and it secretly surges in the deep valleys.

It is never defeated, only repositioned.

In 2019, Figma began entering the enterprise market.

Their customers were no longer just designers from small teams, but large organizations within multinational corporations.

These organizations had hundreds of designers, thousands of developers, and layers of product managers.

Their projects were no longer single apps but complex ecosystems: mobile apps, desktop clients, web platforms, backend systems.

This meant the complexity of cross-functional collaboration was multiplied.

The unification of language had to be maintained at a much larger scale.

The first challenge was internationalization.

Figma was born in the United States; its design philosophy originated in Silicon Valley minimalism.

But when it entered Asian and European markets, the difficulty of unifying language was further amplified.

In Japan, designers are accustomed to extremely fine pixel alignment and have near-punishing demands for typography.

In Germany, developers' adherence to standards and insistence on stability far exceed Silicon Valley's flexibility.

In India, product managers must contend with a vast and diverse user base, with requirements changing frequently and variably.

The same term—"consistency"—meant different things in different cultures.

In Japan, it meant consistency of visual details;

In Germany, it meant strict consistency of processes;

In India, it meant maintaining usable consistency amid chaos.

The Figma team realized that cross-functional unified language was not only about aligning design, development, and product, but also had to span cultures and time zones.

Complexity once again lurked behind language.

The second challenge was permissions and scale.

In small teams, unified language is relatively easy.

Everyone is on the same canvas, communicating face-to-face, and conflicts are quickly resolved.

But in large companies, the hierarchy of permissions multiplies complexity.

Designers do not always have access to all files, and developers are not always able to modify critical parameters.

Product managers must manage permissions to ensure security, but this makes communication slower.

A single misconfiguration of permissions can prevent the entire team from accessing key files.

A missing permission can prevent designers from seeing developers' latest implementations.

Complexity is no longer technical, but organizational.

Figma's solution was to introduce "team spaces."

Different teams have their own canvases, but can reference each other via links.

It's like the provincial system of an empire: each province self-manages, but all operate under the same legal framework.

Complexity is managed in layers, rather than being compressed all at once.

The third challenge was the exacting demands of enterprise customers.

The product development process in large enterprises is often assembly-line-like.

Product managers propose requirements at one end, designers draw up solutions in the middle, and developers implement them at the other end.

Figma's ideal was that all three participate simultaneously, but the reality in enterprises is a clear division of labor and strict boundaries.

This division makes it difficult for the benefits of a unified language to be realized.

Designers are still required to deliver "final drafts," developers still wait for handoffs, and product managers still track progress in Excel spreadsheets.

Complexity accumulates in these gaps.

Figma had to find new ways to let such assembly-line organizations also benefit from a unified language.

They introduced a "design system"—a shared component library.

It was not just a collection of graphical elements, but the institutionalization of a language.

Buttons, input fields, and navigation bars were no longer pixels drawn at will, but components with clear definitions.

Developers know a button's states, designers know a button's styles, and product managers know a button's scenarios.

The three parties establish consensus through components, not verbal descriptions.

This was another unification of language.

It turned complexity from freely growing weeds into orderly cultivated fields.

These challenges did not completely defeat Figma.

On the contrary, they pushed the unification of language to a higher level: from tools to institutions, and from institutions to culture.

The Figma team gradually realized:

The unification of language is not a one-time victory, but a continuous negotiation.

It needs to find resonance across different cultures, balance across different permission levels, and common ground across different processes.

Complexity still exists, but it has lost its most dangerous form —being hidden.

As long as complexity is exposed on the negotiating table, it is no longer a disaster but a manageable object.

"Unifying language does not eliminate complexity.

Its significance lies in making complexity visible and giving humans the opportunity to negotiate.

A civilization without a unified language can only collapse in misunderstanding."

For us iOS developers, Figma's story is not merely the evolution of a design tool.

It reveals a deeper truth:

A cross-functional unified language is fundamental to reducing complexity.

In our daily work, complexity often does not come from technology, but from communication:

- What a product manager calls "simple" is completely different from what a developer understands as "simple."
- The "consistency" that designers draw is worlds apart from the "consistency" that developers implement.
- What developers call "performance" is, in the product manager's eyes, merely an "insignificant detail."

Every misunderstanding is a point where complexity grows.

Every act of translation is an opportunity for complexity to lie in wait.

Without a unified language, these misunderstandings accumulate into debt and eventually crush the team.

With a unified language, these misunderstandings are exposed as conflicts and are resolved through negotiation.

Figma's success is not because it is faster than its competitors, but because it is clearer.

It leaves complexity nowhere to hide and makes negotiation part of everyday life.

It turns cross-functional collaboration from consumption into creation.

This is the power of a cross-functional unified language.

Complexity will not disappear because of language, but language can determine the trajectory of complexity.
In misunderstanding, it is poison; in negotiation, it is nourishment.
The future of civilization depends on whether humanity can share a common language.

PART NINE

THE POWER OF KEEPING IT SIMPLE

CHAPTER 43
WHY THE MOST BORING CODE IS THE MOST POWERFUL

The strongest fortress does not lie in high walls, but in clear paths.

The most enduring code does not lie in showy techniques, but in restraint.

Complexity often appears wearing the mask of a miracle.

It makes people feel grand, feel intricate, feel as if they stand at the pinnacle of technological civilization.

However, when the storm passes, what remains is often not a miracle, but ruins.

The story of Basecamp is a footnote to this.

While countless internet companies around the world chase scale, chase funding, chase so-called "future technologies," Basecamp's choice seems almost contrarian.

They refuse to pile on complex features, refuse blind technology migrations, refuse to sacrifice stability for "looking advanced."

Their creed is a single line: keep it simple.

This company does not pursue glamour.

Their product UI has long been criticized as "boring," and their features are always one step behind competitors.

Their code is also often mocked by external developers as "conservative."

However, it is precisely this seemingly boring choice that has kept their systems almost free of catastrophic outages for more than a decade, and has kept their team small yet highly productive.

In Basecamp's engineering culture, the most emphasized point is:

"Complex things die; simple things live longer."

In the context of SwiftUI, this philosophy equally applies.

SwiftUI gives developers infinite freedom — declarative composition can be nested layer upon layer, state management can expand without bounds, architectural choices can be switched at will.

However, it is precisely this "freedom" that most easily leads to the inflation of complexity.

When a team develops with SwiftUI, they are easily tempted:

They want to abstract all state, modularize all logic, apply all architectural patterns.

Thus, an originally simple interface ends up hiding five levels of abstraction, a dozen derived states, countless dependency injections.

In the end, developers are no longer writing features, but explaining why a state needs so many intermediaries to update the UI.

Complexity quietly takes root here.

Basecamp's founder Jason Fried once said, "Complex systems always bring more complex problems, while simple systems only bring simple problems."

Behind this sentence lies a plain but often overlooked truth: complexity never appears out of nowhere; someone always has to pay the cost of understanding it. When you write an "elegant" abstraction, you are merely shifting the future burden onto the person who reads the code. When you introduce an "advanced" architecture, you are just postponing future complexity to the maintenance phase.

Simple code may be boring, but it minimizes the future cost of understanding. It is like a straight road—perhaps lacking scenic twists, but getting people to their destination the fastest.

At an internal technical review at Basecamp, an engineer asked, "Should we try a more modern front-end framework to keep up with industry trends?"

Jason Fried's answer was brief and firm: "We don't need to follow trends; we need stability."

Stability is time's friend. Showing off is often the fuse for complexity.

This answer sparked a lot of controversy at the time, but as time passed, more and more people understood: stability is not conservatism, but a form of restraint. It means choosing boring technologies and rejecting the illusion of complexity.

In the world of SwiftUI, what does keeping it simple mean?

It means not abstracting prematurely, not abusing architectures, not nesting infinitely just because you can. It means accepting some "repetition," accepting some "plainness," accepting some "boringness." Because boringness implies clarity; because clarity means future developers can quickly understand.

Another famous choice by Basecamp is Ruby on Rails. The philosophical core of that framework is also "convention over configuration." Rails does not pursue extreme performance or extreme flexibility; it pursues simple paths. Those paths may seem "not flashy enough" in the short term, but in the long run they reduce the cognitive load of countless decisions.

Rails has been criticized by many as "outdated," yet it remains active today. The reason is that it chose simplicity, it chose boringness. It does not chase trends; it chases understandability.

The civilization of software lies not in showing off, but in continuity.

The opponent of complexity has never been the advancement of technology, but the restraint of the mind.

Those who choose boredom are often the ones who go the farthest.

We have seen Basecamp's choice, seen how they stood by simplicity in the face of complexity's temptations.

Going forward, complexity will continue to probe, temptation will continue to appear.

And the real test of the power of keeping things simple is only just beginning.

The temptation of complexity never arrives wearing the face of an enemy.

It comes as an ally, promising miracles, promising efficiency.

Until people discover they have lost themselves in the illusion.

Complexity's greatest skill is not frontal assault, but disguising itself as the illusion of progress.

It will make you feel that new technology can solve everything;

It will make you feel that more abstractions will reduce chaos;

It will make you feel that merely keeping up with trends will prevent obsolescence.

Basecamp's history is precisely a history of repeated struggles against this illusion.

In the 2010s, mobile internet swept the globe.

Almost every company expanded rapidly, forming large mobile teams and chasing the future of so-called "full-featured apps."

New frameworks emerged one after another: cross-platform

React Native, Flutter, and even short-lived fads like PhoneGap were touted as "the only answer for the future."

For Basecamp, the temptation was enormous.

Their users began to demand parity between mobile features and the web.

Competitors continuously released flashy new features, using animations, real-time collaboration, and intelligent recommendations to attract the market.

Their engineers also privately discussed, "Are we too behind? Should we try more advanced technologies?"

Complexity appeared at that moment; it did not call itself complexity.

It called itself progress, trend, future.

Yet Basecamp's leadership chose silence.

Jason Fried and David Heinemeier Hansson (the creator of Rails) repeatedly emphasized one idea:

"We're not here to win trends; we're here to win time."

At an internal meeting, they even explicitly rejected some proposals that "looked cool":

An engineer wanted to introduce a new real-time collaboration engine to compete with Google Docs.

Jason's answer was:

"Our users don't need to be typing in a document with ten people at the same time.

What they need is for this document to still be reliably open three years from now."

This remark left the meeting room silent for a moment.

Because it pointed out a harsh fact:

Showing off satisfies the vanity of the moment, while stability guards future survival.

This choice, when placed in the context of SwiftUI, is no less thought-provoking.

The charm of SwiftUI lies in its ability to let you achieve complex effects with very little code.

Animations, transitions, state bindings — they're almost at your fingertips.

So teams are often tempted: "Since we can do it, we must do it."

Thus a simple button is no longer just a button, but a component with three layers of transition animations and a complex state machine.

A form is no longer just a form, but a super-module with dynamic validation, asynchronous loading, and intelligent predictions.

In the short term, this makes the team feel "advanced." But in the long term, these "advancements" become new shackles.

Every small change must traverse complex abstractions; every iteration risks breaking the chain of animations.

Future maintainers face not clear logic, but a tangle of trend-driven complexity.

Basecamp's approach is: they never pay for "can be done"; they only pay for "needs to be done."

They reject over-design, reject over-abstraction, reject blind technology migrations.

They'd rather let the code seem boring than allow complexity to sneak into the future.

This "boringness" is a deliberate choice.

It's not laziness, but restraint.

It's not incompetence, but wisdom.

At a product discussion, someone suggested, "Should we use AI to automatically generate task priorities? That way users wouldn't have to sort manually."

Jason's reply was again concise and stark:

"This is not our responsibility.

Our responsibility is to enable users to manage tasks in an orderly way, not to think for them.

Making the system 'smart' on its own will only make future maintenance stupid."

So that "cool" proposal was rejected. Instead, they implemented the simplest sorting feature: users can drag to reorder.

Ten years later, that drag-and-drop still works reliably. Most systems that relied on "smart" features have long been forgotten.

This culture of "rejecting complexity" later came to be called "Basecamp-style boredom" by outsiders. Their apps don't look flashy and were even mocked as "outdated." But it is precisely this "boringness" that makes their systems extremely reliable. While other companies are busy refactoring, migrating, and fixing collapses caused by complexity, Basecamp keeps moving steadily forward.

This philosophy is exactly what the SwiftUI team urgently needs. The SwiftUI ecosystem is still growing; many patterns and tools are in exploratory stages. Developers can easily fall into a kind of anxiety: "Are we falling behind? Do we need to bring in more libraries, more architectures, more abstractions?"

That anxiety is the illusion of complexity. It makes you feel you must keep adding new things to avoid being outcompeted. But the fact is: those who get truly left behind are not the ones who choose to be boring, but the ones who are addicted to complexity.

History proves this. Seemingly outdated Ruby on Rails still runs stably in countless companies; the seemingly simple Basecamp still remains profitable and keeps its users; the seemingly "boring" code is still understood and maintained by new engineers decades later.

Meanwhile, those complex frameworks once touted as "the future" have long become footnotes in the archives.

In SwiftUI practice, keeping things simple means:

- Don't introduce a large architecture for a one-off requirement.
- Don't abstract away all the details for the sake of "elegance."
- Don't blindly migrate just because it's "trendy."

- Don't feel compelled to "must do" something just because you "can do" it.

Keeping things simple is rejecting the illusion of complexity. Keeping things simple is admitting the limits of human cognition. Keeping things simple is ensuring that your future self can still understand your current self.

The temptation of complexity will appear again and again. Basecamp's story tells us: the key is not a single choice, but the persistence of countless choices. Every time you reject complexity, you reduce a liability on the ledger of the future. Every time you insist on being boring, you preserve a fresh spring in the team's collective mind.

An empire's longevity relies not on glorious battles but on secure supply lines.

The continuity of software does not depend on dazzling technical feats but on boring clarity.

The illusion of complexity will reappear again and again, but history will eventually discard it. What truly survives over time is never the flashiest technology but the most stable systems. In the world of software, a system is the structure of the code; the continuity of the system is the code's comprehensibility.

When other companies struggle repeatedly with refactors, Basecamp's system keeps running stably. More than a decade later, their team remains small yet supports millions of users worldwide. They haven't been mired in "technical debt," nor stalled for months by "architecture upgrades." Their secret is one sentence: choose the most boring code so complexity has nowhere to hide.

The power of this philosophy became especially apparent during an industry upheaval.

In 2015, Silicon Valley sparked a "microservices" craze.

Countless companies broke monoliths into dozens or hundreds of microservices, claiming this would improve scalability and increase team autonomy. On stage, presenters displayed dazzling architecture diagrams in which every arrow stood for some technological "advancement."

Basecamp was asked, "Will you adopt microservices? Will you refactor to keep up with the future?"

Jason Fried's answer was as calm as ever: "We don't have problems that complex, so we don't need such complex solutions."

They kept using a monolithic architecture and maintained a small, steady codebase. To others, this approach seemed "outdated." Yet years later, when countless companies collapsed under the communication and debugging hell of microservices, Basecamp remained unscathed.

Complexity always disguises itself as the future. The real future belongs to those who choose boredom.

The world of SwiftUI is undergoing a similar wave. Architectural patterns proliferate: Redux-style approaches, TCA, variants of MVVM, and a variety of state-management tools... Each claims it can solve "complexity." However, complexity will not be eliminated; it will only be shifted.

Introducing a new architecture means introducing new new boundaries, new semantics, and new Cognitive Loads.

In small teams and simple projects, that complexity can be heavier than the problem itself.

Like with microservices: one well would have been enough to solve the drinking water problem;

Instead people dug a hundred wells and built a hundred pipes, and the effort spent on maintenance far exceeded the act of providing water.

In SwiftUI practice, keeping things simple means:

- When a View can solve the problem, don't be eager to create a new "layer."

- When state can be expressed directly, don't abstract it into patterns no one understands for the sake of "elegance."
- When a feature is stable enough, don't blindly migrate just because it's trendy.

The simple path may seem boring, but it lets your future self understand immediately.

The complex path may look advanced, but it will cause your future self to get lost in a maze.

Basecamp's philosophy also has a huge cultural impact.

They've kept their teams small.

They don't try to hire thousands of engineers or build massive departments.

Because they know: people themselves are amplifiers of complexity.

When headcount increases, communication becomes a new burden;

when modules multiply, coordination becomes new complexity.

So they choose small teams, deep modules, and clear boundaries.

Everyone can quickly grasp the whole and be responsible for the system.

This "cognitive saving" is precisely the reason for their long-term stability.

This choice is highly aligned with the SwiftUI team's organizational philosophy.

SwiftUI is essentially a contraction of UIKit's complexity.

In the UIKit era, engineers had to shuttle between controllers, delegates, data sources, and notifications, which imposed a huge mental burden.

SwiftUI's declarative design gathers that complexity into a single, state-driven source of truth.

Its power is not that it can do more, but that it makes understanding faster.

This is the power of "the most boring code."

It doesn't chase flashy tricks, but seeks cognitive savings.

It doesn't care about momentary vanity, but cares about long-term understanding.

Historians have summarized a rule: an empire is most vulnerable not when its borders are at their widest, but when it has forgotten its "grain." Software is most dangerous not when it has the most features, but when it has forgotten "understanding."

Keeping things simple is guarding the grain, it is guarding understanding. It may seem boring, but it is the only moat of civilization.

In 2020, Basecamp launched an email product called Hey. In an already crowded market, they did not chase Gmail's smart recommendations, nor did they mimic Outlook's enterprise integrations. They simply built a simple and stable product: a clean interface, a reliable inbox, and predictable interactions. Outsiders still mocked them as "boring," but users responded: "Finally an email tool that doesn't make me lose my way."

This is the power of boredom: when everyone else chases complexity, simplicity becomes scarce. When everyone else is addicted to illusions, stability becomes the true advantage.

When we review Airbnb's cross-platform experiment and then look back at Basecamp's choice, we find two paths and two outcomes. Airbnb tried to counter complexity with complexity and was ultimately consumed by it; Basecamp chose to resist complexity with boredom and ultimately survived within that boredom.

The truth about complexity is laid bare here: it does not need miracles, it needs restraint. It does not need glorious campaigns, it needs clear roads.

SwiftUI developers must understand: the most boring code is the most powerful code.

Boring code means:

- No flashy abstractions, yet immediately understandable.
- No complex dependencies, yet the system runs reliably.
- No trendy illusions, yet it stands the test of time.

This kind of code won't become material for talks or win short-term applause. But it will become a lifeline for future developers and the cornerstone of team stability.

At the end of this section, we must remember: complexity will not disappear, but it can be restrained. True strength does not lie in creating complex miracles, but in persisting in boring clarity.

The most boring code is the most powerful code. Because it can travel through time, resist illusions, and safeguard civilization.

The enemy of complexity is not new technology, but old restraint.
Restraint is boredom, and boredom is strength.

CHAPTER 44
NATIVE'S LONG-TERM ADVANTAGE

The road in the short term is often smooth; the road in the long term is often rugged.
But only the rugged road can reach the summit.

The desert of complexity has no end.

Some people choose to build temporary oases in the desert, using the illusion of cross-platform to shield themselves from the sandstorms;

some choose to walk slowly along the river, accepting hardship but not betraying the real terrain.

Native is exactly that river.

The story of WeChat is a journey along the river.

When WeChat was born in a Shenzhen office in 2011, it was not a grand imperial epic.

Its starting point was an experiment: against the backdrop of QQ already dominating the desktop world, Tencent needed a new entry point for the mobile era.

The initial WeChat was simple: one-to-one messaging, a bit of voice, a bit of images.

Like countless instant messaging apps at the time, it was not destined for greatness.

However, complexity was waiting.

As the user base leapt from millions to tens of millions, then to hundreds of millions, every decision in the system was amplified.

Any delay, any stutter, any inconsistency in details would be experienced by thousands upon thousands of users and quickly spread through public opinion.

At this point, technology choices were no longer just engineers' preferences, but a civilizational choice.

In 2012, the WeChat team discussed cross-platform solutions.

They saw the lure of cross-platform: faster feature coverage, lower development costs, more unified code management.

At the time, HTML5 was sweeping the industry, and many apps tried to use WebView as the cross-platform container.

Facebook's Mark Zuckerberg even publicly admitted, "Our biggest mistake was relying too much on HTML5."

The WeChat team did not immediately embrace HTML5.

They experimented with using web technologies to implement some lightweight features, such as simple news pages and event entry points.

However, when they tried to hand core scenarios like the chat interface to cross-platform solutions, performance bottlenecks immediately surfaced: input method latency, janky scrolling, and image rendering stutters.

In a high-frequency application, such experience gaps are a line between life and death.

The team quickly made a decision: core functions must be Native.

This was a critical choice.

They abandoned short-term unification and chose to shoulder the long-term complexity of Native.

The bill for complexity must be paid by someone.

Choosing cross-platform hides complexity in the bridging and compatibility layers;

Choosing Native spreads the complexity across two platforms, forcing the team to face it. The WeChat team chose the latter.

That meant they had to cultivate two strong teams:

One proficient in iOS, familiar with Objective-C's memory management and every detail of UIKit;

The other proficient in Android, able to reconcile the conflicts between resolution and performance across countless fragmented devices.

It was also a burden.

Every new feature had to be implemented twice;

Every architectural evolution required bilateral coordination.

In the short term, it was undoubtedly more "clumsy" and "inefficient" than cross-platform.

But in the long term, it brought clear boundaries:

Every bug could be traced within a single platform;

Every performance optimization could be pushed to the extreme for specific hardware characteristics;

Every system upgrade could stay in sync with the platform's cadence.

WeChat's user growth outpaced all expectations.

In 2013 it surpassed 300 million users; in 2016 it passed 800 million; today it exceeds 1.2 billion.

Such a massive user base cannot tolerate the slightest instability.

Complexity, like sandstorms, rapidly amplifies at the scale of hundreds of millions.

Only Native can ensure the levee remains firm when each storm arrives.

There was a saying inside the team: "In WeChat, 1% lag is the anger of millions."

That anger is not emotion but market force.

It is enough to shake an empire.

The choice of Native also brought another unexpected benefit: being in sync with the platform ecosystem.

Whenever iOS introduced new features—Touch ID, Face ID, ARKit, Widgets—WeChat could integrate them immediately.

Whenever Android updated its permission model, its push mechanisms, or its storage strategies, WeChat could quickly adapt.

They were not constrained by a bridging layer but stood directly on the platform's front lines.

This meant WeChat was not just an app; it was also a showcase of a platform's potential.

Apple and Google both need such partners.

The value of Native is not just performance, but also ecosystem strategy.

But complexity does not yield easily.

Native dual-platform development still implies a huge workload and coordination costs.

The WeChat team had to confront questions like:

- How to ensure features remain consistent on both sides?
- How to synchronize bug fixes across both sides?
- How to prevent architectural divergence?

They gradually developed a methodology:

At the core layer, maintain consistent protocols and interfaces;

At the presentation layer, fully leverage each platform's characteristics.

This is not "complete unification" nor "complete splitting," but a balance.

This balance is not elegant, but it is extremely pragmatic.

It sacrifices some development efficiency in exchange for long-term stability and clarity.

The Native path is arduous.

It requires the team to endure more repetitive work and bear higher short-term costs.

But it also lets the team keep control over complexity, sparing them the betrayal of illusions in the long run.

WeChat's choice validates an old truth:

Simplicity is not free; simplicity is bought at a price.

Native is precisely that price.

This is only the beginning of the story.

The desert of complexity still lies ahead; WeChat will face new challenges: Mini Programs, Channels, Payments…

Each expansion is a new trial.

But at least on this rugged road, they chose to face reality rather than retreat into illusion.

A true empire does not reject outside winds, but must have sturdy walls.

Expansion without walls is an illusion; prosperity without boundaries is corruption.

Complexity has never been completely defeated.

It only appears at different times in different guises.

After choosing Native as its foundation, WeChat did gain the protection of stability and performance, but complexity did not retreat.

It began to approach in another form: feature bloat.

When WeChat evolved from a simple chat tool into a "super app," the gravitational pull of complexity suddenly intensified.

Payments, Moments, Official Accounts, Mini Games—each new layer of functionality is an expansion of territory.

As the empire's domain keeps extending, the difficulty of governance rises accordingly.

At this point, the cost of Native became especially heavy.

Every new feature had to be developed twice on iOS and Android;

Every update had to be tested and released in sync;

Every difference could lead to inconsistency in user experience.

For a small feature, that cost may be bearable.

But when the number of features grows exponentially, the repetitive work itself becomes part of the complexity.

The team keeps expanding, communication costs keep rising, and morale begins to be worn down by day-to-day repetition.

Thus, Mini Programs appeared.

In 2017, WeChat publicly launched Mini Programs — an adventure that seemed "cross-platform."

It promised that developers only needed to write one set of code to run inside WeChat's container, covering both iOS and Android.

Externally, it was an ecosystem strategy to empower third parties;

Internally, it was an attempt to reduce the burden of duplicate development.

However, Mini Programs are not a pure cross-platform technology.

They do not try to replace Native, but rather extend atop Native.

The WeChat team built a dedicated runtime environment for this, running Mini Programs in a sandbox where all capabilities are provided via APIs exposed by Native.

This means:

The flexibility and efficiency of Mini Programs come from Native's underlying support.

They do not bypass Native; they leverage Native's stability and performance to create an upper-layer ecosystem.

Here complexity reveals its dual nature.

On one hand, Mini Programs lower the barrier to entry for external developers.

Countless merchants and startup teams can join the WeChat ecosystem at very low cost.

They do not have to develop separately for iOS and Android; they only need to understand WeChat's Mini Program framework.

This greatly expands WeChat's territory.

On the other hand, Mini Programs increase internal complexity for WeChat.

The team must maintain the runtime environment, continuously expand the APIs, and ensure that Mini Programs do not drag down core functionality.

Every system update may affect the stability of millions of Mini Programs.

This is a new burden.

A burden, but also value.

Native's foundation enables WeChat to shoulder this burden.

Had WeChat initially chosen cross-platform as its base, it would have struggled to provide a stable environment at the Mini Program layer.

The uncertainty of the bridging layer, performance fluctuations, and incompatibilities from system upgrades would all make the entire ecosystem precarious.

Precisely because WeChat's core is Native, it can bear the weight of Mini Programs on the upper layer.

This layering is like an empire's walls and its marketplace:

The walls must be strong for the market to prosper.

Without strong walls, the market's clamor is only a fleeting illusion.

Mini Programs brought a deeper revelation:

Native and cross-platform are not an either-or relationship.

They can form a hierarchical structure:

the core must be Native, while the upper layer can be cross-platform.

Only in this way can long-term stability and short-term flexibility be reconciled.

WeChat's choice actually opened a new path:

use Native to build a solid foundation, and use cross-platform mechanisms to expand the boundaries.

This is not escaping complexity, but redistributing it.

However, transferring complexity never means complexity disappears.

The flourishing Mini Program ecosystem brought new challenges:

- Security: how to prevent malicious Mini Programs from stealing user data?
- Performance: how to ensure Mini Programs' experience does not drag down the main app?
- Governance: how to set rules and standards among millions of developers?

These challenges are no longer technical details but institutional choices.

WeChat had to establish review mechanisms, security teams, and governance rules.

Complexity shifted from technology to institutions and still needs to be governed.

The long-term advantages of Native are shown here again.

Because the underlying layer is Native, WeChat can quickly iterate on its review system, optimize APIs, and strengthen security.

They have complete control.

If the base were cross-platform, they would be constrained by the framework's evolution and struggle to respond promptly to new threats.

This control is an irreplaceable value of Native.

It allows the team to remain proactive in the face of complexity, rather than passive.

Complexity is a torrent.

The illusion of cross-platform often promises a quick dam,

but the dam's sand and gravel are loose and cannot withstand a flood's assault.

Choosing Native is like placing heavy stones to build a slow but solid levee.

Floods still exist, but they are guided, diverted, and tamed.

WeChat's Mini Programs are the tributary opened atop that levee.

They did not go against Native's principles, but relied on Native's solidity to create new prosperity.

All of this confirms a single fact:

The cost of Native is heavy, but its value endures.

It makes the team bear repetitive work, yet in return grants control over complexity.

It forces developers to endure short-term inconvenience, but in exchange buys long-term freedom.

Complexity will not be eliminated; it only shifts.

The power of Native lies not in making complexity vanish, but in making it controllable.

WeChat's team knows this well.

In an internal sharing they wrote: "Native is our root. Without this root, our branches cannot bear the weight of Mini Programs."

This understanding is not abstract philosophy but concrete experience.

They earned the weight of that sentence through countless overtime hours, endless bug fixes, and repeated system upgrades.

The cost of Native remains, and the complexity of Mini Programs continues to accumulate.

WeChat must keep moving forward across this desert and keep governing the torrent of complexity.

The real turning point still lies ahead.

The strength of anything is not measured by its growth, but by its capacity for self-restraint.

The longevity of software does not depend on its features, but on its ability to resist the erosion of complexity.

Complexity is an invisible sandstorm.

It will not retreat after one victory; it will gather again in new territories.

After WeChat weathered the Mini Program frenzy, it faced another trial: Channels, Payments, Mini Games, Search, Enterprise Services...

Each feature is an expansion.

Each expansion is a confrontation with complexity.

WeChat Pay was the earliest frontier to strike at complexity.

In the context of instant messaging, payments are inherently heterogeneous.

Message delivery pursues lightness; payment design demands stability.

The former tolerates occasional delays; the latter requires absolute consistency.

The collision of these two needs is like an empire's northern and southern frontiers—climates differ wildly, yet they must be governed by the same laws.

Here the value of Native is fully revealed.

The core security modules of payment must tightly integrate with the operating system's foundations:

iOS's Secure Enclave and Android's various hardware-encryption solutions can only be directly reached by a Native team.

If you rely on a cross-platform bridging layer, such security cannot be guaranteed.

Any tiny delay or anomaly could be exploited by attackers,

and the consequence would be the collapse of the entire empire's financial order.

Thus, WeChat Pay was firmly built on the cornerstone of Native. This brought heavy costs:

- Each new feature had to be implemented separately by the iOS and Android teams;
- Every regulatory update had to be adapted on both sides at the same time;
- Every risk investigation required double the work.

Yet this cost bought something priceless: users' trust.

In the financial world, the cost of complexity is not the team's overtime but the wealth of millions.

Any cross-platform shortcut could turn into a disaster here.

Native's steadfastness allowed WeChat Pay to maintain a solid levee amid the storm.

Channels (Video Accounts) were another storm of complexity.

Their emergence was almost like rowing against the current for the WeChat system.

Video processing itself is extremely performance-hungry.

Smooth playback, fast uploads, real-time recommendations—each link pushes the system to its limits.

If chat is the light cavalry and payments the heavy infantry, then video is a massive battering ram.

It requires a continuous supply of resources and tight coordination with hardware.

Native once again became the only choice.

On iOS, the WeChat team directly leveraged Apple's AVFoundation and Metal to accelerate video rendering and playback.

On Android, they went deep into the hardware decoding layer, tuning for the differences across countless manufacturers' devices.

No cross-platform framework can replace this work.

It requires engineers to face the most primitive complexities directly, to sculpt performance at every register and every piece of graphics memory.

In the short term, this is the most painful path.

Because every optimization is repetitive labor;

Every tuning session is a night-long dialogue with the unknown.

But in the long run, it is the only right path.

When Channels rapidly scale to hundreds of millions of users, any tiny performance gap will be amplified into a global experience disaster.

Only Native can ensure the system remains controllable under such extreme pressure.

Mini Games, meanwhile, are another metaphor for complexity.

They run inside WeChat's containers; on the surface they appear cross-platform, but in reality they rely on Native's protection.

Because the underlying rendering engine, audio-video processing, and input responsiveness are all provided by Native.

Mini Games merely borrow a simplified interface, yet cannot escape Native's framework.

This again confirms a truth:

The prosperity of cross-platform must stand on Native's shoulders.

Without Native's cornerstone, there would be no flourishing of Mini Games.

Like a marketplace's bustle, it depends on the protection of the walls.

As features expand, the torrent of complexity surges again.

Different features are like the provinces of an empire, each with different needs:

- Chat requires lightness;

- Payments require stability;
- Video requires speed;
- Mini Programs require breadth;
- Search requires precision;
- Enterprise services require specialization.

They are like countless rivers flowing into the same sea.

If there are no clear boundaries, complexity will form whirlpools and drag the entire system into the abyss.

Here, Native's long-term advantage becomes the only fulcrum.

Because Native can provide the clarity of layering:

The bottom layer controls the operating system and hardware;

The middle layer offers unified APIs and services;

The top layer hosts diverse features and ecosystems.

This layering is not an ideal, but a necessity of governance.

It allows complexity to be segmented, managed, and constrained.

It enables teams to maintain order within limited cognitive capacity.

However, the Native path is never easy.

It requires teams to continually expand, to endure double the labor, and to tolerate short-term inefficiency.

It requires management to accept higher budgets and a slower pace.

It requires developers to face the rawest complexity, rather than evade it.

It is a rugged road.

But precisely because it is rugged, it is the real road.

WeChat's engineers said in one presentation: "Native is not our choice, but our destiny."

Destiny is not a shackle, but clarity.

They soberly know that complexity will not disappear, and shortcuts will not last.

They are willing to endure present hardships to secure future stability.

The greatness of an empire lies not in the breadth of its territory, but in the clarity of its institutions.

The longevity of software does not depend on how many features it has, but on the sturdiness of its boundaries.

Native is that boundary.

It is like an invisible wall, holding back the torrent of complexity.

It allows humans, within limited cognition, to maintain an understanding of the system.

It enables civilization to persist rather than collapse.

Native's long-term optimality is not because it is easy, but because it is real.

It requires us to face complexity, not to evade it.

It requires us to respect the platform, not to place ourselves above it.

It asks us to trade repetitive labor for clear layering;

to trade short-term costs for long-term stability.

This is the ultimate philosophy of software design:

Architecture is not for show, but to reduce cognitive load.

The reason Native is optimal in the long run is not that it makes things easy, but that it makes them understandable.

WeChat's story is merely a footnote to this.

But it tells us a simple yet profound truth:

The future of software does not belong to illusion, but to clarity.

Complexity will not be conquered, but it can be governed.

Native is the method of such governance.

Complexity is like a desert, illusions like oases.
Only a sturdy wall can allow humanity to dwell there long-term.

CHAPTER 45
AI'S HUMBLE ROLE

When humans encountered machines that could write code, they thought they had met a savior.

But the savior would not design the future for them; it would only amplify their hesitation and desire.

The wind blew through the empty hall, and dust slowly settled.

Complexity still lurked in the sea of sand, and a new force emerged.

It was not another framework, not another platform, but a whole new kind of existence: artificial intelligence capable of writing code for humans.

In 2021, GitHub released Copilot.

Its slogan was highly tempting: "Your AI programming assistant."

Developers wrote half a line of comment in the editor, and it would automatically complete whole blocks of logic.

Within a few months, it had attracted millions of users.

On forums and at conferences, people loudly discussed: "The future of programming has arrived."

This excitement was like an empire that had just discovered a new sea route.

Crossing the ocean no longer required years of exploration; as long as you set a direction, the sails could carry you there.

For the first time, humans felt that complexity might be counteracted by machines.

At large companies like Airbnb, Netflix, and Twitter, many engineers began trying to introduce Copilot into their daily workflows.

But within this wave, the story of a mid-sized team was more typical.

This was a fintech company headquartered in Europe.

Their goal was to refactor a core mobile app with SwiftUI: a digital wallet used by millions of users.

SwiftUI brought them new hope: declarative UI, state-driven behavior, and a unified cross-platform experience.

However, the migration was difficult: old UIKit code needed to be replaced gradually, and the new architecture had to be built slowly.

Just as they hit a bottleneck, Copilot appeared.

A young developer on the team wrote in the Slack channel:

"We can try Copilot. It can autocomplete much of the logic and might speed up the migration."

This proposal instantly ignited everyone's interest.

The first attempt was astonishing.

In SwiftUI layouts, they wrote only a few keywords and Copilot generated the complete structure.

A seemingly complex interface took shape within minutes.

Tests passed and the feature worked correctly.

There was applause in the conference room.

Someone said, "We saved a day's worth of time."

Someone added, "Maybe a week."

The illusion began to spread.

They gradually treated Copilot as an accelerator: it could generate templates for network requests, complete unit tests, and provide solutions to error messages.

It was like a tireless intern, always there, ready to help.

Complexity seemed to be diminished.

Team morale soared, migration sped up, and management's confidence in the project increased.

In those months, they seemed to see the future: AI was not an assistant, but a replacement.

The gap between design and implementation seemed to be bridged.

They even began to imagine: maybe in a few years AI would be able to complete entire applications, with humans only needing to supervise.

However, complexity would not easily disappear.

It had only changed its form and quietly returned to the battlefield.

Real-world cases began to surface.

In GitHub's official report, Copilot usage data showed: it helped developers generate over 40% of their code, significantly improving efficiency.

But at the same time, users also reported a recurring problem: Copilot would generate logic that "looked correct but was actually wrong."

Its illusion was like a mirage in the desert: real enough to lead people astray, and illusory enough to be deadly.

At that fintech company, the problem soon surfaced.

An engineer noticed: a payment validation logic generated by Copilot looked reasonable and passed tests, but failed under extreme conditions.

The bug wasn't discovered by users until after release, causing some transactions to be delayed.

Although the losses were limited, they were enough to raise internal alarms.

Complexity had returned.

Only this time, it wore the cloak of AI.

In the office at night, the project lead sat alone, staring at the screen.

He recalled his early days of programming: writing logic line by line, gradually building systems.

Back then, complexity was traceable; behind every layer of abstraction there was a clear design intent.

Now, however, complexity seemed to have become intangible.

AI-generated code was like stones falling from the sky—quickly stacked, yet lacking an overall design.

It increased short-term efficiency but raised long-term comprehension costs.

He realized:

AI can generate code, but it cannot design.

It doesn't understand the team's boundaries, it doesn't grasp cognitive load, and it doesn't know which abstractions will become traps in the future.

It merely imitates history rather than builds the future.

The team's arguments began to intensify.

Some believed Copilot was a miracle and should be used as much as possible;

Others thought it was a trap and should be cautiously restricted.

Voices rose and fell in the conference room.

One person offered an example: "We completed 70% of the migration work thanks to Copilot."

Another countered: "But we haven't had time to understand that code. How will the next new hire maintain it?"

This debate was the old human problem with complexity, only on a new stage.

In the past, we argued about whether to abstract; now we argue about whether to let AI abstract for us.

In the past we complained about the illusion of cross-platform solutions; now we face the mirage of intelligent assistants.

Complexity watched with detached eyes; it knew it did not need to speak.

Humans would argue and lose their way on their own.

When an oracle becomes too clear, people lose the habit of thinking;

When answers come too quickly, the question itself is forgotten.

Yet complexity does not vanish through forgetting; it grows in the shadow of answers.

The wind felt quieter at night.

In the team's editors, Copilot tirelessly flashed suggestions.

It generated functions, completed text, wrote comments—like an all-knowing scribe.

Humans only needed to nod to receive a seemingly complete solution.

The initial wonder gradually faded, replaced by a reliance.

Young engineers began to feel sluggish without AI.

They opened their editors and found their fingers stiff, their thoughts dull, as if they'd forgotten how to construct logic independently.

Someone joked, "I don't even know how to write a for loop anymore."

There was a hint of unease in the laughter.

This dependence was like an empire's reliance on tribute.

When caravans from the frontier brought grain each year, people in the capital forgot how to farm;

When the tribute stopped one year, famine immediately followed.

AI is such a tribute.

It accustoms people to convenience while weakening the muscles of independent thought.

The real crisis is not individual, but collective.

That fintech company soon faced a major project:

They needed to implement a brand-new "dynamic billing" feature in SwiftUI, allowing users to synchronize billing records in real time across devices.

This was a system-level challenge involving state management, network synchronization, and offline caching.

Here complexity was no longer simple logic, but coordination across multiple layers.

Copilot quickly supplied a lot of code suggestions.

It filled in network request logic, generated templates for caching strategies, and even wrote state-driven update methods.

At first glance, everything seemed orderly.

Team members nodded and accepted them, as if an invisible architect were pulling the strings behind the scenes.

But when they tried to assemble these fragments, problems were exposed.

- State update logic conflicted with one another, causing the UI to occasionally "flicker."
- The caching strategy was incompatible with the synchronization mechanism, resulting in some bills being duplicated.
- The code structure was loose, lacking unified boundaries, and maintenance difficulty rose sharply.

AI did not design the system for them; it only generated code based on historical patterns.

These fragments were each reasonable, yet lacked a unified philosophy.

Like a city where every street is straight, but when they intersect they form a maze.

Complexity revealed a new face here:

It no longer came from branches and inheritance, but from fragmented correctness.

Most of the code Copilot generated could compile and even pass unit tests.

The problem was that they lacked context.

AI didn't know the team's boundaries, which states were the "single source of truth," or which logic should be hidden inside modules.

It only imitated, it did not design.

Thus, complexity was no longer incorrect code, but correct fragments.

Correct fragments are the most dangerous form of complexity.

Because errors get exposed, while correct fragments accumulate.

They accumulated into an incomprehensible whole, causing future developers to lose their way in the maze.

As problems accumulated, the team's atmosphere began to change.

The initial excitement was gone, replaced by argument and doubt.

Some said, "If it weren't for Copilot, we could never have completed 80% of the migration so quickly."

Others responded, "But now all our time is being spent fixing the consequences Copilot brought."

Voices rose and fell around the conference table.

The engineering manager had to intervene; he tapped the table and said slowly,

"We need to figure out whether AI is helping us or dragging us down."

This was humanity's first confrontation with a harsh question:

AI does not take on complexity; it only shifts it.

The ones who truly bear it remain the team.

Cognitive load began to reach its peak.

A newly joined engineer tried to understand the team's billing sync module.

He opened the files and found chaotic logic and blurred boundaries.

Many comments read "Generated by Copilot."

But no one could clearly explain whether these pieces of logic matched the original design intent.

It took him three days to barely figure out how the module worked.

In the retrospective he said something loaded with meaning:

"I'm not reading the team's code, I'm reading AI's code."

The sentence passed like a cold wind; the conference room fell silent.

People suddenly realized they were losing their sense of ownership.

The code no longer belonged to the team, but to an invisible machine.

This sense of alienation was more terrifying than a bug.

A crisis of trust erupted.

In an online incident, some users' transaction records were lost.

After days of investigation, the team found the cause was a flaw in the caching logic — that logic had been generated by Copilot and "quickly approved" during review.

No one could clearly say why it had been accepted in the first place, nor could anyone explain its design intent.

The incident shook leadership's confidence.

Board members questioned the project lead: "How did this happen? Who wrote that logic?"

The lead was silent for a moment and could only answer, "AI wrote it, but we approved it."

This was the irony of complexity:

the real mistake was not the bug, but the disappearance of responsibility.

When humans hand decision-making over to AI, complexity finds a new hiding place.

After this crisis, the team's division became more pronounced.

Some young engineers still firmly believe AI is the future.

They think the problem is not AI, but the team's lack of experience using it.

"If we learn to control it, we can unleash AI's full potential," they say.

Another group of engineers became increasingly conservative.

They began to reject any suggestions from Copilot, insisting on hand-writing logic and enforcing strict boundary design.

They believe only humans can master complexity.

The two voices kept clashing within the team.

The atmosphere in the meeting room grew increasingly tense, and the review process was charged with tension.

Sometimes, a tiny snippet of code could spark a debate lasting for hours.

The empire's chronicles say:

"When the army no longer draws its swords outward but turns them inward, the decline of the empire is near at hand."

Software teams are no different.

The greatest victory of complexity is not causing bugs, but causing division.

Against this backdrop, the project lead began to reflect.

He walked the streets late at night, recalling his former belief:

"Writing code is not just implementation, but design; it is a negotiation with complexity."

However, AI made people forget design and remember only generation.

They were like a king with endless slaves, who no longer knew how to govern the kingdom.

He wrote in his notes:

"The problem with AI is not that it is wrong, but that it is too right.

Every answer it gives is reasonable.

But when you add them together, they lack a soul."

All of this is not only the predicament of one team, but a reflection of the entire industry.

According to GitHub's report, millions of developers are using Copilot.

Some are made more productive by it; others are lost because of it.

It is both a gift and a curse.

It is both an assistant and an illusion.

Complexity once again proves: it will not disappear.

It has merely changed its disguise, from branches of if-else to the mirage of AI.

It has merely changed its battlefield, from cross-platform bridging to the black box of generative models.

Night deepened, and the team's project kept moving forward.

The SwiftUI interface grew richer and the features more complete.

But the weight of the code grew heavier and heavier.

They began to realize they must redefine the role of AI.

AI cannot be the architect.

AI cannot be the designer.

It can only be an assistant.

True design still requires humans.

Machines can predict, but they cannot decide.

Decision is the weight of humanity, the price of complexity.

If decisions are handed over to machines, humanity will lose its future.

After the dust settles, there is always a silence.

After the fintech company's incident, the air seemed dusted with gray.

Engineers still tapped at their keyboards, screens still flickered, but everyone knew: a change had to be made.

They held a closed-door meeting.

The meeting room door was shut, the curtains drawn, and the air was heavy.

There was no coffee on the table, only stacks of printed incident reports and review records.

The lead spoke: "Today we will not discuss schedule, nor features. We will discuss only one thing — the place of AI in our team."

The debate began again.

Some insisted, "AI has provided enormous productivity. Without it, our migration would not have been completed so quickly."

Others countered, "Yes, but we are being swallowed by the complexity it produces. The code is no longer ours, it is its own."

Voices grew louder and emotions more intense.

Finally, a silent senior engineer — highly respected in the team — spoke.

"AI is not wrong," he said, "we are. We treated it as the architect, not as an assistant. We forgot that design is a human responsibility."

Silence fell.

The sentence, like a stone dropped to the ground, sent echoes through everyone's hearts.

They decided to rebuild their relationship with AI.

First, the team established a clear rule:

AI may generate code, but it may not decide the architecture.

Any suggestion provided by AI must undergo strict review.

The goal of the review is not to check for syntactic correctness, but to confirm whether it aligns with the team's boundaries and philosophy.

Second, they created a special tag for content generated by Copilot.

In commit messages, any AI-generated part must note its source.

This way, future developers reading the code can clearly distinguish which logic was the team's decision and which was the machine's product.

Finally, they redefined the role of AI:

It is suitable for writing boilerplate, generating tests, and completing comments;

But when it comes to design, state management, and defining boundaries, humans must take the lead.

This was not a simple set of rules, but a rebuilding of culture. They no longer regarded Copilot as a savior, but as an assistant. An assistant can improve efficiency, but cannot decide the direction.

The same trend can be seen in GitHub's data. Reports show Copilot is most often used for writing repetitive logic, test cases, and documentation. In areas involving architecture and system design, the real value still comes from humans.

This is AI's humble role: it can reduce labor, but it cannot reduce complexity. It can provide answers, but it cannot make decisions. It can imitate history, but it cannot create the future.

The team's practices gradually began to show results.

In the new iteration, they had Copilot generate the wrappers for network requests. These wrappers were repetitive and tedious—boring for humans to write, but easy for AI to produce. The time saved was used by engineers to rethink the boundaries of state management, ensuring the billing-sync logic was clear and stable.

They also had Copilot generate unit-test templates. Tests still required human design, but the templates made the process more efficient. As a result, test coverage rose and the team's confidence was restored.

Most importantly, the engineers regained control of design. In meetings they no longer argued about whether AI was right or wrong, but discussed the clarity of boundaries. AI was no longer the protagonist, but a tool. Complexity still existed, but it was exposed again to the light rather than hidden in the machine's shadow.

In an internal talk, the project lead summarized their shift: "AI is an amplifier. It amplifies our strengths and it amplifies our blind spots. When we hand design to it, it amplifies complexity; when we hand repetitive work to it, it amplifies efficiency. What determines its role is not the AI itself, but how we position it."

The sentence spread through the team and was written on the meeting-room whiteboard: 'AI is an amplifier. Responsibility is ours.'

Historical footnotes often only become apparent in hindsight.

A few years later, the fintech company's SwiftUI refactor was completed successfully.

Their digital wallet app became a market benchmark—stable, efficient, and with an excellent user experience.

In the postmortem, they all agreed the most critical decision was not choosing SwiftUI, nor adopting AI, but making a clear choice about the boundary between humans and AI.

This was not just a team's story, but an allegory for the entire industry.

In 2023, AI tools sprang up like bamboo shoots after rain: ChatGPT, Copilot, various code generators, design assistants.

Each release drew both amazement and fear.

Some predicted, "In ten years, programmers will disappear."

Others countered, "Without humans, AI will not write any meaningful software."

Complexity laughs.

It knows it cannot be eradicated.

Whether frameworks, platforms, or AI, none can make it vanish.

It will only shift, disguise itself, and wait.

The real enemy is not bugs, not platform differences, not scope creep,

but humans forgetting their role.

The humble positioning of AI is not a technical issue, but a philosophical one.

The essence of software is not to run machines, but to make humans understand.

The essence of design is not pursuing the shortest path, but reducing cognitive load.

AI does not grasp these; it can only predict the next word, not foresee humanity's future.

Therefore, the value of AI lies in:

- It can reduce pointless labor, giving humans more time to think.
- It can provide reference options, enabling humans to make decisions more quickly.
- It can be an intern, but it can never be the architect.

A humble AI is a useful AI.

An arrogant AI will only create new complexity.

At the delivery celebration, the project lead raised his glass and spoke calmly:

"Our victory was not because we used AI, but because we tamed AI.

We did not let it replace us; we made it serve us.

Complexity remains, but we have regained direction."

Everyone present understood: this was not the end, but a new beginning.

There will be new tools, new illusions, new temptations in the future.

But they had already learned the most important lesson:

Humans are the designers, AI is the assistant.

It tells us:

- AI can write code, but it cannot do design;
- The illusions around AI create complexity, but a humble positioning can unlock value;

- The essence of software is always human cognition, not machine output.

The wind settles again.

Complexity still lurks, but humans know that, at least this time, they have gained the initiative.

The greatest wisdom is not to create an all-powerful tool, but to know the tool's limits.
The greatest team is not the one that blindly embraces the future, but the one that clearly defines it.
AI is an amplifier. Responsibility is ours.

CHAPTER 46
MAKING CODE HUMAN-FRIENDLY

Great architecture is not about how much weight it can support, but whether it allows people to live there with peace of mind.

Great code is not about how long it can run, but whether it can be understood.

Complexity is like the dark matter of the universe.

It cannot be seen or touched, yet it pulls everything with its invisible weight.

Empires collapse because of complexity, teams split because of complexity, code sinks because of complexity.

Behind all these stories, there is always an unspoken truth:

Code is not written for machines, code is written for people.

Machines don't care about your indentation, nor whether your patterns are elegant.

Machines only recognize high and low electrical signals, the zeros and ones of binary.

The ones who will truly live with the code are future developers, you debugging bugs, the newcomer who takes over the project months later.

If code makes it impossible for humans to understand, then it is bad code, even if it runs perfectly on machines.

The philosophy of software architecture has been moving toward this conclusion.

From assembly language to high-level languages, from procedural to object-oriented, and then to declarative and reactive.

Each evolution, on the surface, has been to improve efficiency, but in fact to reduce cognitive load.

Compilers are getting more powerful, interpreters becoming smarter, frameworks increasingly abstract.

Behind all of this, the same question is being answered:

How to make it easier for humans to understand.

The arrival of SwiftUI is a continuation of this trend.

It turns complex UI update logic into declarative state bindings.

Developers no longer need to track every button's events one by one, nor manually manage the view tree.

It is not for "elegance", but to make it easier on the human mind.

This philosophy has also been thoroughly implemented in another domain.

Nintendo.

In the world of video games, Nintendo's position is unusual.

Their hardware performance often lags behind competitors.

PlayStation chases extreme visuals, Xbox emphasizes raw performance, but Nintendo always chooses another path:

Not to make machines stronger, but to make games easier for people to understand.

Nintendo developers once said:

"We do not pursue complex controls; we pursue letting players feel the fun within the first minute."

This sentence aligns perfectly with the philosophy of software architecture:

We should not pursue complex abstractions; we should pursue letting developers understand the intent of code at a glance.

In 1985, Super Mario was born.

It only had simple jumping and running, yet became one of the most classic games in history.

Why?

Because its design philosophy is "immediate understanding."

Players don't need a tutorial; they just press a button and can understand the game's rules.

The same philosophy can be applied to code.

A good architecture isn't one that requires long documentation to explain; it's one that lets someone open a file and immediately grasp the intent.

This is "making code human-friendly."

Fast forward to 2006.

Nintendo released the Wii.

It was a console whose performance lagged far behind competitors, yet became a sales miracle thanks to its unique interaction method.

Why?

Because it abandoned complex button combinations, allowing players to experience games with the most intuitive motions.

It lowered the learning threshold, hiding "complex calculations" inside the system so players only felt simplicity and intuition.

This is identical to the goal of software architecture:

Complexity must exist, but it should be hidden in deep modules, not exposed to users.

Users should only see simple interfaces; developers should only see clear boundaries.

Complex logic should be buried deep inside, not scattered across shallow fragments.

The opposite of this philosophy also exists.

In many software projects, we often see another scene:

- Feature-complete, but with convoluted entry points.
- Documentation heavy, but hard to follow.
- Architecture fancy, but impossible to comprehend.

This is like some games: menus piled upon menus, controls complex and obscure; players spend a lot of energy learning the rules and have no time to enjoy the fun.

Such games are often short-lived.

Such software is also doomed not to last.

Nintendo's case reveals a truth:

True innovation isn't in stacking complexity; it's in taming complexity so humans can use it easily.

This is also the ultimate philosophy of software architecture:

Make code human-friendly.

But to achieve this, the cost is extremely high.

When Nintendo developers design games, they must constantly discard "complex features" and keep only the "core experience."

They spend a great deal of time testing and observing players' reactions, stripping away any detail that might increase cognitive load.

This self-restraint is extremely painful.

The same is true in software architecture:

Removing a "clever abstraction" is often harder than writing it;

abandoning a "potential reuse" is often more painful than implementing it.

The most seductive thing about complexity is that it makes developers feel smart.

But true wisdom is doing subtraction amid complexity.

SwiftUI is important not because it is more advanced than UIKit, but because it brings UI logic closer to "human intuition."

You only need to describe state to get the result.

This pattern is not showmanship; it is compassion.

It buries complexity inside the framework and leaves simplicity to the developer.

Like Nintendo's Wii, which hides complex motion-sensing algorithms in the system and leaves the intuitive swing to the player.

Yet, real-world teams often find it hard to follow this philosophy.

Because "complex" is always better at masquerading as "progress" than "simple" is.

A complex architecture looks profound;

a complex abstraction makes people feel brilliant;

heavy documentation makes the team seem more professional.

But complexity is never progress; it is merely debt.

Real progress is reducing the burden on human minds so future developers can understand.

Nintendo's story is a mirror of the software world.

It reminds us:

The ultimate purpose of technology is not to please machines, but to serve humans.

The highest state of architecture is not complex patterns, but comprehensible simplicity.

In the desert sea of complexity, the only oasis is human understanding.

The mission of architecture is to guard that oasis.

As a system grows, complexity billows like sand from all directions.

No design can completely block it; all one can do is protect the oasis amid the storm.

Complexity will not vanish because of a single aphorism.

It is like wind in the desert — it always exists.

Even if a team vows to "make code human-friendly," complexity will still find cracks to seep through.

The real test has never been in small-scale prototypes, but in the process of an empire's expansion.

Nintendo knew this well.

Their hardware often lagged behind competitors, yet they consistently created enduring classic games.

The reason was not performance, but that they always put the "player's experience" first.

However, this philosophy was not always easy to follow.

Market pressure, the lure of technology, and team expansion had all once led them off course.

In 2002, Nintendo released the GameCube.

In terms of hardware performance, it closely chased the PlayStation 2 and Xbox, but it lost in the market.

Many commentators believed this was because Nintendo tried to imitate their rivals: pursuing stronger graphics and more complex features.

They temporarily forgot their philosophy.

The failure of the GameCube became a turning point that brought them back to the path of being "human-friendly."

This story is equally true in the world of software architecture.

When a team faces competitive pressure, someone will always propose:

"We need a more complex architecture to support the future."

"We need more general abstractions to accommodate various requirements."

"We need more sophisticated design to prove our capabilities."

So the code's complexity gradually ballooned.

In the short term, it seemed reasonable: more complex abstractions appeared more powerful.

In the long run, however, it trapped future developers in quicksand.

A hypothetical iOS team may illustrate this phenomenon.

A company decided to rewrite their core app using SwiftUI.

At first, they followed the "human-friendly" principle:

each view was simple and direct, state was clear, and the logic was obvious at a glance.

When new members joined, it only took a few days for them to understand the core code.

Team morale soared and releases came quickly.

However, as demands grew, complexity began to exert pressure.

The product manager proposed:

"We need more personalized interfaces."

"We need complex dynamic animations."

"We need a unified component library for reuse across multiple projects."

Developers began introducing layer upon layer of abstraction.

They built complex state managers to handle various scenarios in a unified way.

They created numerous helper utility classes, scattering common logic across different files.

They wrote clever protocol compositions hoping to cover future changes.

In the short term, these abstractions seemed efficient.

- New members could no longer understand the code in a few days; they needed weeks.

- A simple requirement required changes to multiple files to ensure consistency.
- When debugging, the logic was like a maze and had to be traced layer by layer.

Complexity had reclaimed power.

The "human-friendly" philosophy was gradually consumed by the pressures of reality.

Nintendo's history reflected this again.

After the failure of the GameCube, they reconsidered their direction.

They discovered that pursuing performance and complexity only dragged them into the same mire as their competitors.

The path that truly belonged to them was to reduce complexity and focus on the experience.

So, in 2006 the Wii was born.

It did not have the strongest hardware, but it had the most intuitive interaction.

It brought their philosophy back on track: players first, machines second.

This is the lesson software architecture must learn: developers first, machines second.

The temptation of complexity comes not only from feature bloat, but also from team expansion.

A small team can often maintain clear boundaries.

Communication among a dozen engineers is enough for them to share the cognitive load.

But when a team grows to hundreds, complexity multiplies.

Management often pins its hopes on "architectural unification."

They establish an "architecture committee" and set elaborate standards, trying to suppress complexity through process.

However, such systems themselves become amplifiers of complexity.

Every meeting, every document update adds to the Cognitive Load.

Developers stop focusing on solving problems and start following processes.

This scenario is common in many large tech companies.

The larger the team, the more complex the architecture;

the more complex the architecture, the more fractured the team.

Complexity has not been reduced; it has merely taken another form that weighs on everyone.

When Nintendo faced team expansion, they chose a different path.

They kept core teams small to prevent complexity from growing out of control.

In the development of The Legend of Zelda: Breath of the Wild, they broke the vast open world into modules small teams could understand.

Each team only needed to focus on their own patch of land, yet together they formed a harmonious world.

This "deep module" philosophy is identical to the software architecture principle of "information hiding."

A good architecture does not manufacture uniformity through layer upon layer of abstraction; it allocates cognitive load through clear boundaries.

It lets each team own its module without being crushed by the entire system.

This, that is true "human-friendliness."

The ultimate test of complexity comes from time.

Many teams can remain clear and simple in the short term.

But as time passes, requirements change, and members turn over, complexity will inevitably make a comeback.

Nintendo's philosophy again offers insight.

Their games often span decades and remain understandable and beloved.

Mario, The Legend of Zelda, and Animal Crossing evolve

across different hardware platforms yet always preserve a core simplicity.

In each iteration they held to the principle: do not let complexity devour the player's experience.

Software architecture must be the same.

It is not a one-off design but a long-term stewardship.

The real test is not whether the first version is elegant, but whether the code remains human-friendly five or ten years later.

Complexity is like a sea of sand.

It is everywhere and will not disappear.

The philosophy of being "human-friendly" is not a one-time victory but an eternal vigil.

Teams must, at every decision, actively choose:

- Whether to introduce a new abstraction;
- Whether to add a new dependency;
- Whether to chase short-term showmanship at the expense of long-term understandability.

Each choice is like erecting a stone tablet in the sandstorm.

Those tablets form the civilization of the architecture.

> *All designs will ultimately be judged by time.*
> *Splendor fades, speed slows, and only comprehensibility can leave a spark amid the ruins.*

The story of complexity has never had a true ending.

Like windblown sand, it always exists, only in different forms.

Airbnb's cross-platform experiment proves that shortcuts can turn complexity into new shackles.

The struggles of countless large teams prove that scale magnifies the weight of complexity.

Nintendo's philosophy proves that even in environments

with insufficient performance and limited resources, as long as one holds to being "human-friendly," one can still create classics that transcend eras.

In the development archives for The Legend of Zelda: Breath of the Wild, there is a detail.

The development team had originally planned to add more complex systems: weather affecting equipment, hundreds of food recipes, enemies with highly advanced AI.

But they ultimately removed most of those ideas.

Because in extensive playtesting they found that players became confused.

Players had to spend too much mental effort understanding the systems instead of enjoying the pleasure of exploration.

So the team made a difficult decision: abandon complexity and preserve intuition.

This is the price of being "human-friendly."

It requires designers to constantly negate themselves and repeatedly subtract in the face of temptation.

It is the most painful choice, but also the wisest.

The same choices repeatedly appear in software architecture.

A team builds a huge state manager intended to unify the logic.

Later, they find new members cannot understand it, and debugging time multiplies.

So the architect asks, "Should we abandon this complex mechanism and return to more intuitive state flows?"

This is a real test.

Choosing to stick with complexity can preserve a short-term illusion: the system looks powerful, the architecture appears avant-garde.

Choosing to return to simplicity, however, means admitting that the initial investment was wrong and rebuilding from scratch.

But only the latter can truly protect future developers.

Here, the philosophy of architecture overlaps with Nintendo's: remove complexity, preserve intuition.

The ultimate battlefield of complexity is time.

Imagine a morning ten years from now.

A newly joined engineer opens the project's source code.

She faces not a machine, but words.

Are those words clear?

Are the logic and flow obvious at a glance?

Are the boundaries intuitive?

These things determine her mood for the day, the team's productivity, and the project's future.

Code is not written for machines; machines only recognize zeros and ones.

Code is written for humans—for the future you, for newcomers who have not yet joined, for future maintainers.

If they cannot understand it, then the architecture has failed.

The rise of AI makes this point even more pronounced.

Today, AI can write a fully functional piece of code, generate tests, and help you search APIs.

But it cannot judge whether that code will be easy for your future self to understand.

It cannot evaluate whether that architecture will crush the team five years from now.

It will only produce syntactically correct answers and will not reduce the cognitive load for future humans.

Therefore, in the AI era, the architect's mission is not to reduce the amount of code that needs to be written, but to ensure the code remains human-friendly.

AI can be an assistant, but it cannot be a philosopher.

Because the philosophical question is: for whom are we writing code?

The answer is always: for humans, not for machines.

The philosophy of Native also finds its explanation here.

The temptation of cross-platform development always promises efficiency.

But behind efficiency often lies a transfer of complexity.

The real cost is reflected in the future cost of understanding.

The value of Native is not that it is faster, but that it is clearer.

It moves with the platform's rhythm and reduces an extra layer of cognitive overhead.

It lets developers understand one set of platform rules instead of a three-layer bridging maze.

This is another form of being "human-friendly."

All these clues converge over the long arc of time to the same conclusion:

The ultimate goal of software architecture is not to make machines run faster, but to make it easier for humans to understand.

This sentence sounds ordinary, but it is the spark of civilization.

Because speed can be replaced by hardware, performance can be surpassed by the times, and patterns can be swept away by trends.

Only "comprehensibility" can span ten or twenty years and become the cornerstone of the future.

In future archives, it might be recorded this way:

One team failed because of flashy architecture;

one team collapsed chasing illusions;

one team endured because it held to simplicity.

History will forget flashy patterns, forget complex abstractions, forget fleeting trends.

But history will remember architectures that are human-friendly.

Just as people still remember Mario's jump and Zelda's exploration, not some long-forgotten rendering parameter.

Nintendo's philosophy, SwiftUI's philosophy, and the philosophy of software architecture are essentially one:

Hide complexity, expose simplicity;

respect humans rather than machines;

make understanding the core, not a byproduct.

Therefore, all chapters of this book ultimately point to this.

Complexity is destiny.

Cognitive load is the boundary.

Architecture is negotiation.

A team is an institution.

AI is an assistant.

Native is a home.

They may seem independent, but they all revolve around the same question:

How do we make code human-friendly?

As you read this, you may ask:

Is this too simple? Surely complex patterns, exquisite architectures, and advanced tools matter, don't they?

They matter.

But their value does not lie in themselves; it lies in whether they make it easier for humans to understand.

If they increase cognitive load, they are bad;

if they reduce cognitive load, they are good.

This is the only metric.

Therefore, this book offers the following as the maxim of its final chapter:

- The sole goal of software architecture: reduce complexity.
- The only standard for judging good code: can your future self quickly understand it?
- Boundaries are not walls, but bridges.
- AI is a tool; developers are the designers.
- Native is a friend of time.
- The greatest code is not a flashy marvel, but understandable simplicity.

The wind still blows.

Complexity still lurks in the shadows.

But when you close this book, may you remember:

the true ultimate philosophy is not to fight complexity, but to make code human-friendly.

Empires will fall, tools will be replaced, patterns will change.
But as long as humans are writing code, "comprehensibility" is the single ember.
It is our source of water, our shelter, our oasis.
It renders complexity powerless to devour civilization.
It ensures that people in the future can still understand our voice.

PART TEN
APPENDIX

CHAPTER 47
DAILY REMINDERS FOR DEVELOPERS

Cognitive load is an enemy every developer encounters daily.

It is not like a bug that can be reproduced, nor like a crash that can be located.

It hides in the wording of meetings, hides in the corners of requirements, hides in the structure of code.

It is invisible, yet it can drain a whole day's mental energy.

The following quick checklist is not a cold set of rules, but the sighs and experience of countless civilizations.

They are both admonitions and daily talismans.

Before every build, every review, every argument, silently read a few of them.

They will become small shields against complexity.

When you are reading a piece of logic and need to keep more than three things in your head at once, stop.

Because the brain's capacity is limited; beyond that, all understanding becomes diluted.

Historically, Airbnb's team, when debugging React Native,

often needed to understand JavaScript logic, iOS memory management, and Android thread scheduling at the same time.

They were not lacking intelligence, but because no one can hold three maps at once.

The first reminder about cognitive load is: don't carry three maps at the same time.

When you find you need to draw a complex flowchart to understand a function or module, be warned.

Flowcharts are not the problem; the problem is that the logic has exceeded what natural memory can bear.

An empire's bureaucracy also relies on charts to survive, but when charts are more complex than actions, the empire is already beyond cure.

Reminder: if the logic cannot be described in one breath, it is overloaded.

When you hear colleagues repeatedly explain a concept in a meeting, but different people understand it differently, stop immediately.

Because this means the term has lost a single meaning and its boundaries are blurred.

Complexity's favorite trick is to make the same word mean different things to different people.

Reminder: in any discussion, first agree on terminology.

When you face an abstraction, if you cannot explain its value in one sentence, then it is redundant.

Abstraction is not aesthetics; it is an investment in cognition.

Excessive abstraction is like an empire's elaborate rituals: seemingly solemn, but actually wasteful.

Reminder: if an abstraction does not reduce cognitive load, it is the burden itself.

When you notice the team increasingly using "we'll deal with it later" as a decision, be cautious.

Because "later" is complexity's favorite hiding place.

Historical failures have rarely been because a problem couldn't be solved, but because too many problems were postponed.

Reminder: any "we'll deal with it later" decision should be recorded and given a deadline.

If during a code review you can only rely on intuition and cannot fully understand the intent of the changes, stop.

Because this means the cost of understanding has exceeded acceptable bounds.

Understanding should not be a mysterious intuition but a clear path.

Reminder: if even reviewers cannot easily understand it, future maintainers will be in an even worse position.

When you notice that newcomers to the team cannot understand the core modules within a week, be wary.

This means the module is no longer a deep and simple well, but a shallow and fragmented beach.

The continuation of civilization depends on knowledge being transmitted quickly.

Reminder: the quality of a module is not measured by the speed of veterans but by whether newcomers can master it.

When you are optimizing performance and keep getting bogged down in tiny numerical comparisons, stay calm.

The trap of performance optimization is that you think you're pursuing speed, but in fact you're creating complexity.

True optimization is stability, not extremes.

Reminder: don't let performance fanaticism devour cognitive clarity.

If you find a problem requires many people to discuss to solve, but in the end no one can make a call, be careful.

This is not the difficulty of the problem but a lack of boundaries.

If an empire's frontiers have no clear governor, they will eventually fall into chaos.

Reminder: fuzzy responsibility boundaries let complexity spread without limit.

When you notice meetings getting longer while decisions slow down, reflect.

This means complexity is no longer a technical issue but an organizational one.

Reminder: communication cost is complexity.

If you feel tired but cannot say why, suspect cognitive load.

Fatigue is often not because of hours worked, but because the mind is forced to switch among too many contexts.

Reminder: mental switching is consumption; respect the scarcity of attention.

When you face AI-generated code and feel relieved and excited, be cautious.

AI can bring convenience, but it can also create new black boxes.

If you cannot understand the logic it generated, you are merely shifting cognitive load to the future.

Reminder: AI is a tool, not a free pass.

. . .

When you discover that implementing a feature requires crossing multiple frameworks, multiple tools, and multiple domains of knowledge, stop.

Because this means future maintainers will also have to bridge the same chasms.

Reminder: any implementation that crosses more than two knowledge boundaries is a future liability.

When you notice heroism in the team—one person always solves problems others cannot—stay calm.

The existence of heroes is a signal of boundary failure.

A civilization should not rely on heroes but on institutions.

Reminder: if a system must depend on heroes, it is already unsustainable.

When you see a large number of "notes" or "caveats" in the documentation, stop.

Because this means the design itself can no longer prove its safety and must be patched by external memory.

Reminder: a truly good design does not require many warnings.

When you hear someone say "this is the framework's magic," be immediately alert.

The flip side of magic is a black box.

A framework is not sorcery but a tool; if its behavior cannot be explained, it is a potential disaster.

Reminder: do not rely on magic unless you can explain its cost.

• • •

When you find more and more helper utilities appearing in a project, stop at once.

Helpers are an illusion of convenience that often become a breeding ground for complexity.

Reminder: the number of helpers is the thermometer of complexity.

When you keep hearing "this is just a small issue" in discussions, be cautious.

The accumulation of small issues is how large problems take shape.

Reminder: the flood of complexity always begins with countless small cracks.

These reminders are not meant to stop you from moving forward, but to keep you clear-headed as you do.

Cognitive load is inevitable, but it can be managed.

It is like an empire's taxes: it will not disappear, but it can be fairly distributed.

It is like the desert wind: it will not cease, but vegetation can be used to slow it.

It is like the passage of time: it will not stop, but temperance can extend a civilization's lifespan.

Keep this checklist in your mind.

When you are debugging late at night, when you are arguing in meetings, when you hesitate before documentation, recall these reminders.

They will not solve your problems for you, but they will keep you from losing direction.

Memory is limited; complexity is infinite.
The only wisdom of civilization is to conserve memory.

CHAPTER 48
TEAM GUARDRAIL CHECKLIST

Guardrails are the last defense between the team and complexity.

They are not weapons, but systems;
not techniques, but constraints.

Just as an empire endures by law rather than force, a team must rely on clear guardrails to avoid being lost in the sandstorm of complexity.

The following checklist is not a cold regulation, but a warning left by civilization.

Each item is a warning distilled from real ruins.

If a team can hold these boundaries in daily practice, complexity will not destroy the mind.

When the continuous integration pipeline fails, stop immediately.

The pipeline is not an accessory, but the lifeblood of the empire.

If the lifeblood no longer flows, all construction is an illusion.

Reminder: without stable CI, all commitments are empty promises.

• • •

When code review becomes a formality, remain alert.

Review is not to find faults, but to make it possible for future readers to understand.

If an empire's archives go unchecked, its histories lose their meaning.

Reminder: the goal of review is to reduce future cognitive load.

When tests are skipped merely because "this feature is small," oppose it firmly.

Bugs in small features are often the most deadly cracks.

The fall of an empire often begins with seemingly trivial tax loopholes.

Reminder: no matter how small the feature, it must be validated by the guardrails.

When a PR is so large that it overwhelms reviewers' attention, split it immediately.

Attention is scarce; an overloaded review is no longer a guard but a free pass.

Reminder: every submission must fit within a person's cognitive capacity.

When the habit of "anyone can merge directly" appears in the team, stop it immediately.

Merging is not a power, but a contract.

If the contract is no longer respected, the empire's laws become meaningless.

Reminder: merging without a two-person rule is equivalent to abandoning future safety.

. . .

When CI only checks for successful compilation but not quality, question it.

Compilation is only the lowest threshold; quality is the foundation of civilization.

Reminder: CI must guard quality, not merely the build.

When code review descends into personal arguments instead of addressing future readers, stay calm.

Review is not a debating arena, but an archive.

Reminder: all reviews should use "whether future readers can understand" as the sole criterion.

When you discover the team is relying on memory to carry out processes rather than on systems, be concerned.

Memory fades; systems endure.

Reminder: guardrails must be encoded in tools and processes, not in minds and verbal promises.

When automation is seen as a burden and manual processes are romanticized, oppose it firmly.

Automation is kindness to the future; manual work is indulgence to the present.

Reminder: every repeatable process must be handed to machines, not people.

When review time is compressed merely to keep up with release cadence, stay alert.

Short-term speed inevitably yields long-term stagnation.

Reminder: sacrificing reviews is taking on debt for the future.

. . .

When a team lacks clear boundaries—who owns which module, who guards which contract—fill them in immediately.

Ambiguous boundaries are complexity's favorite breeding ground.

Reminder: one module = one guardian.

When CI results are ignored and the team adopts a "merge first, deal with it later" habit, sound the alarm immediately.

If an empire ignores its border alarms, invasion will arrive silently.

Reminder: a failing pipeline must be repaired ahead of everything else.

When the team discusses boundaries, regard them as invalid if there is no final written contract.

Verbal promises cannot withstand complexity; only written agreements endure.

Reminder: all boundaries must be captured in documentation.

When architectural designs aren't reviewed and instead rely on authority's decree, remain skeptical.

If an empire depends on individuals rather than systems, it is bound to decline.

Reminder: architecture review is the team's contract, not an individual's ruling.

When you notice reviewers gradually losing the courage to ask questions, reflect immediately.

Psychological safety is the foundation of guardrails.

Reminder: if the team fears questioning, the guardrails are already a sham.

When feature testing depends on manual effort and lacks automated regression, stay alert.

Manual testing is short-term cheapness; automation is long-term wealth.

Reminder: automated tests are a guardrail, not an ornament.

When modules lack clear interfaces and rely on implicit behavior to communicate, fix it immediately.

Interfaces are the language of boundaries; if the language is vague, boundaries will collapse.

Reminder: boundaries must be visible, testable, and enforceable.

When CI does not include security checks, performance checks, and style checks, question it.

If the pipeline only verifies that code runs but not that it is understandable, it is equivalent to abandoning clarity for the future.

Reminder: CI's duty is to guard clarity for future readers, not to protect speed for present development.

When a team is accustomed to bypassing guardrails in crises while relying on them in normal times, be wary.

Once guardrails can be bypassed, their authority will be eroded.

Reminder: the power of a system lies in its non-negotiability.

• • •

When a team lacks regular retrospectives and cannot examine whether the guardrails are still effective, reflect.

Systems age; contracts become outdated.

Reminder: guardrails must be periodically reviewed, otherwise they themselves will become part of the complexity.

These checklists are not meant to stifle creativity, but to protect it.

Guardrails are not walls, but bridges.

They free people from the deluge of complexity, allowing attention to be devoted to true design and thinking.

If an empire has no laws, it can only rely on tyrants and heroes.

If a team has no guardrails, it can only rely on overtime and geniuses.

And truly lasting civilizations rely on systems, not miracles.

Remember:

Continuous integration is not a tool, but the lifeblood of civilization.

Code review is not trivial, but the archive of the future.

Boundary contracts are not a formality, but the team's defensive line.

By holding these guardrails, your team can go further in the sandstorm of complexity.

Guardrails are not constraints, but an act of mercy.
They keep civilization from sinking and allow the future to endure.

CHAPTER 49
ANTI-PATTERN RED LIST

The truly terrifying thing about complexity is that it never announces itself with a loud crash.

It is more like an undercurrent lurking beneath a sea of sand, quietly waiting for a crack to widen.

The following anti-patterns are the precursors to those cracks.

Once they appear in a team, you must immediately reduce the burden, otherwise destruction is only a matter of time.

When an "all-purpose manager" class appears in the team and all logic is concentrated in one place, immediately reduce the burden.

This is the illusion of the "God object."

It promises unity but brings paralysis.

In such an object, the cognitive load inflates without limit, and any change feels like prying up a boulder.

Reminder: any object that claims to be "all-powerful" is a disaster by its existence.

• • •

When the architecture diagram grows more and more complex, arrows crisscrossing like a web, immediately reduce the burden.

Architecture is not meant to display complexity, but to tame it.

A web-like set of dependencies is a sign that the team is heading toward collapse.

Reminder: if the dependency graph cannot be explained clearly to a newcomer, it is a danger signal.

When the team begins to abuse inheritance, putting all problems on parent classes, immediately reduce the burden.

Inheritance was once the banner of object-orientation, but it has also become the trap of countless empires.

Deep inheritance chains are like royal bloodlines—complex, fragile, and hard to maintain.

Reminder: when the inheritance chain exceeds three levels, the sword of complexity is already hanging overhead.

When Helper tools spread like weeds and every module has a "Utils" or "Helper," immediately reduce the burden.

Helpers are the most common form of laziness; they move logic from the core to the corners but never truly solve the problem.

In the end, the shadows in the corners devour all the light.

Reminder: the number of Helpers is the thermometer of complexity.

When more and more promises of "refactor later" appear in meetings, immediately reduce the burden.

"Later" is the refuge of complexity.

Each postponement is a new debt.

Debt itself is not terrifying; what is terrifying is that it is never repaid.

Reminder: if there is no clear deadline, "later" is synonymous with destruction.

When module boundaries become blurred and a module simultaneously handles networking, storage, presentation, and other responsibilities, immediately reduce the burden.

Blurred boundaries are the points where complexity seeps in.

If an empire has no clearly defined provinces, rebellions will only continue to grow.

Reminder: if a module's responsibilities cannot be described in one sentence, it has already failed.

When code reviews gradually become a formality, reduced to polite "LGTM"s, immediately reduce the burden.

Reviews are not etiquette, but a system.

If the system loses its binding force, the empire's archives become little more than scrap paper.

Reminder: if reviews do not reduce future cognitive load, they are a hollow ritual.

When the team relies on a single hero to solve every difficult problem, immediately reduce the burden.

The existence of a hero signifies a missing system.

If an empire is held together by one general, it is destined to collapse when that general falls.

Reminder: if a team must depend on a hero, it is already on the road to decay.

• • •

When a bug keeps appearing in the same place, fixed again and again but never truly resolved, immediately reduce the burden.

This is not a bug, but a cycle of complexity.

The real problem is not the symptom, but the structure.

Reminder: recurring bugs are the architecture's distress signal.

When tests are treated as a burden and the team keeps skipping them to "save time," immediately reduce the burden.

A system without tests is like a city without a firewall.

The flames may not come at once, but they will inevitably consume everything.

Reminder: without tests, civilization will perish.

When requirement reviews repeatedly use vague words—"more or less," "whatever," "something like"—immediately reduce the burden.

Vague language is the seed of chaos.

Once sown, complexity will run rampant in the code.

Reminder: vague requirements inevitably lead to vague implementations.

When a cross-platform framework promises "write once, run everywhere," remain immediately skeptical.

History has proven time and again: complexity does not vanish because of slogans.

It only shifts, from two platforms into a three-layered system.

Airbnb's experience is the clearest footnote.

Reminder: cross-platform promises often come at the cost of multiplied complexity.

. . .

When performance optimization turns into a frenzy over numbers and engineers become obsessed with chasing milliseconds, immediately reduce the burden.

Performance is not speed, but stability.

Chasing extremes, like an empire overextending, only causes the frontiers to collapse.

Reminder: if stability is sacrificed, performance optimization is an illusion.

When project documentation has failed and the latest knowledge exists only in the mouths of a few, immediately reduce the burden.

Monopoly of knowledge is the corruption of civilization.

Documentation is an extension of the system; a system without documentation can only rely on the fragility of oral transmission.

Reminder: when documentation is outdated, complexity will flourish.

When team culture begins to make people afraid to ask questions or voice doubts, immediately reduce the burden.

The loss of psychological safety is more dangerous than any bug.

Because it means future mistakes will no longer be discovered in time.

Reminder: a team without questions is doomed to a silent ruin.

When technology choices are over-packaged—chosen because "it's more popular" rather than "it's clearer"—immediately reduce the burden.

Technology is not fashion; it is governance.

Chasing trends is the beginning of an empire's decline.

Reminder: if a technology choice cannot reduce cognitive load, it is the wrong choice.

When processes are frequently bypassed in the name of speed, immediately reduce the burden.

Once systems fail, complexity will invade silently.

Reminder: the illusion of speed exchanges for the reality of debt.

When architecture documents diverge severely from actual implementation, immediately reduce the burden.

If the blueprint and the city do not match, the empire will perish.

Reminder: if architecture cannot be verified, it is no longer architecture.

When a team has grown accustomed to the presence of complexity and no longer senses its weight, immediately reduce the burden.

Habit is the most dangerous poison.

Once complexity becomes the norm, destruction has already begun.

Reminder: do not compromise with complexity, or you have been assimilated by it.

These red lists are not threats, but warnings.

They are not prophecies of the future, but facts already played out in countless civilizations.

Once these signals appear, you must act immediately: reduce the burden, refactor, establish boundaries, restore systems.

Otherwise, the flood of complexity will silently drown everything.

Among the ruins of empires you will always find the same inscription:

It was not external enemies that destroyed them, but complexity.

The same sentence will be carved on the graves of teams.

Hold fast to these red lists.

They are not constraints, but beacons for survival.

If you can see them when the sand rises, you may still lead your team out of the sea of sand.

Complexity will not defeat you; it will wait for you to forget.
Keep the red list, and you will remember: destruction always begins with neglect.

ABOUT THE AUTHOR

I'm Hui Wang, an author focused on the intersections of history, warfare, business, and technology. My mission is to explore the forces that shape our world, both past and present, through rigorous research, clear logic, and compelling storytelling.

I hold dual Bachelor's degrees in Computer Software Engineering and Business Administration from the University of Electronic Science and Technology of China, one of the country's leading engineering universities. I also hold certifications from Apple and Google, and have completed coursework in psychology at Yale University to better understand human behavior and decision-making.

Over the past decade, I have written extensively about how wars are fought and won, how empires rise and fall, how businesses succeed or collapse, and how technology transforms society. I combine historical insight with analytical thinking to provide readers with reliable knowledge and lasting perspective.

In a time of information overload, I aim to provide clarity, depth, and trust. If you are seeking thoughtful, well researched, and engaging content, I invite you to explore my work.

www.ingramcontent.com/pod-product-compliance
Lightning Source LLC
Chambersburg PA
CBHW050519240926
51846CB00003B/618
9789189998995